Praise for *The Lyme D*

Anita Bains and Tracey Middleton have marshaled their extensive personal and professional experience into creating a remarkably powerful, resourceful, and comprehensive self-care guide for those (more than 300,000 new cases each year in the U.S. alone) who are afflicted with Lyme and other tick-borne diseases. These illnesses can bring a happy, productive life to its knees, and Bains and Middleton show you how to use energy psychology and other state-of-the-art resources to re-empower yourself and to address your physical symptoms in ways that complement conventional treatments."

David Feinstein, Ph.D.
Co-author, ***The Promise of Energy Psychology*** and ***The Energies of Love***

"This wonderful workbook will prove exceptionally helpful to the Lyme's sufferer in transcending suffering and achieving wellness. It contains many concepts and processes that will prove beneficial to people suffering from other maladies as well. I highly recommend that you read it in depth and apply the helpful exercises along the way. This workbook will teach you how to use EFT, Energy Psychology, and Mindfulness practices to overcome the common distress that occurs as a result of conditions such as Lyme/TBDs."

Fred P. Gallo PhD, DCEP, author of ***Energy Psychology*** and ***Energy Tapping for Trauma,*** Founder of Advance Energy Psychology, and President of the Association for Comprehensive Energy Psychology (ACEP)

"Anita and Tracey did a good job of describing EFT in a thorough and understandable way and providing a step by step approach that Lyme patients can follow. I did find it interesting. They did a good job explaining and describing the therapy and providing real life examples that might help doubters overcome some of their skepticism. It will be a valuable addition to the Lyme library."

David Hunter, Lyme Advocate, Facilitator of the Greater Manchester Lyme Disease Support Group; Chairman of the Bedford Lyme Disease Council

"If you suffer from Lyme/TBDs and desire to move forward toward a happy and fulfilling life, but can't get unstuck – read *The Lyme Disease Workbook* by Anita Bains, MS, RN, and Tracey Middleton, LCSW-C. This is far more than a workbook. Anita and Tracey bring together every wise insight and life-changing practice they've learned during a combined 34 years in the mental health field, as well as in their own recovery from Lyme/TBDs, in order to help you foster a dynamic process of change and growth. *The Lyme Disease Workbook* is a passionate contribution by two extraordinary practitioners who have much to offer even those who believe they've tried everything. Don't miss it. Allow the exercises in *The Lyme Disease Workbook* to enhance your healing and recovery."

Donna Jackson Nakazawa, author of ***Childhood Disrupted, The Last Best Cure, The Autoimmune Epidemic***

THE LYME DISEASE WORKBOOK

THE LYME DISEASE WORKBOOK

Tapping into a Wellness State of Mind

Self-Help Tools and Mindfulness-Based Techniques for People Living with Lyme, Flea, and Other Tick-Borne Diseases

Anita Bains, MS, RN & Tracey Middleton, LCSW-C

The Lyme Disease Workbook
Tapping into a Wellness State of Mind

Anita Bains, MS, RN & Tracey Middleton, LCSW-C

DISCLAIMER: The information in this book is based upon the research and personal and professional experiences of the authors. It is not intended as a substitute for consulting with a healthcare professional. Should you have any questions concerning the appropriateness of any information provided, the authors of this work suggest consulting a professional healthcare advisor.

The case narratives in this book are derived from actual and combined stories of client experiences as reported over time. Names have been changed and identifying information has been removed to protect the privacy of the individuals.

ISBN-13: 978-0-692-72820-8

Book cover design and illustrations by David Terry • dterry509@gmail.com

Book interior design and typesetting by Laura Piazza • www.piazzacreative.com

"A Personal Story of Resilience in Action" by Katina Makris on page 46 is included with permission of Katina Makris.

"Coping with Emotional Stress Scale" on page 37 is reprinted with permission of Whole Person Associates.

"Fire-Love" exercise on page 107 is reprinted with permission of Vir McCoy.

This workbook is dedicated to all of you who are recovering from Lyme and other tick-borne diseases (TBDs) and the people who journey with you. May you always search for answers, keep persisting until you find lasting relief, invite your community to walk with you, and cultivate unyielding hopefulness that fosters the inner transformation that transcends Lyme/TBDs.

Contents

Appendices

Foreword

Not long ago I was asked by a medical colleague and friend, "What is the one thing in the field of medicine that frustrates you the most after these many years of medical practice?"

I thought for a moment and replied, "I think today's medical profession still has not fully comprehended how to help patients learn to use their own innate healing powers to regain health and vitality. We have a disease-oriented culture of people who have become highly dependent on things we medical doctors prescribe for them. Our medical approach works well for some things like acute illnesses, trauma, and many surgical conditions. However, for many chronic disorders, our medical techniques do little more than cover up distressing symptoms. And, sadly, these methods rarely lead to lasting restoration of good health."

For many years, many practitioners who attempt to help those with chronic Lyme disease and other tick-borne diseases (Lyme/TBDs) have been missing a vital link in providing truly comprehensive treatment for our patients. This is why I am excited to introduce *The Lyme Disease Workbook: Tapping into a Wellness State of Mind.* Now, for the first time, there is a workbook that offers its users highly effective self-help tools and mindfulness-based techniques for overcoming the painful emotional issues and trauma specifically related to Lyme/TBDs.

Both authors - Anita Bains and Tracey Middleton - are highly qualified, licensed psychotherapists. In this groundbreaking book they reveal the critical importance of addressing the painful emotional problems that Lyme/TBDs infections often create in their victims. Fortunately, adequately dealing with these emotional issues may represent a major healing opportunity for patient afflicted with Lyme/TBDs.

On a personal note: like me, Anita and Tracey have made their own life-changing journeys through Lyme/TBDs and felt inspired to share the powerful lessons they learned as they made the crossing from illness to recovery. With great warmth, compassion, and skill, they teach their readers valuable self-help tools and mindfulness-based techniques for literally tapping into a wellness state of mind for the healing and recovery of the whole person: mind, body, and spirit.

The emotional struggles created by Lyme/TBDs are indeed very real and extremely common. Of course, stuff happens to all of us, but we can benefit and grow from our experiences if we are open to learning the lessons of life. During the eight-year struggle it took me to regain my health, I had this recurring thought: *If I could only create a healthy internal environment—mind, body and spirit— then this devastating sickness could not successfully remain within me.* In other words, my goal was to become an inhospitable host to whatever disease process was causing me the misery I was experiencing. The plan was to become a thriving *human* garden where "wellness ecology" ruled and where disease was unwelcome. Mine was a life-changing journey through which I learned the tools and keys that would unlock a new healing vitality within me.

With *The Lyme Disease Workbook,* people who have Lyme/TBDs now have the self-help tools and mindfulness-based techniques they need to develop their own "wellness ecology" right at their fingertips. The Bains and Middleton approach to recovery from Lyme/TBDs uses and expands upon the very same principles that were so critical to my own healing and recovery from Lyme disease.

During my journey to wellness, I learned that my emotional traumas were eroding my internal environment. My unhealthy mindset and emotions were disrupting the appropriate function of my immune system so that it failed to properly support my healing process. The "emotional weeds" could not be effectively removed from my internal garden until I learned to deal with my unfruitful feelings of bitterness and resentment. We all have different issues of course, but for me, learning to utilize the healing power of forgiveness was a major key in my recovery.

It took a lengthy amount of time before the connection between my emotional trauma, stress, and physical illness finally became clear to me. Over the years of Lyme/TBDs practice, I have observed that this is often a very difficult connection for many people to make. Let's be honest - in our society we're not accustomed to making that connection too easily. It is my firm belief that *The Lyme Disease Workbook* can help you to effectively and expeditiously work through your own "emotional weeds" so that you can overcome the psychological stress and trauma that all too often come with "hard to diagnose" illnesses such as Lyme/TBDs.

Drawing on extensive medical studies, their own work as licensed psychotherapists, and their personal experiences of recovering from Lyme/TBDs, Anita and Tracey show how the mind and body influence each other and why, in their words, "cultivating a wellness state of mind is so foundational to recovery." Using this workbook, you will learn, as my own recovery taught me, that as you shift from an unhealthy to a healthy state of mind, your physical body will soon follow suit.

Published scientific studies have given us a growing knowledge of the relationship between one's mind—our beliefs, perceptions, thoughts, and emotions—and one's physical health. This new understanding relates to how one's mind influences the behavior of the cells in one's body. Here is how it works. Our DNA inside our cells contains genes. The genes contain codes or patterns, which tell our cells what to do. Directed by this genetic code, the cells carry out their functions. When trillions of cells directed by their genetic codes are expressing themselves, this becomes our mind-body state.

What medical research has discovered is that the human mind can have a direct influence over which genes are expressed and which ones are not. That means by affecting the genes in the body's cells, the mind can determine how those cells operate, function, and express themselves. Ultimately, therefore, your mind has the power to determine your state of health and direct your recovery from illness through its effect on your genes.

This, too, is why *The Lyme Disease Workbook* can serve as a valuable resource for your recovery efforts. The tools that you will learn are intended specifically to help you release unresolved emotional pain. And the effect that this has on your genes has the potential to also decrease your stress levels, reduce pain and inflammation, and improve your response to treatments through cultivating an overarching wellness state of mind.

A growing body of scientific evidence that shows how chronic stress brought on by painful emotions can have serious adverse effects on healing and recovering from multiple illnesses, including cancer. Numerous studies showed that emotional conditions like chronic stress, depression, hopelessness, and lack of support can help to create a cancer-friendly environment within the body. For example, hormones released during the stress response can even activate survival genes that protect cancer cells from radiation.

There are also numerous studies from the field of psychoneuroimmunology—mind-body medicine showing that a wellness state of mind can result in different cellular and genetic processes that strongly contribute to positive healing outcomes. As a practitioner who treats people who have Lyme/TBDs, it is obvious to me that with reduced emotional baggage, less stress, and a minimized sense of helplessness, the process of recovery tends to be much more rapid and complete.

The Lyme Disease Workbook provides an array of powerful modalities for releasing the unresolved emotional pain and related stress that may be interfering with your own healing and recovery from Lyme/TBDs. Having referred many of my patients with Lyme/TBDs for these same holistic methods, I can say with certainty that the self-help tools and mindfulness-based techniques offered in this workbook are extremely beneficial for promoting healing and recovery from Lyme/TBDs and other chronic illnesses.

Clearing the "emotional weeds" from your own internal garden is critical to restoring your health. With this groundbreaking workbook, Anita and Tracey teach you how you can use Emotional Freedom Techniques (EFT) and mindfulness-based tools to reduce the stress, pain, and inflammation that come with Lyme/TBDs and to build a wellness-based plan of recovery.

My colleagues in health care—Anita, a Licensed Advanced Practice Registered Nurse (APRN), past-president of the Psychiatric Advanced Practice Nurses of Maryland; and Tracey, a Licensed Certified Social Worker-Clinical (LCSW-C)—are both integrative psychotherapists and EFT experts. They each have private practices and substantial experience working with Lyme/TBDs patients.

With the wisdom of experience and the expertise of practice, Anita and Tracey teach you the fundamental practices for building the foundation of your recovery by cultivating a wellness state of mind. In addition to the many self-help tools Anita and Tracey offer in this workbook, they provide twenty-one deeply inspiring case narratives, which include extended global tapping sequences to get you started that teach you how to clear the "emotional weeds" that choke out the possibilities for recovery.

I highly recommend this workbook as a support for your own recovery and healing process and as a means of supporting others you may know who are also struggling with Lyme/TBDs. It can be easily used as a self-help tool, with a therapist, in a recovery group, and/or with others who will help support your wellness endeavors.

Kenneth B. Singleton, M.D., MPH,
author of *The Lyme Disease Solution*
www.lymedoctor.com

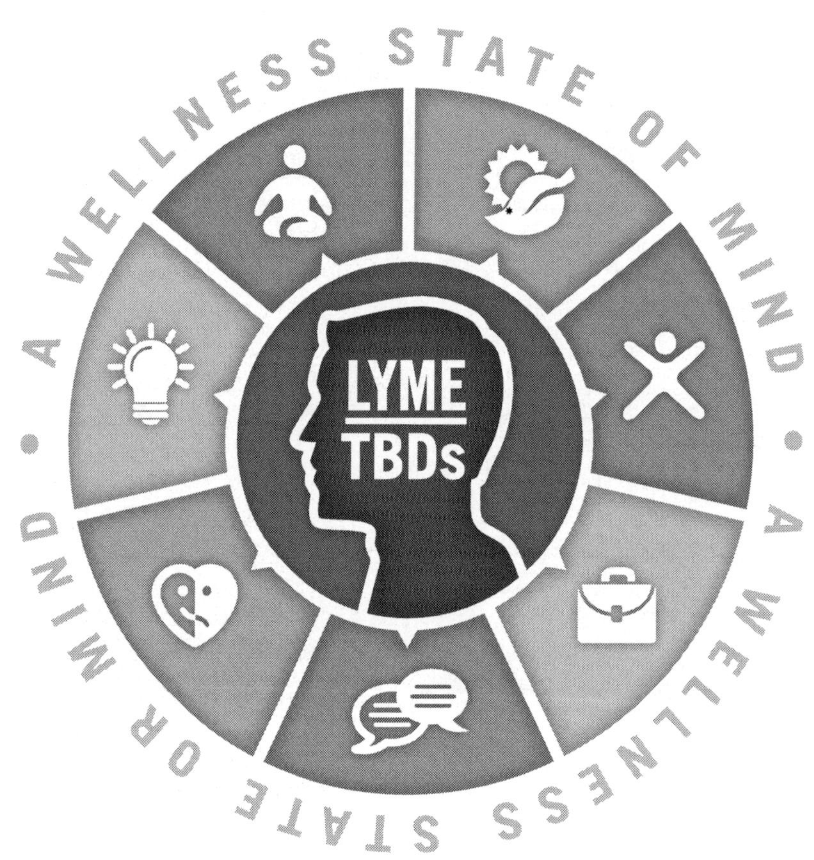
A WELLNESS STATE OF MIND
A WELLNESS STATE OF MIND
LYME
TBDs

Navigating This Workbook

We have gone through a three-year extensive search to find educational material and a variety of self-help tools that you can choose from to be emotionally supportive in cultivating a wellness state of mind that is a vital component for recovery. Since every reader has different preferences in learning and topics of interest, we have made every effort to provide a wide range of topics in this workbook for you to choose from.

We invite you first to skip around, look through the table of contents and go directly to the chapters that interest you. This is not a workbook where you have to start on the first page and read it to the very end. The way we have presented the information makes it possible for you to start wherever you want to based on your interests, emotional issues, and the amount of time and energy you have to address them. You can always choose when to go back to chapters you skipped to learn more.

- We also prompt you throughout the workbook within certain chapters with choices that you can make to continue reading or skip to another specified chapter to address similar emotional issues that may have surfaced for you while reading the content and then be able to choose which self-help tool you would like to use in that process.
- If you are interested and able to learn in-depth information about the concepts we present, you may enjoy reading continuously from the first page onward.
- You may also be interested, but may not have the time or energy to learn more in-depth information about the issues and concepts presented. You can still take positive action to help yourself to more effectively cope and reduce stress by choosing to:

- Skip straight to page 86 to learn **4/8 Diaphragmatic Breathing (Belly Breath)** to reduce the intensity of your stress, regulate your emotions, and ground yourself in the present moment. You can use this technique by itself or in combination with EFT.
- Start by using the featured tool, **Emotional Freedom Techniques (EFT)**. First, you will need to learn the **Modified EFT Basic Recipe** and **tapping acupoints** used with EFT in Chapter 13 on page 121.
- Then, skip to Part 4 on page 151 to **begin using EFT**. Choose a chapter that reflects the Global Issue you would like to address. Read the case study and follow along with the global extended tapping script to gently get you started using EFT. There are twenty-one to choose from!
- As mentioned earlier, at some point, when you have the time, energy, and interest to learn about how to most effectively use EFT, then it is important to understand the main concepts throughout the chapters in Part 3. Return to each of them at a later time when you want to learn more. For now, the following is a road map for skipping around within each part of this workbook. Just have fun with it!

Part 1: Preparation Starts on Page 15

If you are not in a place to read all the information in this part, we suggest you start by skipping to and completing the exercises offered, which can enhance your awareness of what may be mentally supporting and possibly inhibiting your recovery:

- Identify which components within the **Seven Dimensions of Wellness** are active in your life now and which ones you would like to enhance starting on page 26.
- Complete the **Coping with Emotional Stress Scale** on page 37.
- Complete the exercise **Your Qualities of Resilience** on page 47.
- Fill out the **Lyme/TBDs-Related Change/ Loss Inventory** on page 57.
- Fill out the **Lyme/TBDs-Related Belief Inventory** on page 66.
- Complete the exercise **Developing Self-Awareness Around Stress** on page 73 to help you become more aware of how the universal conditions of stress may be impacting you.

You can use the information you discover about yourself that might be inhibiting your recovery with any of the self-help tools and mindfulness-based techniques in your toolkit in Parts 2–4 to help resolve them. These tools can also be used to enhance existing Empowering Beliefs and strategies that support a wellness state of mind.

Part 2: The Toolkit, Supportive Tools Starts on Page 79

You can choose to use any of these self-help tools presented throughout the chapters at any time to support shifting yourself into a wellness state of mind. Skip around and try different ones!

- You can skip to Part 2 starting on page 81 at any time and choose one of the **mindfulness-based tools** to help you reframe disruptive thought patterns.
- Skip to page 86 and use **4/8 Diaphragmatic Breathing (Belly Breath)** at any time for stress reduction, to reduce the intensity of painful emotional states, and to help you feel grounded again. This technique can also stimulate a relaxation response that reduces anxiety, heart rate, and blood pressure.

Part 3: The Toolkit, Featured Tool EFT Starts on Page 113

Chapters 13 and 14 provide detailed explanations of each step in **The Modified EFT Basic Recipe** process and how to get the most benefit in using it. If you are new to EFT, it can be quite overwhelming to read through all of this information for the first time! The good news is that you don't have to. To get started using EFT right away:

- Skip to Chapter 13 on page 121 to learn the **Modified EFT Basic Recipe** and **tapping acupoints** used with EFT.
- Then, skip to Chapter 14: **The Modified EFT Basic Recipe: Sample Tapping Script** on page 131 to follow along through the awareness questions and global tapping script to start experiencing EFT.
- At the end of Part 3, we strongly encourage you to skip to page 147 and complete the exercise **My Commitment to Cultivating a Wellness State of Mind** to develop a wellness plan for yourself.
- Then, skip to Part 4 on page 151 to begin using EFT. Choose a chapter that reflects the issue you would like to address reflected in its title. Read the case study and follow along with the global extended tapping script to gently get you started using EFT. There are twenty-one to choose from!

Part 4: Case Studies and Extended Global Tapping Scripts Start with Chapter 19 on Page 167

For preparation, read the beginning of Chapter 18: **Getting Started Using EFT** on page 153.

- Look through the chapter titles of **Global Issues related to Lyme/TBDs** listed on page 153 or in the table of contents, and choose one that reflects an issue you would like to address and tap through. Have fun skipping around!
- **Write Your Own Tapping Scripts** on page 153.
- **Two Ways to Track Your Progress** on page 154 to learn how to use the worksheets **List of Titled Specific Events** and the **EFT Tapping Log** on page 155.

In the following chapters, we have added more information and exercises about their topics:

- Chapter 21: **I'm so Angry!** on page 185 for a deep exploration into anger and your anger communication style.
- Chapter 34: **Eat to Live or Live to Eat?** on page 321 to learn more about how to use nutrition to support your Lyme/TBD recovery.
- Chapter 36: **My Body Betrayed Me!** on page 347 to identify beliefs you may have about your body image.
- Chapter 39: **I Can't Afford to Be Sick!** on page 377 to explore your beliefs about money.

Part 5: An Introduction to the Science Starts on Page 389

You may enjoy learning more about the science underlying some of the concepts presented in this workbook by skipping to Part 5 whenever you would like. Look through the table of contents to see the chapter topics included in this section.

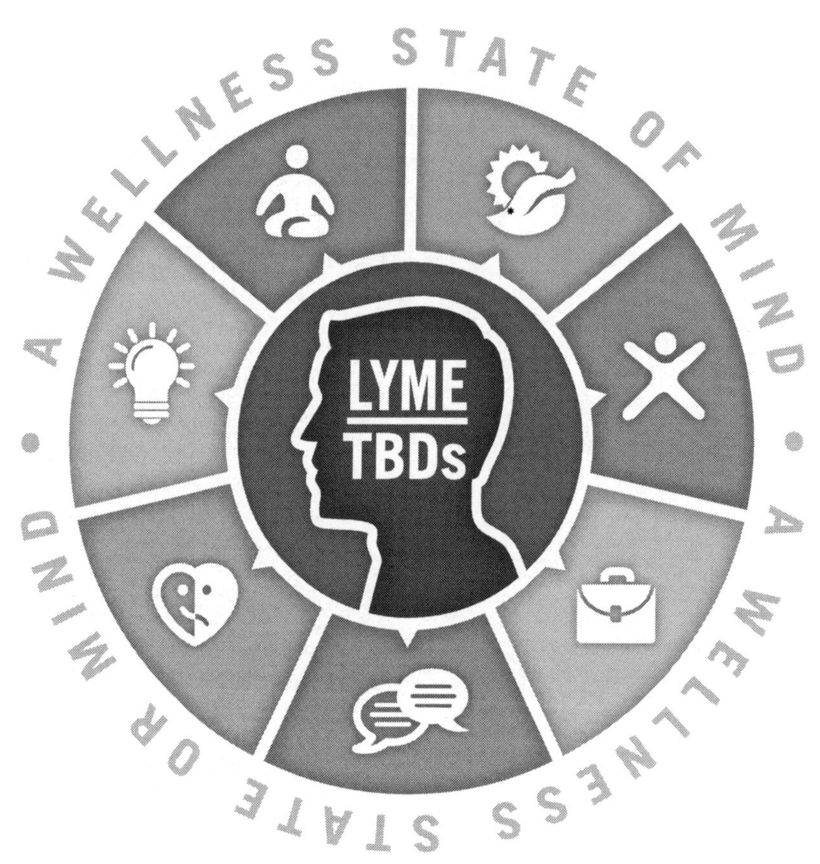
A WELLNESS STATE OF MIND
A WELLNESS STATE OR MIND
LYME
TBDs

Introduction

Have you become discouraged by treatment attempts that don't work? Are you tired of being sick and hearing doctors tell you that there is nothing wrong with you and that your symptoms are all in your head? Do you worry about your ability to work and the toll Lyme disease and other tick-borne diseases (Lyme/TBDs) have taken on your relationships and in all dimensions of your life?

You Are Not Alone

What you are experiencing is the very real life altering impact of Lyme/TBDs and the emotional pain that can come with it. We understand! We are there, too. As integrative psychotherapists who are making our own journey through illness towards recovery from Lyme/TBDs, we recognize the psychological complexity of these illnesses. We also know that among the greatest barriers to healing and recovery are the psychosocial stressors and emotional pain that so many people experience when Lyme/TBDs take hold of their body and take over their life.

Experiencing the benefits in our healing process and seeing it in our clients have convinced us that addressing the emotional issues that Lyme/TBDs often create by "tapping into a wellness state of mind" is a critical missing link to current approaches to treatment. It is far too often the case that the emotional component of these illnesses is overlooked. The result is that patients are left to face their emotional challenges alone without any support and without any education regarding the fact that what they are feeling is a normal human response to the crisis of a serious illness. Lack of effective support to process the emotional issues that typically come with Lyme/TBDs has been shown to weaken the body's capacity for healing while contributing to poor treatment outcomes.

Anybody who has Lyme/TBDs understands that these illnesses have a profoundly negative impact on each dimension of your life:

 **social**

 **intellectual**

 **spiritual**

 **emotional**

 **physical**

 **environmental**

 **occupational**

In fact, there just isn't a single area of your life that Lyme/TBDs don't touch. Sometimes, it can seem as though everything has been turned upside down and that nothing will be right again. This is why tapping into a wellness state of mind is so foundational to recovery: it gives you the means to manage and process the multitude of stressors and painful emotions that can otherwise interfere with healing and prevent recovery from Lyme/TBDs.

Much of what makes Lyme/TBDs so emotionally challenging is that with no specific pattern and so many complicating factors, these illnesses remain a mystery to physicians and researchers alike. In fact, they are highly controversial with many practitioners still claiming that chronic Lyme/TBDs are more a product of a person's imagination than real and treatable illnesses. In the face of a medical and insurance industry that remains woefully misinformed about Lyme/TBDs, it's easy to get discouraged and lose hope. This is especially true when a person is experiencing the chronic pain and emotional destabilization that comes with inflammation of the joints and the brain that can make Lyme/TBDs so debilitating.

Without a proper understanding of Lyme/TBDs and their complexities, practitioners often misdiagnose related neurological symptoms as mental illness. Being misdiagnosed with a mental illness is traumatic and can lead to further stigma and inappropriate treatments. Then there is the fact that many insurance companies don't cover most of the available treatments. This is all very overwhelming and creates enormous emotional and physical stress. If the emotional impact of all of these psychosocial stressors is left unaddressed, it can impede the body's ability to heal. This is why we believe that tapping into a wellness state of mind that cultivates hope and enhances healing is foundational to recovery.

A wellness state of mind is rooted in Empowering Beliefs that stimulate your body's innate ability to heal. It is from a wellness state of mind that you can nurture, grow, and harvest the resilience, fortitude, and hope needed to build and sustain your recovery from Lyme/TBDs.

In this workbook, we equip you with highly effective self-help tools such as Emotional Freedom Techniques (EFT) and mindfulness-based techniques. These tools will help your mind-body system clear the emotional pain and chronic stress that Lyme/TBDs can generate. Research shows that chronic stress compromises immune function and creates adrenal fatigue (low-functioning adrenal glands), both of which can worsen the symptoms of Lyme/TBDs and weaken the body's innate capacity for healing. You will learn how cultivating a wellness state of mind can:

- Break the cycle of chronic stress
- Reduce inflammation and pain
- Balance and restore vital energy for healing
- Activate your body's own capacity for self-repair
- Release the Limiting Beliefs and painful emotions that block healing
- Improve treatment outcomes

There is hope! We experience firsthand the crippling physical and neuropsychiatric symptoms of Lyme/TBDs. On our lowest days, we felt so anxious and depressed that it was all we could do just to maintain a shred of hope. We are very grateful to have the self-help tools in this workbook at our disposal! We continue to use these tools to tap into a wellness state of mind that cultivate hopefulness when presented with relapses and new diagnoses. They continue to work! We share our personal stories with you on pages 7–14.

Your Emotions Matter!

"Working with the mind and learning to find peace in the midst of pain and suffering is essential when dealing with significant illness."

Dr. Richard Horowitz

Why Can't I Get Better? Solving the Mystery of Lyme and Chronic Disease[1]

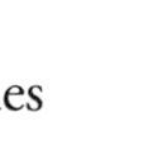

As we address the unresolved emotional issues that create roadblocks in our Lyme/TBDs recovery, we realize that we are also releasing roadblocks in every dimension of our lives. Our journey to recovery has become a catalyst for a level of personal growth and transformation that we could not have imagined possible at the onset of our illnesses.

This process awakened us from deep within ourselves and called us in mind, body, and spirit to a new consciousness that continues to open us to new possibilities in all dimensions of our life. At the beginning of our recovery process, we were able to reprioritize our lives with a focus on what was really important to us. We used these tools to clear the blocks caused by unresolved emotional pain, and were able to make the changes needed to support our recovery process. This created a higher quality of life than we had before we contracted Lyme/TBDs.

Our own personal journeys with Lyme/TBDs showed us what a paradox these illnesses present: how the presence of such powerful and destructive diseases can also be an invitation to go deeper into ourselves to discover what is most important to us, who we are, where we are going, and what we want out of life. How ironic that something so debilitating and painful can also be a path to discovering our true selves: awakening to who we truly are, accepting with compassion and love all that we have endured, and learning how resilient we are!

We Are with You on This Journey

We acknowledge and honor the emotional risk it takes to try something new, especially given the treatment disappointments that so often occur with Lyme/TBDs. At the same time, we encourage you to take a healthy risk now in using this workbook, knowing that it helped our clients and us and that we believe it will help you, too. Here in these pages, you will find many inspirational stories of people who themselves have lived through and overcome the emotional pain and challenges of Lyme/TBDs just as we did. With the daily use of the self-help tools such as EFT and mindfulness-based techniques, you, too, will experience the healing and personal transformation that tapping into a wellness state of mind can bring to Lyme/TBDs recovery and to every dimension of your life.

We invite you to walk with us on the journey to Lyme/TBDs recovery, knowing that you will be part of a community of others who are walking with you. For it is in a community where we can share our stories and offer compassionate witness to one another's trials, so that we can best heal and recover. We encourage you in whatever way you can to reach out to a family member, friend, or another person with Lyme/TBDs or even other chronic illnesses who can support you when you need assistance, conversation, or a quiet compassionate presence. We also recommend that you share this workbook with others, even a therapist, and allow them to support you on days when using the self-help tools seems like too much. They, too, will receive a healing benefit as they help you through your process to recovery.

What's in This Workbook for You

As mentioned, this workbook is essentially a self-help toolkit that contains powerful stress-reducing tools and techniques for releasing the Limiting Beliefs that accompany unresolved emotional issues that can create stress and slow down healing and recovery from Lyme/TBDs. While the tools and techniques are well grounded in theory and practice with emerging research to support them, they are not a substitute for other necessary treatment protocols. Used in conjunction with your current treatment, these self-help tools and techniques can facilitate the emotional healing that will help to activate your body's own mechanisms for repair.

You can use the toolkit anytime and anywhere to either feel better in the moment or to go deeper into core, unresolved emotional issues that may be adding stress to your life and interfering with your healing process.

> This workbook is also relevant for people who have other serious illnesses or conditions.

Whether you are at the beginning of your healing journey or well on your way, this workbook will provide you with an opportunity to use the power of your thoughts and the mind-body connection to enter into a life-changing course that can cultivate recovery and transformation. Using this workbook you can:

- Learn tools and techniques to cultivate a wellness state of mind that is foundational to healing and recovery
- Reduce your stress level in the moment
- Resolve a specific distressing issue
- Resolve a larger, more global life issue
- Release Limiting Beliefs and painful emotions that block healing and recovery
- Develop self-awareness (mindfulness) and self-compassion
- Reframe destructive thought patterns toward enhancing ones
- Identify and build on your strengths and resiliency
- Establish Empowering Beliefs that reduce stress and promote healing
- Reframe Lyme/TBDs as a call to personal growth and transformation
- Strengthen your support system
- Maintain daily wellness practices for creating the recovery you seek
- Create and maintain a wellness-based lifestyle

Emotional Freedom Techniques (EFT): The Featured Tool

The featured tool offered in this workbook is Emotional Freedom Techniques (EFT), and it is presented in Part 3. Often referred to as "acupuncture for the emotions without the needles," EFT is a powerful stress-reduction modality that pairs the tactile manipulation (tapping) of acupoints with the venting of distressing events to disrupt and calm elevated states of fear, anger, and anxiety.[2]

EFT is grounded in energy psychology—a therapeutic approach that combines well-established Western psychological techniques with ancient Eastern healing practices to counteract the distressing thoughts and emotions that can arise from upsetting and traumatic events.[3] Over time and without resolution, distressing thoughts and emotions can create a mind-body state of chronic stress that worsens Lyme/TBD symptoms, compromises the immune system, decreases your response to treatment, and weakens the mind-body system's capacity for healing and recovery. EFT has demonstrated much promise as a means of targeting and processing these Limiting Beliefs and painful emotional states.[4,5,6] Quite simply, EFT comprises an effective and versatile set of tools for:

- Restructuring memories and the release of their painful emotions
- Processing and releasing mental and emotional barriers to healing
- Reducing the stress associated with distressing thoughts and emotions
- Generating a mind-body state of relaxation that facilitates healing
- Enhancing prayer and **meditation**
- Increasing self-awareness and clarifying needs, priorities, and goals
- Cultivating a wellness state of mind rooted in Empowering Beliefs that support, sustain, and enhance Lyme/TBDs recovery

Indeed, we continue to experience both professionally and personally the power of EFT to clear the Limiting Beliefs that accompany unresolved emotional issues, beliefs that can keep any of us locked in a mind-body state of suffering that can interfere with both our recovery from Lyme/TBDs and any other goals we have for ourselves. We have also learned to use EFT as a form of daily emotional hygiene for stress reduction. EFT is so versatile that it can even be used as a spiritual practice to enhance **meditation** and prayer. The more you practice EFT, the more you will be able to literally tap into a wellness state of mind. And this is the reason we present EFT as the primary tool for addressing the emotional component of Lyme/TBDs.

Getting the most benefit from EFT begins with good preparation. This is why we have included in your toolkit a variety of other self-help tools and mindfulness-based techniques in Part 2 that will support you in using EFT to its fullest potential. These mindfulness-based techniques are grounded in established Western therapeutic techniques and from the ancient traditions of the East. Learning and practicing them first will help you to:

- Become more aware of your emotional states in relation to what is happening in the moment
- Regulate your emotional states and arousal levels, thus reducing stress
- Cultivate compassionate acceptance of yourself and what is happening in the moment by reframing negative thoughts and painful emotions to a possibility-based perspective
- Strengthen your resilience
- Identify unresolved emotional issues to use with EFT
- Reduce the stress and tension that weakens the body's capacity to heal

Once learned, all of the self-help tools and techniques offered in this workbook become your personal toolkit. These tools can be used individually or in combination, at any time, to cultivate a wellness state of mind and to build a solid foundation for your recovery from Lyme/TBDs and foster personal growth and transformation.

Case Narratives and Tapping Scripts

Part 4 on page 151 contains twenty-one chapters; each chapter includes an inspirational case narrative that demonstrates the power of EFT to help target, process, and release the distressing perceptions, thoughts, emotions, experiences, and physical symptoms that can come with having Lyme/TBDs. These case narratives are derived from both actual stories and client experiences as reported over time. The names are fictitious and no identifying information is included.

Each case narrative gives you an opportunity to walk with another through the complex process of peeling away the emotional layers of the unresolved issues that can undermine your healing and recovery from Lyme/TDBs. We invite you to journey with the authors and the resilient and courageous individuals who used EFT to establish their own recovery from Lyme/TBDs.

Following each case narrative is an extended global tapping script that will gently guide you through using EFT for your identified Global Issue to get you started. As authors, we cannot assume what your own unique experience of Lyme/TBDs has brought into your life. This is why each global tapping script is followed by an exercise called **Going Deeper with EFT**, which you can use when you feel ready to address the root causes of your Global Issues. The exercise is designed to help you identify the Specific Events that make up the root causes so that you can then tap through them to resolution. We strongly encourage you to go at a gentle pace that allows you to maintain your emotional stability and safety.

Potential Risks & Recommendations for Risk Reduction

While EFT and the mindfulness-based techniques offered in this workbook can break down the potential mental and emotional blocks to Lyme/TBDs healing and recovery, it is important to understand some of the risks inherent in their use and the use of this workbook in general. These risks are related to a number of issues that can arise when using any self-help technique to process and resolve distressing thoughts and emotions related to challenging life events.

The risks are presented below, as identified by Dorothea Hover-Kramer in her book *Creating Healing Relationships: Professional Standards for Energy Therapy Practitioners.*[7] They apply to the use of all of the tools and techniques included in this workbook:

- Particularly distinct or traumatic memories may dissolve, having a potentially adverse effect on your ability to provide legal testimony regarding a harmful or traumatic incident.
- Painful unresolved memories and related emotions may rise to the surface, creating unanticipated feelings and physical sensations that can trigger additional unprocessed material.
- A variety of emotions may continue to surface following the use of EFT and the other tools and techniques offered in this workbook,

indicating the presence of other issues and events that need to be addressed.

With these risks in mind, we strongly recommend that you use this workbook in conjunction with the support of a licensed mental-health therapist, preferably one who is also a certified EFT practitioner, in the following cases:

- If you have been diagnosed with a psychiatric disorder related to the neuropsychiatric symptoms of Lyme/TBDs or were diagnosed prior to getting Lyme/TBDs
- If you experience overwhelming emotions related to depressive and/or anxious states, panic attacks, psychotic episodes, and/or dissociative states
- If you are unable to self-regulate your emotions, ground yourself, and maintain safety
- If you have been diagnosed with post traumatic stress disorder (PTSD)
- If you are having suicidal and/or homicidal thoughts and/or intentions
- If you are currently mentally unstable or currently decompensating
- If you self-injure or engage in other self-harming behaviors

Use of the self-help tools and techniques included in this workbook may worsen some of the symptoms associated with a psychiatric disorder. This risk can be minimized by working with a licensed mental-health professional, ideally one who is also a certified EFT practitioner. Such a professional can provide you with skilled guidance and support as you go through the process of identifying, targeting, and releasing any unresolved emotional pain that may be interfering with your recovery.

A trained and empathic therapist can advise you on the risks and benefits of tapping through certain emotional issues as well as help you to assess when you are ready to address them. A mental-health professional with advanced EFT training can teach you how to contain emotions (emotional regulation) that may otherwise overwhelm you (emotional flooding) and to ground yourself. They can also show you how to break down emotional issues in a way that decreases the likelihood of re-traumatization so that you can safely process and release them.

To locate a certified EFT practitioner in your area, visit www.eftuniverse.com, www.thetappingsolution.com, or www.energypsych.org. You may also contact us (Anita Bains and Tracey Middleton) by visiting our respective websites: www.anitabains.com and www.traceymiddleton.com. We are available to work with individuals in person, over Skype, or on the phone, as well as with groups.

Given that many therapists (even many of those who are certified EFT practitioners) are not familiar with Lyme/TBD issues, it may be a challenge to find a Lyme-literate therapist in your area. However, this does not mean that the person you do find is unable to help you. This workbook is a great resource for helping your therapist understand the neuropsychiatric and emotional impact of Lyme/TBDs. You and your therapist can also work together in using this workbook to create an individualized strength-based treatment plan that will support you in cultivating a wellness state of mind for generating the healing and recovery you desire. When using this workbook, whether it be on your own or along with a therapist, we strongly encourage you to identify those people you can call for emotional support when you need it.

Again, we want to encourage you to understand that you are not alone in your struggle with Lyme/TBDs. There is hope, even in the most challenging situations. In the following two sections, we share our personal stories of Lyme/TBD recovery, relapse and new diagnoses and how we continue to use these tools to tap into a wellness state of mind as new challenges present themselves. They work for us and we also believe that they can work for you, too.

Anita's Story

In 1997, I experienced persistent and often piercing immobilizing pain, sleeplessness, and brain fog that left me nearly disabled. Doctors from a variety of specialties evaluated me in an attempt to find out what was wrong. I was eventually diagnosed with polymyalgia rheumatica (PMR), an inflammatory disorder that causes moderate to severe muscle pain and stiffness in different parts of the body. I was treated with prednisone for six months, and miraculously my pain disappeared! It was such a relief, but short lived. To my dismay, after the prednisone was discontinued, my symptoms reappeared! My doctor did not have other recommendations for treatment. He even told me that my disease might be "psychosomatic in nature." I took this to mean that he believed my symptoms were all in my head.

But I knew that something was physically wrong with me. I realized then that Western medicine alone would not be enough to help me recover. This realization was a wake-up call for me to take more responsibility for my recovery and motivated me to seek alternative therapies in order to enhance the conventional treatments being offered to me.

I began to design my own recovery plan. I became a sponge -- learning as much as I could about alternative practices including Emotional Freedom Techniques (EFT), meditation, sound therapy, self-hypnosis, and other mindfulness-based techniques. I felt compelled to use every tool at my disposal to cultivate "a new wellness state of mind." I worked on my diet and implemented an exercise plan that accommodated my symptoms. I reprioritized my professional life in order to support my recovery. I let go of a very stressful part-time job and put my energy into a part-time teaching position and my psychotherapy practice, which were enjoyable and rewarding.

Emotional Freedom Techniques (EFT) were the most powerful life-changing tools I utilized. I used EFT to tap into my wellness state of mind, and to hold onto my hope for a full recovery. At first, I doubted that such a silly-seeming technique could work. However, I was desperate to feel better so I persisted in using EFT to release painful emotional states of sadness, frustration, and anger as they surfaced. EFT helped me to reduce my stress and, as a result, my symptoms began to improve. My pain, brain fog, and sleeplessness lessened. I noticed that I had more energy. The practice of using EFT to cultivate the core belief that I was going to recover became foundational to my healing. My symptoms of polymyalgia rheumatica gradually diminished and after almost two-and-a-half years, they were gone! I have no doubt that cultivating a wellness state of mind was foundational to my return to health.

I became passionate about sharing EFT with others through teaching. In my psychotherapy practice I used EFT to support others in cultivating a wellness state of mind that could be foundational in creating wellness in every dimension of their lives.

My introduction to Lyme disease came through working with my psychotherapy clients who had Lyme disease. They both educated and inspired me with their resiliency to recover as they shared stories and used EFT, along with other mind-body techniques, to work through their struggles with having these complex diseases.

I was deeply touched by their stories and felt compelled to learn all that I could about Lyme/TBDs in order to support them. I was dismayed by the many stories I heard first hand of people who were being misdiagnosed and dismissed by doctors who assumed they were making up their symptoms. Many of my clients were traumatized by these painful events, at the same time that they were coping with the ravages of their diseases. It became a personal and professional passion for me to support them in cultivating a wellness state of mind by using the integrative mind-body techniques offered in this workbook to help foster recovery. I was honored to witness the tremendous benefits they experienced. I had no idea at that time that I would soon be embarking on my own personal journey of recovery from Lyme/TBDs.

Then, in the early spring of 2013, I discovered a small insect bite on the back of my knee. Soon after that, I began experiencing dizziness, joint aches, and general malaise. Knowing the horror stories of so many people whose experience with Lyme/TBDs began with flu-like symptoms, I was concerned I might have one of the diseases. I was hesitant to go to a doctor because I was afraid he or she might think I was making too much out of nothing, especially since I did not have the signature bull's-eye rash. I even rationalized at one point that I was personalizing my symptoms as a result of intensively researching Lyme/TBDs and working with people who had them. Still, I decided to honor my concerns and get evaluated as soon as possible by a Lyme-literate doctor. I was so grateful to get an appointment with one who respectfully listened to my concerns, asked detailed questions, and evaluated my body. At the end of my appointment, he ordered all the appropriate tests to rule out Lyme and other tick-borne diseases (Lyme/TBDs). Still, I was not expecting to hear that I had anything more than an insect bite. To my surprise, the tests came back positive and I was diagnosed with both Lyme disease and Rocky Mountain spotted fever (RMSF)! I am so grateful that I listened to my body. I give so much credit to the members of the Lyme/TBD communities who advised me about what to do and who to see for help. I am so grateful that a compassionate, informed doctor correctly diagnosed me.

Although I had learned a great deal from my clients, through the research I had done, and from patients and colleagues in the Lyme/TBD community, I was about to learn firsthand the life-changing impact Lyme/TBDs would have on my own life. Once again, I had to cultivate the belief that I could heal and recover my sense of emotional and physical well-being, despite the difficult nature of these seemingly intractable diseases.

As I experienced one layer of deep emotional pain after the next, I was grateful that I knew how to use EFT to process and release my intense feelings as they surfaced. Some examples of thoughts I experienced were: "How can I get a second debilitating disease or maybe it was Lyme disease all along? Who knows anything! I am so angry to be going through something as debilitating as this again! Am I being punished? Who's going to care for me if I'm disabled? I'm furious with myself and my body for making me sick after I worked so hard to get well! I am scared! I don't know how this is going to change me? Will I find the treatments that work for me? How much suffering will I have to go through this time? Is there any hope for me?"

I used EFT almost daily to process the feelings of disbelief, anger, fear, and sadness that naturally surfaced while I faced my new diagnosis of having Lyme and RMSF.

I do want to acknowledge and honor all of those patients who feel a deep sense of relief and validation upon finally receiving a correct diagnosis. My experience of being diagnosed right away is, unfortunately, not the norm. By working with my clients who have Lyme/TBDs, I've learned that once the relief of knowing what is wrong is absorbed, it is common for all of us to experience emotions of anger, fear, confusion, and sadness. These feelings often resurface at different times as patients face the debilitating symptoms, myriad treatment options, and search for the right doctor(s) whom they can trust to compassionately support them to a successful recovery.

The practice of using EFT became my lifeline

through this process; one I reached for on a daily basis to help me address my emotional issues so I could support my body's recovery. EFT helped me to cope and hold onto the belief that recovery was, once again, possible for me. By reducing my fear and stress levels, my body's ability to respond to treatment was enhanced, which in turn made my symptoms more manageable in my day-to-day life.

Through many months of treatment, I tapped through my Limiting Beliefs, anxiety, pain, doubt, anger, sadness, and confusion as each feeling or thought surfaced. After clearing and resolving these emotional layers, I experienced the sense of calm and mental clarity that I needed in order to keep taking positive steps to help myself recover.

I remember one day when my mood had become darkened by the pain and fatigue that enveloped my body, I began tapping through and resolving the identified Limiting Beliefs that were at the root of my fears – focusing on the anger I held against my body for betraying me by getting sick again. I lost track of time as I tapped through to resolution. Eventually, new Empowering Beliefs and insights emerged that allowed me to compassionately forgive and accept my body for all that it was doing on my behalf to recover.

Then, in 2016, I received another unexpected diagnosis; one that further taught me how important my EFT practice had become in helping me in my journey as a patient, and as a human being through the inevitable vicissitudes of life. My doctor diagnosed me with Bartonella, another vector borne disease, as well as mold illness. He was unsure if these had been quietly affecting me all these years, as I struggled to recover from Lyme, or if I had been re-infected. But because I had a strong EFT practice in place, I was able to face this daunting diagnosis without becoming overwhelmed, panicking or blaming myself. My strong foundational practice in tapping into a wellness state of mind helped me to continue to practice healthy lifestyle choices and experience a sense of self-worth despite my newly revealed health challenges. As my healing unfolds I realize that I cultivated a newfound inner strength, confidence and faith that I will find answers and recovery. The realization of how much stronger I had become emotionally and spiritually – even when faced with physical suffering -- brought me great joy and relief.

Recovering from Lyme/TBDs has been a transformational process that has stimulated my personal development. It has called me to go even deeper into my core sense of self to address the challenges I've faced. I became much more aware of the significance of my spiritual life in my recovery process. I embraced the idea, posed by many, that we are spiritual beings having a physical experience. The recovery process for me has become about rediscovering and living as my authentic self, while being open to the invitation to go deeper into experiencing the Divine that I believe is within me, and within each of us.

The most Empowering Belief for me has been the recognition that I am not alone, and that God is available to help me heal and co-create the life I want to live. The process of recovery from Lyme/TBDs has led me to a deeper sense of connection with God, and a greater love for my whole being – mind, body and spirit. I accept the sacred process of life and the way in which it offers me new experiences to help me clarify who I am and what I want out of my life as my interests and abilities evolve. I have the faith that, when I ask for help, I will receive the assistance I need. And I know that it is my responsibility to be aware and open to new possibilities that may be presented for my best and highest good -- and to release whatever is standing in the way of that happening.

I have been fortunate to have access to Lyme-literate physicians throughout my illness, but I know that even with that help, I could not have recovered without cultivating a wellness state of mind that fosters hope and promotes healing. Processing and clearing the Limiting Beliefs and unresolved emotional pain that Lyme/TBDs have triggered in me has been a lifestyle choice I've made throughout my healing process, and it has made a profound, life-changing difference.

My hope is that by using the EFT Techniques we offer in the pages that follow, you too will be able to find new layers of hope, transformational healing and well-being.

Tracey's Story

Like Anita, I did not know that I had Lyme disease and now believe I had it for many years. I was a collegiate athlete and high school teacher/coach of fifteen years before I went back to school to become a clinical social worker. I also spent many summers co-facilitating summer retreats at a center located in Missouri. Then, I did not know anything about Lyme/TBDs. With that said, I was not concerned when a couple of former retreat participants called saying they believed they were infected with Lyme disease while on retreat. I spent summers in those woods with no knowledge of Lyme prevention or risks. I do not have a memory of being bitten by a tick, but like most people, I didn't know what to look for. There were countless days when I was covered in bug bites and I assumed they were just from mosquitoes.

During the years I facilitated summer retreats, I had episodes of sudden and mysterious physical and mental health symptoms unlike anything I have ever experienced. My mood would become unstable and I experienced migrating body pains that I attributed to being a former athlete. I just kept ignoring my symptoms and managing the inconveniences they created. For years, I managed by seeing doctors sporadically for a specific symptom; like having gall bladder attacks and eventually having it removed but never putting all the symptoms together. My episodes intensified through the years until I became debilitated by joint and muscle pain, severe fatigue, depression, and anxiety and almost daily overwhelming full body sweats.

I went to a gynecologist to see why I was having hot flashes. She ran tests and said that I was in full menopause at the age of forty-two. I was told that I would start to feel better with estrogen and progesterone replacement, which did not happen. The night sweats, brain fog and fatigue continued. Then, came the diagnosis of Hashimoto's disease: a disease in which the immune system attacks the thyroid, causing it to become underactive (hypothyroidism). My doctors thought for sure this was my main problem.

A couple of years later as my symptoms continued, I was prescribed prednisone for nine months and had injections in my back to alleviate the debilitating nerve pain I was experiencing, even though my MRI read normal. After stopping prednisone, my symptoms continued and I was bedridden for a week, unable to walk or even make it to the bathroom. I was then hospitalized for three days because my liver enzymes reached dangerously high levels, my right knee was swollen (even though I had no injury) and I had fluid in my right hip causing excruciating pain that made walking impossible. My rheumatologist could not figure it out. I was a mystery to him and his colleagues.

I felt depressed and confused. It was horrifying to have the interns and residents at the hospital walk into my room multiple times a day and look at me as if I was an experiment in a petri dish because they could not find the cause. They drained the fluid from my hip. Nobody knew why the fluid had so suddenly appeared. Looking back, I realized that the fluid from my knee and hip should've been tested for Lyme disease. I didn't know to ask and the medical team did not suggest it. I had already received two negative CDC (Centers for Disease Control) Lyme tests. I didn't know that it is common to receive a false-negative test for Lyme disease.

Then came the multiple surgeries. Within a six-month period, when I was forty-four years old, I endured a total right knee replacement (triggered by mysterious uncontrollable swelling that was too thick to be drained after many attempts), cervical fusion (due to multiple compressed discs), and surgeries on both shoulders. The doctors were chasing my pain with a scalpel, and I still did not improve. I continued to have severe mood swings, which led my doctors to refer me to a psychiatrist who diagnosed me with bipolar disorder!

I started on psychotropic medications that only made me feel worse. I continued to have mood swings with depression and anxiety. I did have some good days that brought relief, but they were confusing. I noticed that I began to be fearful when I was feeling better because I was waiting for my body to ambush me again with the debilitating mood swings, extreme fatigue, body sweats and rotating body pains. I learned not to trust my "good days" for fear of being disappointed when my symptoms reappeared, which they always did.

After a while, there was just no point in seeing doctors who could not help me. I had become their difficult patient (by not getting better) and *needed only a psychiatrist* to treat my supposed bipolar disorder. Friends and coworkers commented that I looked healthy and insinuated my symptoms must be in my head. I soon learned to keep how I was feeling to myself, thus becoming more isolated and alone.

In the meantime, I was working with some clients as a psychotherapist, who themselves had Lyme disease and other tick-borne illnesses. I was astonished by how similar their stories were to mine. I began to research Lyme disease and went to a Lyme rally in Washington, D.C. It was there, after hearing so many inspirational stories and becoming more educated about Lyme disease, that I saw my own story in theirs. I found a Lyme-literate integrative physician who confirmed for me through a more sensitive test that I, in fact, was suffering from Lyme disease. I could not have been happier to be diagnosed with Lyme disease at this point! Now, at least, I could prove that it was not in my head!

At the same time, getting diagnosed with Lyme disease seemed to have opened an emotional floodgate. All of the physical and emotional pain I had endured during those many years of undiagnosed illness came pouring into my consciousness. My emotions were all over the board, in the wake of my diagnosis, I believed I was the victim of an attack on two fronts: by my own body and by the medical establishment who had let me down for years. These traumatic experiences led me to blame myself for causing my physical and emotional problems. I felt sad that all this suffering and disappointment led me to rejecting my body.

As an integrative psychotherapist, and EFT expert, I knew that to heal my body and mind I had to shift from a state of mind that was controlled by the Limiting Beliefs of fear, helplessness, isolation, and despair. EFT and the other mindfulness-based tools included in this workbook, helped me release these painful emotions and Limiting Beliefs. I was then able to shift into a wellness state of mind based on Empowering Beliefs. These beliefs reconnected me to my body, and cultivated hope for recovery.

I made the positive changes necessary to remain compliant with my treatment plan even when I didn't feel like it. Dr. Singleton's Lyme Inflammation Diet,[11] helped to reduce my inflammation, irritability, and depression. I had no idea that I had developed food sensitivities that were making my symptoms worse until I read his book *The Lyme Disease Solution.*[12] I also used *Recipes for Repair* by Gail Piazza and Laura Piazza that features easy to follow and delicious recipes for the Lyme Inflammation Diet. (See Chapter 34, **Eat to Live or Live to Eat?** on page 321 to learn more about it.)

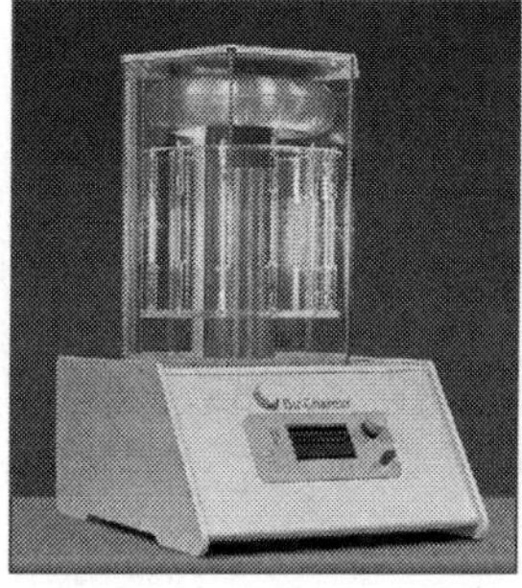

Read about some soft data collected on the use of the BioCharger NG™* in a small group of people with Lyme disease in the appendix on page 419.

To learn more about the Biocharger NG, go to biocharger.com

I also included in my recovery plan the use of the BioCharger Plus. I had researched Rife machines and found that this one offered more. The BioCharger Plus™ is the previous model to what is now the upgraded model on the market called the BioCharger NG™.. These models are described below by the developers.

It is a high voltage multi-frequency, resonant transformer (modified Tesla Coil) that wirelessly and simultaneously transmits pulsed waves of electromagnetic, electrodynamic and photonic energy. The transmitted energy stimulates and invigorates the entire body to optimize and improve potential health and wellness. It is completely non-invasive, and has proven to restore strength, stamina, coordination and mental clarity. It embodies a revolutionary technology when compared to the antiquated analog technology of existing Rife machines, multi-wave oscillators and various Photonic light therapies.[13]

I put together a holistic daily treatment plan for myself, and after only six weeks of following my plan, I was symptom free! It consisted of:

- Applying EFT and the other mindfulness-based tools included in this workbook to cultivate a wellness state of mind
- Using the BioCharger Plus™ (3-4 x week)
- Taking antibiotics and supplements as prescribed
- Getting proper nutrition via the Lyme Inflammation Diet™ (LID)

After twelve weeks, I had moved into early remission. I was thrilled to be free of my symptoms of bipolar disorder, after being successfully treated for Lyme disease. I was safely and gradually taken off all the psychotropic medications with no return of any bipolar symptoms. Much later, I was re-evaluated and was told that I had been misdiagnosed with bipolar disorder and my health record was corrected to reflect this updated information. The justification for this was my sudden onset of mental instability, nonresponsive to psychotropics, the sudden elimination of symptoms (once Lyme disease was properly treated) and continued mental stability! I was both ecstatic and angry at the same time reflecting back on all that I had gone through. I used EFT to help me heal and release the painful emotions associated with being misdiagnosed for years.

Having Lyme disease took me on a spiritual journey that led me back to myself. I used this crisis as a "wake-up call." I could no longer afford the luxury of living a high-stress life that was costing me my health and wellbeing. The level of pain I experienced invited me to reprioritize my life and to let go of a high-stress job, as well as, unhealthy relationships and ways of being that were no longer serving me. My body told me, "No more," so I had to learn a new way of living.

In early 2016, after more than 1 1/2 years of being in remission, I was diagnosed with Babesia and toxic mold illness. I had been very sick in the past year with high liver and pancreatic enzymes, and hospitalized three times with no known cause. I experienced a resurgence of hot flashes, fatigue, rotating body aches and mood instability. Without knowing it, I was being exposed to toxic mold for over 10 months which compromised my immune system and possibly activated persister cells that were dormant. I am now learning about the relationship between toxic mold illness and chronic Lyme/TBDs. It is imperative that I heal from the mold to strengthen my immune system to recover from Babesia. I am currently undergoing integrative treatments for both of these conditions.

I am now using the new BioCharger NG several times a week, along with conventional IV and oral medications that are helping me to recover. (We had donated the Biocharger Plus to a friend for research purposes over a year ago.) I am already experiencing improvement in my symptoms. My experiences continue to teach me that caring for the emotional and spiritual body is just as vital to recovery as is treating the physical body. We are whole beings— mind, body, spirit, and soul—whom need holistic recovery plans. I welcome this next round of healing knowing that this is another opportunity to continue personal and spiritual development and to keep fostering a lifestyle of wellness in all dimensions of my life. I have the tools that I need presented in this workbook to keep tapping into a wellness state of mind to enhance my responsiveness to treatments. I have no doubt that I will recover and go into remission again! I am so deeply grateful for the magnificence of my body and the endless grace of God.

PART 1
Preparation

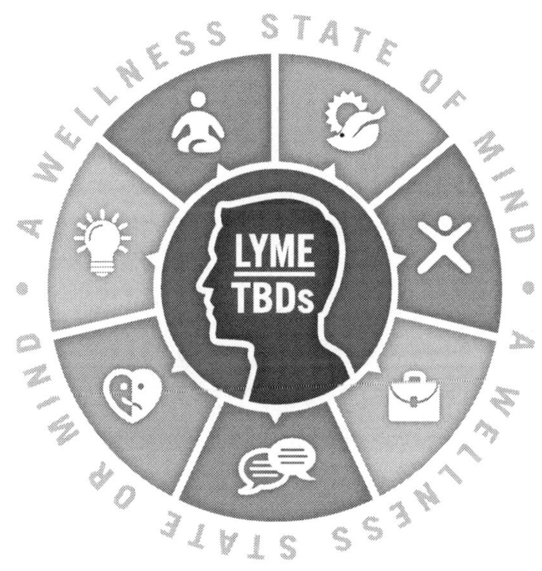

CHAPTER

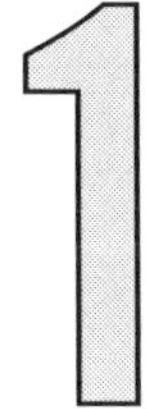

Introduction to the Neuropsychiatric Symptoms of Lyme/TBDs

We know how hurtful and stigmatizing it is when medical professionals and others imply with their words and body language that you are "crazy" or that there is nothing wrong with you physically, that your symptoms are merely "psychosomatic." This is the reason we think it's important to present some of the scientific research and anecdotal evidence from Lyme-literate doctors that demonstrate the very real destructive impact Lyme disease and other tick-borne diseases (TBDs) can have on neurological functions and mental and emotional states.

In *Why Can't I Get Better? Solving the Mystery of Lyme and Chronic Disease,* Dr. Richard Horowitz points out that there is a "complex interaction between psychosocial factors such as stress and trauma and the nervous, cardiovascular, endocrine, and immune systems."[14] When neurological issues are at play, added disruptions in mood and thinking can occur, and focused care needs to be taken to ensure that those with Lyme/TBDs receive the proper treatment for these issues.

Emotional Freedom Techniques (EFT), along with the other self-help tools and mindfulness-based techniques offered in this workbook, provide an effective means of disrupting and calming elevated states of stress, fear, anxiety, and hopelessness, regardless of the source.[15] They belong to a family of modalities that combine Western and Eastern traditions that promote the healing of mind and body by balancing and restoring the energy reserves necessary for our survival and well-being. Horowitz supports these modalities as part of an effective integrative plan of treatment. He notes:

> *People have combined Western and Eastern traditions to help find new solutions for their patients. Working within the framework of the Chinese, Tibetan, and Ayurvedic systems of medicine, doctors work to balance and strengthen the subtle energy channels in the body (known as the energy meridians in Chinese medicine), which when out of balance, lead to diseases of the body and mind. While there is no one right way to resolve an illness, a multidisciplinary approach while working with the mind to clear emotional issues and past trauma is often helpful.*[16]

Horowitz, along with Dr. James Schaller (author of *What You May Not Know About Bartonella, Babesia, Lyme Disease and Other Tick & Flea-Borne Infections*) and Dr. Singleton (author of *The Lyme Disease Solution*), also suggests that medications and/or mental-health treatment may be necessary during the course of treatment.[17,18,19]

It has been our experience that using energy psychology techniques as part of a holistic and integrated plan of care has helped largely mitigate and even clear the emotional distress our clients have experienced in relation to Lyme/TBDs and the impact it has had on their lives.

This chapter familiarizes you with the neuropsychiatric symptoms of Lyme/TBDs and helps you understand how Lyme/TBDs bacteria interferes with neurological functions in such a way that those who are infected can experience a wide range of mild to severe disturbances in mood, cognition, and behavior.

It is our hope that this information will help to de-stigmatize the neuropsychiatric aspects of Lyme/TBDs, particularly when it comes to the use of labels on the part of professionals. If you are someone whom a doctor or other medical professional has dismissed with labels such as "psychosomatic" or "hypochondriac," you can use the information here in conjunction with EFT to clear the negative impact of these labels and to heal any past unresolved emotional pain they may have triggered in you.

If emotional stress increases for you as you go through any section, we suggest:

Skip to Part 2 on page 86 at any time to use **4/8 Diaphragmatic Breathing (Belly Breath)** to reduce the intensity of your stress, regulate your emotions, and ground yourself in the present moment.

An Overview of the Neuropsychiatric Symptoms of Lyme/TBDs

Research into the impact of Lyme disease and other tick-borne diseases (TBDs) on neurological functions points to a strong relationship between the behavior of *Borrelia burgdorferi* (the spirochete bacteria that causes Lyme disease) and inflammation of the brain (encephalopathy). Inflammation of the brain can be associated with:

- Mood swings
- Depression
- Loss of cognitive (thinking) function
- Changes in personality
- Irritability
- Impulsivity
- Poor judgment
- Low frustration tolerance[20]

According to Dr. Robert C. Bransfield, "Thousands of peer-reviewed articles demonstrate the causal association between infections and mental illness and over 300 peer-reviewed scientific articles demonstrate the causal association between Lyme/tick-borne disease and mental illness."[21] The large number of neuropsychiatric symptoms that can come with Lyme/TBDs put people who have these diseases that go undiagnosed at risk for being misdiagnosed with only a psychiatric illness, thus not getting the correct treatment needed to recover. As Richard Horowitz puts it:

> *Apart from physical symptoms, many of my Lyme disease patients complain of mood disorders, especially severe anxiety, depression and post-traumatic stress disorder. Typically, their previous physicians have told these patients that these feelings and emotions are psychiatric in nature and unrelated to their physical health.*[22]

Only recently, in 2015, has the American Psychiatric Association published guidelines that now require psychiatrists and psychologists to rule out Lyme disease during a psychiatric evaluation before making a mental-health diagnosis.[23] Unfortunately, it has come too late for many Lyme-disease sufferers who have already received a misdiagnosis of mental illness. To add to this, many practitioners have not been educated on this change and have not added it to their best practices.

Lyme disease has been known to cause a host of neuropsychiatric abnormalities. In fact, virtually every psychiatric diagnosis listed in the Diagnostic and Statistical Manual (DSM), the bible of mental health diagnosis, can be caused by Lyme disease and associated co-infections.

Dr. Richard Horowitz
Why Can't I Get Better? Solving the Mystery of Lyme Disease[24]

Some compelling research tells a story that is quite different from what many doctors believe. Bransfield found that the activation of cytokines, pro-inflammatory protein molecules, is a major factor in the process of progressive inflammation that contributes to encephalopathy (brain inflammation) and related psychiatric symptoms.[25]

Both he and Dr. Brian Fallon note that spirochetes leave lipoproteins, which are also known to be pro-inflammatory, on the outer membrane of the *Borrelia* cell wall. These lipoproteins then attract neutrophils (white blood cells) that increase the activation of pro-inflammatory cytokines by fifty to five hundredfold.[26,27] This process sets the stage for neurotoxicity and encephalopathy, which can lead to unstable moods, severe emotional states, and impaired thinking and memory.

Cytokines and "Sickness Behavior"

The function of cytokines is to start healing injuries and to fight potential infections. When healing injuries, cytokines initiate a pro-inflammatory response, creating swelling around the affected area to help protect it. The problem arises when the stress response is not turned off and moves into chronic stress, which stimulates an overproduction of cytokines. This creates unnecessary inflammation in addition to the inflammation inherent in Lyme/TBDs, thus worsening symptoms.[28,29]

The role of cytokines in the physiological, psychological, and cognitive responses to chronic disease has also been noted by researchers Suzanne Segerstrom, Denise de Ridder and colleagues, and Margo De Kooker. These researchers point to the role cytokines play in producing what is known as "sickness behavior," which under normal circumstances resolves when an illness goes away but which can be prolonged during chronic illnesses.[30,31,32]

Sickness behavior is the body's adaptive response to conditions such as cold and flu viruses. In the case of a short-lived illness, this response allows the body to slow down and focus on healing. As described by Horowitz, the symptoms of sickness behavior include:

- Weakness
- Malaise
- Lack of concentration
- Depressed mood
- Lethargy
- Little to no appetite[33]

In people with chronic Lyme/TBDs, the persistent presence of these symptoms indicates "a dramatic increase in cytokine production and inflammatory molecules in the body: a kind of inflammation gone wild."[34] The severity and frequency of the symptoms associated with sickness behavior in people with Lyme/TBDs changes according to the frequency and level of activation of cytokines by the lipoproteins produced by the spirochetes.[35]

For physicians who lack experience in treating Lyme/TBDs, the prolonged symptoms of sickness behavior that come with them can easily be misinterpreted as psychiatric illnesses when there seems to be no evidence of a physical disease. This, along with the fact that Lyme/TBDs bacteria are able to mimic a variety of physical and psychiatric disorders, can make accurate diagnosis almost impossible for doctors who are not up to date on how these diseases manifest. For example, many physicians may not know that Lyme/TBDs can cause inflammation of the brain with symptoms that can be easily mistaken for a psychiatric illness unrelated to any organic disease process.[36,37]

Neuropsychiatric Symptoms Associated with Inflammation

Symptoms associated with "inflammation provoked by parasites" during "persistent infection" are gradually increasing mood disturbances and cognitive impairment.[38] "Cognitive symptoms," Bransfield explains, "begin as executive dysfunction and mild cognitive impairment and may gradually progress to dementia."[39] These symptoms can include:

- Lack of mental clarity
- Impaired memory
- Challenges staying focused
- Difficulty comprehending and retaining information
- Confusion while trying to make decisions

Bransfield also notes that early signs of emotional difficulty include:

- Insomnia
- Reduced frustration tolerance
- Irritability
- Dysthymia (mild but chronic depression)[40]

He further states that these symptoms may progress to:

- Anxiety disorders
- Worsening depression
- Impulsivity
- Personality disorders[41]

Addressing Neuropsychiatric Symptoms

Bransfield, Singleton, and Horowitz suggest that treatment for people with Lyme/TBDs who are experiencing the above symptoms include psychotherapy and medication in conjunction with other appropriate treatments. When these psychiatric conditions are interpreted solely as mental illness, they cannot be properly treated.[42,43,44]

According to Horowitz, "Primary modes of treatment for the Lyme patient that presents with neuropsychiatric illness involve a combination of antimicrobial therapies, psychotropic medications, herbal and vitamin therapies, and various forms of psychotherapy and stress reduction techniques."[45] These modes of treatment include EFT,[46] which works like needle-free acupuncture to free the mind-body system of emotional blocks to healing.

These blocks develop over time as part of a pattern of negative thinking and Limiting Beliefs that any of us can fall into in response to a number of emotionally painful and stressful life events. Unless these blocks are addressed, they can intensify the neuropsychiatric and physical challenges that can come with Lyme/TBDs. For example, it is well established that depression and anxiety alone are strongly associated with cognitive impairment (for example, poor concentration, difficulty making decisions, distraction, etc.) and vulnerability to physical challenges (for example, chronic fatigue, heart disease, joint and muscle pain, etc.).

In *The Lyme Disease Solution*, Dr. Singleton states that a major contributing factor to anxiety is the chronic stress caused by infection from the Lyme/TBD bacteria. "It can trigger the release of high levels of 'stress hormones' that can disrupt the mind-body system by causing cognitive impairment, mood disturbance and adrenal fatigue. In addition, some people are anxious to get better and are continually worrying about their health status, which in turn makes them more anxious. Lyme/TBDs actually exacerbate this underlying anxiety issue."[47] Horowitz explains, "Chronic stress markedly increases a patient's vulnerability to poor medical outcomes across a wide variety of mental and medical conditions. Most of my patients notice that when they are under increased stress . . . their underlying Lyme symptoms often come out of hiding, or significantly worsen."[48]

It is important to be aware of the various mental, emotional, and physical factors that can exacerbate the symptoms of depression and anxiety that already exist as a result of the Lyme/TBD bacteria. Take a look at the following factors, which we have adapted from Singleton's work:

Factors That Can Contribute to Anxiety and Depression

- Dr. Singleton: *The Lyme Disease Solution*

Mental/Emotional Factors:

- Financial worries
- Difficulties at work/job loss
- Major life changes
- Treatment failures
- Misdiagnosis
- Relationship issues (spouse/partner, family, friends and colleagues)
- Unresolved trauma from the past with its unresolved guilt, shame and grief

Physical Factors:

- Chronic inflammation
- Chronic Pain
- Allergies (food and environmental)
- Hormonal imbalances
- Nutritional Imbalances
- Poor diet
- Stress
- Certain medications
- EMF (Electromagnectic Field)

Chronic stress related to unresolved emotions, such as anxiety and depression, can easily develop in the face of unresolved emotional pain from past trauma and present-day life stressors. When the destructive effects of Lyme/TBD bacteria are added to the mix, these emotional states intensify, overloading the mind-body system to the point of being unable to balance and manage all that is happening. Horowitz says:

> *I have found that my patients with a history of trauma and abuse will have an exceedingly difficult time healing from Lyme/TBDs. Severe trauma and abuse can affect the immune system. The mind and body do not function separately, and when patients have had trauma or been abused, or if they suffer a loss with unresolved grief, the unresolved conflict usually has a deleterious effect on their immune system and signal it to fail. These people require deep emotional healing and must be willing to gently confront their trauma and learn to transform it, by identifying their own capacity for coping and healing. Skilled psychotherapy and techniques for restructuring memories and painful emotional experiences through EMDR [Eye Movement Desensitization and Reprocessing], the Journey technique (Brandong Bays), Emotional Freedom Techniques (EFT), cognitive behavioral therapy (CBT), and body-centered therapies (i.e., Rosen Method Bodywork) can also be helpful in shifting frozen emotional memories that are stuck in the body, affecting our mood and immunity.*[49]

EFT works to identify the sources of emotional pain and clear them from the system through a simple process of tapping through specific emotion-related EFT acupoints while venting emotional pain. Tapping on these specific acupoints while experiencing the stress response sends signals to the amygdala (the emotional center of the brain) to create a relaxation response instead. Tapping long enough allows the relaxation response to interrupt the stress response to creating a calmer state and helps in releasing frozen emotional states related to trauma. As stress reduces, new patterns of thought—cognitive shifts—can develop into a foundation of Empowering Beliefs that continue to reduce stress and support healing and recovery throughout the entire mind-body system.

Making Sense of the Symptoms

Teasing out whether problems with mood, thinking, and performing activities of daily life are related to Lyme/TBDs or something else is not a small task. A 2008 brochure entitled *Psychiatric Lyme Disease: What Psychiatrists Should Know About Lyme/Tick-Borne Diseases,* published by the International Lyme and Associated Diseases Society (ILADS) states that "when Lyme disease affects the brain, it is often referred to as Lyme neuroborreliosis or Lyme encephalopathy. Usually the patient is totally unaware of its presence. It can mimic virtually any type of encephalopathy or psychiatric disorder and is often compared to neurosyphilis. Both are caused by spirochetes, are multi-systemic, and can affect a patient neurologically, producing cognitive dysfunction and organic psychiatric illness. Such symptoms may be dormant, only surfacing years later."

As the ILADS brochure points out, cognitive impairment and emotional disturbance can occur at any time following a tick bite. Cognitive impairment can include memory loss, poor concentration, and difficulty finding words, while mood disruptions can present as depression, bipolar disorder, anxiety, and/or panic. Proper diagnosis followed by appropriate antibiotic treatment and other supports can improve these symptoms. Dr. Singleton stresses that physicians need to know whether their patients had already been suffering with anxiety and/or depressive disorders prior to becoming infected with Lyme/TBDs, or whether what they are experiencing is a result of Lyme/TBDs alone. "Knowing the answer to this question can make a big difference in terms of effective patient care."[50]

Dr. Schaller's book *What You May Not Know About Bartonella, Babesia, Lyme Disease and Other Tick & Flea-Borne Infections: Improving Treatment Speed, Recovery & Patient Satisfaction* offers extended "checklists that are based on a massive review of thousands of papers over a decade of full-time reading, 2012 science revelations, and/or massive chart reviews."[51] Within the many topics on a checklist, "psychiatric" and "neurological" are included. This is a helpful resource to use when researching possible neuropsychiatric symptoms.

Schaller does note, "The checklists are not meant to be complete or authoritative. It is meant to be used as a starting point, since information about these diseases is constantly emerging and changing. The goal of this checklist is to have you think broadly. You cannot use any of the checklists to diagnose or to rule out a disease."[52]

In their respective works, Drs. Singleton and Horowitz offer general characteristics to consider when you are experiencing psychiatric disturbances and are in the process of ruling out Lyme/TBDs. In *The Lyme Disease Solution,* Singleton writes that there are clues doctors can look for in order to determine whether Lyme/TBDs is the cause of their patients' anxiety. These clues include:

- "That the symptoms occurred at or around the same time as the onset of other symptoms associated with systemic Lyme/TBDs.
- That the symptoms do not correlate with any typical life stressors that might otherwise explain it, such as job loss, family crisis, relationship issues, death of a loved one, or other kinds of common stressors.
- There is only partial and incomplete improvement of anxiety symptoms, despite treatment with usual therapies such as counseling, medications, or other treatment modalities."[53]

Similar clues can also be applied to symptoms of depression. If left untreated, depression can lead to suicidal thoughts and actions. Dr. Singleton recommends that "anyone suffering from ongoing depression admit that they have a problem and seek professional help."[54]

In his book *Why Can't I Get Better?,* Dr. Richard Horowitz presents the following:

Signs That Lyme Is Affecting Your Brain: • Dr. Richard Horowitz: *Why Can't I Get Better*

If you are experiencing psychiatric disturbances along with multi-systemic signs of Lyme disease, then the odds are that the Lyme disease has or is also affecting your brain. The following features have helped make or support a diagnosis of Lyme disease:

1. Atypical features of a psychiatric disorder (e.g., absence of typical early signs or symptoms, unusually acute onset without new traumas or life challenges, and an uncharacteristic constellation of symptoms)
2. Absence of a family history of psychiatric disorders
3. Presentation of a psychiatric disorder at an older or younger age than is typical (e.g., autistic behavior at age six, forgetfulness at age thirty-five, first manic episode at age forty-five)
4. Lack of expected response to psychotropic medication
5. Adverse response to previously well-tolerated psychotropic medication
6. Lack of expected correlation of symptoms to psychological triggers (e.g., mood liability without apparent cause)[55]

The good news is that each of these doctors has found that, when the diseases are properly diagnosed and treated, their associated psychiatric symptoms can be greatly reduced and sometimes cleared completely.

Exercise: State Your Concerns and Needs

We encourage you now to identify issues of concern that may have arisen for you while reading this chapter and that you would like to discuss with your healthcare practitioner(s). In the numbered spaces below, list these issues or concerns. Also identify any symptoms that have yet to be addressed in your treatment, which we encourage you to bring to the attention of your healthcare team.

Issues/Concerns

1. ______________________________

2. ______________________________

3. ______________________________

4. ______________________________

5. ______________________________

Symptoms to Be Addressed

1. __________

2. __________

3. __________

4. __________

5. __________

CHAPTER

Wellness: A Vital Component for Recovery from Lyme/TBDs

Perhaps it seems strange to talk about wellness in relation to Lyme/TBDs. After all, doesn't *wellness* mean healthy? The words are often synonymous, but it raises the question: How can anyone have Lyme/TBDs and truly be healthy, especially in those cases when the disease becomes chronic and more challenging to treat? This assumes that health/wellness is only a matter of *physical* health.

What if it is something much more than that—a state of being that goes beyond the presence of disease and reaches into the relationships we have with ourselves, our bodies, our loved ones, and our environments? How does wellness happen? What type of process might it be—individual or collaborative and creative? What is at the center of this process? Is there anything directing it?

While there are many factors that contribute to health/wellness, there is only one that determines the level and quality of wellness you experience, and that is your state of mind. It is the "food" (your perceptions created by your beliefs and then expressed in your thoughts and emotions) your mind feeds your body that directs how you function and feel at every level of your existence. This is the primary reason that cultivating a wellness state of mind is so critical to your healing and recovery from Lyme/TBDs.

Good News!

Even if you have Lyme/TBDs and the symptoms that go with it, you can still experience a state of wellness!

The UC Davis Student Health Counseling Services (SHCS) describes *wellness* as an "active process of becoming aware of and making choices toward a healthy and fulfilling life" and "a dynamic process of change and growth rather than the mere absence of illness."[56] The SHCS definition not only states that wellness is more than the absence of illness but also presents wellness as a process of opening your options and taking action to improve your overall sense of well-being. That means that wellness is ultimately cultivated through your state of mind!

Wellness is about learning who you are, what you need and want, what your priorities are, and making choices that serve your best and highest good even in the midst of something as challenging and painful as Lyme/TBDs. In fact, the National Institute of Wellness website states: "Wellness is a conscious, self-directed and evolving process of achieving full potential; Wellness is multidimensional and holistic, encompassing lifestyle, mental and spiritual well-being, and the environment; Wellness is positive and affirming."[57]

social

intellectual

spiritual

emotional

physical

environmental

occupational

When we talk about cultivating a wellness state of mind, we are talking about a process of creating a sense of well-being in each of the seven dimensions of life: social, intellectual, spiritual, emotional, physical, environmental, and occupational. From a holistic perspective, these dimensions share an interdependent relationship. Bringing each dimension into balance with the others allows you to create a lifestyle of wellness that nurtures the whole of who you are in mind, body, spirit, and soul. You can do this by using EFT (which you will learn to do in Part 3 on page 113) to identify, process, and clear any Limiting Beliefs that are related to unresolved emotional issues that may be hindering your efforts to achieve optimal health and recovery in each dimension of your life.

The Seven Dimensions of Wellness

We invite you now to explore each of the Seven Dimensions of Wellness individually as they are introduced in the following sections. This is an introduction to what the dimensions are as they apply to life in general. In Chapter 6, you will complete the **Lyme/TBDs–Related Change/ Loss Inventory** on page 57. You will identify how the changes and losses you may have gone through with Lyme/TBDs have more specifically affected your experience with each dimension of wellness. We encourage you to answer the questions and use the space provided below each of the discussions to jot down any thoughts and/or feelings you have regarding your current experience of that dimension.

Social Dimension of Wellness

Social wellness is the ability to be relaxed and comfortable with yourself and other people as well as with the roles you play (for example, partner, parent, friend, sibling, coworker, etc.). Social wellness is also the ability to connect and reach out to others with friendliness and warmth and to cultivate and maintain loving and intimate relationships. It is also the ability to work with others to resolve conflicts while remaining true to your values and beliefs and, at the same time, respecting theirs. Social wellness means loving and accepting yourself while appreciating that, although we all have much in common, we can share and learn from our diversity.

Components of social wellness can include:

- Nurturing and maintaining supportive and loving relationships
- Balancing individual needs with the needs of others
- Acknowledging and communicating needs productively
- Staying connected with others and engaging in community
- Working with others to resolve conflicts in a way that honors both one's own values and the values of those with whom there is a conflict
- Appreciating and respecting commonalities and differences

Exercise: Social Wellness

In the space below, examine how you are experiencing the social dimension of wellness in your life now.

Which components of social wellness are currently active in your life?

Which would you like to enhance?

Intellectual Dimension of Wellness

Intellectual wellness is the ability to think in a way that invites clarity, curiosity, and creativity. It is about lifelong learning, exploring, and taking in new ideas and new ways of seeing things. It is the ability to transfer what you have learned in one setting onto a variety of other settings and seeing how things connect. It is being willing to share your ideas, knowledge, and wisdom with others in meaningful ways. Intellectual wellness includes recognizing that what you believe and think affects your emotions and behavior. It also means understanding the potential of your mind to discover new possibilities for personal growth and development.

Components of intellectual wellness can include:

- Engaging in activities that peak interest and spark creativity
- Keeping an open mind to new ideas and possibilities
- Staying curious and learning new things
- Sharing ideas and life lessons with others
- Appreciating the power of your thoughts to influence your emotions and behavior

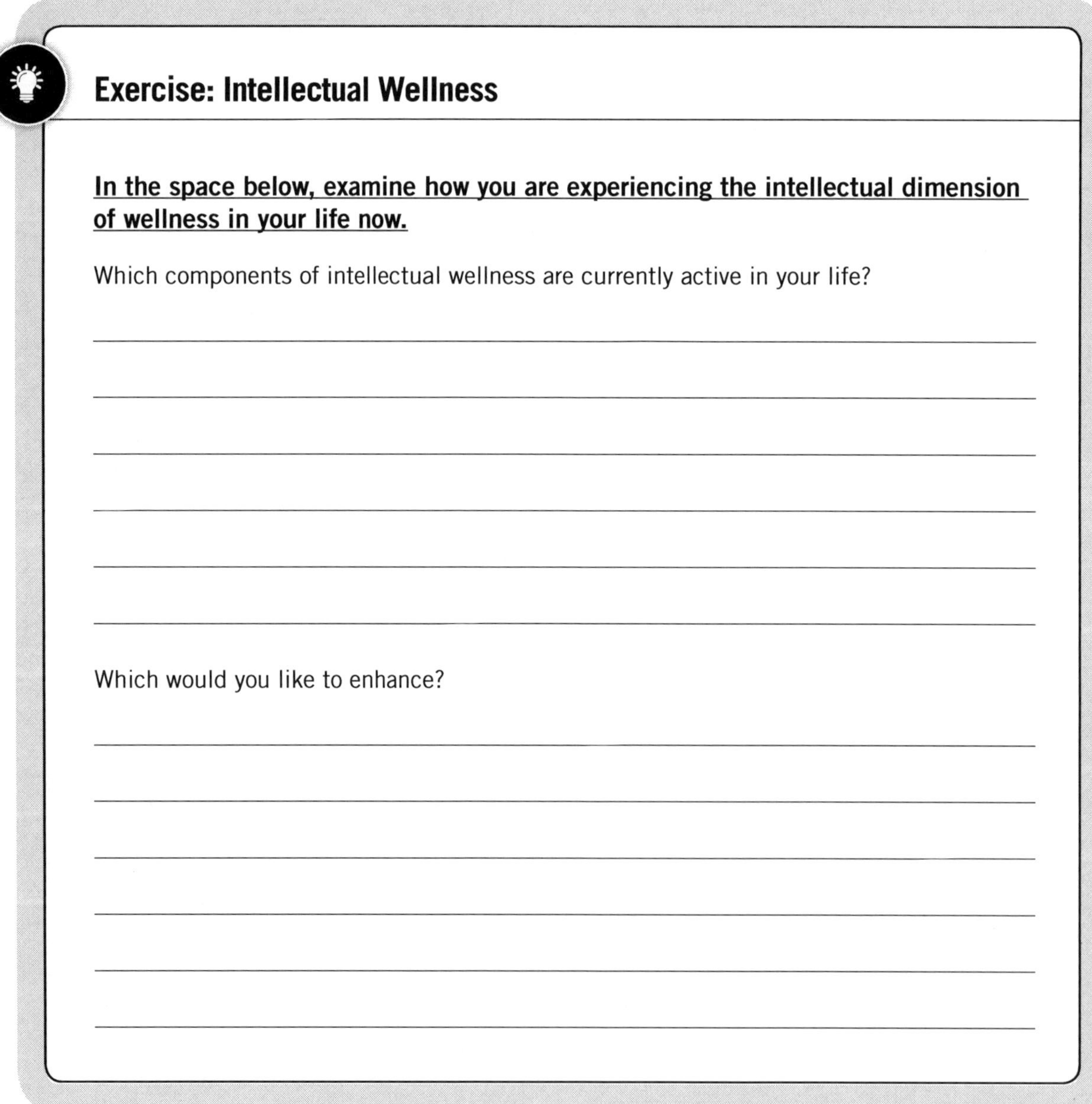

Exercise: Intellectual Wellness

In the space below, examine how you are experiencing the intellectual dimension of wellness in your life now.

Which components of intellectual wellness are currently active in your life?

Which would you like to enhance?

Spiritual Dimension of Wellness

Spiritual wellness is a deep knowing, acceptance, and love of yourself as you are right now. It fosters a mindset of growth that transforms life's many challenges through a heroic inner journey destined for manifesting your authentic self. It is the ability to honor and live as your authentic self with the understanding that you are always growing and evolving. It is the ability to trust your inner wisdom and to be clear about your beliefs, values, and sense of purpose. For many, it includes a belief in God, a Higher Power, or a Universal Force that is greater than oneself. This faith-based belief provides grace, guidance, hope, and healing.

Components of spiritual wellness can include:

- Clarifying values and priorities and growing into yourself
- Living a life that is consistent with your values and sense of purpose
- Cultivating love, compassion, and forgiveness for yourself and others
- Listening to and trusting your inner voice
- Nurturing hope, joy, and creativity
- Practicing gratitude and kindness
- Becoming aware of your connection with all of creation
- Connecting more deeply with yourself and/or God through prayer, relaxation, and/or mindfulness-based practices

Exercise: Spiritual Wellness

In the space below, examine how you are experiencing the spiritual dimension of wellness in your life now.

Which components of spiritual wellness are currently active in your life?

____

____

____

____

____

Which would you like to enhance?

____

____

____

____

____

Emotional Dimension of Wellness

Emotional wellness is a deeply felt sense of well-being that comes from being secure in yourself and having an understanding and acceptance of your own feelings and the feelings of other people. It is rooted in a healthy sense of self-esteem that allows you to acknowledge and accept both your strengths and your vulnerabilities. It is the ability to communicate your feelings and to listen to the feelings of others in a way that nurtures and sustains healthy connection and relationships. Emotional wellness also includes the ability to exercise patience during moments of frustration, to know when to let go, and to develop and use effective strategies for coping with life's challenges and disappointments. It is being emotionally flexible.

Components of emotional wellness can include:

- Practicing "emotional hygiene"—for example, reducing stress with EFT, relaxation, and mindfulness-based techniques; cultivating self-awareness; and processing and clearing unresolved emotional issues with EFT
- Identifying and building on your inner strengths to bolster resilience and increase your sense of self-efficacy
- Acknowledging, accepting, and expressing your feelings in productive ways
- Building and maintaining a support system that connects you with others and fulfills the fundamental human needs to be seen, heard, and understood

Exercise: Emotional Wellness

In the space below, examine how you are experiencing the emotional dimension of wellness in your life now.

Which components of emotional wellness are currently active in your life?

____

____

____

____

____

Which would you like to enhance?

____

____

____

____

____

Physical Dimension of Wellness

Physical wellness supports your overall sense of well-being and is connected with living a lifestyle that helps you to feel good in your body and to experience an optimal level of physical health. It is the ability to recognize and meet your needs for adequate sleep and rest, proper nutrition, and physical activity. It also motivates you to advocate for and receive proper mental and medical treatment. It includes doing no harm to your body and exercising moderation in all things while avoiding substances that your body cannot tolerate or that become too habit forming and disruptive. Physical wellness includes accepting and loving your body and doing all that you can to protect it from injury and strengthen its resistance to infection and disease. It also means being mindful of and respecting your body's own unique requirements.

Components of physical wellness can include:

- Being curious and learning about how to care for your body
- Getting proper nutrition, adequate rest, and as much exercise as you are able
- Avoiding harmful substances and toxins
- Utilizing health and wellness services such as acupuncture, massage, and healing touch in combination with proper medical treatments, as well as learning how to practice mindfulness and use body mechanics in a way that allows your body to relax, repair itself, and respond to a variety of treatments

Exercise: Physical Wellness

In the space below, examine how you are experiencing the physical dimension of wellness in your life now.

Which components of emotional wellness are currently active in your life?

____

____

____

____

____

Which would you like to enhance?

____

____

____

____

____

Environmental Dimension of Wellness

Environmental wellness is the ability to create home, work, and recreational spaces for yourself that promote healing and enhance well-being. This encompasses the emotional, physical, and spiritual aspects of your environment. It includes learning and respecting the nature and function of each space you occupy and understanding how you influence the environment and how the environment influences you.

Components of environmental wellness can include:

- Respecting nature and those species living in it—for example, taking the necessary precautions to prevent tick and flea bites
- Protecting yourself and others from environmental hazards, such as noise, air, and water pollution; secondhand smoke; ultraviolet radiation; toxins, molds, and allergens; and dirty EMFs (electromagnetic fields that can interfere with the energy circuits in the body)
- Creating and using spaces in ways that accommodate your needs and support your recovery in all of the dimensions of wellness

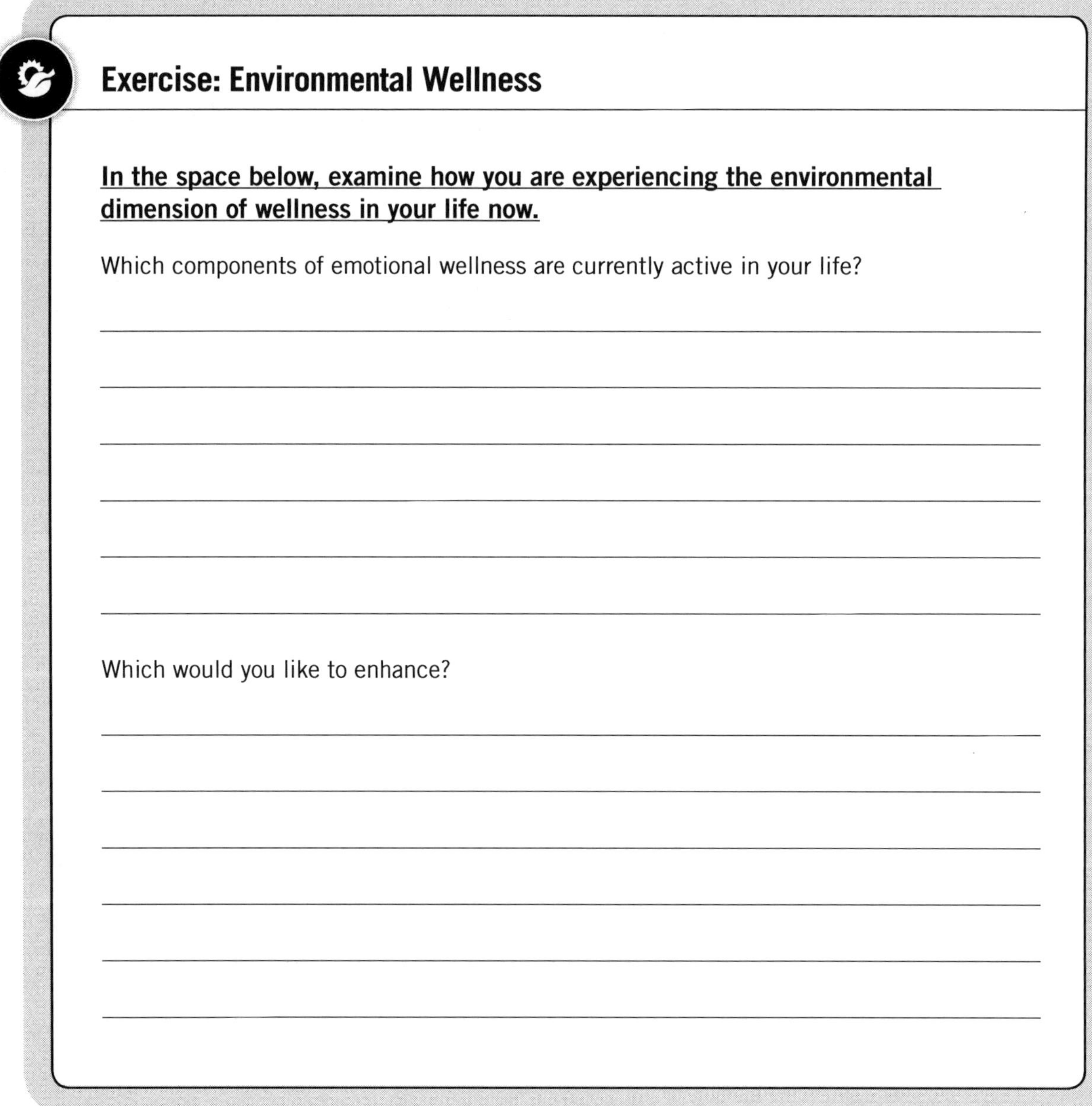

Exercise: Environmental Wellness

In the space below, examine how you are experiencing the environmental dimension of wellness in your life now.

Which components of emotional wellness are currently active in your life?

Which would you like to enhance?

Occupational Dimension of Wellness

Occupational wellness is the strong sense of satisfaction that comes from pairing your values, sense of purpose, and abilities with meaningful and rewarding work and activities. It includes the ability to communicate and work well with others, to cope with work/activity-related stressors, and to create a balance between your work/activities with your home and social life. Occupational wellness means staying committed to your vision and goals while being flexible and open to new possibilities as life circumstances change.

Components of occupational wellness can include:

- Acknowledging, accepting, and appreciating your talents, skills, and abilities
- Clarifying who you are and the contributions you wish to make to the world
- Staying open to new possibilities for meaningful and rewarding work/activities that can accommodate for your needs
- Prioritizing goals and redefining work/activities in relation to your present circumstances
- Building a support system for sharing occupational and financial concerns with others

Exercise: Occupational Wellness

In the space below, examine how you are experiencing the occupational dimension of wellness in your life now.

Which components of emotional wellness are currently active in your life?

____

____

____

____

____

____

Which would you like to enhance?

____

____

____

____

____

____

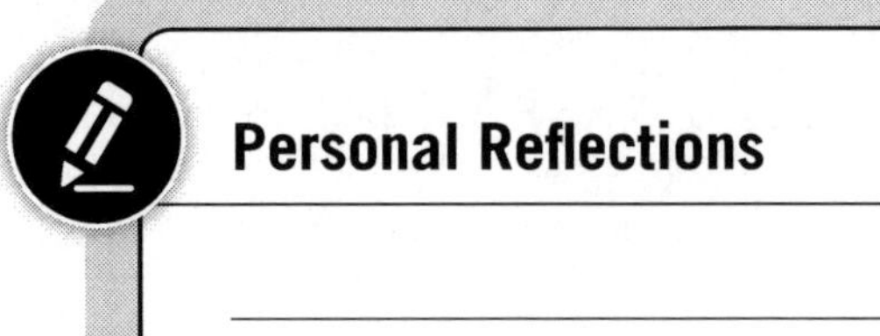

Personal Reflections

CHAPTER 3

Emotions and Wellness

Cultivating a wellness state of mind is foundational to Lyme/TBD recovery. Part of this process is learning the different roles that emotions play, how they impact your body, and developing awareness around how you express and cope with them. Emotional wellness is fostered by taking full responsibility in acknowledging how you are feeling and in making mindful choices around how you respond and express your feelings in ways that promote your healing and recovery.

Emotions play many roles in your mind-body system. They are messengers that carry information that links the major systems of the body into one unit called the mind-body. Candace Pert, author of the book *Molecules of Emotion*, states "Emotions are at the nexus between matter and mind, going back and forth between the two and influencing both."[58] (To learn more about the science on the role of emotions and how they affect the body go to Chapter 40, The Mind-Body Communication Network on page 391.)

In the simplest of terms, emotions give you feedback (which are interpreted as feelings) on how you are experiencing life in any given moment based on how you are relating to your needs being met or not. When your needs are being met, common feelings that can be created are happiness, hopefulness, and gratitude. These kinds of emotional states enhance the immune system and promote the body to be in what the internationally known biologist and author of *The Biology of Belief*, Bruce Lipton, calls a "growth response. This is a relaxed state that allows the body to engage in healthy cell production and maintenance."[59]

When your needs are going unmet, depending on how you are relating to it, painful feelings, such as anger, frustration, and sadness, can be created. These are normal feelings to have. Yet, if sustained or left unprocessed and frozen in the mind-body system, these feelings can put the body in what Lipton calls a "protection response (same as the stress response), thus suppressing the immune system."[60] Lipton states, "The energy the body normally uses to maintain a healthy state has been diverted to defending it against potential threats. The body cannot be in both a growth and a protection response at the same time."[61] (To learn more about the body's growth and protection responses, skip to Chapter 7 on page 71.)

Refer to Appendix F on page 410 for an expanded **List of Needs and Feelings** adapted from the work of Marshal Rosenberg, Ph.D.[35]

Emotions, the type and intensity, may also signal the kind of bacteria you may have and if Lyme/TBDs treatment needs to be started, maintained, or adjusted. Given the neurological impact of Lyme/TBDs as discussed in Chapter 1 on page 17, you may experience episodes of unpredictable and disruptive mood changes beyond your ability to manage alone. If you find yourself experiencing prolonged periods of painful emotional states, we strongly recommend that you communicate this to your healthcare provider(s) and/or support system and get treatment immediately.

Whatever may be happening in the moment, you do have choices in how you interpret, respond, and express your emotions. Whether you react to your emotions in a destructive way or respond to them in a constructive healing way depends on what you "say" and "do" about them—that is, the meaning you give them and whether you choose to feel and acknowledge them or stuff them down.

You first learn how to express your emotions from your primary caregivers. The choices you make around how you acknowledge and express emotions originates from the rules and expectations of your cultural, ethnic, and family system of origin. If you grew up in a culture that believes girls shouldn't express anger because it's not "feminine" and not "pleasing" for a lady to raise her voice or that boys shouldn't cry when they get hurt because it's "girly" and "weak," you may find it difficult to express feelings such as hurt, anger, and sadness. If, like many people, you grew up in an environment where any expression of emotion was just not allowed, then you might find it difficult to even acknowledge them. Repressing emotions (stuffing down) may be an adaptive response to this kind of environment that did not support them. But, sooner or later, they will need to come out and are commonly triggered by current life stressors.

> Repressed painful emotions can be triggered by any life and body stressor, thus contributing to increased overwhelming emotional states, whether or not it is related to Lyme/TBDs.

In severe cases, repressing emotions while experiencing painful or traumatic events can be a resilient act at the time. It can allow you to focus on the problem solving needed to get through it and, in extreme life or death cases, to survive. This protective response is not meant to be sustained over long periods of times, but rather only long enough to get through. Then it is important to shift your mind-body from a protection response (by releasing painful emotional states) to a growth response that enhances your body's innate ability to heal and repair itself. (Parts 2 through 4 of this workbook are dedicated for you to do just that with the use of the mindfulness-based techniques and EFT.)

Experiencing emotional stress while recovering from Lyme/TBDs is a given. It is important for you to be aware of how well you are coping with your emotions and then you can make mindful decisions on what to keep doing and what may need to be added to support the emotional wellness needed for Lyme/TBD recovery.

We invite you now to take a moment to complete the **Coping with Emotional Stress Scale** provided on the next page. This scale is helpful in identifying how well you are coping with your emotions. You can also use it to track your progress by completing the scale again at a later time after you have put EFT and the other mindfulness-based tools and techniques into daily practice for tapping into a wellness state of mind. An additional copy of this scale can be found in the appendix on page 414 for you to use at a later time. We are grateful to Whole Person Associates for granting us permission to reprint.

> **Please note:** Within the Profile Interpretation below, Low and Moderate Range, it reads "Complete the following exercises to develop greater emotional wellness." This refers to exercises in the *Coping with Everyday Stressors Workbook.* Given that we have included the scale here for your use, this statement is also relevant to following the exercises in this workbook toward developing greater emotional wellness.

Coping with Emotional Stress Scale • Introduction and Directions

Maintaining your emotional wellness is critical in living a stress-free life. Emotional wellness includes awareness of your emotions at any given time, the ability to maintain an even emotional state regardless of what is happening around you, and the ability to control your emotions.

This assessment contains 20 statements related to your emotional wellness. Read each statement and decide whether or not the statement describes you. If the statement *does* describe you, circle the number under the TRUE column next to that item. If the statement *does not* describe you, circle the number under the FALSE column next to that item.

In the following example, the circled number under "TRUE" indicates the statement is descriptive of the person completing the inventory.

	TRUE	FALSE
I have difficulty identifying my feelings	①	2

This is not a test. Since there are no right or wrong answers, do not spend too much time thinking about your answers. Be sure to respond to every statement.

Coping with Emotional Stress Scale

	TRUE	FALSE
I have difficulty identifying my feelings	1	2
I have fairly consistent emotional states	2	1
I usually understand how others are feeling	2	1
I am able to maintain intimate relationships with others	2	1
I often am unable to express my emotions clearly	1	2
I adjust to change and cope with the stress of daily life	2	1
I tend to be positive most of the time	2	1
I have inner peace and contentment	2	1
Minor setbacks cause me stress	1	2
I don't waste time or energy dwelling on the past	2	1
I am unable to stay focused on the present	1	2
I am aware of my personal limitations	2	1
I have a hard time valuing and accepting myself	1	2
I manage my emotions well	2	1
I am aware of how my negative emotions affect others	2	1
I worry a lot about failure	1	2
I find it easy to forgive others	2	1
I am not able to laugh at myself	1	2
I can appropriately express my feelings	2	1
I have a hard time accepting constructive criticism	1	2

Scoring Directions

The *Coping with Emotional Stress Scale* is designed to help you explore how you are managing your emotions in this stress-filled society.

Add the numbers that you circled on the scale. This will allow you to get your Emotional Wellness score. You will get a total in the range from 20 to 40. Then, transfer this total to the space below:

EMOTIONAL WELLNESS TOTAL = ______

Profile Interpretation

Scale Score	Result	Indications
20 to 26	Low	Low scores indicate that you are rarely able to manage your emotions well. Complete the following exercise to develop greater emotional wellness.
27 to 33	Moderate	Moderate scores indicate that you sometimes are able to manage your emotions well. Complete the following exercises to develop greater emotional wellness.
34 to 40	High	High scores indicate that you are pretty effective in managing your emotions.

Exercise: Process Your Results

EMOTIONAL WELLNESS TOTAL = ______ Date ____________

What ways of managing your emotions are supporting your recovery?

What ways of managing your emotions could be inhibiting your recovery?

What ways of managing your emotions would you like to develop?

What ways of managing your emotions would you like to improve or enhance?

It is foundational to cultivate a wellness state of mind to support Lyme/TBD recovery. This workbook is filled with exercises to use with the featured self-help tool EFT and the mindfulness-based techniques that help you do just that. These tools also foster an overall sense of self-efficacy and emotional wellness. They empower you to take a proactive stance by helping you clarify and express your emotions and needs in healthy ways. Remember, a healthy mind-body connection is invaluable in terms of recovery. Any steps you take to promote emotional well-being are steps in the right direction for your physical well-being.

CHAPTER

Spirochetes, Crisis, and Transformation

The impact of Lyme/TBDs spans across the globe, draining personal and public resources. One story after another speaks of the devastating impact Lyme/TBDs have had on millions of people throughout the United States as well as in parts of Europe and Asia. It is a crisis, too, for the medical community, which is still deeply divided on the nature and treatment of Lyme/TBDs. We recognize how confusing, difficult, and stressful it can be when diagnosis and treatment are delayed or just plain miss the mark.

On one side is the Infectious Diseases Society of America (IDSA), which takes the position that Lyme/TBDs can be easily diagnosed and treated with short-term antibiotics with little likelihood of becoming chronic. On the other side is the International Lyme and Associated Diseases Society (ILADS), which takes the position that Lyme disease is a multisystemic complex illness that can become chronic and for which there are few accurate tests or simple short-term treatments.

Even though there are disagreements about the serious nature of Lyme/TBDs and treatment protocols, you do not have to wait for them to resolve their disagreements. You can begin using the self-help tools in this workbook to tap into a wellness state of mind to optimize your possibilities for recovery.

Approaching the experience of Lyme/TBDs from a wellness state of mind can open you to seeing it in another light that reveals new possibilities for your healing and recovery. This in no way minimizes the pain, confusion, and heartbreak you may be experiencing. Rather, it is a process of acknowledging and using your experience to turn this crisis into an opportunity to go beyond the limits of disease and illness to restore you to the whole of who you are.

In her book *Conscious Evolution: Awakening the Power of Our Social Potential*, Barbara Marx Hubbard explains that crises are a natural and necessary element, not only for human evolution, but also for the growth and expansion of the entire universe. "Crises," she notes, "precede transformation. When nature reaches a limitation, it does not necessarily adapt and stabilize; it innovates and transforms."[62]

Among nature's greatest innovators and transformers are spirochetes. These long, slender, spiral-shaped bacteria are quite prolific; there are also numerous species of them. The best known are the parasitic types that cause syphilis and Lyme disease. *Borrelia burgdorferi* is the spirochete responsible for Lyme disease.

Spirochetes have been on the earth much longer than humans. They have a lot to teach us about how to thrive even in a biologically compromised environment. Looking at their capacity for flexibility, change, and persistence, we came to understand that these same organisms that are causing sickness can teach valuable strategies for creating a wellness-based mind-body environment that supports healing and recovery.

What a paradox! The very organisms that are making you sick could also reveal characteristics of how to stimulate personal growth and transformation that goes beyond anything we could have imagined. There is a lot we can learn from spirochetes! Let's take a look.

The Wisdom of the Spirochetes

Spirochetes are organisms that have been living in nature for millions of years and have become quite good at adapting and doing whatever is necessary to ensure their own survival. At first glance, it may seem as though nothing can stop them from wreaking havoc in all dimensions of a person's life. But if we stay open and ask, What is happening? there is a lot we can learn from how the spirochetes operate to survive that may be adapted to any recovery plan. For example, they may actually have a formula for resilience that we can use to help us cultivate a wellness state of mind.

Author of *Healing Lyme: Natural Healing and Prevention of Lyme Borreliosis and Its Coinfections*, Stephen Buhner writes, "It is most accurate to realize that Lyme spirochetes are opportunistic parasitic organisms with a great deal of intelligence and experience in promulgating themselves in the wild, as they have done for some 100 million years. . . . Whatever works they will do and they are exceptionally good innovators."[63]

Spirochetes instinctively do whatever they need to do for their own well-being and survival. In this way, they reflect what nature has given all living organisms: the drive to thrive! Buhner goes on to say that spirochetes are constantly experimenting with various alterations so that, at any moment, they can "evade host-immune responses" and "enhance colonization of different parts of the body."[64] These hardy bacteria also have the ability to rapidly release from their bodies any drug designed to harm them. Now, in the table to follow, let's break down these strategies for resilience and see how they can be used to create a wellness state of mind to promote your own recovery from Lyme/TBDs.

Strategies of the Spirochetes	Strategies for Creating a Wellness State of Mind
Learn from experience: Do what works! They stay persistent!	Learn from experience: Do what works! Be persistent!
Remain flexible: Adapt and change to meet the demands of their environment.	Remain flexible: Adapt and change to meet the requirements of your recovery.
Innovate: Move, shift, and reinvent to meet the demands of a changing environment.	Innovate: Shift perspective(s) and use new strategies when things change or treatments don't work.
Evade host-immune responses.	Avoid that which feeds the spirochetes and worsens inflammation and pain.
Release: Rapidly excrete medication and other substances designed to harm them.	Release: Detox the physical body. Use EFT and the other tools to detox the "emotional body" (process and release Limiting Beliefs and painful emotions that create stress, suppress the immune system, and impede healing). Also use other methods for detoxing the body to clear out debris left from the die-offs of bacteria during treatment.
Enhances survival: Colonize throughout different parts of the host body to proliferate and thrive.	Enhance repair and recovery: Use a holistic and integrative multisystem approach that addresses all the dimensions of wellness and complexities of Lyme/TBDs. Build a supportive community of family, friends, and others in recovery.

Spirochetes are remarkably resilient and almost chameleon like in their ability to alter their structures and blend in with their hosts' biological environment. With 100 million years' worth of experience in learning how to dodge host-immune responses, spirochetes have developed the capacity to change their shape and avoid medication that will harm them. In essence, they maintain an "awareness" and "acceptance" of the fact that their survival and growth requires attention, flexibility, change, and persistence. And they have had eons to practice and perfect these strategies.

Well, humans have also been on the earth for quite some time. Although we have not been here as long as the spirochetes have, we share their ability to assess and adapt to the demands of our environment. Just as the spirochetes can alter themselves to sustain and thrive within their environment, you can do the same by shifting your perspective when treatments don't work so that you can continue to remain open to using new treatments that can possibly best serve your recovery. To do this, it is helpful to resolve the disappointment you may still have by using EFT. If you would like to, you can now:

- Skip to Chapter 13 on page 121 to learn the **Modified EFT Basic Recipe** and **tapping acupoints** used with EFT.
- Then skip to the global tapping script **Discouraged by Treatment Disappointments** on page 251 in Part 4 to begin using EFT to address any emotional distress you may be experiencing in relation to this issue.

Shifting Perspectives

In learning how resilient spirochetes are in surviving and thriving, it shocked the both of us into facing how we related to having them in our bodies. Initially, this new information made us feel, in a weird way, a new respect for them. But how can this be? At the same time, we both felt a similar resistance to this perspective because we acknowledged that we had been "unconsciously at war" against the spirochetes. Trying to "kill them" was a very familiar way that we "rallied" through treatments and tolerated Herxheimer reactions (a detox reaction that causes short-term flu-like symptoms), believing they had died.

For me, Anita, I also realized that the anger I held at the spirochetes for making me sick slowly and unintentionally shifted to anger toward my body. There were times when I blamed and rejected my body for being sick or felt as though it had abandoned me. An unconscious and destructive perspective was created that justified a "me versus them (my body) stance." My body was now the object of my anger. For me, I desired peace and harmony within and about my body and explored what it would feel like to create peace with the spirochetes to support this.

"Making Peace with the Spirochetes" on the following page is a visualization I experienced that allowed me to see how I was relating to the spirochetes and how that was negatively affecting how I related to my body. This process gave me a profound shift in perspective that opened me to self-acceptance, newfound hope, and, as a result, decreased the symptoms I was experiencing.

If you experience yourself "at war" with the Lyme/TBD bacteria in your body and the added emotional stress that it can cause and want to shift it, you can:

- Skip to Chapter 13 on page 121 to learn the **Modified EFT Basic Recipe** and **tapping acupoints** used with EFT.
- Then skip to the global tapping script **I Am at War with Lyme/TBDs** on page 369 in Part 4 to begin using EFT to address any emotional distress you may be experiencing in relation to this issue.
- You can also skip to the **Fire-Love meditation exercise** by Vir McCoy on page 107. Vir describes two ways of Liberating Lyme disease: love and fire. He leads you through a transformative **meditation** to support this liberation. Use these tools often, and you will begin to notice changes in yourself.

We acknowledge that this idea of making peace with bacteria is "way out of the box" of conventional thinking. We simply offer it as a suggestion if you believe it will support your wellness state of mind. If this concept does not feel supportive to you, use the "law of two feet" and move on to something that does.

Making Peace with the Spirochetes • By Anita Bains

I woke up one morning with nausea and pain searing through my body. I could barely move my arms. I had been grappling with the suggestion put forth by Dr. Stephen Harrod Buhner that essentially suggested healing is more likely to occur if we stop waging war on Lyme and make peace with the bacteria that has chosen us for its host.

I thought, *All I've wanted to do is kill the bacteria in my body, and it's been exhausting. How many times have I rejected my body because of the bacteria that keeps attacking me?* I realized then that the bacteria had not entered my body with an intention to harm me but just wanted a place to live. I began thinking, *I don't want to kill the bacteria. We share the same body, and they want to live just as I do.* Yes, they do harm me, but I saw that we were now part of one body and that I needed to find a way for us to share a peaceful coexistence.

I began with some focused but gentle breathing. I then started visualizing the bacteria. I saw them, evicted from their natural habitat, in need of a new home. I realized that like me, they wanted to survive. They were not my enemy; they just wanted a place to live, like all other living things.

The next image that came was a butterfly. I thought, *Of course!* Butterflies symbolize transformation. Bacteria, like all other living things, are a form of energy, and energy takes on different forms. I thought, *Maybe the bacteria could take on a new form that would allow it to coexist peacefully with my body rather than as an antagonist causing me to suffer. What if they learned that they could survive in a different form and agreed to do this?*

Then I got to thinking about how bacteria can go dormant. *What is this dormancy really about? I wondered. Are they sitting around waiting to attack, or can we create a natural harmonious cohabitation?* I remembered: "It is what we say it is."

I thought about how the body holds an unlimited number of microbes that can create both illness and wellness. In wellness, these microbes and the rest of the body are in a state of balance. *What if dormancy is a form of balance? If so, then how can I create this state of balance with the bacteria in my body?*

As I deepened my **meditation**, I noticed a negative voice saying, "They hurt me! I don't want to be in harmony with them! Am I crazy?" I immediately noticed fear and anger toward the bacteria. "It's me against them!" I was not feeling peaceful. This meant that my body was becoming stressed and producing chemicals that inhibited my immune system. I realized that, if I wanted to heal, I was going to have to make a choice between being in a fearful and angry state of mind (illness) and being in a peaceful state of mind (wellness). So I began tapping on my anger and resentments.

Even though I was having lots of doubt and uncertainty about this whole process, I realized it was time for me to "stand down" and call a truce. Only in this way could I enter into a wellness state of mind and create for myself a "**Large Mind**" story grounded in a balanced, peaceful coexistence with the bacteria. The **meditation** gave me clarity on what I needed to do to heal, but I still had a lot of tapping to do on this issue!

I began by focusing on the fear and uncertainty I had about making peace with the bacteria in my body and tapped on these for a long time. After tapping through many emotional layers, these distressing emotions subsided. I was now free to focus on restoring my body to a balanced state, one in harmony with all of the organisms living within me. Tapping cleared my fear-based beliefs and shifted me into a "**Large Mind**" story of working with the bacteria in my body to create new possibilities for healing.

This shift in perspective did not mean that I stopped treatment. I continued to follow my treatment protocol, but what was different was that my inner emotional battle against my body (which was misdirected and projected anger from being at war with the bacteria) was over.

I invited peace with the bacteria in my body. When I stood down and stopped "thinking" about waging war, I felt them standing down, too! What an incredible feeling I had! My whole body seemed to relax at a very deep level. I was astonished by how my state of mind immediately shifted and focused on wellness, harmony, and balance.

CHAPTER 5

It's All About Resilience!

Spirochetes have an abundance of resilience and persistence. This is the reason they have survived for millions of years. Lessons they can teach us are learn from experience, build resilience, stay persistent, avoid harm, and let go of anything that interferes with your well-being. In fact, this is not only a formula for how *you* can recover from Lyme/TBDs but also for how you can use your recovery as an opportunity to thrive.

The primary difference between the spirochetes and you is that they don't have an emotional filter through which they interpret their experiences. When a medication that is designed to eliminate them is introduced into a person's body, they don't get caught up in what this might mean for them or why anyone would want to hurt them; they simply "see" what's happening and adjust accordingly. We humans, however, are more emotionally complex in this regard, and so we need to be aware of the fact that the choices we make in relation to an event are a direct result of our state of mind—the beliefs, thoughts, and emotions that determine how we perceive and experience that event.

Nearly everything related to your recovery from Lyme/TBDs hinges on your state of mind. Your state of mind is the foundation from which everything else follows. It is in itself a truly powerful force that can either wear you down or build you up. A wellness state of mind cultivates the resilience needed to be persistent in the pursuit to resolve and evolve through the many challenges that come with Lyme/TBDs.

Resilience in Action

Studies show that when faced with some form of adversity, resilient people are those who:

- ✔ **Maintain sense of self:** Resilient people have strong self-esteem, self-confidence, and a positive self-concept. They recognize that who they are is separate from any hardship they may experience. Life's storms come and go as scenes in their story, but their identity and sense of purpose remain intact.
- ✔ **Cultivate self-awareness:** Resilient people listen to their bodies and pay attention to how their thoughts and emotions are influencing them. They are aware of and responsive to their needs, meeting them in healthy and productive ways.
- ✔ **Go with the flow:** Resilient people believe that change is a part of life. They meet life's changes with emotional flexibility and stay open to new possibilities. When a crisis comes, they remain calm and assess the situation rationally, listening for the answers and trusting they will come rather than trying to force them. They accept change and go with the flow in an active and empowered way.
- ✔ **Explore possibilities:** Resilient people question what they are telling themselves about their experiences. *What is happening? How can I look at this in a way that cultivates hope and helps me feel better? What might this mean for me? What are my options? What would be most helpful to do right now? Where can I get support? What new treatments out there could help me recover?* They stay open to new possibilities to advocate and help themselves.
- ✔ **Maintain hope:** Resilient people do more than survive; they thrive. They have the expectation that they can recover from adversity and can use it as an opportunity for personal growth

and transformation. With the belief that they can transcend, and even grow from, the most challenging of circumstances, resilient people can cultivate hope in the present moment and maintain it through future challenges.

✔ **Stay empowered:** Resilient people have a strong sense of personal power and believe that they can change things for the better. They see their possibilities, remain persistent, and choose those options that best serve their well-being and the well-being of others.

✔ **Build support:** Resilient people believe that we are "all in this together" and that it is okay to ask for help. They engage in positive and mutually supportive relationships that include common goals, acceptance, love, trust, and encouragement. They continue to reach out to others to find the support they need.

✔ **Practice mindfulness and relaxation:** Resilient people know the importance of being able to breathe, relax, and just be in the present moment without negative judgment. They are willing to sit quietly with themselves and listen to their inner voice, allowing and accepting with compassion while actively minimizing the thinking that creates hopelessness. They focus on "what is" rather than "what if." Resilient people are proactive and stay in tune with their mental, emotional, and physical states using stress-reduction techniques to stay in balance.

✔ **Practice self-care:** Resilient people listen and respond proactively to their needs in all the dimensions of wellness. This includes practicing "emotional hygiene"—that is, recognizing, processing, and releasing any Limiting Beliefs embedded in unresolved emotional pain that may be interfering with their sense of well-being and their capacity to overcome a challenge.

A Personal Story of Resilience in Action • By Katina Makris

Katina Makris, CCH, CIH, is the author of the award-winning book *Out of the Woods, Healing Lyme Disease, Body, Mind & Spirit,* and *Autoimmune Illness & Lyme Disease: Mending the Body, Mind, and Spirit.* Below, Katina shares in her own words a piece of her inspirational story of moving out from the debilitating changes and losses due to Lyme disease to radical transformation. She is a resilient person in action.

Life in the countryside was rewarding and exactly what I have dreamed of. Nothing lasts forever and little did I know every shred of my cherished existence would be ripped away. Lyme disease stripped me of everything: my career, income, home, marriage, and health. The trauma of the Lyme experience required healing. My inner journey of healing was as profound as the physical ministerings. It would become a trial in loss; it would also become a healing passageway through transformative changes and rebirth.

It took five years of fortitude, commitment and hard work, and I healed 100 percent, learning to walk again at year one, drive a car in year two! Additionally, deep spiritual healing attention was needed to reclaim my very fragile psyche. Learning to let go of what I thought mattered on the material plane and coming to understand myself as a deeply creative being, with deep wellsprings of willpower and the capacity to use affirmations, prayer, vision, intention, and belief, became healing tools at an energetic level that triggered the mind-body healing pathway and have been just as instrumental as the nutritive supplements and anti-microbial agents I took. I needed to consciously tend to my thought and belief patterns on a daily basis, relying on **meditation** and mindfulness to keep myself moving toward light and a healthier tomorrow. Lyme disease forced me to change, to dig deep, to reflect, and to grow into a person of greater wisdom and clarity. I feel blessed to have a second chance at life.

Exercise: Your Qualities of Resilience

Building and strengthening resilience is cultivating the wellness state of mind necessary for recovering from Lyme/TBDs and other major life challenges. We invite you now to consider each attribute of resilience in relation to how active it is in your life today.

There may be some elements you have yet to cultivate, and there may be some you already possess and would like to enhance. Responding to the questions in this exercise will help you acknowledge and celebrate where you are most resilient and will bring to your attention where you need a boost.

Maintaining a Sense of Self

Describe your self-concept.

____

____

____

____

In what ways do you believe that you have a positive self-concept in spite of having Lyme/TBDs?

____

____

____

____

State (if applicable) those ways that Lyme/TBDs have compromised your sense of self.

____

____

____

Cultivating Self-Awareness

In what ways do you feel positively connected to your body?

____

____

____

____

Your thoughts?

Your feelings?

What attributes/habits do you notice about yourself that could benefit from using mindfulness-based techniques?

Going with the Flow

Do you see yourself as emotionally flexible?

In what ways are you able to proactively go with the flow through all of the changes that Lyme/TBDs bring?

In what ways do you see yourself being open-minded?

What areas of your life could benefit from being more emotionally flexible?

Exploring Possibilities

What do you notice about yourself that is not open to new possibilities for treatment and recovery from Lyme/TBDs?

What evidence do you have that you are open to new possibilities for treatment and recovery from Lyme/TBDs?

What new possibilities do you see for yourself right now?

What new possibilities do you see for yourself in the future?

Maintaining Hope

How hopeful are you in recovering from Lyme/TBDs?

In what ways can you use your recovery from Lyme/TBDs as a catalyst for personal growth and development?

What are you hoping for? Describe in detail your hopes for recovery.

Staying Empowered

In what ways do you feel empowered to take positive action toward recovery from Lyme/TBDs?

What specific Empowering Beliefs are you aware of that are supporting your recovery from Lyme/TBDs?

What specific Limiting Beliefs are you aware of that could interfere with your recovery? (If you need assistance, refer to the **Lyme/TBDs–Related Belief Inventory** on page 66.)

Building Support

Who is in your support system?

How strong is your support system? Describe the ways you feel supported.

Is there anyone you would like to invite into your support system?

What kind of support do you need to add?

Practicing Mindfulness and Relaxation

How committed are you to using the mindfulness-based and stress-reduction techniques offered in this workbook to support your wellness state of mind?

What barriers might you have to using mindfulness-based and stress-reduction techniques as part of your strategies to cultivate recovery from Lyme/TBDs?

Practicing Self-Care

In what specific ways do you practice self-care?

What barriers do you notice in yourself that prevent you from practicing daily self-care?

If there are some barriers, what specific changes are you willing to make so that self-care is a priority in your daily life?

In the midst of such devastating illnesses like chronic Lyme/TBDs, it can be difficult at times to see that you are being, and can be, resilient. The truth is that by facing the difficult challenges you have already met and by persistently pursuing your recovery (for example, reading and doing the practices in this workbook), you *are* being resilient! Cultivating a wellness state of mind that strengthens and sustains that resilience is crucial to firmly establishing and maintaining the recovery you desire.

Making use of EFT as part of a daily "emotional hygiene" routine is a great way to strengthen your resilience. Refer to Chapter 17: **Commit to Cultivating a Wellness State of Mind** on page 145 to learn more!

CHAPTER

Make Sense of the Crises That Come with Lyme/TBDs

Lyme /TBDs can turn your life upside down and your mind inside out. This is especially true when the illness becomes chronic, lasting for years and even decades for some. The unpredictable nature, frequency, intensity, and duration of symptoms can make life chaotic and difficult to manage. As Lyme/TBDs become chronic, they can take a serious toll on all dimensions of your life. Families are disrupted, friendships are at risk, and jobs are threatened and often lost as unpredictable and debilitating symptoms make it increasingly difficult to perform previously simple tasks and expected roles.

There just isn't a single area of life that Lyme/TBDs don't touch. This is because every dimension of life (social, intellectual, spiritual, emotional, physical, environmental, and occupational) is part of an interwoven whole in which the events that occur in one dimension affect all of the others. For example, Lyme/TBDs related changes that occur on the physical level can set off changes in every other dimension. (Turn to page 26 in Chapter 2 for a quick review the Seven Dimensions of Wellness.)

Clarifying the Chaos

One day, everything is as it's always been. The next, you just don't feel right. Maybe it's a touch of the flu or some virus that's been going around. Time passes, and then comes the day when you're in so much pain you can barely move and your head is full of brain fog and you can't even think your way through the simplest task. Then you realize that the symptoms you're experiencing are completely unpredictable. Not even the doctors can figure out what's happening. Days, weeks, months, and even years may pass as the landscape of your life morphs into something you no longer recognize and could never have imagined. The terrain has become slippery, and it may even seem as if there is no stability at all. Previously established roles, expectations, and routines give way to a new unknown reality for which there is no map or guidebook. This is the chaos in the crisis that comes with having Lyme/TBDs for so many people.

When life as you knew it is gone and you're thrown off balance, the challenges you face can somtimes seem insurmountable. You may find yourself feeling anything from shock and confusion to anger and fear to sadness and despair. You may ask yourself many times over: *What's happened to me? Why did this happen to me? Who am I now that I have Lyme/TBDs? What do the changes and losses I've experienced say about me? What am I going to do about it?* And then there may be thoughts like, *I don't like my life anymore. This isn't fair! I want things to be the way they used to be!* Sometimes it's hard to see, but due to the debilitating symptoms of Lyme/TBDs, you may be grieving what you can no longer do and ways of expressing and experiencing yourself that you had been used to.

How you grieve depends a lot on your core beliefs about yourself, others, and the world as well as on the traditions and values of your family, culture, and faith. While many of these can support you through your grief, you may also be carrying unhealed emotional wounds that are triggered by current changes and losses that make life even more challenging. Acknowledging that you may be grieving the changes and/or losses from your life's reality before getting Lyme/TBDs is a great first step.

Unacknowledged grief can manifest emotionally as anger, sadness, and/or self-blame. For some people, the changes and losses occur so frequently that the focus is on just adjusting to the new challenges at hand, which is where it is most supportive to have your focus. This is a form of resilience! And, at some point, it is helpful to just stop and allow yourself to grieve the changes and losses you have experienced with a state of mind of acceptance and compassion when appropriate and emotionally safe to do so. We know firsthand that this is easier said than done. That's why we have written this workbook and provided you with many self-help tools to choose from to help you through the healing process.

Addressing the Multidimensional Impact of Lyme/TBDs

We have worked with many people who find themselves reeling from Lyme/TBDs-related changes and losses. These changes and losses create disruptions that we refer to as psychosocial stressors. Psychosocial stressors are disruptive events that vary in intensity from person to person and can occur in some or all of the Seven Dimensions of Wellness. Present-day psychosocial stressors like the changes and losses that can come with Lyme/TBDs can frequently trigger unresolved painful emotions from the past that make the present-day situation even more stressful.

Some of the participants in our EFT for Lyme/TBDs recovery groups have shared that having a way to identify the many ways their illness has affected their lives has helped them to better understand what they have been going through, thus developing self-empathy and self-compassion. Others identified how their experiences have triggered old wounds, adding to their current distress. After completing the "Lyme/TBDs-Related Change/Loss Inventory," which is presented on the next page, one participant spontaneously yelled out to the group, "I am taking this home to show to my husband so he can see all that I have been going through! This will help him understand."

Another person shared that using the "Lyme/TBDs-Related Change/Loss Inventory" was "a real help in giving me a more complete picture of the ways that Lyme is negatively impacting my life and that this has been difficult to recognize on my own." This same person spoke with regard to herself about "how eye opening it was to realize that Lyme creates an 'environment' that is similar to aspects of my childhood that negatively affected me. The roots that this disease triggers can be so deep."

Indeed, those roots can run deep, but when you can acknowledge, process, and release your own past emotional pain and allow yourself to grieve your past and present losses, you can "weed" out some of the sources of your suffering and cultivate a wellness state of mind that expects and promotes healing in every dimension of your life.

The inventory lists some of the most common changes and losses that can occur in each of the Seven Dimensions of Wellness related to having Lyme/TBDs. The dimensions are identified in the left column. We encourage you to take a moment to put a checkmark next to those changes/losses that have occurred with your own experience of Lyme/TBDs. We have also provided room at the bottom of the inventory to write in any other changes/losses you have/are experiencing that are not included.

Exercise: Lyme/TBDs-Related Change/Loss Inventory

Dimensions		Self-Check
Psychosocial stressors: Social	**Change/loss in quality engagement with family, friends, and/or community**	
	Difficulty participating in relationships	❑
	Difficulty communicating	❑
	Interrupted sexual intimacy	❑
	Possible conflict with family and friends	❑
	Isolation, loneliness	❑
	Fear of being outdoors	❑
	Avoidance of outdoor activities	❑
Psychosocial stressors: Intellectual	**Change/loss in learning new things**	
	Diminished pleasure in previously enjoyed activities	❑
	Loss of creativity	❑
	Decreased interest in reading and/or writing	❑
Psychosocial stressors: Spiritual	**Change/loss in the meaning of personal identity and life purpose**	
	Who am I now? I'm no longer the person I thought I was.	❑
	Who am I now with Lyme disease/TBDs?	❑
	Who am I now without doing the work I have always done?	❑
	Who am I now if I can't be the partner I have always been?	❑
	Who am I now if I can't parent the way I have always parented?	❑
	Why has God/Higher Power/Universe forsaken me?	❑
	Rejection of a Higher Power	❑
	Angry with "God" or the Universe	❑
Psychosocial stressors: Emotional	**Change/loss in ability to process emotions in healthy and productive ways**	
	Unhealthy coping strategies, such as destructive behaviors	❑
	Rejection of self and/or others	❑
	Generated fears	❑
	Change/loss in emotional resilience	
	Diminished self-esteem (self-acceptance/ self-love)	❑
	Helplessness (despair)	❑
	Change/loss in ability to cultivate joy, hope, peace, love, happiness, contentment	
	Hopelessness (despair)	❑
	Depression	❑
Psychosocial stressors: Physical	**Change/loss in the healthy functioning of the body**	
	Change/loss in hearing (earaches; ringing)	❑
	Change/loss in eyesight (double or blurred vision)	❑
	Change/loss in mobility (muscle weakness, muscle spasms, twitches, muscle coordination, tremors)	❑
	Change/loss in energy (tired to severe, debilitating fatigue)	❑
	Change/loss in sensory integration (touch, sound, and light sensitivity)	❑
	Change/loss of libido (sex drive)	❑
	Change/loss in restorative sleep	❑

(continued on the next page)

Dimensions		Self-Check
Psychosocial stressors: Physical	**Change/loss in mental functioning: neuropsychiatric**	
	Mild/moderate/severe depression	❑
	Mild/moderate/severe anxiety (irritability to panic attacks)	❑
	Psychosis (hallucinations, delusions, and paranoia)	❑
	Impulsivity	❑
	Mild/moderate/severe mood swings	❑
	Hypomania, mania	❑
	Misdiagnosis with a mental illness	❑
	Emotional rigidity	❑
	Overwhelming emotions: anger/rage episodes, anxiety/panic attacks, depressive episodes	❑
	Racing thoughts	❑
	Rigid thinking	❑
	Change/loss in cognitive functioning	
	Difficulty formulating thoughts (brain fog)	❑
	Confusion	❑
	Forgetfulness	❑
	Loss of concentration (shorter attention span)	❑
	Difficulty absorbing new information	❑
	Disorientation (getting lost in familiar places or going to the wrong places)	❑
	Speech errors (unable to retrieve words and/or using the wrong word)	❑
	Memory loss (dementia spectrum)	❑
Psychosocial stressors: Environmental	**Change/loss managing environmental conditions**	
	Increased sensitivity to electromagnetic fields (EMFs)	❑
	Increased vulnerability to bacteria/viruses	❑
	Increased sensitivity to allergens (food, perfumes, cosmetics, dust mites)	❑
	Additional environmental sensitivities (sound, light, touch)	❑
Psychosocial Stressors: Occupational	**Change/loss in ability to function adequately at work and/or at home**	
	Underperforming	❑
	Demotion	❑
	Loss of employment	❑
	Occupational identity challenged	❑
	Disruption and/or inability to parent efficiently	❑
	Change/loss of income	
	Challenges/inability to pay bills	❑
	Challenges/inability to access medical care and treatments	❑
	Challenges/inability to provide food, clothing, housing	❑

List any other changes/losses you have/are experiencing that are not included above:

Exercise: Processing the Inventory

What was it like for you to complete this inventory?

___

___

___

(Describe any beliefs, thoughts, feelings, and/or body sensations that you experienced.)

___

___

Which (if any) changes and/or losses that you have experienced and identified here feel emotionally unresolved:

From the past:

1. ___

___

___

2. ___

___

___

3. ___

___

___

4. ___

___

___

5. ___

___

___

From the present:

1.________________________________

2.________________________________

3.________________________________

4.________________________________

5.________________________________

What do the changes and/or losses you have experienced say about you?

State which ones you would like to emotionally resolve/heal using the self-help tools in this workbook:

What (if anything) about this inventory:

Supported you?

Was not supportive to you and why?

What (if anything) about this inventory:

Fostered self-empathy and self-compassion?

Surprised you?

Overwhelmed you?

If you need to take a break and put this book down for now, that is okay. If you are feeling emotionally overwhelmed or stressed and want relief, you can:

- Skip directly to page 86 to begin using **4/8 Diaphragmatic Breathing (Belly Breath)** for stress reduction. Use this breathing pattern until you feel more relaxed and grounded.
- Use any of the other **mindfulness-based tools in Part 2** on page 79 to help you reframe the disruptive thought patterns and emotions that can be triggered with Lyme/TBDs-related changes/losses.
- Skip to Chapter 13 on page 121 to learn the **Modified EFT Basic Recipe** and **tapping acupoints** used with EFT.
- Then skip to the global tapping script **I Feel Overwhelmed By All of These Changes and Losses!** on page 177 in Part 4 to begin using EFT to address any emotional distress you may be experiencing in relation to this issue.

Once you are ready to move on, you can continue reading this chapter and then complete the **Lyme/TBDs-Related Belief Inventory** at the end of this chapter to identify any Limiting Beliefs you may have in relation to any Lyme/TBDs-related changes/losses that may be contributing to doubts you have about your prospects for recovery. You will also be invited to identify the Empowering Beliefs you currently have that are enhancing your recovery. Once you have completed that inventory, you can refer back to it at any time to target and tap through any of the Limiting Beliefs you identified and to enhance the empowering ones.

Find Meaning in the Chaos

What does it mean when you are no longer able to feel and do what you have always felt and done before? How do you maintain a sense of self when you can no longer play the roles you have always played as partner, parent, sibling, friend, and professional, doing the things that once gave you a sense of purpose and identity? Sometimes it can feel as if the ground of your being is literally dissolving beneath your feet.

In the search for meaning and stability, you may find yourself asking questions like:

- Why did this happen to me?
- What does this change/loss say about me?
- Who am I now with Lyme/TBDs?
- Where is all of this taking me?
- How do I live my life now?

These are common questions some people ask themselves when faced with chronic and debilitating illnesses like Lyme/TBDs. We sure did! With so much pain and confusion, it can be difficult to see that hidden within these questions is the ultimate gift of all crises and the chaos they bring: the opportunity for self-transformation.

When Lyme/TBDs began taking their toll on us, we, too, were reeling from the changes and losses we experienced. Even though we are psychotherapists, we were literally unexpectedly thrown off our feet by this illness! How were we supposed to work with so much pain and unpredictability? What were we to say to people when we had to cancel yet another appointment or event? How could we explain why one day we could have it together and the next we just couldn't do a thing and had to rearrange our schedules to accommodate? Question after question went racing through our minds, bringing us face to face with our own painful sense of inadequacy. And so it was that Lyme/TBDs created for us a healing crisis that ultimately reshaped our lives.

We noticed that prior to getting sick, we had maintained a high level of personal and professional success despite the fact that we had been carrying a number of Limiting Beliefs and unresolved painful emotions that we had buried deep within ourselves. Getting Lyme/TBDs and having to cope with all of the challenges they bring brought to the surface an awareness of our own repressed emotional pain. It came pouring out! This was our invitation to acknowledge, resolve, and release the Limiting Beliefs and insecurities that were keeping us locked in discouragement and impeding our healing that at first we did not even know we had.

We needed to shift from a state of mind clouded by pain and limitation to one that was clear and centered on wellness and the possibility of recovery. This is how Lyme/TBDs became for us a catalyst propelling us toward a level of personal growth and transformation beyond anything we might have attained had our lives remained untouched by such an unexpected debilitating force.

For instance, when I, Tracey, was diagnosed with Lyme disease, I chose to let go of a high-stress job when the emotional and physical costs outweighed its benefits. I was the mobile treatment supervisor of a mental-health team that served people in the community who were struggling with severe and chronic mental illness. I was on call 24/7 and facilitated daily crisis interventions that would determine life or death for our clients. This job is one of the most rewarding and stressful jobs in the field of clinical social work. I soon discovered that as much as I valued serving in this way, my job was hindering my ability to recover.

Lyme disease was showing me that I could no longer absorb the impact of high levels of job-related stress without major negative consequences on my mental and physical health, thus on my recovery. What I thought I wanted had to be renegotiated for the betterment of my health. I made the decision to resign my position as a mobile treatment team leader and chose a job with 80 percent less inherent stress that still challenged me as a therapist and provided me with plenty of fuel for my personal passions. I am so grateful to have had Lyme disease in this situation because it required me to make a professional decision that was in my best and highest good all the way around.

Lyme disease brought me to the raw acknowledgment that by holding on to that high-stress job, I was feeding an unconscious need to achieve so that I could feel better about myself. I was caught in the trance of unworthiness. I processed deep grief and failure through many months of tapping sessions, going through emotional layer after layer until I identified the limiting belief that "I was not enough unless I was proving myself."

Wow! My desire to recover from Lyme disease was the catalyst I needed to finally realize that my need to overachieve was really compensation for feelings of unworthiness I had throughout my life. Tapping cleared the limiting belief that "I am not enough" from my mind-body system so that I could let go of the status of the job and still feel worthy and successful, no matter how I chose to serve others.

The "Trance of Unworthiness"

In confronting the emotional pain and insecurities Lyme/TBDs triggered in us, we discovered that we had been living in what Tara Brach, a well-known psychologist and teacher of Buddhist **meditation**, calls the "trance of unworthiness"—a commonly shared unconscious state in humans based in the belief that there is something fundamentally wrong with us. Over time, the trance of unworthiness becomes a veil of negative self-judgment, blame, and insecurity through which we see ourselves, others, and the world. It is sewn together from limiting core beliefs developed mostly in childhood that state we are not lovable, not acceptable, not enough, and/or that we deserve to suffer.

Having peeled away layer after layer of our own Limiting Beliefs with EFT, we were surprised by what surfaced as we sought to answer all the "whys" that Lyme/TBDs brought up for us. We discovered yet unknown layers of unworthiness (not being good enough) and self-blame that we might never have known were there had it not been for this crisis. It was only because we had Lyme/TBDs and became very ill that we chose to face our Limiting Beliefs and the reality that they were actually sabotaging our healing process by eroding our sense of worth and increasing our sense of helplessness.

We came to realize more deeply than ever before the power of our state of mind—the beliefs, thoughts, and emotions that create our perceptions and define our experiences—to either promote or inhibit healing and recovery from Lyme/TBDs. As therapists, we had an intellectual understanding of this, but when it happened to us, we needed to get to the emotional roots of our own experience. That meant practicing what we preached even when we were knocked to our knees by Lyme/TBDs.

Discovering the Missing Link in Treatment

We realized that the missing link in current Lyme/TBD treatment protocols was the cultivation of a wellness state of mind that is rooted in an Empowering Belief system that expects healing and recovery. Clearing the fears and Limiting Beliefs with EFT freed us from our trance of unworthiness and shifted our focus to Empowering Beliefs filled with self-worth, self-love, and the knowledge that recovery was possible. Mahatma Gandhi put it so beautifully:

> *Your beliefs become your thoughts,*
> *Your thoughts become your words,*
> *Your words become your actions,*
> *Your actions become your habits,*
> *Your habits become your values,*
> *Your values become your destiny.*

In other words, it is not simply life events that determine the course and quality of your life, but your perceptions of those events and the beliefs, thoughts, and emotions that come with them. What Gandhi is saying, and what researchers have been discovering, is that your state of mind has a direct effect on your reality! How you believe, think, and feel directs your response to Lyme/TBDs and is critical to how your body both manages the illness and responds to treatment. This is why cultivating a wellness state of mind is so vital to Lyme/TBDs healing and recovery.

Identifying Your Lyme/ TBDs-Related Beliefs

The beliefs you have about yourself, others, and the world originate in the context of family, cultural values, and life experiences. For some people who grew up in a culture where more value was placed on what you do and how you perform rather than who you really are, it's easy to believe that being a person of worth means having a great job, a beautiful house, the "right" friends, and material wealth. It might also mean being the "perfect" spouse and/or parent. In this kind of circumstance, you can come to believe that the measure of your worth is based on what you do, what you own, and how you live up to family and cultural expectations.

With these kinds of beliefs firmly planted in your subconscious mind, you could develop and build your life on a series of related limiting and inaccurate beliefs such as: *I am what I do. I am what I have. I must be what others expect me to be if I want to be loved and accepted.* These beliefs become the foundation for your sense of identity and how you relate to others and the world.

Where once believing that *I am what I do, I am what I have, and I must be what others expect me to be* may have gained you acceptance in your family and motivated you to achieve the material success and relationships sought, these beliefs become a great source of pain, stress, and grief in the face of the many changes/losses that can come with Lyme/TBDs.

If you are what you do, what happens when you can't "do" anymore or as you did before? If you are what you have, what happens if you lose it? If being loved and accepted depends on being who or what others expect you to be, what happens when you can no longer live up to those expectations? If you can allow these questions to surface, they may lead you into a deeper awareness of the specific Limiting Beliefs that could be sabotaging your healing.

We have been amazed by the many new and exciting possibilities that arise for our clients when they use EFT to identify, process, and release those Limiting Beliefs that have blocked their recovery from Lyme/TBDs. One of our group participants put it this way:

"My internal mantra became, 'I can't do it' because I had become so used to the limitations that Lyme had imposed on my life. I also was suffering great shame due to my ineffectiveness in my day-to-day duties. I felt like my thinking ability had become impaired by the disease, and I feared that no one would hire me due to continued cognitive impairments. That is where EFT came into play for me. . . . EFT did bring repeated relief to me. . . . I have no doubt whatsoever that EFT can be a great tool in helping people lessen or even eliminate the suffering caused by Lyme disease."

Practicing EFT helped this person to deepen her awareness of the shame she felt and gave her a means to let go of her negative self-judgment and to develop compassion for herself so that she could increase her self-esteem. We invite you now to complete the following exercise to help identify the beliefs that apply to you. We encourage you to go through them at your own pace.

Exercise: Lyme/TBDs-Related Belief Inventory

Place a checkmark next to each statement that applies to you.

Limiting Beliefs		Empowering Beliefs	
Self-help tools won't work for me.	☐	Self-help tools will work for me.	☐
There are no Lyme treatments that work for me.	☐	I will find the Lyme treatments that work for me.	☐
I don't trust the medical system to help me recover.	☐	I will find the people in the medical system to help me recover.	☐
I can't get the help I need.	☐	I will continue to seek the help I need.	☐
If doctors can't help me, no one can.	☐	I believe there are doctors and people out there who can help me.	☐
It must be all in my head.	☐	I know my body and acknowledge something is wrong.	☐
There is no future for me.	☐	My future is full of new possibilities.	☐
My life is out of control.	☐	I am emotionally flexible and able to move through the changes in my life.	☐
I'll never get better.	☐	I do believe I will recover. It is what it is for now, and it is temporary.	☐
I am useless and/or defective.	☐	I am useful and have value.	☐
Life will always be a struggle.	☐	Life is full of change and new possibility.	☐
It's all my fault that I'm still sick.	☐	I have Lyme/TBDs.	☐
I am filled with guilt.	☐	I am not to blame for this.	☐
I do not believe medications will help me.	☐	I am open to the possibility that medications will help me.	☐
This treatment protocol is too much for me.	☐	I have the resilience needed to heal through this treatment protocol.	☐
My body betrayed me.	☐	My body is doing everything it can to help me heal, and I am grateful.	☐
I don't know who I am anymore.	☐	I am gaining a deeper understanding of myself as a result of going through this.	☐
I'll never get my energy back.	☐	This fatigue is what it is, and it is temporary.	☐
I will be in pain forever.	☐	This pain is what it is, and it is temporary.	☐
I am disconnected from everybody.	☐	I am able to connect with others, even though I am in pain.	☐
There is no way that I can give up my favorite high-inflammatory foods.	☐	I am able to choose foods that support my healing and recovery.	☐
Nobody understands what I am going through.	☐	I am able to find people who can understand what I am going through.	☐
I'll never be able to work again.	☐	I believe I will be able to work again in the future. It is what it is for now, and it is not forever.	☐

Limiting Belief		Empowering Belief	
Lyme/TBDs are taking everything away from me.	☐	I accept the loss I experience and believe new possibilities surround me.	☐
I don't have any friends I can count on.	☐	I am able to and will find friends I can count on.	☐
My family doesn't understand what's happening to me.	☐	My family understands what is happening to me to the level that they are capable.	☐
I have failed my spouse/partner and/or kids.	☐	I am doing the best I can for my spouse/partner/kids based on where I am and how I feel.	☐
I am not carrying my weight.		I can only do so much and accept that it's okay for now.	
I can't cope with the stress of Lyme/TBDs.	☐	I am able to cope with the stress related to Lyme/TBDs by using the self-help tools suggested in this workbook.	☐
I'll never enjoy being in the outdoors again.	☐	With the right precautions, I can enjoy the outdoors.	☐
I will never get out of this depression.	☐	My depression is what it is for now, and it is temporary.	☐
I don't have enough money to make it.	☐	I am capable of figuring out my finances, and I am open to creative solutions.	☐
Life will always be a struggle.	☐	I accept where I am now, learning what I need to learn for my best and highest good.	☐
There's no hope for me.	☐	There are always new possibilities for me.	☐
Add any additional Limiting Beliefs you may have:		Add any additional Empowering Beliefs you may have:	

My Top-Five Limiting Beliefs (if any):	My Top-Five Empowering Beliefs (if any):
1.	1.
2.	2.
3.	3.
4.	4.
5.	5.
How do you **FEEL** right now while reflecting on the Limiting Beliefs you have identified?	How do you **FEEL** right now while reflecting on the Empowering Beliefs you have identified?
Do you believe that it is possible that the Limiting Beliefs you have identified could be inhibiting your recovery from Lyme/TBDs? If yes or no, describe in what ways.	Do you believe that it is possible that the Empowering Beliefs you have identified could be enhancing your recovery from Lyme/TBDs? If yes or no, describe in what ways.

Whenever you are ready to address and release any identified Limiting Beliefs, you can:

- Skip to Chapter 13 to learn how to use the **Modified EFT Basic Recipe** and **Tapping Acupoints** used with **EFT** on page 121.
- Then, skip to Part 4 on page 151 to begin using **EFT**. Choose a chapter that reflects the issue you would like to address. Read the **case study** and follow along with the **global extended tapping script** to gently get you started using EFT.
- You can then use the **Lyme/TBDs-Related Belief Inventory** to track your cognitive shifts by noting the Empowering Beliefs that emerge for you as you tap through, process, and release your current Limiting Beliefs. (We have provided another **Lyme/TBDs-Related Belief Inventory** in Appendix H on page 412 for you to complete at a later time to track your progress of releasing Limiting Beliefs and cultivating empowering ones that sustain a wellness state of mind.)

Radical Self-Acceptance

As long as there are any remaining emotional layers of the Limiting Beliefs that stem from a core sense of not being loveable or acceptable enough, there is the risk of seeing all experiences through the trance of unworthiness. It is from this conscious and unconscious state of mind and perceptive lens through which people create meaning and experience their lives. And it is one of the major reasons that a crisis like having Lyme/TBDs can so quickly pull some people down into the self-doubt, self-blame, and self-judgment that weakens their capacity for hope, healing, and recovery. If this is true for you, it is time to break the trance!

In the *Mindful* magazine article "Feeling Overwhelmed? Try 'RAIN'" by Tara Brach, the author shared how the discouragement and unhappiness she felt through the pain and fatigue of a particularly difficult past period of chronic illness awakened her out of her own trance of unworthiness: "In my view, I was terrible to be around—impatient, self-absorbed, irritable, gloomy." She explains that while she was meditating, she heard an "embittered" voice saying, "I hate living like this." And then a moment later, "I hate myself!" She writes:

> *The full toxicity of self-aversion filled me . . . Not only was I struggling with illness, I was at war with the self-centered, irritable person I believed I had become. Unknowingly, I had turned on myself and was held captive by the trance of unworthiness. But in that moment of recognizing and allowing the suffering of self-hatred, my heart began to soften with compassion.*[65]

Brach's experience is a movement toward what she calls "radical acceptance," accepting what is—no matter what it appears to be—and approaching it with a nonreactive and loving presence, holding it in kindness and tending to it with loving care.

If you find that you, too, have been living under the "trance of unworthiness," you can use EFT and the other self-help tools and mindfulness-based techniques offered in this workbook to become more aware of what is happening with you in the moment and to develop greater compassion for yourself, accepting whatever is in your heart, knowing that you have the tools to change your perspective and to cultivate a wellness state of mind.

When you can experience the present moment as it is without negative judgment, you can open yourself to a new way of being and quality of living that honors and holds with compassion all that you have endured with Lyme/TBDs. With the practice of radical acceptance, the veil of fear and negative self-judgment is lifted, revealing the truth of who you are, the gifts you never knew you had, and the possibilities for healing you never knew existed.

CHAPTER

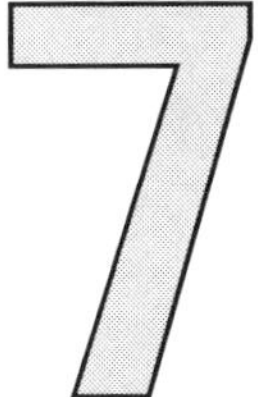

Lyme/TBDs and the Stress Factor

The previous chapter introduced the many psychosocial and physiological stressors that can come with having Lyme/TBDs. Stressors like these are more than minor discomforts; if left unresolved, these stressors can overtax your entire system. This is why understanding the impact of stress on your body and using EFT and the other mindfulness-based tools to reduce your stress is so critical to your recovery from Lyme/TBDs.

We have discovered in our work as psychotherapists that many people do not know what stress really is and how it can affect them. Many people assume that all stress is bad, but there is actually a form of healthy stress called eustress. Eustress is the energy you experience in response to something thrilling like a roller-coaster ride or when you are preparing for an important event like a job interview or a wedding. This type of stress adds spice to your life and energizes and motivates you to give your best to something that has meaning for you.

Chronic stress or what some call negative stress or distress, however, occurs when too much stress is experienced over a prolonged period of time. It can contribute to high blood pressure, immune and endocrine dysfunction, digestive issues, and an intensification of symptoms related to an already existing illness such as Lyme/TBDs and an interference with the body's response to treatments. Naturally, this makes dealing with the symptoms of these illnesses that much more challenging. Let's take a closer look.

Stress

The word "stress" is frequently used in our culture to describe everything from daily annoyances to emotional upheaval over major events. More accurately, stress is our mental, emotional, and physical response and adaptation to a stressor that is commonly perceived as threatening. This perception of threat will activate the stress response.

The level of stress you experience is influenced by how you perceive and relate to what is happening. For example, while one person who has Lyme/TBDs might experience eustress or healthy stress in anticipation of trying a new treatment, another might become distressed, believing that the treatment is bound to fail as all previous attempts have failed. (To learn more, skip to Chapter 8: What's Happening and **How am I relating to it?** on page 81.)

The Stress Response

When the mind-body system is confronted with stress, the brain registers this as a change in the body's internal equilibrium. To restore balance, the brain immediately initiates the stress response. This signals the endocrine system to release a variety of chemicals (for example, adrenaline, cortisol, and glucose) that work to enhance our focused attention on survival. With survival being the body's priority, it reduces the need for such things as eating, digestion, sex, and sleep, since focusing on these lessens the chance for immediate survival.

At the same time this is happening, the immune system releases a large number of protein molecules called cytokines. For a more detailed explanation of the role cytokines play in inflammation and healing, read Chapter 41: The Stress Response in Action on page 395.

In the case of acute or short-term stress, the brain signals the endocrine, immune, and all other systems to "stand down" once the stressor has been resolved. In the case of chronic stress, however, the stress response is extended so that the brain stays on red alert causing the body to remain in a stress-induced defense mode.

Fight, Flight . . . or Freeze

The stress response is frequently referred to as "fight or flight," by which our mind-body system prepares us to confront our fear head on (fight) or run away (flight). Dr. Robert Scaer, author of *The Trauma Spectrum: Hidden Wounds and Human Resiliency*, includes the freeze response as part of the fight-flight stress response and refers to it as fight/flight/freeze response.[66] The freeze response can occur when you feel helpless and hopeless as a result of frequent treatment disappointments, and it may explain the state of a person with Lyme/TBDs who gives up on treatment altogether. When the body interprets major stressors as threatening, the fight/flight/freeze response can be activated.

Distress/Chronic Stress

Distress is what we experience when we believe that the demands of our situation exceed our personal and social resources for coping with that event. In other words, we experience distress when we are overwhelmed by the challenges we are experiencing. Distress can be experienced in relation to either an ongoing overwhelming stressor such as chronic pain and/or as a result of too many stressors occurring in multiple areas of life at the same time, which is very common for those with Lyme/TBDs.

Chronic stress is a mind-body state of too much distress. It is an ongoing state of being overwhelmed in which the mind and body are constantly on guard, attempting to protect us from one distressing event after another. As long as we are distressed, the body's stress response stays on so that our neural, endocrine, and immune systems become overtaxed, fatigued, and unable to properly function. This is backed by researchers and practitioners alike who have found that chronic stress highly correlates with dysregulation of both the immune and endocrine systems. These systems play a critical role in the prevention of and recovery from illness. Disruptions in these and other major systems can worsen Lyme/TBDs symptoms while making you more vulnerable to new illnesses and relapses. Additionally, Lyme/TBDs and the emotional distress they can create often form the perfect storm for chronic stress. It's a vicious cycle for anyone suffering from Lyme/TBDS.

When chronic stress occurs, these systems become overloaded with adrenaline, cortisol, glucose, and pro-inflammatory cytokines. The results can be:

- Dysregulation of the endocrine and immune systems
- Increased inflammation and Lyme/TBD symptoms
- Digestive dysfunction
- Increased fatigue
- Increased anxiety and depression (feeds back into above conditions)
- Vulnerability to new illnesses and relapses
- Decreased responsiveness to Lyme/TBD treatments

The following figure illustrates the impact chronic stress can have on you when you are suffering from Lyme/TBDs.

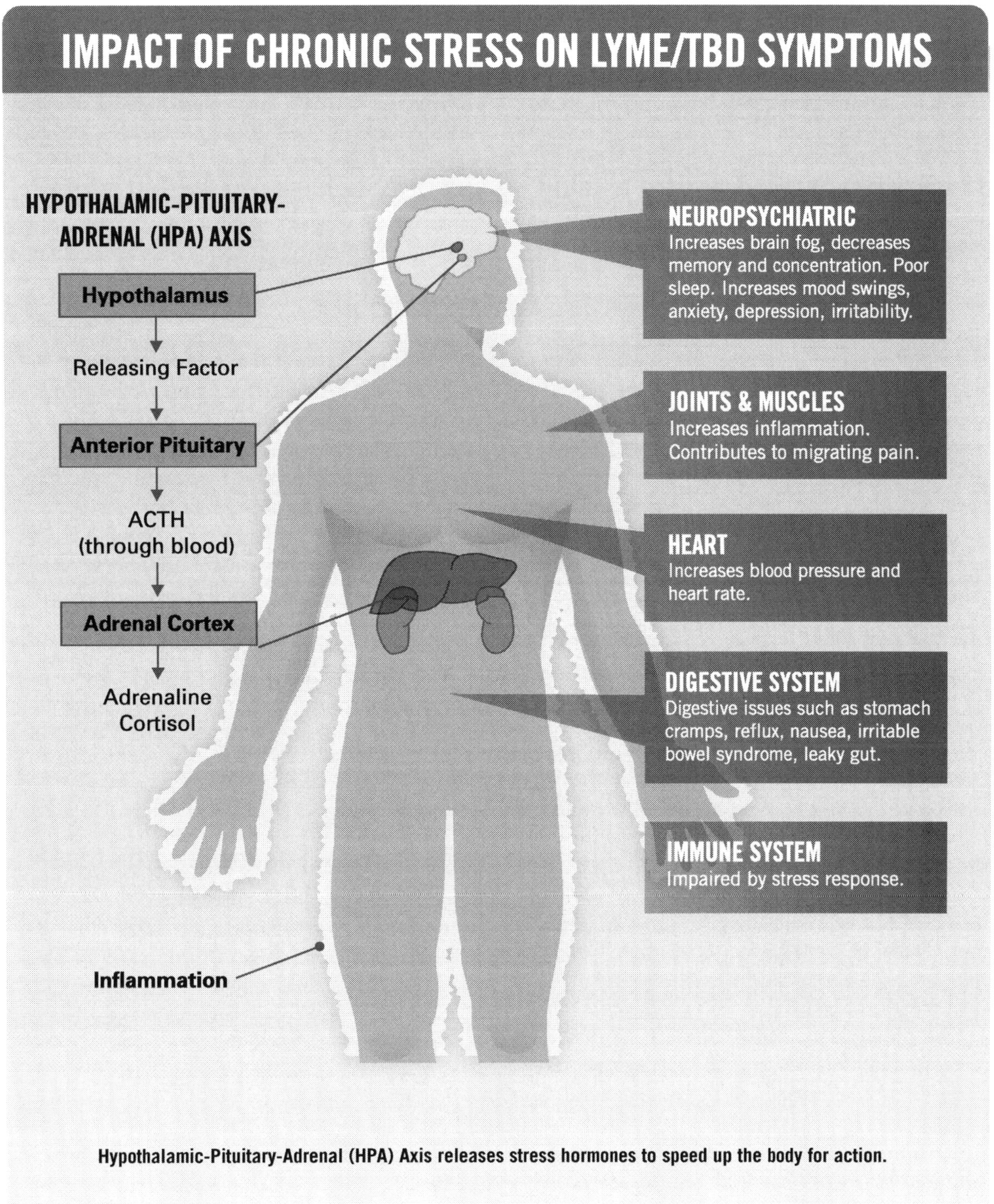

Hypothalamic-Pituitary-Adrenal (HPA) Axis releases stress hormones to speed up the body for action.

Lyme/TBDs, Perception, and Chronic Stress

Your state of mind plays a major role in creating either a thriving or an ailing biological state. The same applies for creating an internal environment that either promotes or inhibits your healing and recovery. Bruce Lipton explains that your body can be in only one of two states at any given moment:

1. **Protection response** (same as the stress response): energy the body normally uses to maintain a healthy state has been diverted to defending it against potential threats, OR

2. **Growth response** (similar to homeostasis—the body's ability to regulate and maintain itself for survival): the body is relaxed and can engage in healthy cell production and maintenance.[67]

How you think and feel about things, says Lipton, has a direct impact on your cells. He explains that your perceptions of life events largely contribute to whether your internal biological state supports or hinders healthy cell growth and function.[68] By extension, a wellness state of mind helps your cells to flourish and produce the proteins your body needs for maintenance and repair, as well as strengthens the immune system. To counter that, a state of chronic stress brought on by unresolved distressing thoughts and emotions can deprive your cells of the nutrients they need to grow and inhibit the function of the immune system.

Need a break? Go to Part 3 and try 4/8 **Diaphragmatic Breathing (Belly Breath)** on page 86 for a great way to reduce stress and relax!

When you are in a state of chronic stress, your cells, deprived of the nutrients they need to thrive, can actually begin to mutate in a way that creates infection and other illnesses. According to Richard Horowitz, author of *Why Can't I Get Better? Solving the Mystery of Lyme and Chronic Disease*:

> Chronic stress markedly increases a patient's vulnerability to poor medical outcomes across a wide variety of mental and medical conditions. Most of my patients notice that when they are under increased stress (psychological/emotional, physical, contracting a new illness such as an upper respiratory tract infection or sinus infection), their underlying Lyme symptoms often come out of hiding, or significantly worsen.[69]

Horowitz later notes that "patients will occasionally need to see a therapist to help them deal with significant depression, anxiety, trauma, and PTSD. I have found that my patients with a history of trauma and abuse will have an exceedingly difficult time healing from Lyme disease. Severe trauma and abuse can affect the immune system. The mind and body do not function separately, and when patients have had trauma or been abused, or if they suffer a loss with unresolved grief, the unresolved conflict usually has a deleterious effect on their immune systems."[70]

Any unresolved emotional pain and trauma you may have from the past can greatly hinder your ability to recover from Lyme/TBDs in the present. This is because, as Horowitz explains, you carry your emotions in your body. He highlights the "complex interaction between psychosocial factors such as stress and trauma and the nervous, cardiovascular, endocrine, and immune systems," noting that "high levels of the stress hormone cortisol can trigger cell death of white blood cells and other changes in inflammatory processes during traumatic experiences. In this way, the mind and body work as one. Psychiatric medications can be helpful with symptom relief, but they do not address deeper emotional wounds and the way they affect our immune system."[71]

Four Factors of Lyme/TBDs-Related Stress

In essence, Lyme/TBDs often create four factors common to stress: 1) uncertainty, 2) conflict, 3) lack of control, and 4) lack of information. These conditions can be particularly destabilizing and stress producing. When combined with other present-day life stressors, they trigger unresolved emotional pain from the past.

Acknowledging those places in your life now where you feel stressed because of uncertainty, conflict, lack of control, and/or lack of information is another opportunity for you to see both how resilient you have been through the difficult conditions that can come with Lyme/TBDs and which emotional issues you may need to resolve in relation to these conditions of stress. We invite you now to review the table, insert a checkmark next to those that apply to you, and complete the exercise that follows.

Four Factors of Lyme/TBDs-Related Stress		Self-Check
	Place a checkmark next to each one that applies to you.	
Uncertainty	Unpredictability of illness	❑
	Questions about the future	❑
	Anxiety about managing daily life	❑
	Lack of trust in self, others, treatment providers, and the treatment process	❑
Conflict	Being at odds with treatment providers and insurance companies about treatment options and coverage	❑
	Misunderstanding and confusion at home, at work, and/or among friends	❑
	Feeling caught between competing priorities and changing roles	❑
	Feeling angry and out of sync with self and others	❑
Lack of control	Feeling overwhelmed by symptoms	❑
	Lack of choices in treatment	❑
	Decreased physical functioning	❑
	Memory impairment and difficulty keeping track of things	❑
Lack of information	Difficulty understanding what's happening	❑
	Conflicting research and treatment guidelines for Lyme/TBDs	❑
	Misdiagnoses	❑
	Challenges finding resources for managing family, medical, occupational, and financial issues	❑
	Not knowing where to turn for support	❑

Exercise: Developing Self-Awareness Around Stress

Using the table above, identify any issues you may have in relation to the four factors of Lyme/TBDs-Related Stress by completing the following statements (skip any that do not apply to you):

You are uncertain about:

This reminds you of a time when:

____

____

____

____

____

____

____

____

____

This makes you feel:

You have coped with this by:

You have shown resilience by:

You feel unresolved about:

You are in conflict with:

This reminds you of a time when:

This makes you feel:

You have coped with this by:

You have shown resilience by:

You feel unresolved about:

You don't have control over:

This reminds you of a time when:

This makes you feel:

You have coped with this by:

You have shown resilience by:

You feel unresolved about:

You don't have information about:

This reminds you of a time when:

This makes you feel:

You have coped with this by:

You have shown resilience by:

You feel unresolved about:

We recommend that you make note, as you did in Chapter 5, of any unresolved issues that may have arisen for you while completing this exercise. At this point, you can:

- Skip to the **List of Titled Specific Events** on page 156 in Part 4 where you can title each unresolved issue to tap on at a later time.
- Skip to Chapter 13 on page 121 to learn the **Modified EFT Basic Recipe** and **tapping acupoints** used with EFT.
- Then skip to the global tapping script in Chapter 26, **I'm Not Seen, Heard, or Understood** on page 241 in Part 4 to begin using **EFT** to address any emotional distress you may be experiencing in relation to this issue.

Personal Reflections

PART 2
The Toolkit: Supportive Tools

Introduction to Using the Toolkit

The mindfulness-based tools presented in this part support a wellness state of mind. They will help you to begin identifying the Limiting Beliefs and unresolved painful emotions that can be triggered by Lyme/TBDs-related events and also serve as self-help tools for stress reduction and grounding yourself in the present moment. Practicing these mindfulness-based tools also facilitates your use of Emotional Freedom Techniques (EFT) by giving you the means to quickly identify any mental and emotional barriers you may have to overcoming Lyme/TBDs, so that you can effectively process and release them from your mind-body system.

Once learned and practiced, all the tools and techniques offered in this workbook can bc used individually or in combination to generate healing and recovery in every dimension of your life.

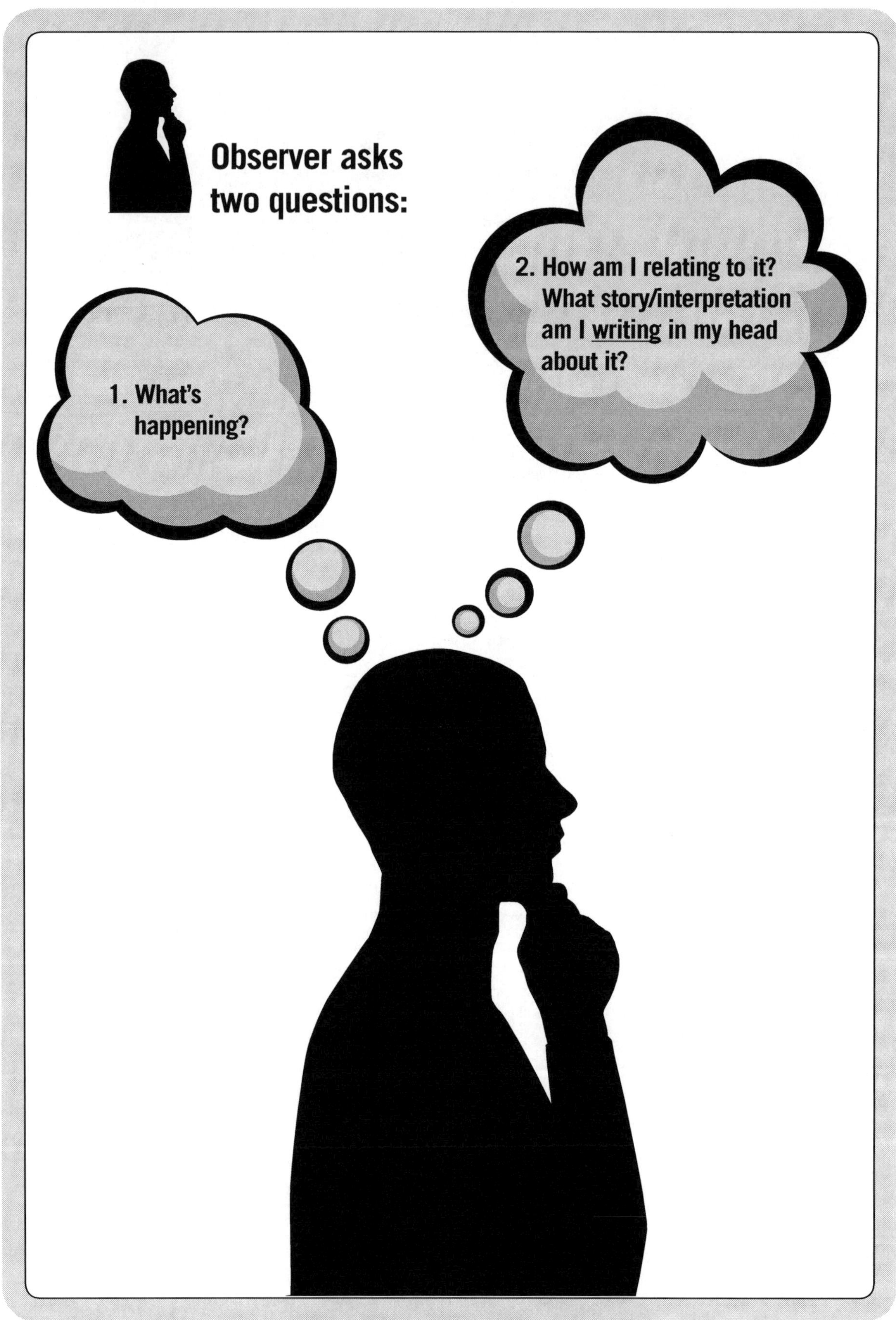
Observer asks
two questions:
1. What's
happening?
2. How am I relating to it?
What story/interpretation
am I writing in my head
about it?

CHAPTER

What's Happening and How Am I Relating to It?

In this chapter, you will learn to use the first two supportive tools in your toolbox: the **Body Scan** and **Stop-Drop-Breathe**. The **Body Scan** is a technique that focuses your attention on your body, allowing you to observe what is happening. You will use this technique in an abbreviated form in the beginning and throughout each of the EFT extended global tapping scripts in Part 4. These **Body Scans** will help you monitor your progress as you tap.

Stop-Drop-Breathe is another technique for becoming mindful about what is going on inside you in the present moment. This technique requires that you ask yourself two questions: **What's happening?** and **How am I relating to it?** (Stop-Drop). Once you have become mindful of the fact that how you are relating to something is creating overwhelming emotional states, you will be guided to use **4/8 Diaphragmatic Breathing (Belly Breath)** as the last step—Breathe—to reduce them.

4/8 Diaphragmatic Breathing (Belly Breath) is explained on page 86; it is a very important skill to learn. It can be used by itself or in combination with **Stop-Drop-Breathe** and/or EFT to:

- reduce stress
- reduce blood pressure
- reduce heart rate
- reduce anxiety and other overwhelming emotions
- regulate your emotions
- help ground yourself safely in the present moment

There Is Power in the Present!

Only in the present moment, when your awareness is no longer clouded by unresolved emotional pain from the past and future fears, can you access your knowledge, strength, and abilities to make choices that promote healing and that are in your best and highest good.

Supportive Tool #1: The Body Scan

The **Body Scan** is a great technique to support self-awareness of your mind-body state. While you focus your attention, starting at the top of your head and moving down your body, identify what you notice: beliefs, thoughts, feelings, and body sensations. You may not notice all of these and document only the ones you do.

Exercise: Body Scan

- Take a couple of minutes to notice what you are experiencing in your body.
- Sit or lie down in a comfortable place.
- You can close your eyes or leave them open with a relaxed gaze on a point in the room.
- Focus on your breathing. Notice the beginning of your inhale, the pause at the end, the beginning of the exhale, and the end of the exhale. Allow yourself to mindfully focus on the detailed movements of your full breaths, inhaling and exhaling. Do this for one or two minutes.
- Then bring your attention to your body, starting at the top of your head and slowly moving downward to each part of your body. Scan each part using the questions below. (This variety of questions is offered to include the diversity of experiences a person could have. It is common for people to not have awareness around every question asked. Focus on which questions you are able to answer, and let go of the rest.)

What beliefs do you notice about yourself?

What are you thinking?

What are you feeling?

Imagine that your feelings and body sensations you identified have tangible properties such as a location in your body, a temperature, and/or a texture. Describe each in detail:

Location:____

Temperature: ____

Texture: ____

Form: ____

Color: ____

What images come to mind?______________________________

____

____

____

A mindfulness state of observing what you are experiencing in your body allows you to cultivate the space to:

- Embody yourself (awareness that you are in your body)
- Continue observing with compassionate presence
- Radically accept awareness "as is" (without criticism, judgment, or blame)
- In a mindfulness state of accepting, you can also assess if you need to shift to a healthier mind-body state in order to:
- Reduce or release painful physical states
- Release painful emotional states
- Reduce stress and trigger the relaxation response
- Regulate your emotions
- Resolve internal and external conflicts through creative problem solving

In a mindfulness state of taking ownership of how you feel, you can then make decisions to take positive action to help yourself in those areas you identified by choosing any of the self-help tools in this workbook that feel supportive to you in addressing any of the above issues.

As mentioned at the beginning of this chapter, you will use the **Body Scan** in an abbreviated form at the beginning and throughout each of the EFT extended global tapping scripts in Part 4 to help you monitor your progress.

Supportive Tool #2: Stop-Drop-Breathe

Stop-Drop-Breathe is a technique for becoming mindful about how you are in the present moment. When we were in elementary school, many of us were taught to "stop-drop-roll" if our clothing caught on fire. This simple set of directives was given to us so that we could be empowered to take positive actions for our own preservation and well-being during a crisis. Building on this concept, we developed **Stop-Drop-Breathe** as a means of teaching valuable tools for mindfully resolving emotional challenges.

Included in this set of tools is diaphragmatic breathing—a stress-reduction technique adapted from yoga and various forms of **meditation** that uses deep breathing to relax the mind and body. The benefits of this technique include reduced stress, lower blood pressure and heart rate, increased clarity of mind, and an improved emotional state.

Stop-Drop-Breathe is a three-in-one tool. You can use the tools individually or all together in the present moment to quickly shift out of the stress response and into a wellness state of mind. You'll have a chance to practice this tool at the end of this chapter, but first let's break it down:

1. **Stop!** Observe what is happening. "Stop" literally means stop! Stop what you are doing, check in with yourself, and become the "observer." Becoming the observer is a way of stepping back from your emotional reaction to an event and looking at it rationally as if you were a reporter whose job it is to assess only the facts of the situation. Becoming the observer is a way of shifting your mind into a neutral state. In this neutral-mind state, the tools of the observer include asking yourself the following two questions: **What is happening?** and **How am I relating to it?**

John Sullivan, author of *Living Large: Transformative Work at the Intersection of Ethics and Spirituality*, presented the "observer" as an effective and easy-to-use tool for quickly assessing and reframing an event in terms of empowerment and possibility rather than powerlessness and suffering. Asking, **What is happening?** and **How am I relating to it?** gives you an opportunity to put your mind in a neutral state and your emotional reaction to an event on "pause." This gives you the space needed to make a mindful choice about how you perceive, interpret, and respond to a situation so that you can move forward rather than become stuck in a state of emotional distress.[72]

> "We don't see things as they are, we see them as we are."
>
> — **Anaïs Nin**

One of the most important concepts to understand here is that your thoughts, feelings, and physical responses to an event are directly related to how you interpret that event. You are emotionally responding to your thoughts about the event, not to the actual event itself. The event "is what it is" (neutral) until you give it meaning and power. Really think about that! Knowing you can choose how you interpret an event and take full responsibility for how that interpretation makes you feel empowers you to become proactive. Rather than automatically reacting to whatever happens, you have the option of consciously choosing a response that opens your possibilities for healing, growth, and expansion.

Having a choice is empowerment! If you stop when you are in an emotionally challenging situation and ask yourself, **What is happening?** and **How am I relating to it?** you will likely feel yourself becoming emotionally unhooked from the event and start to calm down. These two questions interrupt the thinking that creates distress and helps you to move from a reactive state to a responsive state, observing where choices can be made with an awareness of their costs and benefits. Here is the process of "Stop!" in detail:

- **What is happening?** (Just the facts. No interpretation. The "it is what it is" neutral state of mind.)
- **How are you relating to it?** (Your interpretation of the facts.)
- How does your interpretation make you feel?

- What body sensations do you notice?
- Do you feel tension?
- Where do you feel tension?
- Are you in a stress or a relaxation response?

2. **Drop.** Bring awareness down to your belly. Become the observer (adopt a neutral state) and then drop your attention down to your belly (stomach). The observer watches events, maintaining a neutral state of mind.

3. **Breathe.** Inhale and exhale slowly, deeply, and fully. The breathing technique we have found most helpful is called **4/8 Diaphragmatic Breathing (Belly Breath).** Here's how to do it:

   1. Inhale on a count of 4. With your awareness on your belly, take a deep breath in through your nose, letting the air push down on the diaphragm. Feel your stomach being pushed outward like an inflating balloon.
   2. Pause at the end of the 4 count inhale.
   3. Exhale slowly out of pursed lips for a total of an 8 count. It is very important to double the length of your exhale. (This massages the vagus nerve, helping it to generate the relaxation response. A part of the vagus nerve can be found just behind the stomach, and it is from this point that the relaxation response is initiated. From its initiation point, the relaxation response spreads upward to the tip of the vagus nerve at the base of the brain and then moves down through the rest of the body.)
   4. Repeat the process until you feel more relaxed.

The Benefits of 4/8 Diaphragmatic Breathing (Belly Breath)

- Counting in the mind acts as an interference pattern for the brain. It interrupts the thinking that triggers a painful emotional response. It is hard to think and count at the same time.
- Belly breathing shifts us from the hind brain where the stress response—fight, flight, or freeze—is initiated to our frontal lobe, which is our thinking and problem-solving center. This allows you to make a mindful choice about how to proceed.
- Inhaling deeply and pushing the diaphragm downward into the belly (like inflating a balloon) helps the stomach to massage the dorsal vagal nerve that resides just behind it to send relaxation signals up the vagus nerve to the amygdala in the brain. (The vagus nerve is the longest of all our cranial nerves. It is essentially an information superhighway running up the spine connecting the nervous system with the brain. It plays a critical role in heart rate, blood pressure, digestion, and overall organ function.)
- An extended exhale, twice the count of the inhale, stimulates the ventral vagal nerve at the base of the skull to also support relaxation signals going to the amygdala (located in the limbic system of the brain) to help shift it from a stress response to a relaxation response.
- The amygdala is the part of the brain that is responsible for emotions and motivations, particularly related to survival: fear, anger, pleasure. Emotional distress causes the amygdala to initiate the stress response, which disrupts the normal function of our organs.
- Diaphragmatic breathing calms the amygdala, thus creating stress-reduction and the healthy function of our organs. It tells the brain that "all is well," thereby reducing stress (lowering heart rate and blood pressure), bringing awareness back to the present moment, and improving the emotional state (that is, relieves anxiety and lifts mood).

Exercise: 4/8 Diaphragmatic Breathing (Belly Breath)

If this type of breathing is new to you, it is helpful to place one hand on your chest and the other on your belly when you first begin practicing. When you correctly execute a belly breath, the hand on your belly will rise as you inhale, and the hand on your chest will remain still. If the hand on your chest rises upward as you inhale (instead of the one on your belly), then you have taken a shallow chest breath; try again to take a deep belly breath. Learning this technique takes some practice, but the benefits are worth it! Go ahead and practice now.

1. Inhale on a count of 4. With your awareness on your belly, take a deep breath in through your nose, letting the air push down on the diaphragm. Feel your stomach being pushed outward like an inflating balloon.
2. Pause at the end of the 4-count inhale.
3. Exhale slowly, through pursed lips, for a total of an 8 count. It is very important to double the length of your exhale.
4. Continue **4/8 Diaphragmatic Breathing (Belly Breath)** for 1–2 minutes. Then complete another **Body Scan** and describe what you notice:

We invite you now to practice **4/8 Diaphragmatic Breathing (Belly Breath)**. We encourage you to use it while tapping, as a break between tapping rounds, and any time you experience an emotionally intense event. In fact, you can do this breathing exercise whenever you feel the need to relax and reduce stress—no matter where you are.

Exercise: Stop-Drop-Breathe

Now put **Stop-Drop-Breathe** together to experience how these steps can be used as one very powerful tool for changing your perspective. We recommend using this mindfulness-based tool whenever you feel the need to bring yourself to the present moment, observe what you are experiencing, and, if needed, to make the choice to reduce your stress and ground and center yourself (initiate the relaxation response).

1. **Stop!** Ask yourself:

   What is happening? *(Just the facts. No interpretation. The "it is what it is" neutral state of mind.)*

   ____

   ____

   ____

   ____

   ____

   How am I relating to it? *(My interpretation of the facts.)*

   ____

   ____

   ____

   ____

   How does my interpretation make me feel?

   ____

   ____

   What body sensations do I notice?

   ____

   ____

   Do I feel tension?______________________________

   Where do I feel tension?__________________________

   Am I in a stress or relaxation response?_______________

2. **Drop:** Drop your awareness to your belly (stomach).

3. **Breathe:** Do the **4/8 Diaphragmatic Breathing (Belly Breath)** for a few minutes. Then complete another **Body Scan** and ask yourself:

   What thoughts am I noticing now?

   ___
   ___
   ___
   ___
   ___
   ___
   ___

   What feelings am I noticing now?

   ___
   ___
   ___
   ___

   What body sensations am I noticing now?

   ___
   ___

   What changes am I noticing now?

   ___
   ___
   ___
   ___
   ___

If you are still feeling distressed, continue **4/8 Diaphragmatic Breathing (Belly Breath)** for a few more minutes until you feel noticeably less tension throughout your body. It takes as long as it takes.

CHAPTER

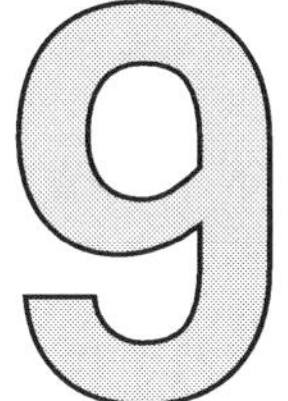

Small Mind and Large Mind

The daily lives of people who have Lyme/TBDs can contain any number of illnesses and life-related psychosocial stressors in which a person can easily become emotionally ensnared. You may find at times that this is true for you. And who wouldn't feel distressed by the painful and challenging symptoms, emotional upheaval, and unpredictability that so often come with the experience of Lyme/TBDs? To help reduce the intensity of distress you are feeling in the present moment, it is first necessary to be aware of how you are responding to it (your interpretation).

When you take the time to **Stop-Drop-Breathe** (see page 84),and assess the situation, you give yourself the space you need to make mindful choices about how you want to respond. When you are able to move from reacting to life events (increased stress) to being mindful with the ability to choose your response, it is really important to understand one important fact:

It is the story you are telling yourself in the form of thoughts (your interpretation) about what is happening that create your feelings; it is not the event itself!

> It is your interpretation of the facts of an event, and not the actual event itself, that determines your emotional response to that event.

Really think about this and take in the wisdom and freedom that this fact has for you. How many people have you heard say, "You make me angry!" This is a delusion, a false belief or opinion appearing real. The truth of reality that can set you free is that nobody can make you angry but yourself. Your story (your interpretation) of the other person's behavior is what you are responding to and is what creates your anger. Something in them triggered something in you, which then surfaces as an emotion. In reality, their behavior "is what it is" until you give it meaning.

The interpretation (the story) that you give is based on your belief system that then produces your thoughts and the emotions you feel, which are a direct expression of those beliefs. How we feel is an "inside job"! It is very freeing and empowering to know that you are responsible for how you are feeling, and your happiness is not left in the hands of other people or life circumstances (disempowerment). The quality of your mindset is your responsibility, not others, which means it is within your power to change it (empowerment).

Rather than getting stuck in an emotionally distressing and disempowering story filled with Limiting Beliefs, such as "No one can help me, and I'll never get better," you can begin to gently question the story you are telling yourself so that you can see where it might be taking you. How does it feel to believe and think this? Yes, you got it: hopeless and helpless. This is critical to understand.

Stories based in Limiting Beliefs can rob you of hope and diminish your sense of self-efficacy, while stories rooted in Empowering Beliefs can give you hope and strengthen your resilience.

Supportive Tool #3: Small Mind/Large Mind

Being able to shift your mindset from one that is contributing to your distress to one that empowers you is a mindfulness-based skill that is needed for emotional wellness. In fact, John G. Sullivan, PhD, developed a mindfulness-based tool for the "observer" that helps reframe limited thinking (which he calls "Small Mind") into expansive thinking (which he calls "**Large Mind**").[73]

Our own success using this **Small Mind/Large Mind** tool for ourselves and our clients has convinced us that engaging in this mindfulness practice on a daily basis is essential for cultivating the empowerment, self-acceptance, and resilience that create a wellness state of mind. Let's explore how to use this tool deeply and effectively.

Let's begin by reviewing the tools of the "observer." The purpose of the "observer" is to be able to ask yourself two questions: **What is happening?** and **How am I relating to it?** These questions help you to:

- Distinguish fact from your interpretation (story).
- Identify your interpretation.
- Make a choice about what you think, which affects how you feel and respond.

Sullivan distinguishes the "kinds" of stories you tell yourself (your interpretations) that you make as being either Small Mind or **Large Mind**. When we speak here of Small Mind stories, we are not talking about being a "small-minded" person. Rather, we are referring to a fixed mindset in which Limiting Beliefs create fear-based thoughts that then create distressing emotions.

Small Mind creates high levels of distress that can compromise the immune system and interfere with the body's innate ability to heal and recover from Lyme/TBDs. It also can contribute to feelings of hopelessness and helplessness that too often lead to quitting treatment too soon.

Large Mind is a growth mindset that is made up of quality thoughts that can open you to new possibilities (hopefulness) and stimulate your body to heal and respond to treatments. This is an example of the mind-body connection. By interpreting events from a **Large Mind** perspective, you are cultivating a wellness state of mind which is resiliency!

The following table adapted from Sullivan's work reflects the characteristics of Small Mind and **Large Mind** stories. Remember, the quality of your thoughts directly affect the quality of your emotions, which in turn affect the quality of your response to any given event. As you review these characteristics, ask yourself if you are relating to any experience of Lyme/TBDs in a way that, based on its outcome, creates a Small Mind story or a **Large Mind** story.

Is Your Story Small or Large?

As something is happening, asking yourself, **What is happening?** and **How am I relating to it?** allows you to create a mindful pause between observing and responding. As you maintain the stance of the "observer," you can ask whether the story you are telling yourself is a Small Mind or a **Large Mind** story and then make a choice on how to direct your attention and response. Here's an example:

Joyce was really excited about trying a new treatment that she had learned was tremendously helpful to other people who have Lyme disease. However, the treatment did not work for her, and she felt deeply disappointed and discouraged. She began saying to herself, "I've tried so many treatments, and none of them have worked. I just can't find anyone or anything that can help me. I may as well just give up."

Joyce's reaction and the story she is telling herself are completely understandable. Who wouldn't feel disappointed and discouraged by yet another treatment failure? However, if Joyce sticks with

Small Mind Versus Large Mind Stories

Adapted from Living Large: Transformative Work at the Intersection of Ethics and Spirituality by John Sullivan (2004)

Small Mind (fixed mindset)	Large Mind (growth mindset)
Breaks down	Builds up
Keeps us asleep	Awakens us
Automatic and reactive	Responsive, mindful, and proactive
Creates disconnection (egocentric and individualistic)	Creates connection ("us" centered in service, partnership, and community)
Disempowers	Empowers
Focuses on lack	Focuses on abundance
Closes possibilities	Opens possibilities
Labels and judges	Accepts and understands
No room for humor	Incorporates humor
Destroys	Heals
Creates Walls (story is concluded)	Creates Windows (story remains open)
Hard Eyes (critical)	Soft Eyes (compassionate and understanding)

this story, she may never find anything that will help her because she does not believe that is possible. This is why it is a Small Mind story: it takes away her hope and blinds her to new possibilities for herself.

A **Large Mind** story for Joyce might be something like, "Yes, I have had a number of treatment failures, but there are still other treatments I haven't tried. Maybe I can work with my doctor or find another one who can help clarify what is happening with me and what treatments offer the best possibilities for me." This **Large Mind** story is hope inspiring, realistic, and empowering. It offers Joyce the strength and resilience to remain persistent in seeking and exploring new treatments that may in fact help her.

A Small Mind story rooted in fear, pain, and limitation breaks you down and closes you off to possibilities. A **Large Mind** story, rooted in empowerment, choice, resilience, and hope builds you up and opens you to new possibilities. When you create a **Large Mind** story for yourself, you are cultivating a wellness state of mind that will promote your recovery from Lyme/TBDs and nurture your personal growth and development.

Whether you create a Small Mind or a **Large Mind** story for yourself depends on how you relate to what is happening, the meaning you give to an event. Whatever you may be going through—pain, fatigue, family issues, difficulty getting medical care, or challenges at work—you will experience the event, not as it is, but as it is reflected in relation to your core beliefs (your interpretation) and the thoughts and emotions they generate. These are the conscious and subconscious beliefs, learned in childhood and throughout life, that form the foundation for how you create meaning about yourself, other people, and the world.

Infants and small children whose emotional needs are met tend to develop a high level of self-esteem believing that they are lovable, acceptable, and enough, while children whose emotional needs went unmet tend to develop low self-esteem, believing that they are not acceptable, lovable, or enough. (See the discussion on the "Trance of Unworthiness" on page 64 in Chapter 6 for a reminder of how this happens.) The beliefs you have about yourself, others, and the world are always actively creating your perception even if you are not aware of them. Empowering and Limiting Beliefs can remain stable or change, depending on whether or not life events seem to validate or disprove them.

Large Mind is a Wellness State of Mind.

Choose Large Mind!

Exercise: Feel the Shift from Small Mind to Large Mind

When you become caught in a Small Mind story, it is generally a sign that you are holding some Limiting Beliefs and unresolved emotional pain that have yet to be identified, processed, and/or released. These Limiting Beliefs are the source of all Small Mind stories. As a supportive mindfulness-based tool, acknowledging that you are in Small Mind can help you to identify unresolved issues that can then be used with EFT (which you will learn to do starting on page 113) to effectively clear from your system so that you can create a new **Large Mind** story for yourself: one of acceptance, empowerment, and hope that opens you to new possibilities for making choices that promote your healing and support your recovery.

Being able to reframe from a Small Mind story to a **Large Mind** one is also a tool in itself to be used in the moment as a life event is happening to increase the likelihood of a positive outcome. Below is a helpful guide that shows you how to quickly move from Small Mind to **Large Mind** and thus radically change your perspective and feelings. As you read through the examples of cognitive reframes (changes in the quality of thoughts), focus on how you feel when you go from Small Mind to **Large Mind**.

Reframing Distressing Thoughts Example

Small Mind (fixed mindset)		Large Mind (growth mindset)
Breaks down: I'm never going to get better.	REFRAME	**Builds up:** I know that my body is doing all that it can right now to heal.
Disconnects us: I don't trust that any doctors can help me.		**Connects us:** I am open and willing to find somebody who can help me.
Creates walls: I feel shut down and disappointed.		**Creates windows:** I choose to listen for the answers and trust that they will come.
Destroys: My body betrayed me!		**Heals:** I am grateful for all my body is doing for my well-being and recovery.
Closed to possibilities: There is no treatment that will work for me.		**Open to possibilities:** I am open to the possibility that the tools in this workbook will support my recovery.
Lack: I am never going to have the money I need.		**Abundance:** I am open to creative solutions for finding the financial resources I need.

Exercise: Processing the Shift

Describe your experience of going from Small Mind to **Large Mind**:

____

____

____

____

Describe if you noticed anything change in your:

Thoughts: _______________________________________

____

____

____

Feelings:____

____

____

____

Body sensations:__________________________________

____

How did the Small Mind statements make you feel?

____

____

____

How did the **Large Mind** statements make you feel?

____

____

____

Exercise: Reframe Small Mind to Large Mind!

We invite you now to enhance your resilience by practicing reframing the quality of your thoughts from Small Mind to **Large Mind** with with a Specific Event (see page 122) of your choosing. In the space provided below, title (see page 122) your Specific Event and complete each column with a Small Mind and **Large Mind** statement of your own that reflects each characteristic. Notice how your feelings change as you shift from Small Mind to **Large Mind**.

Title of Specific Event:____________________

Small Mind (fixed mindset)	REFRAME	Large Mind (growth mindset)
Breaks down:	→	Builds up:
Disconnects us:		Connects us:
Creates walls:		Creates windows:
Destroys:		Heals:
Closed to possibilities:		Open to possibilities:
Lack:	→	Abundance:

After you have filled in the statements and practiced shifting from Small Mind to **Large Mind**, take a few minutes answering the following mindfulness-based questions.

How did the Small Mind statements make you feel?

What Limiting Belief (see page 119) can support this?

How did the **Large Mind** statements make you feel?

What Empowering Belief (see page 119) can support this?

Describe if you noticed anything change going from Small Mind to **Large Mind** in your:

Body sensations:

Thoughts:

Feelings:

What did you notice about your ability to reframe from Small Mind to **Large Mind** thoughts?

What did you learn about yourself in this exercise?

____

____

____

____

____

____

____

____

What did you learn about the power of your thoughts?

____

____

____

____

____

____

____

____

The more you practice reframing the quality of your thoughts from Small Mind to **Large Mind** in the present moment as a life event is happening, the more easily you will be able to cultivate and sustain a wellness state of mind. Also using this mindfulness-based tool will support your use of EFT by helping you to quickly identify any Limiting Beliefs (see page 119) and unresolved emotional pain that can lock you into living a Small Mind story. Using EFT (starting on page 121) to process and release the Small Mind story will naturally shift your thinking so that you can create and live a new **Large Mind** story. This will strengthen your resilience and enhance your well-being in all dimensions of wellness, which is foundational for Lyme/TBD recovery.

To help guide you deeper through this process at any time, complete the following worksheet, Exercise: **Cultivate Large Mind**. (An additional copy of this worksheet is included in the appendix on page 416 for use at any time.)

Exercise: Cultivate Large Mind

Specific Event Title (see page 121) ______________________________

As a specific life event is happening and you notice yourself *starting* to feel negatively defensive or reactive, **STOP! Ask yourself:**

1. *What is happening?* (State just the facts. No interpretation.) ______________________________

____

2. *How am I relating to it?*

   My perception/interpretation of the facts (my story) is: ______________________________

   ____

   As a result, **my** strategies for responding/behaving are: ______________________________

   In this situation, **am I** in Small Mind or **Large Mind**?______________________________

3. *Do* I *want to continue to believe, think, feel, and respond the way that* I am *doing?* ____

Self-Inventory to Develop Mindfulness About Small Mind

If you are in Small Mind and answered "NO" to question number 3:
BE CURIOUS and EXPLORE the impact of your choices by completing this self-inventory with compassionate understanding.

A (if any) Limiting Belief (see page 119) that may be supporting **my** Small Mind interpretation is:

____

____

My Limiting Belief (if any) makes **me** feel (see page 119): ______________________________

As a result of **me** believing in this Small Mind way, **my** Small Mind thoughts are: ________

____

____

As a result of having **my** Small Mind thoughts:

I am making **myself** feel: ______________________________

____

I am making **my** body feel (body sensations): ______________________

____

The visual image (if any) that **I am** creating for **myself** is: ______________________

____

My visual image is making **me** feel: ______________________

My strategies for responding/behaving are: ______________________

The needs (see page 410) that **I am** not honoring **in myself** by using these strategies for responding/behaving are: ______________________

These **make me** feel: ______________________

The needs (see page 410) that **I am** not honoring **in others** by using these strategies for responding/behaving are: ______________________

These **make me** feel: ______________________

Now that you are more self-aware of the impact of Small Mind, you are ready and ABLE to make a CHOICE! Ask yourself a new question: *Do* I choose *to continue to believe, think, feel, and respond the way that* I am *doing?* ______If NO: ______________________

____

Choose Large Mind!

Self-Inventory to Develop Mindfulness to Cultivate Large Mind

Choose mindfulness to reframe and/or use EFT in the present moment to cultivate **Large Mind**, which is a wellness state of mind.

1. Use Mindfulness to Reframe

Restate what is happening. (State just the facts. No interpretation.)______________________

____

How am I relating to it now? ______________________

My Large Mind perception/interpretation of the facts is: ______________________

____

As a result, **my Large Mind** strategies for responding/behaving are: ______________________

____

An (if any) Empowering Belief (see page 119) that supports **my Large Mind** interpretation is: ______________________________

____

My Empowering Belief (if any) makes **me** feel: ______________________________

As a result of **me** believing in this **Large Mind** way, **my Large Mind** thoughts are: __________

____

As a result of my choosing Large Mind thoughts:

I am making **myself** feel: ______________________________

I am making **my** body feel (body sensations): ______________________________

____

The visual image (if any) that **I am** creating for myself is: ______________________________

____

My visual image is making **me** feel: ______________________________

____

My strategies for responding/behaving are: ______________________________

The needs (see page 410) that **I am** honoring **in myself** by choosing these strategies for responding/behaving are: ______________________________

These choices **make me** feel: ______________________________

The needs (see page 410) that **I am** honoring **in others** by choosing these strategies for responding/behaving are: ______________________________

These choices **make me** feel: ______________________________

2. Use Emotional Freedom Techniques (EFT)

You can use EFT to tap just on your Small Mind thoughts, feelings, and behaviors in the present moment for a quicker reframe to **Large Mind**.

You can also use EFT to resolve the Limiting Belief(s) within unresolved painful Specific Events to naturally cultivate a Large wellness state of mind (see Chapter 15 on page 137). By doing this, reframing is no longer needed since you will have resolved the underlying issues that originally created Small Mind.

Personal Reflections

CHAPTER 10

The Kind of Question You Ask Determines the Kind of Answer You Get

You now have a foundational understanding of the importance of reframing your thoughts from a Small Mind perspective to a **Large Mind** one. Now, if you would like to do more than just reframe, you can learn to focus your mind by asking the right kinds of questions that facilitate the **Large Mind** perspective you desire. We have another tool to offer you in this chapter that we find extraordinarily helpful and that we hope can guide you on your way. Let's take a look.

Supportive Tool #4: Afformations®

Developed by Noah St. John, bestselling author of *The Book of Afformations* (www.noahstjohn.com), **Afformations** are empowering, open-ended **Large Mind** questions that state what you desire as if you have already realized its fulfillment—for example, "Why is it possible for me to have hope today?" The question assumes that it is, in fact, possible to have hope, and it focuses the brain on finding evidence to support it.[74]

Afformations work by engaging the brain in finding **Large Mind** solutions to a problem. Whenever a person asks this kind of open-ended question, the brain automatically looks for validating information from both within your personal belief system and in external events to answer it. Asking open-ended questions about what you want as if you already have it shifts the mind from a state of lack to a state of abundance. The process happens quickly and without a person's conscious awareness. **Afformations** teach the brain to focus on finding positive solutions from within and outside themselves.

Afformations work on the premise that the kinds of questions you ask reflect the kinds of answers you get! If you ask a Small Mind question like, "Why do bad things always happen to me?" the brain will have to **focus** on the Limiting Beliefs you have about yourself and on external events that happened in the past that validate the truth of those beliefs, to come up with a Small Mind answer like, "Because I deserve it."

The opposite is true as well. If you ask a **Large Mind** open-ended question like, "Why is it possible for me to overcome this?" the brain will have to **focus** on the Empowering Beliefs you have about yourself and on external events that happened in the past that validate the truth of those beliefs to come up with a **Large Mind** answer like, "Because I am strong and resourceful."

Which focus do you prefer and which question is more likely to manifest your desires?

The Difference Between Afformations and Affirmations

Though the word *Afformations* sounds a lot like *affirmations,* this is where their similarity ends. **Afformations** are **Large Mind** intentions framed as open-ended questions that require the brain to focus on Empowering Beliefs in the subconscious mind, thus bringing them to the conscious to be answered. Once the empowering belief is conscious, it becomes the lens through which external events are interpreted, thus justifying them into **Large Mind** existence. On the other hand, affirmations are positive statements that people repeat to themselves as an attempt to change a self-limiting perspective into a self-affirming one that supports the truth of what they want to believe and do. For example, a person might repeat a statement from the conscious mind like, "I am going to recover."

Positive thinking and making affirming statements are excellent tools, of course, but if there are Limiting Beliefs in that person's subconscious mind that contradict this statement, such as "Not true! I'll never get better!" or "This is it for me!" then it is unlikely that repeating, "I am going to recover" will be successful in the long term because the subconscious mind, which is 90 percent stronger than the conscious mind, will always trump the conscious mind.

Afformations at Work

Some people are well practiced, consciously and unconsciously, at focusing on Limiting Beliefs that validate a Small Mind perspective in what they see, think, and speak. **Afformations** offer an opportunity to refocus by helping to bring Empowering Beliefs from the unconscious mind into the conscious mind where they can serve your best and highest good. They work especially well in the midst of a distressing event to shift your focus to what you desire instead of what you might be dreading.

Energy flows where attention goes.

Afformations are:

- Intentions framed as open-ended questions as if they have already happened. This trains the brain to operate out of a focus on cultivating abundance, rather than lack. Lack creates a stress response and closes us to new possibilities.
- Tools that teach the brain to **focus** on what you desire so you can then create it.
- A way to bring Empowering Beliefs from the subconscious mind to the conscious mind and build skills in perception to look for external validating evidence of **Large Mind** in everyday life events.

Here's one example of an Afformation: "Why is it so easy for me to choose an anti-inflammatory diet?" Even if the answer is not immediately available, the brain will remain fixed on answering the question by focusing on the Empowering Beliefs that you have about yourself getting well and on benefits of nutrition to support this question. (By the way, to learn more about an anti-inflammatory diet, go to Chapter 34, **Eat to Live or Live to Eat?** on page 321 in Part 4.)

We suggest adding the phrase, "Why is it so easy" to some of your **Afformations**. Why not? We are used to things being hard. Why not get used to things being easier? What do you have to lose? Look at all that you can gain by training your mind to not only **focus** on what you want in yourself and in your life but to also activate you in manifesting it! Once you use an Afformation, let it go. Know that your mind will continue to work on finding the answer and direct your focus to seeing it actualize.

Sample Afformations for Cultivating a Wellness State of Mind

You will have a chance to create your own **Afformations** in the exercise to follow. First, to help you get started, take a look at the sample **Afformations** below. Pay close attention to how you feel as you read them and how they feel in your body. Once you get comfortable with these **Afformations**, feel free to use them in addition to any you create on your own. We also invite you to use them while tapping with EFT if they address your particular issue.

Afformations for Release of Pain

- How is it possible for my body to reduce my pain?
- Why is it safe for me to relax and let go of this pain now?
- Why is it okay for me to forgive my body?
- Why is it okay for my body to forgive me?
- Why is it possible for me to accept that my pain is what it is for now and it is not forever?

Afformations for Encouragement

- Why is it so easy to be grateful for all the good people and things in my life?
- Why am I grateful for the help I am receiving?
- Why does my body respond so well to the love I am giving it?
- Why is it easy for me to believe that I will find the treatment that will help me to heal fully?
- How is it possible for me to have hope today?

Afformations for Healing

- Why is it easy for me to choose to heal?
- Why is it easy for me to be grateful for the healing that is happening right now?
- Why is it possible for me to be open to new treatments that help me heal?
- Why is it easy for me to know that my body knows how to heal?
- Why is it easy for me to give my body permission to heal?
- How is it possible for me to heal?

Exercise: Creating Effective Afformations®

1. Think of something you **DESIRE** for yourself (beliefs, thoughts, or actions).
2. Voice your **DESIRE** in the form of an open-ended **QUESTION** as if you **ALREADY HAVE IT**. Keep it positive.
3. Formulate it in the **PRESENT** tense.
4. Write your **Afformations** in the space below:

   Why is it so easy to:____

   ____

   ____

   ____

   ____

   Why is it possible: ____

   ____

   ____

Why am I so grateful for: ______

Why do I enjoy: ______

Why am I: ______

Why do I: ______

5. Observe. Watch as the answers you desire arise from within yourself and as evidenced in your life.

To practice focusing your mind on what you desire, choose a couple of **Afformations** each day to repeat to yourself as often as you remember to do so. See if you notice anything different. As mentioned earlier, you can also use **Afformations** while tapping with EFT. The last round of tapping at the end of each extended global tapping script in Part 4 includes **Afformations** to support your practice.

An Overview of Mindfulness Meditation and Transformative Imagery

This chapter offers a powerful pair of mindfulness-based tools you can use individually or in combination to cultivate a wellness state of mind. These tools, alone or combined with the ones you've learned in the previous chapters, can help you work through distressing events, painful emotions, and Limiting Beliefs. All of the mindfulness-based tools are quite powerful in their own right, but they are even more powerful when you have identified your Limiting Beliefs and use them for the content of your EFT sessions. (You are almost there!) First, let's take a look at the last two supportive tools and their accompanying exercises.

Supportive Tool #5: Mindfulness Meditation

Mindfulness **meditation** is another highly effective tool for cultivating a wellness state of mind. This popular **meditation** technique fosters resiliency, improves the quality of your perceptions and increases recovery time from stressful events. There are many resources for learning mindfulness **meditation**. Once resource we like is Tara Brach's website (www.tarabrach.com).

Brach is a clinical psychologist, teacher of Buddhist and mindfulness **meditation**, and author of *Radical Acceptance: Embracing Your Life with the Heart of a Buddha.* She offers visitors to her website a free PDF download on how to do mindfulness **meditation** as well as powerful guided **meditations** for stress reduction, self-acceptance, and self-awareness.

We encourage you to stay open to exploring mindfulness **meditation** by giving it a try and making it a part of your plan for recovery. Here are some of the benefits you may experience:

- Reduced stress and increased relaxation
- Increased higher order problem solving
- Decreased pain and inflammation
- Lowered blood pressure
- Decreased anxiety and depression
- Improved sleep
- Enhanced self-awareness and acceptance
- Increased quality of life

Jon Kabat-Zinn, a leader in the field of mindfulness and health and the founder of the Center for Mindfulness at the University of Massachusetts, has defined mindfulness as, "The awareness that emerges through paying attention on purpose, in the present moment, and nonjudgmentally to the unfolding of experience moment by moment."[76]

Kabat-Zinn is speaking here of accepting with openness and curiosity all that you feel, think, and experience in your body here and now in the present. Mindfulness Based Stress Reduction, developed by Kabat-Zinn, is a powerful tool for reducing the stress that comes with any illness. According to the Center for Mindfulness **Meditation**:

> *Mindfulness-Based Stress Reduction (MBSR) over the past 35 years has shown consistent, reliable, and reproducible major and clinically relevant reductions in medical and psychological symptoms across a wide range of medical and psychological diagnoses. It has been recognized by the Substance Abuse and Mental Health Services Administration (SAMHSA) as an evidence-based program through the National Registry of Evidence-Based Programs and Practices (NREPP). Mindfulness is an active area of scientific research with new studies on MBSR being shared on a regular basis.*[77]

Practice Mindfulness Meditation

Mindfulness **meditation** works best with daily practice. We recommend meditating for at least 10 to 15 minutes a day. If that seems too long, you can begin with 5 minutes a day and then gradually lengthen your **meditation** and strengthen your practice at a pace that feels comfortable to you. If you struggle with quieting your mind, we suggest using EFT to tap the first 5–10 minutes before starting your **meditation**. This can facilitate the release of stress and trigger the relaxation response, thus support you in arriving into the present moment for **meditation**. You can even use **4/8 Diaphragmatic Breathing (Belly Breath)** to focus on your breath while meditating.

Using this easy **meditation** technique will help you to relax and reduce your stress. With regular practice, mindfulness **meditation** can help you to open to new possibilities for yourself and improve your perspective. Mindfulness **meditation** is a powerful tool for cultivating a wellness state of mind and enhancing your quality of life in a way that supports your healing and recovery from Lyme/TBDs.

Through the relationship of mind-body medicine, and the intermediary of psychoneuroimmunology, if we can integrate the practice of mindfulness **meditation** (Kabat-Zinn), calm abiding **meditation**, or other stress reduction techniques into our daily routines, we will not only be providing a way to better cope with our illness, but also will be helping to decrease stress as another factor driving the inflammatory response.

Dr. Richard Horowitz

Why Can't I Get Better? Solving the Mystery of Lyme and Chronic Disease[75]

Exercise: Mindfulness Meditation

- **Sit so that your spine is as straight as possible without causing too much discomfort.** You may choose to sit on the floor with or without the use of a cushion, in a chair, or on your bed with your legs crossed or straight out. You can also lie down on your bed as long as it does not induce you to fall asleep. The most important thing is that you find a comfortable pose that you can maintain for 5 to 15 minutes.
- **Focus on your breathing.** Review the steps for **4/8 Diaphragmatic Breathing (Belly Breath)** on page 86. On a count of four, take in a full, gentle breath through your nose, noticing how your belly inflates like a balloon. On a count of eight, gently exhale through pursed lips, noticing the fall of your belly as you exhale. Mindfulness **meditation** is all about the breath. Focusing on your breathing will keep you focused on the present and allow your mind and body to relax.
- **Become the "observer" and allow your thoughts to come and go**. Simply notice them without judgment as they flow in and out of your awareness. If you find that you are becoming engaged with your thoughts, simply let them go without judgments and return to being the observer. The act of disengaging your thoughts and returning to the neutral state of the observer is an important skill for developing a wellness state of mind.

Supportive Tool #6: Transformative Guided Imagery

Transformative guided imagery is a visualization process that helps us to realize our desires. It works because our subconscious mind accepts what we imagine as being just as real as what we experience. We can actually shift our emotional and physical states toward healing and recovery by visualizing ourselves as already there!

Visualization is often used by athletes to improve their sports performance. In fact, many athletes spend time every day visualizing themselves making the plays and the moves that will put them at the top of their game. The perfectly executed pitch, pass, putt, goal, or first-place finish is more often than not the result of an athlete's repeated visualization of success. Repeated visualizations train the mind in a way that positively impacts reality. Transformative guided imagery can also help you achieve your desires to get well.

In Chapter 4 on page 44, Anita offers a transformative imagery that she used while tapping called, **Making Peace with the Spirochetes.** "I desired peace and harmony within and about my body and noticed that being 'at war' with the spirochetes interfered with that. I used this to help create the peace I desired and much more."

Below is a powerful exercise called "Fire Love" by Vir McCoy, which is also included in his upcoming book, *Liberating Lyme*, with coauthor Kara Zahl. Vir, who has recovered from Lyme disease, is a healing arts practitioner trained in massage therapy, neuromuscular reprogramming, and Reiki. He incorporates **meditation** and visualization in his practice, using "the power of fire and the energy of love" to stimulate healing and promote recovery. Vir has generously granted us permission to include the "Fire Love" exercise in this workbook so that you can start benefitting from it right away. For more information about Vir McCoy and his work, visit www.virmccoy.com.

Exercise: "Fire-Love"

The following exercise appears in the book Liberating Lyme *by Vir McCoy and Kara Zahl.*

We are going to work with "Fire" in the belly (Hara, Tan Tien, Prana, Chi center, etc.) and love for healing ourselves. The first part of our **meditation** is a modified "microcosmic orbit" (see Matak Chia's excellent book *Awaken Healing Light*) for further study. I call this the "Fire-Love" exercise.

To get the fire in your belly started we are going to use the analogy of a car engine. Imagine that the liver is an oil tank with fuel oil—the gall bladder the regulator with a valve—and the fuel pump will squirt fuel oil onto the spark plug located in your belly or hara center where oxygen from your breath will ignite the fire and get your engine going. Then once the engine is running and the fires burning in the belly we will bring the fire up the spine (transmission) to the head and then bring it back down the front of the body through the heart (the radiator) cooling the energy, back through the belly and out the tailbone (exhaust). From the side it will look like a large loop. Fire up, Cool down.

It is helpful to gaze at a fire, a candle, or best is the sun during sunset and/or sunrise.

Part 1: The Fire Love Generator

1. Find a quiet place and sit upright, either cross-legged, in a chair or on your back.
2. Warm Up. Gently rock the lower part of your body back and forth like a cat stretch but not as intense. As your back arches forward inhale, and as your back arches back exhale. This loosens up the lower spine and gets the breath ready. 60 times. Rest for

a moment and focus on your upper body. Place the tips of your fingers on the outside of your shoulders like wings. Begin to flap them back and forth like butterfly wings. Opening the chest and coming forward, touching the elbows together. This warms the upper body. Notice the natural exhale as arms come together, inhale as they come back. 60X. Rest.

3. Begin by breathing in and out slowly from your belly. Start by exhaling all your air out and flattening your belly. Sit straight up. Now bring the inhalation as low into your belly as you can. On inhalation your belly becomes a big balloon. Then again on exhalation bring the abdominal muscles tight to the back as much as you can. Continue this slow belly breath for 15 breaths. As you are doing this begin to expand on the breath by exaggerating the movement of the lower part of your body (like cat stretch—where your back arches forward on the inhale and back on the exhale) back and forth with the inhalation and exhalation.

4. As you're doing this imagine and feel with your senses and focus with your mind into a spot just below your navel and towards the back of the spine where your "spark plug" or little fire is. Focus the heat you are creating to this hot spot. This is the center of chi or your Tan-Tien. Another image is to imagine you are going to make a fire by twirling a stick back and forth on a little bit of tinder the traditional native way. See it burst into flames and create a fire in your "inner stove." Feel the heat.

5. Touch your thumbs together and the tips of all your fingers together and place over your fire center (looks like a triangle). These are liver mudras to open the "valves" of your gallbladder so the "fuel oil" can move through into your fire.

6. Rest for a moment from this and begin to pulse the mulabanda or "Root Lock." These are the perineal muscles or your "poopoo and peepee" muscles. Squeeze as if you were trying not to pee or poop. This is the "oil pump" to get the oil moving and hold in the fire once we get the engine going. Squeeze the Root Lock back and forth for 15x.

7. Breath of Fire or Kopalabati. Begin a series of quick exhales and thrusts of breath through the nose. The belly will come back and the stomach muscles tighten during the exhale. The inhale will be a byproduct of the exhale as the belly will naturally come back out. Now add in the Liver mudra as above and add in Root lock holding it the whole time. 15x. This is "oxygen" to help ignite the spark plugs and get the fires burning. If you feel sexually aroused let that happen and add in the energy to your fire focus spot.

8. Now do the same thing but slow the breath. Breathing slowly as before, rock the hips back and forth, add in the Liver mudra, and Root Lock. The difference is only do the Root Lock on inhalation as your abdomen and belly come forward. Continue this for 15x.

9. Now that the belly fires are hot and burning and the "engine" is running, we are going to bring the fire up the spine. Imagine that each vertebra is like a tea candle and that your fire from the belly is going to light each candle all the way up to your head.

10. Start to take a belly breath; squeezing Root Lock, arching your back forward and focus the fire spot coming to the spine near the kidneys and lighting the vertebra like "tea candles." Keep inhaling. As we inhale bring the breath all the way up from the belly into the chest and as high up as you can. Let the breath move your body as you inhale. The chest will expand at the peak of the inhalation and the belly will flatten out some. Visualize or see the fire following the breath up the spine all the way to the center of the head. Imagine each tea candle lighting another as the fire goes up the vertebra to the pineal and pituitary glands. Fill your body with as much breath as you can. Root Lock should be held the whole time. This is the fire up.

11. When you have filled the body with as much oxygen as you can bring the chin down to the chest (chin lock) and hold this lock and the Root Lock with a full body of air. Hold the breath and lock for a moment, in effect "sealing" your body with energy and oxygen. This is a good moment to set a prayer or intention for what it is you want. Rest and go on to 12 when comfortable with the inhalation part.
12. Repeat the inhalation and with the locks in place, place the tip of your tongue to the roof of your mouth. This will be the channel for the fire energy that rises up to come down. Imagine the hot energy is now being pulled down the front of the body or swallowed. Let go of the Root Lock and begin to gently exhale out your mouth around the tongue, still placed as the energy comes down your tongue and into your chest. Smile.
13. Continue exhaling as the exhalation and energy now flows down the front of your body. Imagine the hot fire that we brought up is now passing into the heart to be cooled in the "radiator." Any negative thoughts can come down here from the mind as well. Allow a gentle sigh of release and relaxation to naturally occur.
14. Let the breath and exhale continue down the front of the body into the solar plexus and intestines with the love feeling generated from your heart. Imagine you are cradling the internal organs and belly gently as you continue to exhale with this blessed energy.
15. Allow for anything that has passed through your heart to now be "digested" in the fire in your belly. Feel the fires burn through and melt any impurities.
16. Let all the air come out and slump back a bit naturally as you finish the exhalation. Feel the energy loop back and cross over to your tailbone as you very gently push the root as if you were going to the bathroom and letting any excess energy pass back into the earth to be recycled.
17. Continue from step 10 again and repeat this cycle as much as you like. When we let the breath guide the movement it ends up looking like a figure eight (from the side) so if it helps you can imagine or emphasize the figure eight movement as you follow the natural course of the breath.
18. This exercise is powerful and very healing as we use the power of fire and the energy of love to heal ourselves.

Part 2: Liberating with Love

After working with the FIRE-LOVE exercise we are now going to apply it to working with Lyme disease or any other "disease."

Many of those suffering with Lyme disease have felt the energy of the Lyme as an "entity" or crude intelligence that can suck the energy out of you. I have felt this before and have seen the Lyme as a "baby alien spider" on an energetic level. Physically we know the Lyme looks like a spiral or corkscrew. However you see it energetically or physically, find an image of what Lyme (or any "disease") looks and feels like to you, separate from yourself.

Our initial response when getting ill with Lyme disease is to both be disgusted and want it out and killed or we go into a fear space and get really afraid of it.

In this **meditation** we are going to look at it from a different angle. We are going to ***thank*** *the Lyme as our teacher,* ***bless*** *the Lyme with all our love and* ***liberate*** *it with our fire.*

After you have warmed up with the FIRE-LOVE exercise, picture the Lyme however you choose—see it as a spider, corkscrew, entity, or whatever works for you. Take this image and begin to feel how it is separate from you. See how it might be similar. Sense the differences. Also sense the connection and the interconnectedness that all life has. See it as a teacher for a moment. What's it trying to tell you? Come from a place of a nonjudgmental witness. Just watching as best as you can. Is it possible to actually consider thanking it? Is it possible it is showing where we have been out of balance?

1. Imagine there is a bright candle in the center of your heart. This is your love, your uniqueness, your spirit center, and the place of light that no one can ever take from you. Keep breathing and increasing the heart fire through the breath and felt sense in the center of your heart. *Feel* the things you love for a moment. Picture babies, people you love, trees, rivers, pets, Jesus, whatever it is you know you just love. Imagine cradling your own heart as if it's the most sacred beautiful thing in the world. Keep generating the feeling of unconditional love.
2. BLESS THE ENEMY. Now when you have created love and are centered in your heart, take the image of the Lyme again and *love the Lyme with all your heart.* Either on the cool down part of the FIRE–LOVE exercise or just with your heart *invite the Lyme in to be blessed.* Invite it in to your heart to get all the love you can give it. Take the image you have of the Lyme and hold it like a baby. Cradle it, kiss it, bless it, cherish it, rock it, *and melt* it in love. Take your hands and gently brush your body as well. No matter how disgusting, how vile, how much fear or separation there is, hold it. See it as part of the universe with a purpose. Keep returning to this again and again. Keep loving it with all your heart. Invite it in to be *liberated* or freed in the love of your heart. *Picture it and feel it melting in your love.*
3. The mind will rebel against this exercise but keep returning again and again to this idea. This is a powerful exercise. Love heals. Love the Lyme again and again. Whenever you feel fear, frustration, anger, and hopelessness, stop and feel your heart. Think of what you love and *pull the thoughts and the Lyme into the center of your heart to be blessed and transformed by love.* When we do this exercise the Lyme begins to lose power over you. How can something hurt you when you love it so much? This is an ancient exercise used by many monks, priests, holy ones, avatars, Jesus, Buddha, etc. "Love thy enemy."

In my own experience with this it took some time but I kept returning to this again and again. At a certain point I actually began to feel *compassion* for it. You can use this exercise for other "enemies" including thoughts and beliefs that you find are disempowering. Pull them into your heart to be transformed. *Then we can liberate it with our Fire.* . Then it is much easier to pull out the "sword of liberation"(see below). Always bless the "enemy" first as a part of creation, then if it still wants to hurt you, we in a sense "free" it back to the universe.

Part 3: Liberating with Fire

This exercise focuses on the hot fire coming up the spine and down to "burn"away disease.

After doing the FIRE-LOVE exercise and the LYME BLESSING exercise return to the feeling of hot fire in your belly. In the center of our earth is a hot molten ball of lava. In the core of our belly is a fiery molten core of lava that can *transmute* or melt anything back into its base. Imagine you are Frodo from Lord of the Rings dropping the ring (Lyme) from your heart back into the fire of your core to melt away. This is why exercise and any herbs or other tools that get the fire in the body going are so important.

1. Do the FIRE up exercise with Fire breath, Root Lock, Mudra and Spine rocking. Allow yourself to feel *Angry* if it helps as a motivator. Set your intention. Imagine you are a

tiger about to pounce on a gazelle. Feel this warrior fire or liberating flame in the belly and when you're ready, hold the Root Lock, inhale and bring the energy up the spine.

2. With an image of "golden sword of transmutation" inhale and bring the energy up the spine as before, pause and set your intention, and on the exhale open your mouth wide and exhale like a dragon. As if you were breathing pure fire. Now drop whatever is left into the belly fire. See all the hot fire you have generated, burning and melting the Lyme. Cut through it with your "golden sword of liberation." Another great image is picturing your belly like a giant composting digester (it is) and see whatever you have dropped in it being transmuted in this hot compost.
3. On the exhale out exhale through your mouth. Imagine you are a dragon or tiger and growl, hiss, gurgle (as if you were vomiting) on the exhale. Feel the sensation of warrior burning anything in your way. You may feel like vomiting and so on the final part of the exhalation curl up forward and *feel* how disgusting the Lyme makes you feel and go through the motions of a vomit if needed and be sure to spit out what comes up.
4. This is where you "liberate" anything that wants to harm you. State your boundaries. Claim your body. Guard your temple. Light your fire. Stand firm against anything that would harm you. Stomp the ground. Roar. Go warrior/shaman—use your sword. Push it off you. Kick it in the ass. Burn it. Men *feel* your testicles like a bull and women *feel* your ovaries like Kali.
5. As before, let any excess energy drain out the tailbone at the end of the exhale back into the earth for composting.
6. Rest and see this fire you have generated pour into the red marrow in your bones, and see the immune system with all the white blood cells and other warrior cells come to eat and digest any Lyme invaders.
7. Return to the FIRE-LOVE part of the exercise and again bring the energy down into the heart, again blessing and loving the Lyme with all your heart as described before.
8. As the energy comes back down into your belly, see whatever that may be left melted in the hot lava core in the belly. Digest it. Break it back down. Gently cool down.
9. Alternate back and forth on the exhalation part of the exercise between liberating with love and liberating with fire.

We have described two ways of "Liberating" Lyme disease: love and fire. Use these tools often and you will begin to notice changes in yourself. These are powerful physical and energetic exercises and when used in conjunction with exercise, diet and medicines can help heal you of Lyme disease.

Further practices for Fire

Yoga, Drumming, Dancing, Exercise, Martial Arts, Pilates, Weight Lifting, Pranayama, Kundalini Yoga.

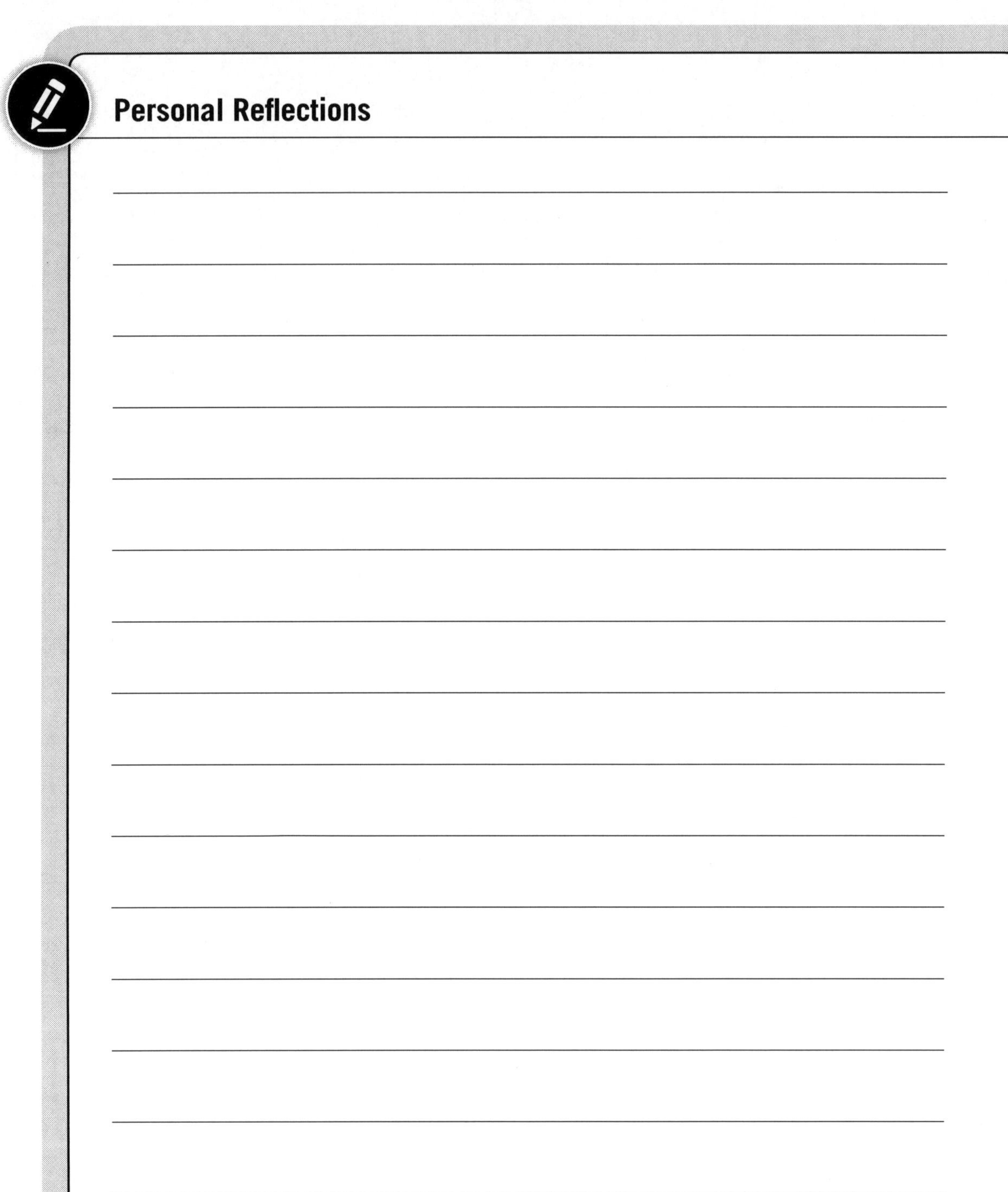
Personal Reflections

PART 3
The Toolkit: Featured Tool EFT

CHAPTER

12 An Introduction to Energy Psychology and EFT

Emotional Freedom Techniques (EFT) comes from the field of energy psychology. Energy psychology is described by the Association for Comprehensive Energy Psychology (ACEP) as "a family of integrative approaches to psychotherapy, coaching and healthcare treatment that work with the mind-body connection."[78] More simply, energy psychology techniques such as EFT can be described as "acupuncture for the emotions without the needles."

Energy psychology is grounded in Traditional Chinese Medicine as well as more recent Western-based psychotherapeutic approaches to wellness. Wildly accepted and practiced throughout the United States and in other countries, energy psychology works from the premise that our emotional well-being is largely dependent upon the balance and flow of energy needed by the mind-body system to function and thrive.

As with all living things, humans contain and emit their own bioenergetic patterns (energy frequencies), which are in constant circuit throughout the neurobiological system. When the bioenergetic system is disrupted, so, too, are one's thinking patterns (Limiting Beliefs), emotions (anger, fear, and sadness, etc.), and physiological functions (impairment of the endocrine and immune systems). To go deeper into the science of this, skip to Chapter 40: **The Mind-Body Communication Network** on page 391 to learn more.

When painful and/or traumatic events occur in a person's life, the associated energy can become frozen in the mind-body system, blocking the healthy flow of energy (the way a clog stops up a drain, for instance). Unless those events are processed and released from the mind-body system, they will continue to generate the Limiting Beliefs that trigger the unresolved emotional pain and thus create a state of chronic stress that can compromise the immune system. If you are interested in going deeper into the science about this, read more in Chapter 41: The Stress Response in Action in Part 5 on page 395.

EFT Summarized

EFT is a novel treatment that combines three essential ingredients: exposure (focusing on a Specific Event), somatic stimulation (tapping on acupoints, or "acupoint stimulation"), and cognitive reprocessing (reframes such as going from Small Mind to **Large Mind**; see page 89). The technique involves tapping on designated EFT acupoints (which we sometimes refer to as EFT tapping points, as shown in the following illustration) while "venting" a specific distressing problem or issue.

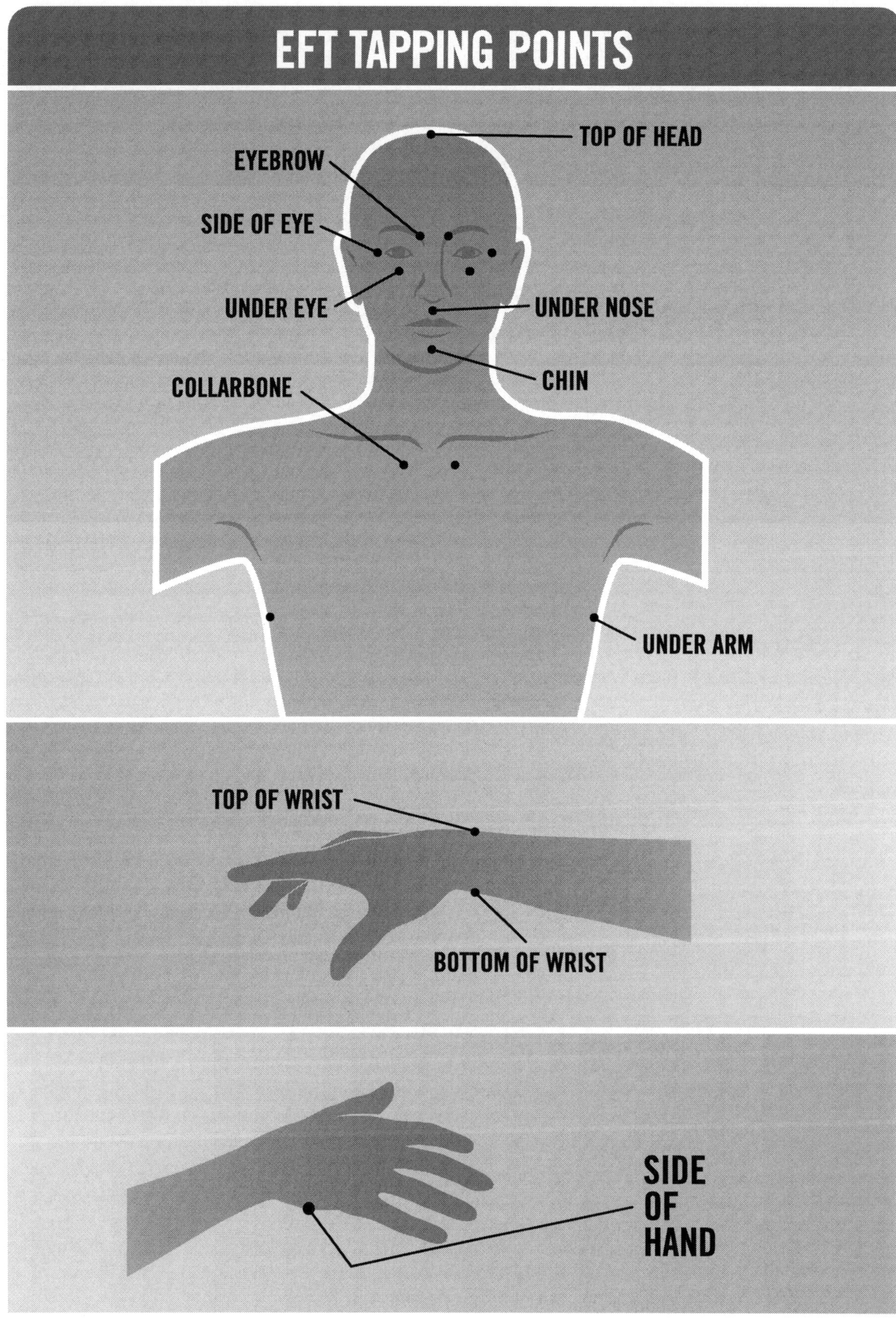
EFT TAPPING POINTS
TOP OF HEAD
EYEBROW
SIDE OF EYE
UNDER EYE
UNDER NOSE
CHIN
COLLARBONE
UNDER ARM
TOP OF WRIST
BOTTOM OF WRIST
SIDE OF HAND

This approach engages both the body and the mind in identifying, processing, and releasing distressing thoughts and emotions to significantly reduce stress and restore the balance and flow of energy needed by the body for optimal function and repair. It is a highly effective form of exposure therapy for treating anxiety and posttraumatic stress disorder (PTSD) because it works to reduce the production of distressing emotions such as fear, anger, and panic triggered by the arousal of the amygdala during the stress response.

Here is what you can expect to be able to do while using EFT:

- Identify, process, and release Limiting Beliefs that interfere with recovery.
- Significantly reduce the stress that worsens symptoms, compromises the immune system, and can impede healing.
- Support the processing and releasing of painful emotions from the mind-body system.
- Cultivate a wellness state of mind with Empowering Beliefs that strengthen resiliency, nurture self-acceptance and compassion, and promote recovery on all seven dimensions of wellness.

Additional Ways to Use EFT

Emotional First Aid for Stress Reduction

Some days, you may not have the time or energy to tap through the root causes of your emotional distress. That's okay! EFT is a great form of emotional first aid! Using EFT only on a global level can still stimulate stress reduction and create a relaxation response. Tapping for a few minutes globally can help you contain and reduce emotional flooding when something is triggered inside you that is creating a painful emotional response.

Sometimes just lowering the intensity level and distress caused by an upsetting event is enough to do in the moment. It helps you to regroup and mindfully make choices on how to respond that supports your best and highest good. For full resolution and to reduce the frequency of being triggered, it is still necessary to return to addressing the underlying causes with EFT at another time.

Emotional First Aid on the Go
Wherever you are, just start tapping on what you are feeling until you feel the relaxation response kick in and you are able to ground yourself. You can tap in a bathroom, bedroom, in your car (pulled over to a safe place), in an empty room, during a walk, or with a friend or family member.

Embracing a Spiritual Uplift

Since EFT is so versatile, you can also use it while praying to support going deeper; before/after **meditation** to support mindful relaxation; stating only positive, uplifting statements, and/or **Afformations** (see page 101) to start or end your day to help focus the mind on manifesting what you desire. The only intention and expectation of this kind of tapping is to enhance how you feel in the present moment; it's like getting a mind-body tune-up. But this not a substitute for the need to release unresolved emotional issues that can return and sabotage the positive effects from the tune-up, so be sure to tap on your issues when appropriate.

Feel Like Tapping Is Just Too Much to Do Right Now? TAB IT!

On days when fatigue, pain, or disinterest makes it too hard to tap, you can use Touch and Breathe (TAB). TAB is an energy psychology technique developed by John Diepold, PhD, which we have adapted for your use in this workbook.

TAB uses the same acupoints as EFT but *replaces* tapping with gently putting your first two fingers on the acupoint (review the EFT Tapping Points on the previous page). As you hold your fingers on the point, emotionally tune in to your issue while completing one full cycle of **4/8 Diaphragmatic Breathing (Belly Breath)** (see page 86), then move on to the next point. Continue TAB through each of the EFT Tapping Points and then assess your SUD levels (see page 124) on the Aspects you have identified. TAB is great to do while reclining in a chair or lying in bed. Instructions for the step-by-step TAB process are provided in the appendix on page 411.

To Start Using EFT Right Now

To make this workbook as comprehensive as possible, we have included detailed explanations for each step of the **Modified EFT Basic Recipe** in Chapter 13. However, you do not have to read through everything right now if you are ready to get started. At some point, though, when you have the time, energy, and interest to learn all the nuances of EFT to get the most out of this technique, come back to the parts you skip. For now, you can:

- Skip to Chapter 13 on page 121 to learn the **Modified EFT Basic Recipe** and **tapping acupoints** used with EFT.
- Then, skip to Chapter 14: **The Modified EFT Basic Recipe: Sample Tapping Script** on page 131 to follow along through the awareness questions and global tapping script to start experiencing EFT.
- Then, skip to Chapter 18: **Getting Started Using EFT** on page 153, to begin using **EFT**. Choose a chapter that reflects the issue you would like to address reflected in its title. Read the **case study** and follow along with the **global extended tapping script** to gently get you started using EFT. There are twenty-one to choose from!

Mind-Body Concepts at the Root of an Issue

The following is a list of mind-body concepts defined, along with examples of how to apply them, which you will need to understand in order to resolve the root causes of your emotional distress with EFT. This will enable you to make the most effective use of EFT for creating the lasting results you desire.

Subconscious Mind: The subconscious mind is like a computer that records and stores the memories of our lived experience. Within each recorded memory are the Empowering and Limiting Beliefs that were learned or reinforced as a result of that memory, along with the thoughts, feelings, body responses and behaviors that reflect the expression of those beliefs. To be efficient, the subconscious mind makes instantaneous connections between similar memories to draw conclusions that validate Empowering and Limiting Beliefs as being true. This forms the core of our belief system and our operating system (subconscious mind). These connections develop into behavioral, emotional, and physical response patterns that we can call programs. When triggered they are instantly activated to play the pre-recorded programs for a quick and precise response to new life events as they happen. All of this is happening just below the level of our conscious awareness (subconscious). This is evident when you notice that you are responding to a current life situation in the same way you did in the past. This can be a helpful or hurtful dynamic, depending on the kind of beliefs, Empowering or Limiting, that are being triggered from your operating system that dictate which programmed response will be used. The subconscious mind is the operating system for our perceptions and stored programmed responses that affect the meaning and quality of our life. It is very important to note, that the subconscious mind is 95 percent stronger than the conscious mind, thus it overrides conscious intent and desires that are contrary to it. This can create an internal conflict. An example of an internal conflict can be when the conscious mind is believing one way with an Empowering Belief like, *I can find a doctor who can help me to recover*, while the subconscious mind believes a Limiting Belief such as, *I don't trust the medical system to help me to recover*. Since the subconscious mind is 95 percent more powerful than the conscious mind, it overrides the conscious mind and can result in self-sabotaging behaviors such as not being compliant with treatment, conflicts with a doctor due to lack of trust, the body's inability to respond to treatment, and/or the decision to stop treatment all together. Using EFT to clear the Limiting Beliefs by resolving the unresolved Specific Events that created them helps to re-set your operating system to using Empowering Beliefs to create a wellness state of mind that fosters the life and recovery you desire.

Conscious Mind: The conscious mind observes and responds to environmental stimuli, is self reflective, creative, observes behaviors, plans for the future, expresses desires, and is responsible for decision making and reasoning. It allows you to think about the past as well as the future.

It is the creative part of you that develops new ideas and the willpower to carry them out. It takes self-awareness to notice the tension that is created between the conscious mind's willpower to operate through Empowering Beliefs, at the same time the triggered Limiting Beliefs in the subconscious mind's programming are overriding it. You may be successful in using the conscious mind's willpower to override the Limiting Beliefs in the subconscious mind for a short period of time, but the tension created eventually gives way to you resorting back to old limiting programed responses. The good news is that you are not doomed to keep repeating past destructive behavioral, emotional, and physical response patterns from the subconscious. You can take positive action to use the mind-body technique EFT to systematically collapse and remove Limiting Beliefs from the subconscious mind, thus creating new Empowering Beliefs. This directs the conscious mind to create the life you desire through pursuing new possibilities and enhancing your body's innate ability to heal and recover.

Global Issue: A Global Issue is a generalization about something that is upsetting to you. It involves painful emotions that you may have about yourself, others, and/or at a situation that you find yourself in that is not meeting your needs. Some examples of a Global Issue can be: *I'm so angry! I feel so overwhelmed by having Lyme/TBDs. I'm not seen, heard, or understood. I'm on empty.* Notice that these statements are generalizations and lack the specifics of why you believe, feel, and think as you do. A Global Issue can also be a Limiting Belief and/or made up of Limiting Beliefs. It is important to explore and identify any Limiting Beliefs that may be hidden at the root of a Global Issue and use EFT to resolve them.

Belief: A belief is a concept that one accepts as true or real. It can be a firmly held opinion or conviction that something is true. The beliefs you have about yourself, others, and the world originate in the context of family, cultural values, and life experiences. Beliefs dictate your perception, the lens through which you look through when interpreting and creating meaning about yourself, others, and your life circumstances. They dictate your state of mind (thoughts and feelings), physical state, behaviors, and actions. Beliefs can be both Empowering and Limiting. Current science exploring the dynamics within the mind-body connection explains how beliefs, both Empowering and Limiting, may have a direct affect on the health of your body and its ability to heal and recover. (See Chapter 40 on page 391.)

Empowering Belief: An Empowering Belief is a conviction that supports and fosters prosperity, success, healing, and wellness. It directs your perception to seeing and creating new possibilities that are optimistic and expansive. Empowering Beliefs about healing stimulate your body's innate ability to heal. Empowering Beliefs about yourself create a positive self-image that supports resiliency, optimism, love, joy, hope, faith, and the confidence needed to overcome challenges. Empowering Beliefs about others foster intimacy, connection, and allow for creative problem solving that can create new possibilities and attract abundance. Empowering Beliefs are foundational to cultivating a wellness state of mind.

Limiting Belief: A Limiting Belief is a generalized negative conclusion that can be made about yourself, others, and life circumstances in response to creating meaning about unresolved pain. Limiting Beliefs develop in response to repeated painful Specific Events that may have happened in childhood and/or throughout life that remain unresolved, thus supporting a negative conclusion as being true. They interfere with your body's innate ability to heal and recover, thus fostering and maintaining illness. Limiting Beliefs about yourself can create low self-esteem and a negative self-image. They can focus your perception on what is lacking and wrong in yourself and others, while missing new possibilities for abundance and healing. Limiting Beliefs negatively impact the quality of your state of mind (thoughts and feelings), physical state (stimulating stress responses that compromise the immune system, sending messages to cells that healing is not possible), and behaviors that are self-sabotaging. (See page 391). Limiting Beliefs can also become global in nature and present as a Global Issue. When these are not resolved, they can foster illness, prevent recovery, and ultimately mental states of hopelessness, helplessness, and despair.

A few examples of when a Limiting Belief can present as a Global Issue are as follows:

- There's no one who can help me to recover.
- There's Something Wrong with Me!
- I'll never get better.
- My body betrayed me!

A Global Issue/Limiting Belief can limit your awareness to any new possibilities that could be available to you and can actually prevent your body from healing. Limiting Beliefs can be the root cause of an illness state of mind that can prevent wellness and recovery from occurring. The greatest benefit of EFT is when it is used for releasing the Limiting Beliefs from within the subconscious and allows new Empowering Beliefs to emerge that cultivate a wellness state of mind.

* In this workbook, Global Issue/Limiting Belief will be stated together at times to acknowledge that they are one and the same.

A WELLNESS STATE OF MIND

CHAPTER 13

Learn How to Tap Using the Modified EFT Basic Recipe

EFT (tapping) involves a number of steps, but once you learn what those steps are and tapping through the guided practices presented in this workbook, you will be able to effectively put them all together. In this chapter, we will begin by presenting a modified version of the Basic Recipe, along with a breakdown of how to use each step in detail. You will learn exactly how to use EFT, a powerful mind-body approach, to resolve Limiting Beliefs through resolving the painful Specific Events that validated them as being true for you, thus creating New Empowering Beliefs that cultivate a wellness state of mind. The Terms in the previous chapter on page 118 will go more in depth about why this is so important. *If you want to use EFT for just resolving a painful Specific Event **only**, then skip the Preparation, and move right into Step 1. Then disregard identifying a Limiting Belief in the exercises that follow throughout this chapter.*

The Modified EFT Basic Recipe: The Steps

Preparation: Identify a Limiting Belief/Global Issue you desire to resolve using EFT.

Step 1: Identify a Specific Event and give it a title. Be Specific.

Step 2: Subjective Units of Distress (SUD) #1: Rate the intensity of distress that you feel.

Step 3: Setup Statement: State the problem combined with a statement of acceptance, repeating three times while tapping on the Side of Hand.

Step 4: Two rounds of tapping with Reminder Phrases to keep you focused on your Issue.

Step 5: Subjective Units of Distress (SUD) #2: Rate the intensity of distress that you feel now.

Preparation: Identify a Limiting Belief/Global Issue You Desire to Resolve Using EFT

Identify a Limiting Belief that you desire to resolve using EFT. Beliefs form your perception, which directly influences the quality of your thoughts, feelings, behaviors, the health of your body and how it responds to treatment. (To review, refer back to page 119.) Limiting Beliefs are easily identified when they present as a Global Issue (see page 119). When these are the same, we will identify this relationship by using the terms together, such as Global Issue/ Limiting Belief. Other times, a Limiting Belief may not be the same as a Global Issue, but rather hidden at the root of a Global Issue. In this instance, the terms will be used separately, thus indicating that it is necessary to identify at least one Limiting Belief to resolve that is at the root of your Global Issue. Identifying, processing, and resolving a Limiting Belief with the systematic use of EFT by resolving the painful Specific Events that created and validated it is the best possible way to allow for new Empowering Beliefs to emerge.

Step 1: Identify a Specific Event and Give It a Title. Be Specific.

A Specific Event is an incident that you lived that created a memory that has a beginning, middle, and end. The focus of using EFT will be to resolve the painful Specific Events from your past that helped create and validate your identified Global Issue and Limiting Belief as being true for you. For example:

Global Issue: I am so angry at the medical system for not helping me!

Limiting Belief: I don't trust the medical system to help me recover.

Specific Event #1: Doctor saying, "There is nothing wrong with you."

Specific Event #2: False negative Lyme Test

Specific Event #3: My partner telling me, "I look too healthy to be sick."

Specific Event #4: When I was 10 years old, my mother made me go to school when I was sick because she thought I was faking it.

If the Limiting Belief, *I don't trust the medical system to help me recover*, is not resolved, it could lead to not being persistent in seeking out the treatment needed to recover. The systematic use of EFT is the best way to identify, process, and resolve painful Specific Events that created and validated Limiting Beliefs. This allows for new Empowering Beliefs to emerge naturally. This is the most important concept to understand in making EFT an effective self-help tool in creating new Empowering Beliefs that support a wellness state of mind that fosters healing and recovery.

Don't be surprised if you have many unresolved Specific Events. This is true for all of us. You can use the List of Titled Specific Events worksheet on page 156 to write them down so that you can use EFT to resolve them later when you have the time and energy.

Be Specific with the Event: While replaying the Specific Event over in your mind like a movie, it should last only a few minutes because you are to tune in to only the painful Aspects (details) while you tap. If, for example, the Specific Event was a twenty-minute doctor visit, you will focus only on the most distressing Aspects (details) of that event when you tap, which could be just a total of a couple of minutes.

Exercise: Identify a Specific Event and Give It a Title. Be Specific.

Identify and write down a Global Issue (if relevant) that is made up of one of the Limiting Beliefs that you may have in relation to Lyme/TBDs that you would like to resolve. (You can refer back to the **"Lyme/TBDs-Related Beliefs Inventory"** on page 66 if you need help choosing one.) Then identify, choose one unresolved Specific Event that supports and validates that Limiting Belief as being true for you, and write it below. (Restate these in the exercises that follow.)

Global Issue:____

Limiting Belief:____

Specific Event Title:____

Give It a Title: Giving your Specific Event a title helps you to stay focused on it while using EFT. If each Specific Event were a book or a movie, what title would you give it? Have fun with it! Whatever you come up with is correct!

Try this now:

Be Specific with the Aspects: Aspects are the painful and emotionally charged details of a Specific Event that can include all or some of the following: cognitive (thoughts), emotional (feelings), kinesthetic (physical sensations), and visual images. Aspects are the details that make up your experience of that unresolved Specific Event and validate your identified Limiting Belief. In resolving a painful Specific Event, it is important to use EFT to tap through all the identified painful Aspects that are relevant to you until they feel released and/or resolved. When tapping, notice how your Aspects can change in detail and intensity. Not every Specific Event has Aspects in all of the categories presented, so just focus your EFT tapping rounds on the Aspects that pertain to your experience.

Exercise: Identify the Aspects of the Specific Event

Take a moment to replay the memory of your newly titled Specific Event in your mind. Take three slow, deep belly breaths as you do a **Body Scan** (see page 81). What Aspects (details) do you notice? Identify only those Aspects, along with their descriptions, that pertain to your Titled Specific Event.

	Description
Specific Event	
Thoughts	
Feelings	
Body Sensations	
Visual Image	

Due to the Generalization Effect, see page 139, you only need to tap to resolution enough of the Specific Events to release the Limiting Belief, thus naturally creating a new Empowering one.

Step 2: Subjective Units of Distress (SUD) #1

Rate the intensity of distress that you feel.

You will be using a Subjective Units of Distress (SUD) scale that allows you to determine for yourself (subjective) the intensity of your distress in regard to the Global Issue (if relevant), Limiting Belief, and the Titled Specific Event, along with each of its Aspects that you identified. This will allow you to track any changes, improvements, and to add any new Aspects as they emerge as you go through the tapping process to resolution.

The SUD scale ranges between 0 (no distress/peaceful) and 10 (highest intensity of distress). Nurses in hospitals use this scale when they ask, "What is your pain level on a scale of 0–10?" A Limiting Belief is resolved when it is no longer true for you with a SUD of 0–2. You know when you are done tapping a Specific Event and it is considered resolved when you can replay it in your mind or retell it aloud with a SUD level remaining at a 0–2, along with its Aspects.

Exercise: Rate the Intensity of Distress That You Feel

- Focus your attention on your titled **Specific Event.**
- Take three slow, deep belly breaths as you do a **Body Scan** (see page 81).
- Restate below: **Global Issue**, **Limiting Belief**, and the **Specific Event**, along with the Aspects that you identified in the previous 2 exercises (see page 122 and 123).
- Using the **SUD scale**, choose a number between 0 (no distress/peaceful) and 10 (highest intensity of distress) to rate the intensity of distress that you feel about the **Global Issue**, **Limiting Belief,** and the **Specific Event**, along with only the **Aspects** (thoughts, feelings, body sensations, and visual image) that apply to you and write them below.

	Description	SUD #:
Global Issue		
Limiting Belief		
Specific Event		
Thoughts		
Feelings		
Body Sensations		
Visual Image		

Step 3: Setup Statements

State the problem combined with a statement of acceptance, repeating three times while tapping on the Side of Hand.

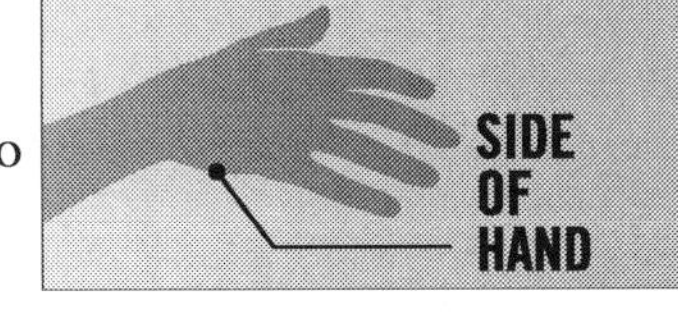

The purpose of the Setup Statement is to address the conflict that can arise when you have subconscious Limiting Beliefs that run counter to your conscious mind's intentions. These Limiting Beliefs are activated when your conscious mind wants to do something that contradicts them (see page 119). To tap without addressing them can sabotage your success by causing your body's energy to remain blocked and thus significantly reducing the benefits of tapping. The Setup Statements we use in EFT correct this problem by balancing out the conflict so that energy can flow freely and facilitate emotional releases.

Saying the Setup Statement while tapping the Side of Hand prepares the mind-body to release any resistance to change. You state the problem (negative) and connect it to a statement of acceptance (positive). Putting a negative and a positive statement together works energetically to clear the emotional blocks that prevent resolution. This is necessary because even though we may tell ourselves that we want change on a conscious level, our subconscious may be holding onto an opposing Limiting Belief that can resist change.

Here is how a Setup Statement is structured:

Stating the problem (Exposure): "Even though I have this problem with [fill in the blank]," combined with a positive statement of self-acceptance (Cognitive Realignment): "I honor and accept myself." Repeat these two phrases in combination while tapping on the Side of Hand.

The Setup Statement can vary in its wording and is stated three times with a repeated emphasis on a particular Aspect of a Specific Event while continuously tapping the Side of Hand. Here is an example:

> **Side of Hand:** *Even though I'm angry that my doctor said there's nothing wrong with me, I honor and accept myself.*
>
> **Side of Hand:** *Even though I'm angry that my doctor doesn't believe me, I honor and accept my body.*
>
> **Side of Hand:** *Even though I feel so angry that my doctor said there is nothing wrong with me, I accept all of my feelings about this.*

Exercise: Create 3 Setup Statements

Using the **Specific Event** you have been working with up to this point, create a few **Setup Statements** of your own.

On the first line, state the problem. On the second line, make a statement of acceptance.

Even though ______________________, I______________________.

Even though ______________________, I______________________.

Even though ______________________, I______________________.

(Sample **Setup Statements** for use in your tapping rounds can be found in the appendix on page 403.)

Step 4: Two Rounds of Tapping with Reminder Phrases to Keep You Focused on Your Issue.

EFT Tapping Points: The first part of Step 4 is to become familiar with the acupoints (EFT Tapping Points). The diagram below illustrates the location of each point.

According to Traditional Chinese medicine, each acupoint on the body corresponds to a different part of the body's energy pathways (the meridian system) and energetically affects different organs and emotional states. Tapping on them stimulates an emotional release.

How to Tap: Tapping is performed using the fingertips of your pointer finger and middle finger. Using the pads of your fingertips, lightly tap each point as long as it feels comfortable and then move on to the next point.

The easiest way to remember the EFT Tapping Points is to practice them in order: start tapping on the Top of the Head point and move downward from the Top of the Head to the Eyebrow to the Side of Eyes to Under the Eyes and so forth. It is okay if you skip some of the points and you can tap around in whatever order feels comfortable for you. Just keep tapping through them. (When you are first learning EFT, you may find it helpful to have the illustration of the tapping points in front of you to refer to if necessary.)

Tapping has been traditionally done using one hand, tapping only on one acupoint at each location on the same side of the body as the tapping hand. This works fine, but we encourage our clients to do bilateral tapping, using both hands to alternately tap those points that are present on both sides of the body. For example, Between the Eyes, Side of the Eyes, Under the Eyes, Collarbone, Under the Arms. The advantage of bilateral tapping is that it may stimulate the right and left brain hemispheres to initiate the release of emotional energy as indicated in the practice of therapeutic approaches such as Eye Movement Desensitization and Reprocessing (EMDR).

Whether you tap with one hand on one side of the body or tap with both hands alternating, you will experience the benefits of EFT.

As you tap, notice which spots seem to have the most or quickest effect for you and incorporate them more often into your tapping sequence. We often hear people say, "I really felt it when I tapped THIS spot!" so be on the lookout for a similar experience. Feel free to skip those points that don't feel supportive to you. Tapping through all of the points one time is considered a Round. Practice now tapping on the different acupoints shown on the EFT Tapping Points diagram for a couple of Rounds.

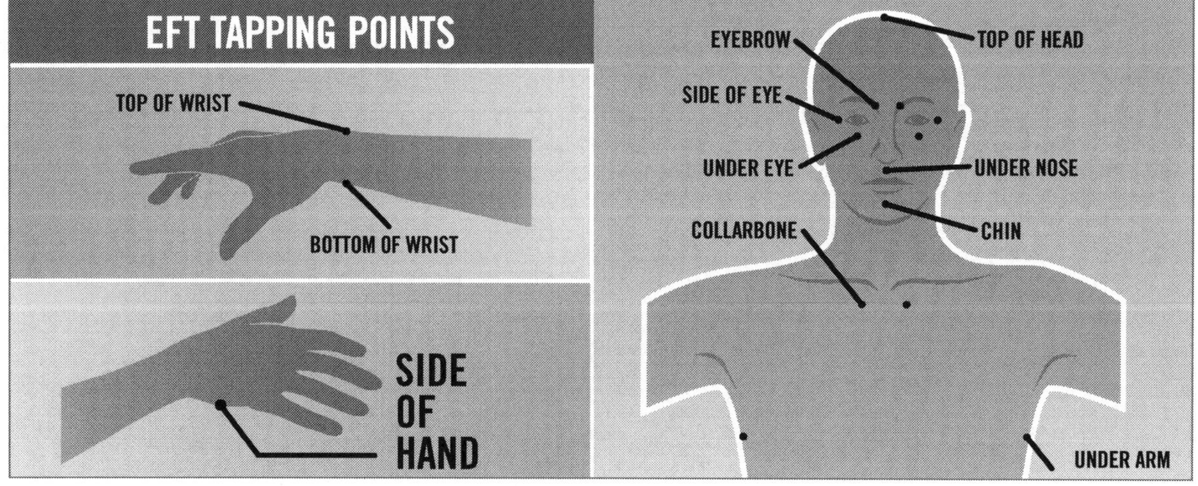

Exercise: Tapping Practice

Tap lightly on each of the following points:

Eyebrow (at the beginning of the eyebrow, just above and to one side of the nose)

Side of Eye (on the bone bordering the outside corner of each eye)

Under Eye (on the bone under each eye and 1 inch below the pupil)

Under Nose (small area between bottom of nose and top of upper lip)

Chin (midway between point of chin and bottom of lower lip)

Collar Bone (beginning of collarbone where the breastbone, collarbone, and first rib meet; to find this spot, place your forefinger where a man would knot his tie and move toward the navel 1 inch and then go to the left and right 1 to 2 inches)

Under Arm (about 4 inches below the armpit, at a point even with the nipple)

Additional Points
Many of our clients have shared that they experienced an added benefit after tapping these additional points. This is why we chose to include them in the extended global tapping scripts provided in Part 4.

Top of Head (center of the head and back about 1 inch)

Top of Wrists Together (where you would wear your watch)

Bottom of Wrists Together (where a watch buckle would be located)

Reminder Phrases: The second part of Step 4 is to create Reminder Phrases from the description of the Aspects that you identified for your Specific Event to help you stay focused on it while tapping. You can even use the title of your Specific Event to repeat as you tap!

"What do I say when I tap after I've said my setup statement?" is one of the most common questions we hear from EFT beginners. The quickest and most liberating answer we can give is that it doesn't really matter what you say as long as you are tuned in to your **feelings** about the Specific Event you've chosen to tap. This is so important that the technique is named emphasizing this, Emotional Freedom Techniques.

Reminder Phrases help you to stay focused on the emotions and other painful Aspects connected to the memory of your Specific Event. This is important because those emotions are what you want to process, resolve, and release from your mind-body system. You can vent and tap, talk and tap, or just go through the memory of the Specific Event silently in your mind as you tap.

Your awareness will naturally shift from one set of Aspects to another as you go from one round of tapping to the next. This is a sign that EFT is working to help you identify and clear all of the Aspects of a Specific Event from your system. The mind-body system stores emotions in layers. EFT has a built-in expectation that, as you go deeper into tapping Rounds through a Specific Event, your awareness will shift from one emotional layer such as anger, to the next, which could be sadness. Along with emotional shifts, come changes in what you are thinking, and how it feels in your body (sensations). The sensation of pain can also change in intensity and its location.

Exercise: Create Reminder Phrases and Practice 2 Rounds of Tapping

Fill in the table below with the same information you identified in the exercise in step 2 on page 124.

	Description	SUD #:
Global Issue		
Limiting Belief		
Specific Event		
Thoughts		
Feelings		
Body Sensations		
Visual Image		

Now, choose from your identified Specific Event along with its **Aspects** to create a Reminder Phrase for each tapping point. Start tapping through each of the acupoints while repeating the Reminder Phrase to complete Round 1. Then Repeat again for Round 2.

Top of Head: ______________________________

Eyebrow: ______________________________

Side of Eye: ______________________________

Under Eye: ______________________________

Under Nose: ______________________________

Chin: ______________________________

Collarbone: ______________________________

Under Arm: ______________________________

Top of Wrists Together: ______________________________

Bottom of Wrists Together: ______________________________

Step 5: Subjective Units of Distress (SUD) #2

Rate the intensity of distress that you feel now.

After tapping through the acupoints for two rounds, STOP. Focus your attention on replaying the Specific Event in your mind. Look for what Aspects have stayed the same and which ones have changed. The directives that you will be given is a variation of the following:

- Focus your attention on your Specific Event
- Take 3 slow, deep belly breaths as you do a **Body Scan**.
- Identify and describe below any Aspects that you notice now.
- Using the SUD scale, choose a number between 0 (no distress/peaceful) and 10 (highest intensity of distress) to rate the intensity of distress that you feel about the Global Issue, Limiting Belief, and the Specific Event, along with only the Aspects (thoughts, feelings, body sensations, and visual image) that you apply to you now and write them below.

Exercise: Rate the Intensity of Distress That You Feel Now

	Description	SUD #:
Global Issue		
Limiting Belief		
Specific Event		
Thoughts		
Feelings		
Body Sensations		
Visual Image		

If your intensity rating for this Specific Event and/or any of its Aspects are still 3 or above on the SUD scale after two rounds of tapping, keep tapping through the remaining Aspects that are in your awareness. Note any changes in the Aspects and use them as your Reminder Phrases in the next round. If your Specific Event is not resolved (that is, if SUD is 3 or above), repeat Steps 3 through 5. KEEP TAPPING.

When you repeat Step 3, use the Setup Statement, but this time, begin with "Even though I still . . . " This acknowledges the fact that you are not done yet. For example, "Even though I **still** have some of this anger, I honor and respect myself." Repeat the Modified EFT Basic Recipe and measure your SUD intensity, noticing any changes in the Aspects after each round.

Tapping through each of the Aspects of a distressing Specific Event helps to desensitize the pain associated with the memory of that event. You know you are done tapping when you can replay the whole event in your mind or retell it aloud with a SUD level remaining at 0–2. With resolution, it is common that a shift in perspective occurs from reliving the memory to one where you are watching it from a distance, like on TV. It is as if the memory as been turned off and can no longer be emotionally triggered. This allows a new perspective that can bring closure represented with new thoughts (cognitive shifts) like, *It's over. It was not my fault. I did the best that I could. That was then, this is now.*

When you have reached resolution or just want to stop a tapping session, we encourage you to finish with tapping a couple of rounds using your new cognitive shifts, positive, hopeful, and/or uplifting statements for the Reminder Phrases. This is an enjoyable way to finish! The last two Rounds of tapping within every global extended tapping script in Part 4 (see page 153) will end with one round of Reminder Phrases that are positive statements and one round of **Afformations** (see page 101).

CHAPTER

The Modified EFT Basic Recipe: Sample Tapping Script

Now that you are familiar with **The Modified EFT Basic Recipe**, we invite you to tap along with this sample tapping script if this issue applies to you. If it does not apply to you, it would be helpful for you to read through it to see how the EFT process unfolds.

Sample Tapping Script

Preparation: Identify a Global Issue (if applicable) and a Limiting Belief that You Desire to Resolve Using EFT. (See page 121.)

Global Issue: I'm so angry at the medical system for not helping me.

Limiting Belief: I don't trust the medical system to help me recover.

STEP 1: Identify a Specific Event and Give It a Title. Be Specific. (See page 122.)

Specific Event Title: There's nothing wrong with you.

- Focus your attention on this **Specific Event.**
- Take 3 slow, deep belly breaths as you do a **Body Scan** (see page 81).
- Identify and describe below any **Aspects** (see page 123) that you notice.

STEP 2: Subjective Units of Distress (SUD) #1 (See page 124.)

Rate the intensity of distress that you feel.

- Using the **SUD scale**, choose a number between 0 (no distress/peaceful) and 10 (highest intensity of distress) to rate the intensity of distress that you feel about the **Global Issue**, **Limiting Belief,** and **Specific Event**, along with only the **Aspects** (thoughts, feelings, body sensations, and visual image) that apply to you and write them on the next page.

	Description	SUD #:
Global Issue	I'm so angry at the medical system for not helping me.	8
Limiting Belief	I don't trust the medical system to help me recover.	8
Specific Event	There's nothing wrong with you.	6
Thoughts	Who does he think he is?	5
	He's so smug!	4
	He's judging me!	6
Feelings	Frustrated	6
	Angry	6
Body Sensations	Pain in left hip	4
	Chest pressure	3
Visual Image	Dark cloud	4

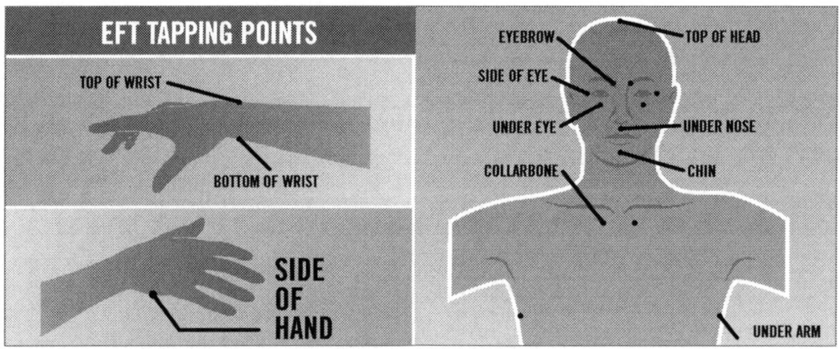

STEP 3: Setup Statements: State the Problem Combined with a Statement of Acceptance, Repeating Three Times While Tapping on the Side of Hand. (See page 125.)

Side of Hand: Even though the doctor said to me "There is nothing wrong with you," I accept my experience and myself.

Side of Hand: Even though he's judging me, I honor and accept myself.

Side of Hand: Even though I'm really angry, I accept all of my feelings.

STEP 4: Two Rounds of Tapping with Reminder Phrases to Keep You Focused on Your Issue. (See page 126.)

Round 1:

Top of Head: There is nothing wrong with you!

Eyebrow: Who does he think he is?

Side of Eye: He is so smug!

Under Eye: I am so angry!

Under Nose: I feel so frustrated!

Chin: He's judging me!

Collarbone: This pressure in my chest.

Under Arm: Pain in my left hip.

Top of Wrists Together: There's nothing wrong with you!

Bottom of Wrists Together: This dark cloud.

Take a deep belly breath, release, and keep tapping.

Round 2:

Top of Head: He's judging me!
Eyebrow: I'm really angry!
Side of Eye: There is nothing wrong with you!
Under Eye: This pressure in my chest.
Under Nose: He is so smug!
Chin: This pain in my left hip.
Collarbone: I am so angry!
Under Arm: I feel so frustrated!
Top of Wrists Together: Who does he think he is!
Bottom of Wrists Together: This dark cloud.

STEP 5: Subjective Units of Distress (SUD) #2 (See page 129.)

Rate the intensity of distress that you feel now.

- Identify and describe below any **Aspects** that you notice now.
- Using the **SUD scale**, choose a number between 0 (no distress/peaceful) and 10 (highest intensity of distress) to rate the intensity of distress that you feel now about the **Global Issue**, **Limiting Belief**, and **Specific Event**, along with only the **Aspects** (thoughts, feelings, body sensations, and visual image) that apply to you and write them below.

	Description	SUD #:
Global Issue	I'm so angry at the medical system for not helping me.	6
Limiting Belief	I don't trust the medical system to help me recover.	7
Specific Event	There's nothing wrong with you.	3
Thoughts	Who does he think he is?	3
	He's so smug!	1
	He's judging me!	1
Feelings	Frustrated	3
	Angry	3
Body Sensations	Pain in left hip	3
	Chest pressure	2
Visual Image	Dark cloud	0

Notice that all of the SUD levels decreased in intensity, while the Aspect of the Visual Image of the dark cloud resolved completely. For SUD levels of 3 or above, continue tapping through the Aspects remaining in the next round.

REPEAT STEP 3—Setup Statements and Keep Tapping

Round 3:

Begin Setup Statements with "Even though I am still . . ."

Side of Hand: Even though I am still angry, I honor and accept all of my feelings.

Side of Hand: Even though I am still frustrated, I deeply accept myself.

Side of Hand: Even though I am still angry with my doctor for saying, "There is nothing wrong with you," I honor all of my experiences.

Top of Head: This remaining anger!

Eyebrow: I still feel angry!

Side of Eye: I am still frustrated with my doctor!

Under Eye: This remaining pain in my left hip.

Under Nose: I still can't believe he/she said that!

Chin: This remaining chest pressure.

Collarbone: I still don't trust the medical system to help me.

Under Arm: I am so frustrated!

Top of Wrists Together: I am still angry with my doctor!

Bottom of Wrists Together: Remaining dark cloud.

Take three slow, deep belly breaths as you do a **Body Scan**. What do you notice now?

	Description	SUD #:
Global Issue	I'm so angry at the medical system for not helping me!	5
Limiting Belief	I don't trust the medical system to help me recover.	6
Specific Event	There's nothing wrong with you.	4
Thoughts	Who does he think he is?	1
	He's so smug!	0
	He's judging me!	0
	He really let me down.	4
Feelings	Frustrated	0
	Angry	1
	Disappointed	5
Body Sensations	Pain in left hip	0
	Chest pressure	1
Visual Image	Dark cloud	0

Notice with this example, how tapping through the Specific Event, "There's nothing wrong with you." the intensity level was down to a SUD of 3 before the last round and now has a higher unresolved SUD level of 4 after this last round. The Global Issue and Limiting Belief are also still unresolved. All of the original Aspects were resolved, yet after Round 3, two new Aspects appeared: the feeling of disappointment with a SUD of 5 and a new thought, "He really let me down" with a SUD of 4. This doesn't mean that EFT didn't work. Actually, EFT did work by uncovering the next emotional layer: the Aspect of disappointment, along with the thought, "He really let me down." When this new emotional layer was triggered, it actually increased the Specific Event's overall SUD level because it had not yet been addressed with EFT. It is necessary to now continue to tap on this Specific Event until these two new Aspects are resolved and no other new Aspects emerge.

Also notice that the Global Issue decreased to a SUD of 5 by tapping on anger and frustration, yet it is still unresolved, along with the Limiting Belief.

To resolve this Global Issue and Limiting Belief, you have to identify other Specific Events that have helped to validate the "truth" of the Limiting Belief for you. Remember, once all of the Limiting Beliefs that are at the root of a Global Issue are identified and resolved, the Global Issue will collapse with it, giving rise to new Empowering Beliefs that cultivate a wellness state of mind. The **Going Deeper with EFT** worksheet will guide you through this process and can be found at the end of each global tapping script chapter in Part 4 starting with Chapter 19 on page 175.

You can keep track of your identified unresolved Specific Events and document when they were tapped and resolved on the worksheet, **List of Titled Specific Events** on page 156 in Part 4. Below is an example of this worksheet filled out for this sample tapping script.

Sample of the List of Titled Specific Events Worksheet

Global Issue	Start SUD #	End SUD #	Titled Specific Events	Start SUD #	End SUD #	Date Tapped
I'm so angry at the medical system for not helping me!	8	5	There's nothing wrong with you.	6	4	1/8/16
Limiting Belief						
I don't trust the medical system to help me recover.	8	6				
Resolution: New Empowering Belief(s)						

Sample EFT Tapping Log

You can also track the progression of your SUD levels through the tapping rounds of a Specific Event using the **EFT Tapping Log** worksheet found in Chapter 18 on page 162.

Date: 1/8/16				**Titled Specific Event:** *There's nothing wrong with you.*			
Starting SUD Scale	**Rounds 1–2 Ending SUD #**	**Round 3 Ending SUD #**	**Round 4 Ending SUD #**	**Round 5 Ending SUD #**	**Round 6 Ending SUD #**	**Round 7 Ending SUD #**	**Done When SUD # is 0–2**
6	3	4					

New Perspectives with EFT

- **Shifts your perception from starring in the "movie" to watching it on a screen.** Unprocessed pain about a Specific Event (the "movie") can sometimes leave you stuck in it so that you keep re-experiencing it over and over in your mind, thus interfering with your perception of current-day events. It's as if you are the star in a movie about yourself! When using EFT to resolution, the movie is turned off emotionally or is desensitized. This shifts your perception from starring in the movie to being separated from it, like watching your movie on a screen. This shift from "star" to "viewer" or "observer" is a powerful change in perspective that can free you from the pain and emotional distress associated with the Specific Event you have addressed. You may not forget what happened, but you can stop reliving the emotional pain.
- **Shifts the quality of your thoughts (cognitive shifts).** Resolving an emotionally charged event means that it will have little to no intensity (SUD 0–2) and that your perceptions and thoughts about the event will have changed for the better from a Small Mind to a **Large Mind** perspective (see page page 89) called a cognitive shift. This is what resolving an emotionally charged Specific Event feels like. Your new thoughts about it may sound something like:

  It's over.

  I am ready to move on.

  It is what it is for now, but it is not forever.

  I'm safe.

  It was not my fault.

  I am open to new possibilities about this issue.

A natural result of collapsing/releasing Limiting Beliefs (Global Issues) is that it shifts your attention to the innate Empowering Beliefs that have been in your conscious and subconscious mind. Empowering Beliefs now dominate the lens of your perception, allowing you to view yourself, others, and life itself in a **Large Mind** way that cultivates a wellness state of mind.

CHAPTER

15 Break Down a Global Issue: Getting to the Root Causes

To facilitate your understanding of how to break down a Global Issue/Limiting Belief by tapping to resolution the unresolved Specific Events that created it, in this chapter, we use an illustration of a table that needs to be collapsed. Later in this chapter, we will look at the concept of Issue Strings, which explains how present-day emotions surrounding a Specific Event can sometimes be "attached" to past-unresolved events. But let's first collapse a table.

Tabletop (Global Issue/ Limiting Belief)

The tabletop is a symbolic representation of the Global Issue/Limiting Belief such as, "I don't trust the medical system to help me recover."

Table Legs (Unresolved Specific Events)

The table legs are the unresolved Specific Events, along with their Aspects, that validate the Global Issue/Limiting Belief as being true. For example, you may have had many experiences of treatment failures that led to the conclusion, "I don't trust the medical system to help me recover." Each treatment failure can be considered a table leg.

It is common to have a tabletop (Global Issue/ Limiting Belief) with many table legs (Unresolved Specific Events) supporting it. There is usually an initial painful event that happened in the past that taught you something limiting about yourself, others, and how your world works. Then following the initial painful event, you may have had many emotionally similar painful events that validated what you initially learned to be true for you. This is how both Limiting and Empowering Beliefs are created.

Global Issue/Limiting Belief Resolved

The aim is to tap through to resolution (SUD level of 2 or below) as many unresolved Specific Events (table legs) as needed to collapse the tabletop with the Global Issue/Limiting Belief being resolved. Once resolved, you should be able to notice a shift in perspective to new Empowering Beliefs, with its thoughts and feelings that foster hope and new possibilities to support your recovery. An example of resolution can sound like: *I believe I can find a Lyme Literate Physician/Practitioner who can help me to recover.* This can be followed with a renewed sense of determination and persistence to make it happen.

Issue Strings: The Connection Between Past and Present-Day Events

As you tap through a present-day Specific Event, you may find that the emotions connected to that event bring to mind other events from the past. At first it may seem as though these events from the past have no connection with the present-day event on which you are focused. But what would happen if you took a moment to look at one of these past events using a skill of the "observer" (see page 90) to ask, "How am I relating to this event?" Most likely you would discover that some of these Specific Events from the past contain unresolved emotional issues similar to those in the present-day event that you have targeted for tapping. The only difference is that the emotional issues from the past event(s) have not yet been resolved. This creates a scenario called an Issue String. An Issue String can be triggered when a present-day stressor that has emotionally similar content to a past unresolved event is triggered and adds to the intensity of your present-day Specific Event. The underlying emotional pain from the past makes the present-day stressor more emotionally intense than it would be otherwise because they are emotionally strung (connected) together.

Every one of us has many Issue Strings, so don't fret! The good news is that you don't have to tap through each and every event on an Issue String that contributed to your Global Issue/Limiting Belief to release the emotional issues on that string from your mind-body system. By resolving the emotional content from the major unresolved Specific Events on an Issue String, the resolution can generalize to all of the other minor events and their related emotional issues along that same "string." This dynamic is called the Generalization Effect, which will be described in more detail at the end of this chapter.

A helpful way to think about the Issue Strings connection between present and past events is to imagine that those past events are like a string of lights. The string represents the shared unresolved emotional issues that connect all of the lights together. When you experience a present-day event that is emotionally similar to that string of past events or Issue String, it can act as a fuse that triggers some or all of the events on that string to be triggered or to "light up." When the emotional pain of unresolved past events is triggered in the present moment, it will add to the emotional pain you are already experiencing from a current distressing event.

If you are not feeling resolved after tapping on a current Specific Event, check in with yourself. Do you feel resolution about the event you were tapping through, yet still feel a level of distress 3 or above on the SUD scale? If the answer is yes, see if you can notice if there is any connection between your remaining emotional distress to a related past unresolved event that could be strung or connected together. If there is a connection, then target that past event as the Specific Event for your next rounds of tapping.

To see this process in action, read the case narrative presented in each chapter within Part 4 starting with Chapter 19 on page 167. You will discover how others have used EFT to resolve some of their deeply held painful issues along an Issue String that was interfering with their own healing, responsiveness to treatments, and recovery from Lyme/TBDs. You will have an opportunity to do this yourself at the end of each of these chapters with an exercise called **Going Deeper with EFT**.

Going Deeper with EFT

In Part 4, we invite you to start tapping with an extended global tapping script that pertains to your issue. This is a gentle way to take the edge off and to decrease the overall intensity of your Global Issue before going deeper. Then, when you have the time and energy, you can choose to tap through the exercise called **Going Deeper with EFT**, which is included at the end of every global extended tapping script. This exercise helps you to identify, target, and tap through the individual Specific Events that are at the root of the Global Issue/Limiting Beliefs you wish to collapse and release from your system. After completing the **Going Deeper with EFT** exercise, you can then use the **Blank Tapping Script** provided in the appendix on page 404 to develop your own tapping script that addresses the Aspects of your Specific Event to facilitate your tapping process.

Caution: For people with an extensive unresolved trauma history, it is possible that tapping on a current Specific Event could trigger the stimulation of many Issue Strings all at once, unleashing overwhelming emotions. This is sometimes referred to as "emotional flooding." Emotional flooding can create dangerously high levels of emotional intensity that make containing and managing your emotions difficult to do by yourself. We suggest that, if you have an extensive history of trauma and are unable to regulate your emotions resulting in frequent episodes of emotional flooding, you seek out a licensed mental-health practitioner who is also a certified EFT practitioner to help guide you through the EFT process safely. They are trained to help you manage and contain these intense emotional states.

As certified EFT practitioners, we are available for appointments if you need extra support. We can meet in person, over the telephone, or via Skype, as appropriate. You can contact us through our respective websites: www.anitabains.com and www.traceymiddleton.com. To see this process in action, read the case narratives in Part 4 to discover how others have used EFT to resolve some of the deeply painful issues along an Issue String that were interfering with their own healing, responsiveness to treatments, and recovery from Lyme/TBDs.

The Generalization Effect: A Side Benefit of EFT

The good news is that you do not have to tap on every Specific Event to resolve the Global Issue/Limiting Belief through the dynamic of the Generalization Effect. You only need to use EFT to resolve enough of the Specific Events to create the resolution you desire. When you single out and tap through to resolution the major Specific Events (table legs) related to a Global Issue/Limiting Belief (tabletop), the other lesser supporting events with their related emotional issues can resolve on their own without tapping them. Without the emotional intensity and the energy to support and keep them alive, the validating Specific Events (the legs) collapse and the Global Issue/Limiting Belief (tabletop) breaks apart and dissolves. All the energy that went into the identified problem is now available for cultivating a wellness state of mind that will support the body's own capacity for healing.

The Generalization Effect also occurs in other ways but can be so subtle that it can be easily missed. People who regularly use EFT often report:

- Increased calm
- Reduced anxiety
- Improved sleep
- Increased energy
- Reduced pain
- Reduced emotional intensity on seemingly unrelated events
- Not being emotionally triggered by events that were previously upsetting

When asked about these positive changes, it is common for people who are new to using EFT to attribute them to something other than the use of it. The most common example we hear from a new client is, *"Talking about it probably made it go away,"* even though they've talked about it before with no relief. Some examples of the evidence that resolution occurred can be seen in statements (cognitive shifts) like these:

- *It's in the past and time heals all things.* (Even though they did not experience this before using EFT, rather only thought it.)
- *It really wasn't a big issue in the first place.* (Even though before tapping they may have rated their intensity on the SUD scale as an 8–10.)

A Review: How to Collapse/Resolve a Lyme/TBDs-Related Global Issue

1. Identify the Global Issue/Limiting Belief (tabletop) you wish to resolve. (For example, I don't trust the medical system to help me recover.)
2. List and title the Specific Events (table legs) that first come to mind that validate the Global Issue/Limiting Belief as true for you. You can add them to the **List of Titled Specific Events** worksheet on page 156 to return to them when you have the time and energy to address with EFT.
3. To help you begin, go to Part 4 and locate a chapter that reflects your personal issue in the title. Read the case study and tap along with the global extended tapping script to get you started. We suggest that you start tapping on the Global Issue first as a gentle way to take the edge off your overall intensity.
4. Then use the worksheet **Going Deeper with EFT** provided at the end of each global tapping script to guide you through tapping to resolution enough Specific Events to collapse your Global Issue/Limiting Belief for full resolution.

CHAPTER 16

Tips to Enhance the Effectiveness of EFT

In this chapter, you will find tips to keep in mind to help enhance the effectiveness you can get from the use of EFT. This is a helpful chapter to refer to if you are first learning EFT and if you have been using it for a while with unsatisfactory results. If you have applied the information presented in this chapter to your use of EFT and you still are not satisfied with your results, contact a certified EFT practitioner who can assist you by going to www.EFTUniverse.com or www.thetappingsolution.com. You can also contact us through our respective websites at www.anitabains.com and www.traceymiddleton.com.

Allow Yourself to Feel Your Emotions as You Tap

For EFT to be effective, it is critical that you stay tuned in to your feelings about a Specific Event. Experience the event you are tapping as if each scene with all of its details were happening right now. We encourage you to involve as many of your senses as you can. This helps to connect you more deeply with your emotional experience of the event while tapping, which allows your emotions to be expressed, processed, and released from the mind-body system.

CAUTION: If your emotional distress is above a SUD level of 6, you are already tuned in. Just start tapping, focusing only on the title of your event until your distress level lowers. **We do not encourage you to make yourself feel any level of distress above a 7 on the SUD scale.** Doing so can be re-traumatizing and overwhelming and can increase your stress level in a way that overtaxes your system.

If you already have a high level of distress, just start tapping globally while focusing only on the title of your event to reduce the likelihood of re-traumatization. Choose a way that does not intensify your level of distress. You might choose to tap silently or to verbalize while tapping. This will allow you to reduce some of the intensity of your distress so that you can tap safely at a lower intensity level as you dive deeper into your issue.

Tap FIRST the Painful Emotions and Negative Thoughts/Beliefs

You may have noticed that in demonstrating how to create Setup Statements and Reminder Phrases, we have been focusing on the painful emotions and "negative" thoughts that can come with a distressing event. This is because using the Reminder Phrases to vent all of your painful emotions and upsetting thoughts *first* is critical to using EFT successfully. This is why we are encouraging you to first focus on the *negative/painful* Aspects while you tap.

Yes, you heard us right! Tapping the *negative/painful* Aspects first ensures your success with EFT. We liken this to treating a wound. The first step is to clean out all the debris before applying a dressing so that it doesn't become infected later. The same applies to treating emotional wounds. With EFT, we engage in a simultaneous process of venting and tapping through negative thought patterns and painful emotions so that they can be processed and released from the mind-body system. Venting emotional pain as Reminder Phrases prevents them from festering, remaining stuck in the mind-body system, and creating more suffering.

We always tap through negative thoughts and painful emotions *first* to clear them. Then you can tap through positive reframes and **Affirmations** (see page 101) to finish. When you get to tapping rounds 4 and 5 of the extended global tapping scripts provided in Part 4, you will be tapping through positive statements and **Affirmations** to finish. You will be directed to repeat tapping rounds 1–3 first until your SUD level about the Specific Event you are addressing is below a 2. You can then move on to the positive tapping rounds 4 and 5.

Avoid "Skipping the Pain"

We call tapping through *only* positive statements while trying to resolve a painful issue "skipping the pain." It may feel good in the moment, but it avoids addressing and releasing the emotional pain at the root of suffering. Left unprocessed, that emotional pain remains lodged in the mind-body system where it can continue to cause high levels of distress when triggered.

Many people who are new to EFT think that the resurfacing of painful emotions associated with a particular issue means that EFT isn't working. This is not the case. It's merely a signal that it may be time to go deeper with EFT to resolve those painful emotions that are at the root of the issue and that continue to create undue stress when triggered.

3 Ways to Determine When You're Done Tapping

1. **Test yourself.** We strongly encourage you to test yourself when you reach a SUD of 2 or below on a Specific Event to see if all of the Aspects have been released and neutralized. If you stop tapping too soon, the unresolved Aspects could be triggered at a later time, making you feel as though EFT did not work. Here's how to test yourself:

   - Replay the Specific Event in your mind as if you are watching a movie. Make it as vivid as possible as you play it through from beginning to end, checking to see if any Aspects (see page 123) still have an intensity of a SUD level of 3 or above. If they do, focus on them for your next round of tapping until all the Aspects are at a SUD level of 0–2.
   - Tell the story out loud to yourself or someone else.
   - Do a **Body Scan** (see page 81) while tuned in to your Specific Event and notice any discomfort in different parts of your body.

Notice if you experience any distress as you imagine being in the same place or with the same people when the event originally occurred. Recalling these details may remind you of new Aspects that did not come to mind while you were tapping the first time. Tapping through your Specific Event for the first time may have triggered more deeply layered emotional content that is only just coming into your awareness because you have tapped into it. Continue tapping through any Aspect of the event that still holds a SUD level of 3 or more until it reaches a SUD level of 2 or below.

2. **Notice cognitive shifts.** Cognitive shifts are changes in your perception (beliefs) that form the quality of your thoughts and feelings in relation to a Specific Event. Positive cognitive shifts contain **Large Mind** compassionate understanding, forgiveness, acceptance, and closure that will allow you to let go and live in the present moment embedded in hope that there are always new possibilities for your healing and recovery. These shifts in thinking are really a movement from Small Mind to **Large Mind** (see page 89), and it is **Large Mind** thinking that forms the foundation for a wellness state of mind.

3. **Notice common physical signs of release.** Your body will indicate when an emotional release has happened through reflexes that can include the

following: yawning, smiling, laughing, relaxed posture, blushing, deep breath/sigh, and body discomfort decreased or gone.

When EFT Doesn't Work

Asking and answering for yourself the following questions can assist you in addressing issues that may be preventing you from getting the results you desire:

- Are you remaining too global? Are there other unresolved Specific Events that support your Global Issue/Limiting Belief as being true that you have not yet identified? Remember, tapping globally is a good place to start, but you also need to use the exercise **Going Deeper with EFT** (at the end of each chapter in Part 4 starting with Chapter 19 on page 167) to address the underlying root causes of your issue.
- Are you drinking enough water? Emotions are less likely to be released from the mind-body system when you are dehydrated. Drink water periodically during your tapping sessions to remain hydrated.
- Are there any additional Aspects to your Specific Event that you still need to tap through? Remember an Aspect is considered resolved if it is at a SUD scale of 0–2.
- Are you emotionally tuned into your issue? Painful emotions are less likely to be freed from the mind-body system if you are not adequately tuned in to them. That is why this process is called Emotional Freedom Techniques. Tuning in to your emotions while tapping can be supported by the following strategies: raising your voice, exaggerating, swearing, or having a "pity party." Just vent!

Personal Reflections

CHAPTER

17 Commit to Cultivating a Wellness State of Mind

We have all heard how important proper sleep hygiene, physical hygiene, and nutritional hygiene are to supporting Lyme/TBDs treatments and ultimately recovery. We couldn't agree more! And we want to also add the importance of practicing daily emotional hygiene techniques to help clear the mind-body of emotional stresses that may have occurred throughout the day.

By learning and using the self-help tools in your toolkit daily, you have the capacity to cultivate a wellness state of mind with the power to generate all that you need to optimize your healing, promote your recovery, and expand your possibilities for personal growth and development. Practiced regularly as a form of emotional hygiene, the self-help tools in Part 2 along with EFT can empower you to:

- Become calm and centered in the present moment
- Choose mindful responses to life events that reduce stress and conflicts
- Take responsibility for how you feel and have the ability to change it when necessary
- Reduce stress
- Enhance your body's innate ability to respond to treatments
- Strengthen your resiliency
- Shift from a Small Mind to a **Large Mind** perspective
- Think and act on behalf of your well-being and recovery
- Realize your intentions for recovery
- Activate recovery
- Become aware of new possibilities for yourself in all dimensions of your life
- Deepen your connection with who you are and what you value
- Take positive action to create what is in your best and highest good

We encourage you now to make a commitment to cultivating a wellness state of mind for your own recovery from Lyme/TBDs. As you engage in a daily practice of cultivating a wellness state of mind, you will be able to see yourself transforming!

There are many options for creating and maintaining your wellness plan, but it is essential to practice emotional hygiene by tapping (or using TAB when necessary; see page 411) at least 15 minutes each day to reduce the high stress levels that are inherent for most people with Lyme/TBDs.

Emotional Hygiene Practices

The following are some suggested emotional hygiene practices to choose from for cultivating a wellness state of mind that fosters resiliency:

- ✔ Get into the habit. Practice **emotional hygiene** by using **EFT** or **TAB** at least 15 minutes a day. Make a list of titled Specific Events and choose one each day to process and resolve using **EFT** or **TAB** (see page 411). Use the **extended global tapping scripts** in Part 4 to get you started.
- ✔ Find a **tapping buddy** and schedule time to tap together.
- ✔ Check in with yourself each day and do a **Body Scan** (see page 81).
- ✔ Get into the habit of using the tools of the **"observer"** on a regular basis. When something is happening, ask yourself: **What is happening?** and **How am I relating to it?** Be so practiced that these two questions become automatic.
- ✔ Ask yourself often: "Am I in Small Mind or **Large Mind**?" (See page 89.) Then make a choice! Practice choosing **Large Mind** every day!
- ✔ Track your progress daily using the **EFT Tapping Log** in Part 4 on page 162 and/or by keeping a tapping journal.
- ✔ Practice **Afformations**® every day (see page 101). Just choose one and repeat it periodically throughout the day and see if you notice anything new.
- ✔ Practice the **Stop-Drop-Breathe** exercise on page 84 as often as you need to throughout the day when you start to feel stressed. Try to interrupt the stress response early.
- ✔ Each day, list at least three things for which you are grateful. It is helpful to keep a **gratitude journal** for this purpose. Place it by your bed and make your daily list before going to sleep. If you commit to this practice, you will be training your brain to look for things throughout the day that you are grateful for so that you can write them down at night.
- ✔ Explore **meditation** (see page 105). Add in a couple of rounds of tapping before or after meditating to enhance your experience.
- ✔ **Build a support system** by reaching out to others.
- ✔ Go to a Lyme/TBDs recovery group.
- ✔ Stay **open to new possibilities** for treatment and recovery.
- ✔ Practice **self-empathy** every day. Allow yourself to see, hear, understand, and **radically accept** all that you are in the present moment.

Commitment to Practice

The self-help tools and mindfulness-based techniques in this workbook only work if you use them. It takes commitment to practice them, especially when you are distressed and feeling ill. In your low moments, sometimes taking any kind of positive action to help yourself can feel like too much and leave you feeling powerless. If you are there, allow the commitment you are making to yourself to daily emotional hygiene practices to move you to take positive action toward cultivating a wellness state of mind. Remember why you are doing these things, and identify people you can call who can encourage you onward when you're not feeling motivated. You might even consider inviting them to tap with you as a tapping buddy. Feeling empowered in the healing process is a critical element to recovery. Remember, cultivating a wellness state of mind can improve your mind/body response to Lyme/TBDs treatments.

We have offered you a variety of emotional hygiene practices that make up your toolkit for cultivating a wellness state of mind. It is important to have choices and to make the choice that feels right to you in the moment. Give yourself the freedom and flexibility to change your mind, but choose something. If you don't feel like tapping, then commit to **shifting your mindset** from Small Mind to **Large Mind**, using **Touch and Breathe (TAB)**, **meditation**, using **Stop-Drop-Breathe**, or refocusing with **Afformations**. There is always something you can do in the moment to help yourself if you are in distress and/or experiencing Lyme/TBD symptoms.

If you are feeling any resistance to using EFT, we suggest skipping to Chapter 19: **Resistance to Using EFT** on page 167 to explore this issue further and to possibly use EFT on the issue of not wanting to use it! Check it out!

Exercise: My Commitment to Tapping into a Wellness State of Mind

State which daily emotional hygiene practices you commit to using to help cultivate your wellness state of mind and the reasons why.

I commit to the following daily practices:

1. ______________________________ because

____

2. ______________________________ because

____

3. ______________________________ because

____

4. ______________________________ because

____

5. ______________________________ because

____

6. ______________________________ because

____

The person or people I can call for emotional support are:

Person______________________ Number______________

Person______________________ Number______________

Person______________________ Number______________

Person______________________ Number______________

My tapping buddy is ______________ Number______________

My tapping buddy is ______________ Number______________

In case of an emergency, I commit to calling: Person__________ Number__________

**** Call 911 or go to the nearest hospital if your emergency is life threatening. ****

Looking Within

The Golden Buddha is a story that inspires us to take a deeper look inside ourselves and uncover the hidden resources that can help us heal. Our attention is often consumed with the pain and suffering masking the healing possibilities that lie within. Are you ready to look within, as you move forward in the following chapters to tapping into a wellness state of mind? We hope the Buddha story inspires you to do just that.

The Story of the Golden Buddha

During the late eighteenth century, the King of Thailand, fearful of potential unrest in the country's Northern region, ordered that all images of the Buddha that were left in abandoned and ruined temples be brought to his new capitol in Bangkok. Among the many rescued statues was a twelve-foot tall painted and bejeweled Buddha that everyone believed was made of plaster. Not seeing that this particular Buddha statue had much material worth, the king ordered that it be sent to a minor temple where it rested for over 100 years, until that temple was abandoned and the statue had to be moved again.

This time the Buddha was moved to a small temple in Bangkok, but because the statue was so large, the keepers of the temple had to house it under a tin roof so that it could be protected from the rain and other elements that might have destroyed its plaster molding. Roughly twenty years had passed when the keepers of the temple decided it was time to expand. Their giant Buddha, treasured by the monks despite its humble appearance, would finally have a proper place to live.

The day came when it was time to lift the Buddha from its pedestal and move it out of the tin structure that had protected it up to that point. A crane was brought in to hoist the heavy statue from its place, but just as the project got underway, it started to pour. The workers began rushing to complete the job, but their worst fears were realized when a rope broke and the Buddha fell from its pedestal into a pit of mud. The crew decided to cover the Buddha with a tarp until the next day when, in hopes of better weather, they could try again to move it to its new home.

One of the temple monks volunteered to keep watch over the Buddha throughout the night to make sure that its protective tarp stayed in place. This same monk fell asleep and awoke to pounding rain. Getting up in a panic, the monk saw that the Buddha's protective tarp had been ripped away. There was nothing he could do but watch as the torrent of rain battered away at the now defenseless statue. Still, he kept his vigil. Soon a streak of lightning hit the statue, allowing the monk to see that its plaster had been cracked and that there was something shining through the mud in which it was covered.

Bursting with anticipation, the monk climbed into the pit where the statue had fallen and began pulling the mud away with his hands. How astonished he was when it became clear to him that this seemingly minor statue was, in fact, a most magnificent statue sculpted in beautiful detail and made of pure gold! He called all of the other monks from the temple to come help him, and together they worked to uncover the Buddha statue's true nature.

Once believed to be nothing more than a simple plaster representation, the Golden Buddha, the largest gold statue in the world, now stands at the Wat Traimit in Bangkok as one of the world's greatest wonders.

How it happened that such a splendid statue as the Golden Buddha came to be covered in plaster no one knows for sure, but it is quite possible that whoever did it wanted to secure its safekeeping and protect it from harm. Even after centuries of existence, it wasn't until the "perfect storm" came along and the Buddha seemed to be in peril that its true nature came shining through. As long as the Buddha's protective covering remained intact, it could never be known nor be given its rightful place in the world. Only when its layers of plaster were removed and its true "self" was revealed, could it fulfill its ultimate purpose.

What the Golden Buddha Can Teach Us About Lyme/TBD Recovery

Like the storm in the story of the Golden Buddha, Lyme/TBDs can come into our lives and wash away everything we believed ourselves and our lives to be. And like the monk who wakes up in a panic and feels helpless against the storm, we, too, can become lost in believing that our situation is hopeless.

What we learn from the monk, however, is that we can choose to see things in a different way—a way that cultivates hope, opens us to new perspectives and new possibilities. Although the monk is distressed by what has happened, he keeps his eyes and himself open. This is what allows him to look up into the sky, at which moment he sees the lightning and realizes that there is far more happening than he knew. Had he given into his despair, he might never have seen the beauty and abundance hiding beneath the Buddha's plaster façade, which was solid gold.

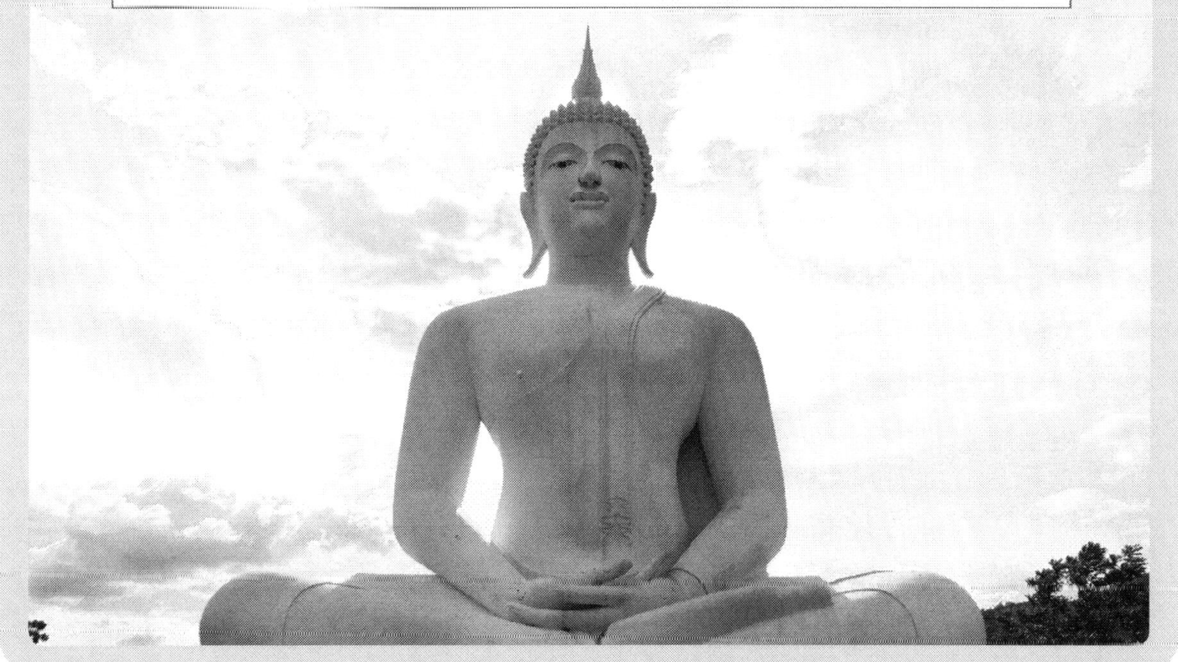

PART 4
Tapping into a Wellness State of Mind

Case Studies with 21 Extended Global Tapping Scripts

CHAPTER

18 Getting Started Using EFT

Review the twenty-one common unresolved Global Issues related to having Lyme/TBDs as reflected in the chapter titles below.

Choose a Chapter and Start Tapping!

Once you have chosen a chapter that reflects your Global Issue, most of them will have a case study reflecting a person who used EFT to address many of the emotional layers at the root of the issue and the resolution they experienced. Then you can start using EFT by tapping along through the global extended tapping script guided by step-by-step instructions to help keep you moving through the process. Tapping globally first is a gentle way to reduce the overall intensity of that issue. Then when you have the time and energy, you will be guided to identify your personal Global Issue/Limiting Belief along with your unresolved Specific Events that are at the root of it by doing the **Going Deeper with EFT** exercise. This will result in the natural emergence of new Empowering Beliefs that support a wellness state of mind! Feel free to skip around!

Write Your Own Tapping Scripts

If it is supportive to you to write your own tapping scripts to follow along with while using EFT, we added two different kinds of worksheets to choose from. You can use either of them to fill in your Reminder Phrases with the Aspects you identified about an unresolved Specific Event you want to tap. Once you have written your script, you can read it while you tap to stay tuned in to your issue.

These are located in the appendix:

- **Blank Tapping Script** worksheet on page 404
- **Vent While You Tap** worksheet on page 409

Two Ways to Track Your Progress

1. List of Titled Specific Events

As you learned in Chapter 15, collapsing a Global Issue/Limiting Belief means resolving many of the Specific Events that created it. (If needed, go back to that chapter on page 137 for a review.) As you identify any unresolved Specific Events that need to be tapped, it is helpful to list them on the **List of Titled Specific Events** blank worksheet, starting on page 156. You can then refer back to them when you have the time and energy to address them. The following is a sample filled out from the tapping script in Chapter 14 on page 135.

Sample: List of Titled Specific Events Worksheet

Global Issue	Start SUD #	End SUD #	Titled Specific Events	Start SUD #	End SUD #	Date Tapped
I'm so angry at the medical system for not helping me!	8	5	There's nothing wrong with you.	6	4	1/8/16
Limiting Belief						
I don't trust the medical system to help me recover.	8	6				
Resolution: New Empowering Belief(s)						

Key Points to Enhance Your List of Titled Specific Events

- Identify and record your Global Issue/Limiting Belief, then title and list the unresolved Specific Events that happened to you that support it as being valid and true.
- Each Specific Event should last only 2 to 3 minutes when replaying in your mind to make sure you have narrowed it down to being very specific. (To review the instructions for each step used in **The Modified EFT Basic Recipe** , turn back to Chapter 13 on page 121.)
- Don't allow yourself to feel overwhelmed because you may have identified many unresolved Specific Events. This is normal for all of us! Keep in mind that a side benefit of EFT is the Generalization Effect (see page 139), so you only need to resolve ***enough*** of the Specific Events to collapse your Global Issue/Limiting Belief. Be persistent!
- Record the dates you tapped and resolved a Specific Event.
- Identify and record any Empowering Beliefs that you become aware of as a result of resolving your Global Issue/Limiting Belief. A new Empowering Belief is a sign that you've resolved that issue resulting in a change in perception and consciousness! Notice, document, and celebrate them!
- Have fun tracking your progress! (If you don't want to use this worksheet, start a tapping journal.)

2. EFT Tapping Log

This log is a helpful way to track your SUD scale changes of the overall intensity of your Specific Event as you tap through the Aspects in each of the rounds to resolution. This is not necessary, but it can be helpful and fun! Some of our clients like to track their progress in detail, so we have included this worksheet as an option for you. The **EFT Tapping Log** blank worksheet starts on page 162. The following is a sample filled out from the sample tapping script in Chapter 14 on page 135.

Sample of the EFT Tapping Log Worksheet

Date: 1/8/16				**Titled Specific Event:** *There's nothing wrong with you.*			
Starting SUD Scale	**Rounds 1–2 Ending SUD #**	**Round 3 Ending SUD #**	**Round 4 Ending SUD #**	**Round 5 Ending SUD #**	**Round 6 Ending SUD #**	**Round 7 Ending SUD #**	**Done When SUD # is 0–2**
6	3	4					

List of Titled Specific Events Worksheets

Global Issue	Start SUD #	End SUD #	Titled Specific Events	Start SUD #	End SUD #	Date Tapped
Limiting Belief						
Resolution: New Empowering Belief(s)						

Global Issue	Start SUD #	End SUD #	Titled Specific Events	Start SUD #	End SUD #	Date Tapped
Limiting Belief						
Resolution: New Empowering Belief(s)						

Global Issue	Start SUD #	End SUD #	Titled Specific Events	Start SUD #	End SUD #	Date Tapped
Limiting Belief						
Resolution: New Empowering Belief(s)						

Global Issue	Start SUD #	End SUD #	Titled Specific Events	Start SUD #	End SUD #	Date Tapped
Limiting Belief						
Resolution: New Empowering Belief(s)						

Global Issue	Start SUD #	End SUD #	Titled Specific Events	Start SUD #	End SUD #	Date Tapped
Limiting Belief						
Resolution: New Empowering Belief(s)						

Global Issue	Start SUD #	End SUD #	Titled Specific Events	Start SUD #	End SUD #	Date Tapped
Limiting Belief						
Resolution: New Empowering Belief(s)						

<table>
<tr><th>Global Issue</th><th>Start SUD #</th><th>End SUD #</th><th>Titled Specific Events</th><th>Start SUD #</th><th>End SUD #</th><th>Date Tapped</th></tr>
<tr><td></td><td></td><td></td><td></td><td></td><td></td><td></td></tr>
<tr><td colspan="7">Limiting Belief</td></tr>
<tr><td></td><td></td><td></td><td></td><td></td><td></td><td></td></tr>
<tr><td></td><td></td><td></td><td></td><td></td><td></td><td></td></tr>
<tr><td></td><td></td><td></td><td></td><td></td><td></td><td></td></tr>
<tr><td colspan="7">Resolution: New Empowering Belief(s)</td></tr>
</table>

<table>
<tr><th>Global Issue</th><th>Start SUD #</th><th>End SUD #</th><th>Titled Specific Events</th><th>Start SUD #</th><th>End SUD #</th><th>Date Tapped</th></tr>
<tr><td></td><td></td><td></td><td></td><td></td><td></td><td></td></tr>
<tr><td colspan="7">Limiting Belief</td></tr>
<tr><td></td><td></td><td></td><td></td><td></td><td></td><td></td></tr>
<tr><td></td><td></td><td></td><td></td><td></td><td></td><td></td></tr>
<tr><td></td><td></td><td></td><td></td><td></td><td></td><td></td></tr>
<tr><td colspan="7">Resolution: New Empowering Belief(s)</td></tr>
</table>

Global Issue	Start SUD #	End SUD #	Titled Specific Events	Start SUD #	End SUD #	Date Tapped
Limiting Belief						
Resolution: New Empowering Belief(s)						

Global Issue	Start SUD #	End SUD #	Titled Specific Events	Start SUD #	End SUD #	Date Tapped
Limiting Belief						
Resolution: New Empowering Belief(s)						

Global Issue	Start SUD #	End SUD #	Titled Specific Events	Start SUD #	End SUD #	Date Tapped
Limiting Belief						
Resolution: New Empowering Belief(s)						

Global Issue	Start SUD #	End SUD #	Titled Specific Events	Start SUD #	End SUD #	Date Tapped
Limiting Belief						
Resolution: New Empowering Belief(s)						

EFT Tapping Logs

Date:				Titled Specific Event:			
Starting SUD Scale	Rounds 1–2 Ending SUD #	Round 3 Ending SUD #	Round 4 Ending SUD #	Round 5 Ending SUD #	Round 6 Ending SUD #	Round 7 Ending SUD #	Done When SUD # is 0–2

Date:				Titled Specific Event:			
Starting SUD Scale	Rounds 1–2 Ending SUD #	Round 3 Ending SUD #	Round 4 Ending SUD #	Round 5 Ending SUD #	Round 6 Ending SUD #	Round 7 Ending SUD #	Done When SUD # is 0–2

Date:				Titled Specific Event:			
Starting SUD Scale	Rounds 1–2 Ending SUD #	Round 3 Ending SUD #	Round 4 Ending SUD #	Round 5 Ending SUD #	Round 6 Ending SUD #	Round 7 Ending SUD #	Done When SUD # is 0–2

Date:				Titled Specific Event:			
Starting SUD Scale	Rounds 1–2 Ending SUD #	Round 3 Ending SUD #	Round 4 Ending SUD #	Round 5 Ending SUD #	Round 6 Ending SUD #	Round 7 Ending SUD #	Done When SUD # is 0–2

Date:				Titled Specific Event:			
Starting SUD Scale	Rounds 1–2 Ending SUD #	Round 3 Ending SUD #	Round 4 Ending SUD #	Round 5 Ending SUD #	Round 6 Ending SUD #	Round 7 Ending SUD #	Done When SUD # is 0–2

Date:				Titled Specific Event:			
Starting SUD Scale	Rounds 1–2 Ending SUD #	Round 3 Ending SUD #	Round 4 Ending SUD #	Round 5 Ending SUD #	Round 6 Ending SUD #	Round 7 Ending SUD #	Done When SUD # is 0–2

Date:				Titled Specific Event:			
Starting SUD Scale	Rounds 1–2 Ending SUD #	Round 3 Ending SUD #	Round 4 Ending SUD #	Round 5 Ending SUD #	Round 6 Ending SUD #	Round 7 Ending SUD #	Done When SUD # is 0–2

Date:				Titled Specific Event:			
Starting SUD Scale	Rounds 1–2 Ending SUD #	Round 3 Ending SUD #	Round 4 Ending SUD #	Round 5 Ending SUD #	Round 6 Ending SUD #	Round 7 Ending SUD #	Done When SUD # is 0–2

Date:				Titled Specific Event:			
Starting SUD Scale	Rounds 1–2 Ending SUD #	Round 3 Ending SUD #	Round 4 Ending SUD #	Round 5 Ending SUD #	Round 6 Ending SUD #	Round 7 Ending SUD #	Done When SUD # is 0–2

Date:				Titled Specific Event:			
Starting SUD Scale	Rounds 1–2 Ending SUD #	Round 3 Ending SUD #	Round 4 Ending SUD #	Round 5 Ending SUD #	Round 6 Ending SUD #	Round 7 Ending SUD #	Done When SUD # is 0–2

<table>
<tr><td colspan="4">Date:</td><td colspan="4">Titled Specific Event:</td></tr>
<tr><td>Starting SUD Scale</td><td>Rounds 1–2 Ending SUD #</td><td>Round 3 Ending SUD #</td><td>Round 4 Ending SUD #</td><td>Round 5 Ending SUD #</td><td>Round 6 Ending SUD #</td><td>Round 7 Ending SUD #</td><td>Done When SUD # is 0–2</td></tr>
<tr><td></td><td></td><td></td><td></td><td></td><td></td><td></td><td></td></tr>
</table>

<table>
<tr><td colspan="4">Date:</td><td colspan="4">Titled Specific Event:</td></tr>
<tr><td>Starting SUD Scale</td><td>Rounds 1–2 Ending SUD #</td><td>Round 3 Ending SUD #</td><td>Round 4 Ending SUD #</td><td>Round 5 Ending SUD #</td><td>Round 6 Ending SUD #</td><td>Round 7 Ending SUD #</td><td>Done When SUD # is 0–2</td></tr>
<tr><td></td><td></td><td></td><td></td><td></td><td></td><td></td><td></td></tr>
</table>

<table>
<tr><td colspan="4">Date:</td><td colspan="4">Titled Specific Event:</td></tr>
<tr><td>Starting SUD Scale</td><td>Rounds 1–2 Ending SUD #</td><td>Round 3 Ending SUD #</td><td>Round 4 Ending SUD #</td><td>Round 5 Ending SUD #</td><td>Round 6 Ending SUD #</td><td>Round 7 Ending SUD #</td><td>Done When SUD # is 0–2</td></tr>
<tr><td></td><td></td><td></td><td></td><td></td><td></td><td></td><td></td></tr>
</table>

<table>
<tr><td colspan="4">Date:</td><td colspan="4">Titled Specific Event:</td></tr>
<tr><td>Starting SUD Scale</td><td>Rounds 1–2 Ending SUD #</td><td>Round 3 Ending SUD #</td><td>Round 4 Ending SUD #</td><td>Round 5 Ending SUD #</td><td>Round 6 Ending SUD #</td><td>Round 7 Ending SUD #</td><td>Done When SUD # is 0–2</td></tr>
<tr><td></td><td></td><td></td><td></td><td></td><td></td><td></td><td></td></tr>
</table>

<table>
<tr><td colspan="4">Date:</td><td colspan="4">Titled Specific Event:</td></tr>
<tr><td>Starting SUD Scale</td><td>Rounds 1–2 Ending SUD #</td><td>Round 3 Ending SUD #</td><td>Round 4 Ending SUD #</td><td>Round 5 Ending SUD #</td><td>Round 6 Ending SUD #</td><td>Round 7 Ending SUD #</td><td>Done When SUD # is 0–2</td></tr>
<tr><td></td><td></td><td></td><td></td><td></td><td></td><td></td><td></td></tr>
</table>

Date:				Titled Specific Event:			
Starting SUD Scale	Rounds 1–2 Ending SUD #	Round 3 Ending SUD #	Round 4 Ending SUD #	Round 5 Ending SUD #	Round 6 Ending SUD #	Round 7 Ending SUD #	Done When SUD # is 0–2

Date:				Titled Specific Event:			
Starting SUD Scale	Rounds 1–2 Ending SUD #	Round 3 Ending SUD #	Round 4 Ending SUD #	Round 5 Ending SUD #	Round 6 Ending SUD #	Round 7 Ending SUD #	Done When SUD # is 0–2

Date:				Titled Specific Event:			
Starting SUD Scale	Rounds 1–2 Ending SUD #	Round 3 Ending SUD #	Round 4 Ending SUD #	Round 5 Ending SUD #	Round 6 Ending SUD #	Round 7 Ending SUD #	Done When SUD # is 0–2

Date:				Titled Specific Event:			
Starting SUD Scale	Rounds 1–2 Ending SUD #	Round 3 Ending SUD #	Round 4 Ending SUD #	Round 5 Ending SUD #	Round 6 Ending SUD #	Round 7 Ending SUD #	Done When SUD # is 0–2

Date:				Titled Specific Event:			
Starting SUD Scale	Rounds 1–2 Ending SUD #	Round 3 Ending SUD #	Round 4 Ending SUD #	Round 5 Ending SUD #	Round 6 Ending SUD #	Round 7 Ending SUD #	Done When SUD # is 0–2

Date:				Titled Specific Event:			
Starting SUD Scale	Rounds 1–2 Ending SUD #	Round 3 Ending SUD #	Round 4 Ending SUD #	Round 5 Ending SUD #	Round 6 Ending SUD #	Round 7 Ending SUD #	Done When SUD # is 0–2

Date:				Titled Specific Event:			
Starting SUD Scale	Rounds 1–2 Ending SUD #	Round 3 Ending SUD #	Round 4 Ending SUD #	Round 5 Ending SUD #	Round 6 Ending SUD #	Round 7 Ending SUD #	Done When SUD # is 0–2

Date:				Titled Specific Event:			
Starting SUD Scale	Rounds 1–2 Ending SUD #	Round 3 Ending SUD #	Round 4 Ending SUD #	Round 5 Ending SUD #	Round 6 Ending SUD #	Round 7 Ending SUD #	Done When SUD # is 0–2

Date:				Titled Specific Event:			
Starting SUD Scale	Rounds 1–2 Ending SUD #	Round 3 Ending SUD #	Round 4 Ending SUD #	Round 5 Ending SUD #	Round 6 Ending SUD #	Round 7 Ending SUD #	Done When SUD # is 0–2

Date:				Titled Specific Event:			
Starting SUD Scale	Rounds 1–2 Ending SUD #	Round 3 Ending SUD #	Round 4 Ending SUD #	Round 5 Ending SUD #	Round 6 Ending SUD #	Round 7 Ending SUD #	Done When SUD # is 0–2

CHAPTER 19

Resistance to Using EFT

Case Study

Note: *Limiting Beliefs are italicized* and **Empowering Beliefs are in bold**.

Treatment for chronic Lyme/TBDs is a process of trial and error that can bring many disappointments when one treatment after another fails to produce the desired effect. As one letdown builds upon another, it forms a chain of disappointing events that creates and reinforces the *Limiting Belief* that *nothing is going to help me*. Over time, this becomes the subconscious filter through which you see and assess each new treatment strategy. On one hand, believing *nothing is going to help me* is a protective and understandable response against future disappointments. On the other hand, it is limiting in that it can close you off to seeking and trying new treatment strategies that could be helpful. Also, *believing that nothing is going to help me* can actually direct the mind-body system up to do just that, by not responding optimally to treatment (see Chapter 40 on page 391).

When you are already skeptical about trying something new, being open to something as seemingly strange as EFT is a real stretch! When introducing EFT for the first time to our clients, we often hear statements of resistance like: *This is silly. This is too weird. If people see me doing this, they're going to laugh at me. I look so stupid tapping! How can just tapping on my body help me when I've got so much going on?* We understand the resistance and doubts that come with uncertainty. Upon first glance, practicing EFT looks weird and doesn't seem like it would do much of anything at all, but as they say, looks can be deceiving.

EFT engages you mentally, emotionally, physically, and spiritually in a process of venting and releasing *Limiting Beliefs* and distressing emotions from your mind and body as you tap. And though it can feel strange at first, it becomes easier and more comfortable the more you do it (much like practicing yoga and **meditation**).

One way you might want to approach it is from what the Buddhists call "beginner's mind." This is a state of being open and curious about doing something only for the experience of it. Just for the moment, can you set aside any preconceived notions you may have about doing something new? Saying yes frees you to relax and just be open to seeing what happens. You always have the "Law of Two Feet": if something isn't serving you, you can walk away at any time and make a different choice. You are in charge!

We want to introduce you to Amber who made a choice to use EFT even though she initially resisted. Find out what happens!

Amber was a client whose many previous treatment failures had her believing that *"Nothing is going to help me"* and that the best way she protected herself from future disappointments was to avoid trying anything new. This is a natural response when your hopes are repeatedly dashed as you move from one treatment to another. Still, it can close the door to discovering new, potentially helpful possibilities. Amber's disappointment had nearly caused her to give up altogether on getting treatment for her Lyme disease. Even so, her remaining desire to get better, along with her husband's encouragement, was enough to persuade her to explore EFT. Here's her story:

Amber entered the office with an air of hesitation. She was simply but stylishly dressed and showed no outward signs of illness, as is so often the case for people who have Lyme/TBDs. Still, her pain was evident in the way she carried herself, the tears in her eyes, and the sadness in her voice.

"I came here today because my husband heard about EFT from one of the Lyme support groups and begged me to try it. I don't want to let him down, but I've tried just about everything a person can do to get better and nothing has worked**. My husband really believes doing this EFT thing could help me**, but *I just don't believe that's possible.* I am only trying it because he wants me to."

Amber acknowledged that she was also scared to get her hopes up about trying something new when everything else she had done did nothing to relieve her pain or help her to recover.

Amber was not entirely open to trying EFT, but she committed to completing one session for her husband's sake because he wanted her to find something that made her feel better. Amber tapped through three rounds on the Global Issue/ *Limiting Belief* that *"EFT won't work for me."* This led to other Specific Events that validated this *Limiting Belief* when she was disappointed by previous treatment outcomes. She tapped through to resolutions her deep disappointment and frustration.

As Amber completed a **Body Scan**, she noticed a significant reduction in the joint pain she came in with and expressed surprise: *"I really didn't believe this was going to work*, but now my pain is almost gone! **EFT does work for me!** This is the **first time in months that I have hope that I can feel better**. I am so glad my husband encouraged me to try EFT."

By allowing her husband's encouragement to try new things, Amber opened herself to the possibility that EFT could help her feel better. And it did! In this way, she empowered herself to use EFT on a daily basis to release her disappointment, to decrease joint pain that resulted from her emotional distress, and to cultivate hope for recovery.

Like Amber, you, too, can use EFT and the other self-help tools in the toolkit to process and release, not only the disappointment that comes with treatment failure, but also the related feelings of frustration, helplessness, and hopelessness that can undermine your recovery process. Resolving these emotional issues cultivates hope and fosters the persistence needed to recover from Lyme/TBDs.

If you have doubts that EFT and the other self-help tools and mindfulness-based techniques offered in this workbook will work for you, we encourage you to become aware of what you are resisting and then tap through to resolution. Yes, you can use EFT on your doubts about using EFT! This is because EFT works to help you uncover and release the *Limiting Beliefs* that are creating the resistance to trying something new. Clearing out common resistance to using EFT for the first time is an important first step.

If the information presented here resonates with you, we invite you to begin with the extended global tapping script that follows. This is a gentle way to get you started and to decrease your overall intensity. Even though the scripted Reminder Phrases may not be reflective of your personal Aspects, we invite you to just go with it, track your progress, and see what happens!

Global Issue Title: EFT Won't Work for Me!

- Focus your attention on this **Global Issue/Limiting Belief** (at times Global Issues and Limiting Beliefs are the same, see page 121).
- Take three slow, deep belly breaths as you do a **Body Scan** (see page 81).
- What **Aspects** (see page 123) do you notice?
- Using the **SUD scale** (see page 124), choose a number between 0 (no distress/peaceful) and 10 (highest intensity of distress) to **rate the intensity** of distress you feel about the **Global Issue/Limiting Belief**, along with only the **Aspects** (thoughts, feelings, body sensations, and visual image) that you notice that apply to you.

	Description	SUD #:
Global Issue	EFT won't work for me!	
Limiting Belief	EFT won't work for me!	
Thoughts		
Feelings		
Body Sensations		
Visual Image		

A WELLNESS
STATE OF MIND

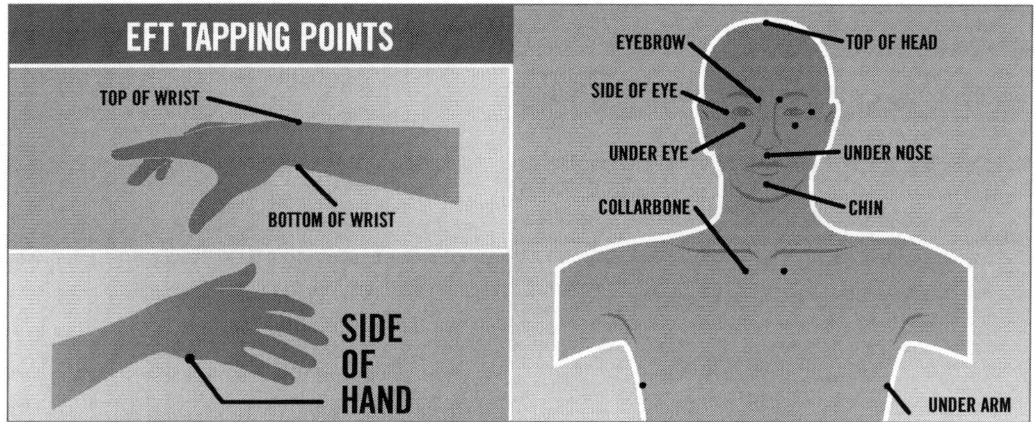

Extended Global Tapping Script: Let's begin tapping **(see page 126)**

Round 1

Setup:

Side of Hand: Even though this EFT isn't going to work for me, I honor all of my beliefs and feelings about this.

Side of Hand: Even though my problems are too long-standing and difficult for this EFT to work, I honor and accept myself.

Side of Hand: Even though EFT looks and sounds too silly, I'm willing to give it a try.

Top of Head: Nothing else worked; why should this?

Eyebrow: EFT isn't going to work for me.

Side of Eye: I don't trust that it's going to help me.

Under Eye: My issues are too deep and long-standing.

Under Nose: I have had so many treatment failures; why will this one be different?

Chin: EFT is too simple to work on my issues.

Collarbone: I am so frustrated trying things that don't work!

Under Arm: I don't want another disappointment.

Top of Wrists Together: This might work for others, but not for me.

Bottom of Wrists Together: Tapping just looks silly and stupid.

Slowly complete a deep belly breath and then keep tapping.

Round 2

Top of Head: Nothing else worked, why should this?

Eyebrow: I'm too frustrated to even try.

Side of Eye: I am tired of trying things that don't work.

Under Eye: EFT is too silly!

Under Nose: My family really wants me to give this a try.

Chin: How can EFT possibly work?

Collarbone: I have had my issues too long.

Under Arm: EFT might help other people, but not me.

Top of Wrists Together: How can something like this really work?

Bottom of Wrists Together: Nothing happens fast, I will be tapping forever.

Take three slow, deep belly breaths as you complete another **Body Scan**. What do you notice now? Note changes to the Aspects and any new ones that may appear below:

	Description	SUD #:
Global Issue	EFT won't work for me!	
Limiting Belief	EFT won't work for me!	
Thoughts		
Feelings		
Body Sensations		
Visual Image		

If your intensity level about this Global Issue/Limiting Belief, along with any of its Aspects, is still 3 or above on a SUD scale, continue tapping with the next round. (If you have a SUD scale of 0–2, skip down and finish by tapping through the positive statements and **Affirmations**.)

Round 3

Setup:

Side of Hand: Even though I still have doubts that EFT is going to help me, I am open to new possibilities.

Side of Hand: Even though treatments have not worked for me in the past, I honor and accept all of my feelings about this.

Side of Hand: Even though I still have a hard time believing EFT will work for me, I am open to using it.

Top of Head: I still have a hard time believing EFT will work for me.

Eyebrow: I hear that it helps others, but I still doubt it will help me.

Side of Eye: All of this remaining doubt.

Under Eye: All of this disappointment from the past.

Under Nose: Nothing that looks this silly can work.

Chin: I really do want to trust that it will work for me.

Collarbone: I will use EFT, but I am sure it is not going to work.

Under Arm: This remaining doubt.

Top of Wrists Together: I guess I don't have anything to lose.

Bottom of Wrists Together: This remaining fear of disappointment.

Take three slow, deep belly breaths as you complete another **Body Scan**. What do you notice now? Note changes to the Aspects and any new ones that may appear below:

	Description	SUD #:
Global Issue	EFT won't work for me!	
Limiting Belief	EFT won't work for me!	
Thoughts		
Feelings		
Body Sensations		
Visual Image		

If your intensity level about this Global Issue/Limiting Belief, along with any of its Aspects, is still 3 or above on a SUD scale, keep tapping through what is in your awareness or move down to **Follow These Steps to Resolution**.

Once you reach a SUD level of 0–2 or when you just want to stop tapping for now and return at a later time, finish up by tapping through the positive statements and **Afformations**.

Round 4 – Now let's tap through some positive statements!

Top of Head: I choose to be open to healing with EFT.
Eyebrow: I am open to trying something different.
Side of Eye: I haven't lost anything if this doesn't work.
Under Eye: It has helped others, so maybe it will help me.
Under Nose: I give myself permission to be open to EFT.
Chin: I've tried other new things and sometimes they do work.
Collarbone: I like that I can do this on myself.
Under Arm: I am open to healing.
Top of Wrists Together: I give myself permission to use EFT.
Bottom of Wrists Together: It is safe for me to take this risk. What do I have to lose?

Round 5 – Tapping with Afformations (see page 101)

Top of Head: Why is it so easy for me to be open to new ways to heal?

Eyebrow: Why is it possible for me to take this risk now?

Side of Eye: Why am I able to do something for my own healing?

Under Eye: Why is it possible for me to help myself with EFT?

Under Nose: Why is it so easy for me to trust the decisions I make?

Chin: Why is it so easy for me to learn new things?

Collarbone: Why is it so easy for me to be willing to take the necessary risks to change and follow my heart's desire?

Under Arm: How is it so easy for me to overcome my fears?

Top of Wrists Together: Why is it so easy for me to be making personal changes for the better?

Bottom of Wrists Together: Why is it possible for EFT to work for me?

Take three slow, deep belly breaths as you complete another **Body Scan**. What do you notice now? Note changes to the Aspects and any new ones that may appear below:

	Description	SUD #:
Global Issue	EFT won't work for me!	
Limiting Belief	EFT won't work for me!	
Thoughts		
Feelings		
Body Sensations		
Visual Image		

If your intensity level about this Global Issue/Limiting Belief, along with any of its Aspects, is still 3 or above on a SUD scale, you need to explore them more in depth and follow the directives in **Follow These Steps to Resolution**, on the following page.

Exercise: Developing Self-Awareness

Describe your experience of tapping through this Global Issue/Limiting Belief.

Which Aspects resolved, decreased, increased, or stayed the same?

In the identified Limiting Belief, state what (if anything) changed or any new ones that emerged.

State any Empowering Beliefs (see page 119) that you notice now.

What Global Issues/Limiting Beliefs need to be resolved (if any)?

Follow These Steps to Resolution

- When you have the time and energy, move on to the next exercise, **Going Deeper with EFT.** Use this to help you identify Specific Events, along with their Aspects, that are contributing to not resolving this Global Issue/Limiting Belief or on any new ones that may have surfaced while tapping. You may identify many, and this is to be expected.
- Just break down one Specific Event at a time and tap it until resolution. Title the rest of the Specific Events that you have identified and add them to the **List of Titled Specific Events** on page 156 so you can return to them at a later time to tap. You can use the **Blank Tapping Script** on page 404 or the **Vent While You Tap** worksheet on page 409 to assist you while tapping through a Specific Event.

Exercise: Going Deeper with EFT

If you just completed tapping through the extended global tapping script, and you still feel that the issue is unresolved, it's time to go deeper. What is keeping it unresolved? Title your Global Issue in the space provided below. Answer the following questions so that you can discover, uncover, and recover from the unresolved Specific Events and related Aspects that created and support the Limiting Belief you wish to resolve.

Global Issue: ______________________________

1. What Limiting Beliefs do you have at the root of this Global Issue? Rate the level of intensity of how true they are for you between SUD 0 (not true at all) and 10 (completely true).

______________________________ • SUD # (0–10): ____

______________________________ • SUD # (0–10): ____

2. Title and list the Specific Events in which you learned the Limiting Belief(s) (you can also add them to your List of Titled Specific Events on page 156).

____

____

____

____

____

____

3. Choose one Specific Event to break down here. Title: ______________________________

____

4. Tune into your titled Specific Event and identify only those Aspects that apply to you, below:

What thoughts do you notice?

______________________________ • SUD # (0–10): ____

______________________________ • SUD # (0–10): ____

Do your thoughts have the quality of Small Mind or Large Mind (see page 90)?______________

Describe your Large Mind thoughts (if any):________________________

____

Describe your Small Mind thoughts (if any): ________________________

____

What emotions are you feeling?

__________________________________ • SUD # (0–10): ____

__________________________________ • SUD # (0–10): ____

__________________________________ • SUD # (0–10): ____

What body sensation do you notice?

__________________________________ • SUD # (0–10): ____

Where is the sensation located?__________________ • SUD # (0–10): ____

Does this sensation have a temperature?____ Describe:__________________

__________________________________ • SUD # (0–10): ____

Texture?______________________________ • SUD # (0–10): ____

Color?______________________________ • SUD # (0–10): ____

Describe a visual image that you have (if any): ________________________

__________________________________ • SUD # (0–10): ____

5. Use the Aspects you have just identified to create your Reminder Phrases.
6. Stay tuned into your titled Specific Event.
7. Start tapping using the Modified EFT Basic Recipe on page 121. You can use the Aspects you have identified here to fill in the Reminder Phrases on the **Blank Tapping Script** on page 404 or the **Vent While You Tap** worksheet on page 409 to assist you in creating your own tapping script.

REPEAT PROCESS IF UNRESOLVED

Be aware of any changes in the intensity of distress you feel in relation to the Aspects, along with any new ones that emerge as you tap through the Rounds of EFT. Continue to tap, repeating the EFT Basic Recipe until your Specific Event, along with its Aspects, is resolved at a SUD level of 0–2. Also be mindful of shifts in Limiting Beliefs and the emergence of any new Empowering ones. To get full resolution of a Global Issue, the Limiting Beliefs must be released by resolving other painful Specific Events that are validating them.

CHAPTER

20 I Feel Overwhelmed by All These Changes and Losses!

Global Issue Title: I Feel Overwhelmed By All of These Changes and Losses

This extended global tapping script was written to address any overwhelming feelings that may have surfaced when completing the **Lyme/TBDs-Related Change/Loss Inventory** on page 57. If you have not done so already, we invite you to go back and fill out this inventory. If any feelings overwhelm you, this is a great place to start by using this extended global tapping script to process them.

- Focus your attention on this **Global Issue** (see page 119).
- Identify one **Limiting Belief** (see page 119) that may be at the root of this Global Issue.
- Take three slow, deep belly breaths as you do a **Body Scan** (see page 81).
- What **Aspects** (see page 123) do you notice?
- Using the **SUD scale** (see page 124), choose a number between 0 (no distress/peaceful) and 10 (highest intensity of distress) to **rate the intensity** of distress you feel about the **Global Issue and Limiting Belief**, along with only the **Aspects** (thoughts, feelings, body sensations, and visual image) that you notice that apply to you.

	Description	SUD #:
Global Issue	I Feel Overwhelmed by All of These Changes and Losses	
Limiting Belief		
Thoughts		

Feelings		
Body Sensations		
Visual Image		

Extended Global Tapping Script: Let's begin tapping (see page 126)

Round 1

Setup:

Side of Hand: Even though I am overwhelmed by so many Lyme/TBD related changes and losses, I accept that's where I am right now!

Side of Hand: Even though I'll never be the same, that's how I feel right now.

Side of Hand: Even though my life is turned upside down with all these changes, I honor and accept myself.

Top of Head: I am overwhelmed when I think about all I've lost!

Eyebrow: I can't imagine recovering from all these changes and losses!

Side of Eye: This is just too much!

Under Eye: I've lost my whole way of living!

Under Nose: Everything in my life has changed!

Chin: I can't do the things that came naturally before.

Collarbone: I've lost so many of my friends. They just don't understand.

Under Arm: I can't even eat the foods I like!

Top of Wrists Together: My whole body is different!

Bottom of Wrists Together: Lyme has taken away the life I had!

Slowly complete a deep belly breath and then keep tapping.

Round 2

Top of Head: There are too many changes and losses.

Eyebrow: I'll never get my life back.

Side of Eye: I've lost so much of myself.

Under Eye: Nothing is the way it was.

Under Nose: It is just so overwhelming!

Chin: I've always had difficulty dealing with change.

Collarbone: I feel so overwhelmed!

Under Arm: I miss the life I had.

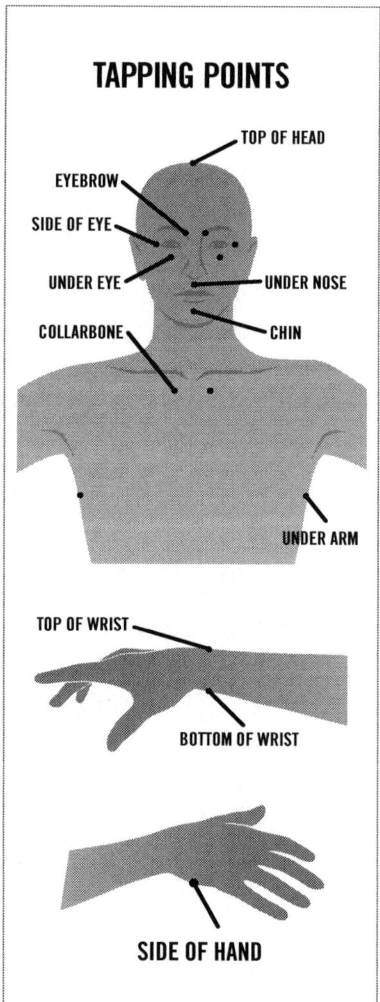

Top of Wrists Together: All these changes make life so hard.

Bottom of Wrists Together: All these losses make life so difficult.

Take three slow, deep belly breaths as you complete another **Body Scan**. What do you notice now? Note changes to the Aspects and any new ones that may appear below:

Aspects	Description of Aspects	SUD #:
Global Issue	I Feel Overwhelmed by All of These Changes and Losses	
Limiting Belief		
Thoughts		
Feelings		
Body Sensations		
Visual Image		

If your intensity level about this Global Issue, along with any of its Aspects, is still 3 or above on a SUD scale, continue tapping with the next round. (If you have a SUD scale of 0–2, skip down and finish by tapping through the positive statements and **Afformations**.)

Round 3

Setup:

Side of Hand: Even though I still feel overwhelmed, I honor and accept myself.

Side of Hand: Even though I still have difficulty dealing with loss, I honor all of my feelings.

Side of Hand: Even though I continue to feel overwhelmed, I am doing the best that I can where I am.

Top of Head: I still feel overwhelmed by all of the changes and losses I've gone through.

Eyebrow: I don't believe I will ever get used to all of these changes.

Side of Eye: I am still overwhelmed!

Under Eye: I have never seen the whole picture of all that I have been through.

Under Nose: This is overwhelming!

Chin: I still miss the life I had before I got sick with Lyme/TBDs.

Collarbone: Change will always be hard for me.

Under Arm: I've had one loss after another.

Top of Wrists Together: I now see where I can focus my healing.

Bottom of Wrists Together: I am stronger than I thought I was.

Take three slow, deep belly breaths as you complete another **Body Scan**. What do you notice now? Note changes to the Aspects and any new ones that may appear below:

Aspects	Description of Aspects	SUD #:
Global Issue	I Feel Overwhelmed By All of These Changes and Losses	
Limiting Belief		
Thoughts		
Feelings		
Body Sensations		
Visual Image		

If your intensity level about this Global Issue, along with any of its Aspects, is still 3 or above on a SUD scale, keep tapping through what is in your awareness or move down to **Follow These Steps to Resolution.**

Once you reach a SUD level of 0–2 or when you just want to stop tapping for now and return at a later time, finish up by tapping through the positive statements and **Afformations**.

Round 4 – Now let's tap through some positive statements!

Top of Head: Change is always happening.

Eyebrow: I just never thought about change before.

Side of Eye: This tapping helps me see the whole picture.

Under Eye: I have more empathy for myself now.

Under Nose: Maybe my husband/wife/partner/friend will better understand why I've had such a hard time.

Chin: I now realize why our relationship has been so hard.

Collarbone: It is hard to see all these changes, but now I understand.

Under Arm: I see the bigger picture now.

Top of Wrists Together: I can heal through these changes and losses.

Bottom of Wrists Together: I honor all the experiences I've had and how well I've coped.

Round 5 – Tapping with Afformations (see page 101)

Top of Head: How is it possible for me to change and heal?
Eyebrow: Why is change easier than I thought?
Side of Eye: Why is it easy for me to see the whole picture now?
Under Eye: Why am I able to accept my losses?
Under Nose: Why is it possible to acknowledge how well I've adapted?
Chin: Why is it easy for me to smile when I notice a positive change?
Collarbone: Why is it so easy for me to accept where I am right now?
Under Arm: Why is it possible for me to feel gratitude for what I have?
Top of Wrists Together: Why is it possible for me to change and grow?
Bottom of Wrists Together: Why is it okay for me to focus on positive changes?

Take three slow, deep belly breaths as you complete another **Body Scan**. What do you notice now? Note changes to the Aspects and any new ones that may appear below:

Aspects	Description of Aspects	SUD #:
Global Issue	I Feel Overwhelmed by All of These Changes and Losses	
Limiting Belief		
Thoughts		
Feelings		
Body Sensations		
Visual Image		

If your intensity level about this Global Issue, along with any of its Aspects, is still 3 or above on a SUD scale, you need to explore them more in depth and follow the directives in **Follow These Steps to Resolution**, on the following page.

Exercise: Developing Self-Awareness

Describe your experience of tapping through this Global Issue.

Which Aspects resolved, decreased, increased, or stayed the same?

If you identified a Limiting Belief, state what (if anything) changed.

State any Empowering Beliefs (see page 119) that you notice now.

What Global Issues/Limiting Beliefs need to be resolved (if any)?

Follow These Steps to Resolution

- When you have the time and energy, move on to the next exercise, **Going Deeper with EFT.** Use this to help you identify Specific Events, along with their Aspects, that are contributing to not resolving this Global Issue/Limiting Belief or with any new ones that may have surfaced while tapping. You may identify many and this is to be expected.
- Just break down one Specific Event at a time and tap it until resolved. Title the rest of the Specific Events that you have identified and add them to the **List of Titled Specific Events** on page 156 so that you can return to them at a later time to tap. You can use the **Blank Tapping Script** on page 404 or the **Vent While You Tap** worksheet on page 409 to assist you while tapping through a Specific Event.

Exercise: Going Deeper with EFT

If you just completed tapping through the extended global tapping script, and you still feel that the issue is unresolved, it's time to go deeper. What is keeping it unresolved? Title your Global Issue in the space provided below. Answer the following questions so that you can discover, uncover, and recover from the unresolved Specific Events and related Aspects that created and support the Limiting Belief you wish to resolve.

Global Issue: ____________________

1. What Limiting Beliefs do you have at the root of this Global Issue? Rate the level of intensity of how true they are for you between SUD 0 (not true at all) and 10 (completely true).

____________________ • SUD # (0–10): ____

____________________ • SUD # (0–10): ____

2. Title and list the Specific Events in which you learned the Limiting Belief(s) (you can also add them to your List of Titled Specific Events on page 156).

____

____

____

____

____

____

3. Choose one Specific Event to break down here. Title: ____________________

____

4. Tune into your titled Specific Event and identify only those Aspects that apply to you, below:

What thoughts do you notice?

____________________ • SUD # (0–10): ____

____________________ • SUD # (0–10): ____

Do your thoughts have the quality of Small Mind or Large Mind (see page 90)?____________

Describe your Large Mind thoughts (if any):______________________________

____

Describe your Small Mind thoughts (if any): ______________________________

____

What emotions are you feeling?

____ • SUD # (0–10): ____

____ • SUD # (0–10): ____

____ • SUD # (0–10): ____

What body sensation do you notice?

____ • SUD # (0–10): ____

Where is the sensation located?__________________________ • SUD # (0–10): ____

Does this sensation have a temperature?____ Describe:________________________

____ • SUD # (0–10): ____

Texture?______________________________________ • SUD # (0–10): ____

Color?____ • SUD # (0–10): ____

Describe a visual image that you have (if any): ___________________________

____ • SUD # (0–10): ____

5. Use the Aspects you have just identified to create your Reminder Phrases.
6. Stay tuned into your titled Specific Event.
7. Start tapping using the Modified EFT Basic Recipe on page 121. You can use the Aspects you have identified here to fill in the Reminder Phrases on the **Blank Tapping Script** on page 404 or the **Vent While You Tap** worksheet on page 409 to assist you in creating your own tapping script.

REPEAT PROCESS IF UNRESOLVED

Be aware of any changes in the intensity of distress you feel in relation to the Aspects, along with any new ones that emerge as you tap through the Rounds of EFT. Continue to tap, repeating the EFT Basic Recipe until your Specific Event, along with its Aspects, is resolved at a SUD level of 0–2. Also be mindful of shifts in Limiting Beliefs and the emergence of any new Empowering ones. To get full resolution of a Global Issue, the Limiting Beliefs must be released by resolving other painful Specific Events that are validating them.

CHAPTER 21

I'm So Angry!

Case Study

Note: *Limiting Beliefs are italicized* and **Empowering Beliefs are in bold**.

June was a married 43-year-old woman with three school-aged children and a full-time secretarial job. After several months of remission, her Lyme symptoms returned, making it difficult for her to manage the demands of work and family. She found herself becoming increasingly angry and unable to manage her emotions. Feeling desperate, June decided to reach out for help and give EFT a try.

June entered the office with a slight limp and a stiff expression on her face. She sat down with a groan and said, "I'm not even sure why I bothered coming in. After three years of having this damn illness, I thought I was finally getting better. Now all of my symptoms are back and I feel even worse than I did before! Everything I've done has failed. I'm so angry all the time that my husband and kids don't even want to be in the same room with me. And when I'm not lashing out at them, I'm either sitting alone crying or getting up at night and raiding the refrigerator. I don't know what to do! I feel terrible about the way I have treated my family. That's not how I was taught to be, but *I can't seem to control my anger anymore*. I hate what Lyme has done to me! It is like Lyme has taken over my entire life and *I can't do anything to change it*."

During therapy June shared that when she was a little girl her parents taught her that it was not acceptable for her to show anger. Her mother would tell her, "*It is not proper for little girls to be angry*," and her father would punish her if she raised her voice or expressed her anger in some other way. June learned then that *anger is "bad" and that it is not safe to express it*. Still, her anger needed to be processed, so she learned to turn it in on herself through self-blame, negative self-talk, and emotional eating—a pattern of behavior that greatly diminished her self-esteem. June continued this pattern into her adulthood, but when faced with Lyme and the unpredictable return of symptoms, she was no longer able to contain her anger.

June noticed that her anger seemed to intensify during active episodes of Lyme disease and that it was during those periods when she would lash out at her husband and kids. She felt terribly guilty in the aftermath of her outbursts, yet unable to control them. "This is not how I was raised. *There is just no way for me to express how I feel!*"

Without knowing it, June was directing all of her unprocessed anger in relation to Lyme disease at her husband and kids. At the same time, her anger and all of the distress it caused only served to create more frequent and intense Lyme-related headaches, sleep disturbance, inflammation, and migrating pain.

As June learned in therapy, the presence of unprocessed anger can trigger an active episode of Lyme/TBDs. The emotional stressors of daily life can then intensify that anger. A vicious cycle can develop in which stressful life events trigger intense emotional responses, which in turn, can activate an episode of Lyme/TBDs-related symptoms that increase and intensify with continued emotional distress. It is also the case that the neurological impact of Lyme/TBDs alone can create states of anger and even rage that make day-to-day life events even more stressful. Either way, *Limiting Beliefs* that are supported by unprocessed anger from the past can be triggered by current life events, greatly increasing one's level of emotional distress.

Using EFT allowed June to realize that while repressing her anger helped her to survive the emotional pain of her childhood, it was now impeding her potential for healing and recovering from Lyme disease. With continued support and tapping throughout the months, June was able to resolve her *Limiting Beliefs* about anger. Processing and releasing long-held anger from the past made it easier for her to let go of her present anger about the impact of Lyme on her life. "I feel so much better now," she said. "Before, I was just so hurt and angry. *I really didn't believe there was anything I could do to help myself* and I was taking it all out on my family. I stuffed a lot of anger inside and tapping through the *Limiting Beliefs* and Specific Events that created it helped me to let it go."

After tapping, I feel more relaxed and calm. There are even times when I'm actually pain free. Before I started tapping, I just believed *there was no way for me to express how I felt.* Now, I know that **it's okay for me to feel and express my anger."**

June also reported that practicing EFT opened her to sharing more with her family and allowing them to support her on those days that were most difficult for her. June's experience with EFT showed her that it was possible for her to confront and work through her emotional pain in a way that transformed her entire perspective from one based in fear, *Limiting Beliefs*, to one grounded in **Empowering Beliefs** that foster forgiveness, self-acceptance, trust, and love—the very foundation of a wellness state of mind.

Exercise: Self-Reflection on Anger

In preparation for tapping, allow the following questions to lead you into a deeper awareness of how you experience and express anger. If you notice anything about your experience of anger that you would like to resolve, change, and/or enhance, use EFT on those things.

What types of people, situations, and events trigger your anger?

____

____

What are you angry about right now? (Just the facts.)

____

____

What interpretation or story are you telling yourself about those facts that are making you angry? (Take ownership of your anger.)

____

____

____

Exercise: Explore Your Anger Communication Style

Everyone communicates anger in a different way. The following is a detailed description of the three most common ways people communicate anger. We encourage you to take a moment now to read through the "Anger Communication Styles" and identify any traits that pertain to you.

Anger Communication Styles			
	Passive*	**Aggressive**	**Assertive**
Traits	*Taking a backseat (fear of confrontation):* • Avoidance • Self-denial • Repressing feelings • Withholding love • Blaming • Complaining • Getting even	*Taking over (fear of vulnerability):* • Controlling • Blaming • Yelling • Criticizing • Threatening • Becoming violent	*Taking responsibility for self (trust and respect):* • Acknowledges and accepts anger • Is nonjudgmental • Clearly and specifically states needs/desires • Uses "I" statements • Listens • Seeks positive solutions
Impact on You	• Anxiety • Resentment • Helplessness • Distrust • Increased stress • Lowers self-esteem	• Distrust • Tension • Increased stress • Potential shame • Potential guilt • Lowers self-esteem	• Empowerment • Confidence • Increased self-esteem • Increased trust in self and openness to others
Impact on Others	• Hurt • Frustration • Confusion • Lack of trust • Feel disrespected • Anger	• Fear • Resentment • Distrust • Humiliation • Hurt • Anger	• Feel respected • Increased trust and connection • Clear understanding of where you stand
Results	• Others may be compelled to make decisions without you. • Others may get their needs/desires met at your expense. • You may feel left out and used.	• Harm to self/others • Others fear you • Others resent you • Destabilizes relationships • Potential abandonment • Decreases the likelihood of others caring or responding	• Acceptance of self and others • Goals achieved with honesty and empathy • Strengthened relationships • Increased likelihood of deeper connection and understanding
Beliefs	*Limiting Beliefs* • It's not safe to be angry. • People won't like me if I get angry. • I'm not allowed to get angry.	*Limiting Beliefs* • I have to yell to be heard. • I have to look out for myself. • I have to fight for what I want. • I have to protect myself with my anger.	**Empowering Beliefs** • I take responsibility for my anger. • I have every reason to feel the way I do. • I can express my anger in productive ways out of respect for myself and others. • I accept my feelings and the feelings of others.

**A combination of passive and aggressive styles may manifest itself depending on your level of stress.*

List the traits (from the table on the previous page) of your identified anger communication style:

What is the impact on you?

What is the impact on others?

What are the results you experience?

What beliefs did you identify about anger?

The Value of Developing Emotional Regulation

How self-aware are you of your inner experience of frustration that, when not productively acknowledged, processed, and expressed, could continue to escalate into severe anger and rage?

SUD scale:	0–2	3	5	7	10
		Mild Frustration	Mild Anger	Moderate Anger	Severe Anger/Rage
				RED ZONE	

Some people with unresolved trauma, neuropsychiatric symptoms of Lyme/TBDs, and/or Limiting Beliefs about feeling/expressing anger can lack skills in emotional regulation. An example of this is when a person can very easily feel no anger (SUD scale of 0) in one moment and, in what seems like a few seconds, be triggered and escalate to the RED ZONE of severe anger/rage.

The **RED ZONE** is what we call a mind-state in which you can experience overwhelming emotions, thus interfering with your perception in a way that can increase the possibility of:

- Acting impulsively by responding with aggressive behaviors
- Lacking awareness of the consequences of expressing anger aggressively
- Saying and doing things that could hurt yourself or others
- Triggering the mind-body fear/stress responses: fight, flight, or freeze
- Increasing the intensity of the stress response, thus interfering with your body's innate ability to heal

To cultivate skills in emotional regulation, it is helpful to learn and practice the mindfulness-based techniques in Part 3 to become more aware of how you are feeling in the moment. The earlier you can notice how you are feeling while at a lower SUD scale intensity, the more likely you can make a choice to take proactive action to interrupt and prevent your emotions from escalating. You can use the skills of the observer to assist you in emotional regulation by asking yourself, **What is happening?** and **How am I relating to it?** (Turn to page 90 to learn more about the observer.)

These two mindfulness-based questions can help create a pause in your thinking that allow you to check in with yourself about how you are feeling and at what intensity. By becoming self-aware in this "pause," no matter where you are on the SUD scale, you can then make a *choice* in how to help yourself decrease your emotional intensity before responding outwardly to others. (Turn to page 84 to review the "**Stop-Drop-Breathe**" exercise and to page 90 to interrupt Small Mind thinking and reframe it to **Large Mind**.)

By decreasing your emotional intensity first, it will increase the likelihood of expressing yourself in ways that are based on your needs (see page 410). For some people, it can be challenging at first to learn and develop skills in emotional regulation. This is to be expected. We strongly suggest making a daily practice of using the mindfulness-based tools offered in this workbook along with EFT to increase your skills.

Exercise: Developing Self-Awareness Throughout the SUD Scale of Anger

We encourage you now to take some time to become even more aware of how you experience anger throughout the SUD scale rating by answering the directives and questions below. Becoming aware will empower you to see more quickly where you are and where you want to go (increase or decrease intensity).

SUD scale:	0–2	3	5	7	10
		Mild Frustration	Mild Anger	Moderate Anger	Severe Anger/Rage
				RED ZONE	

Describe in detail how you experience **Mild Frustration** on a SUD scale of 3.

In your body?____

____

Where do you hold it/feel it?________________________________

____

What does it feel like? Texture, temperature, color?____________________

____

What signs do you notice that let you know you are feeling **Mild Frustration** with a SUD of 3?

____

Describe in detail how you experience **Mild Anger** on a SUD scale of 5.

In your body?____

____

Where do you hold it/feel it?________________________________

____

What does it feel like? Texture, temperature, color?____________________

____

What signs do you notice that let you know you are feeling **Mild Anger** with a SUD of 5?

____

Describe in detail how you experience **Moderate Anger** on a SUD scale of 7.

In your body?____

____

Where do you hold it/feel it?__________________________________

____

What does it feel like? Texture, temperature, color?____________________

____

What signs do you notice that let you know you are feeling **Moderate Anger** with a SUD of 7?

____

Describe in detail how you experience **Severe Anger/Rage** on a SUD scale of 10.

In your body?____

____

Where do you hold it/feel it?__________________________________

____

What does it feel like? Texture, temperature, color?____________________

____

What signs do you notice that let you know you are feeling **Severe Anger/Rage** with a SUD of 10?

____

Additional Reflection Questions

What messages did you receive as a child about expressing anger?

____

____

____

What Limiting Beliefs are you aware of, if any, about feeling and/or expressing anger?

____

____

We suggest that you take a moment now to make a list of the Specific Events that taught you the Limiting Beliefs you may have about expressing anger that lead to nonproductive ways of coping and expressing this emotion. You may find that there are many events, but don't panic! Though it will be necessary to tap through as many events as it takes to resolve the issue, you don't have to tap through every single event you have identified. Thanks to the Generalization Effect (see page 139), you only need to resolve enough of the Specific Events to release the Limiting Beliefs holding you back.

You can add them to the **List of Titled Specific Events** on page 156 or title them and write them down here to tap on at a later time.

Specific Event: ____

Specific Event: ____

Specific Event: ____

Specific Event: ____

Vent While You Tap

EFT becomes more effective when you are tuned into your feelings. The more intense you feel while tapping, the more effective EFT is, ONLY if kept within an emotionally safe range (SUD less than 7). This is key! We invite you to tune in to your anger and give it a voice while you tap. Go ahead! Vent within the level of your comfort and safety. Choose a private and safe place (to avoid upsetting others) where you can even yell as you tap. Yelling or speaking loudly supports the release of deeper stuffed anger and its intensity.

Try it! It is very liberating! And remember to keep tapping through the anger.

You can choose to tap through your current anger or Specific Events related to past unresolved anger. If you choose to tap through your current anger only and still feel as though it is not resolved, this is not because EFT did not work. It may be that the present situation has triggered some unresolved anger from the past. Targeting those past Specific Events with more rounds of EFT will help you to process and clear them so that you can feel a greater sense of resolution.

It is important to be persistent and keep tapping until you feel an emotional release, decrease in intensity to a SUD scale of 0–2, and a **Large Mind** change in perception.

If the information presented here resonates with you, we invite you to begin with the extended global tapping script that follows. This is a gentle way to get you started and to decrease your overall intensity. Even though the scripted Reminder Phrases may not be reflective of your personal Aspects, we invite you to just go with it, track your progress, and see what happens!

Global Issue Title: I'm So Angry!

- Focus your attention on this **Global Issue** (see page 119).
- Identify one **Limiting Belief** (see page 119) that may be at the root of this Global Issue.
- Take three slow, deep belly breaths as you do a **Body Scan** (see page 81).
- What **Aspects** (see page 123) do you notice?
- Using the **SUD scale** (see page 124), choose a number between 0 (no distress/peaceful) and 10 (highest intensity of distress) to **rate the intensity** of distress you feel about the **Global Issue and Limiting Belief**, along with only the **Aspects** (thoughts, feelings, body sensations, and visual image) that you notice that apply to you.

	Description	SUD #:
Global Issue	I'm so angry!	
Limiting Belief		
Thoughts		
Feelings		
Body Sensations		
Visual Image		

If you believe that expressing your anger can lead you to being unsafe with yourself and/or others, do not use EFT alone. We strongly encourage you to seek out a certified EFT practitioner to determine if EFT is an appropriate and safe strategy for you to use. When you are ready, the practitioner can safely guide you through the EFT process.

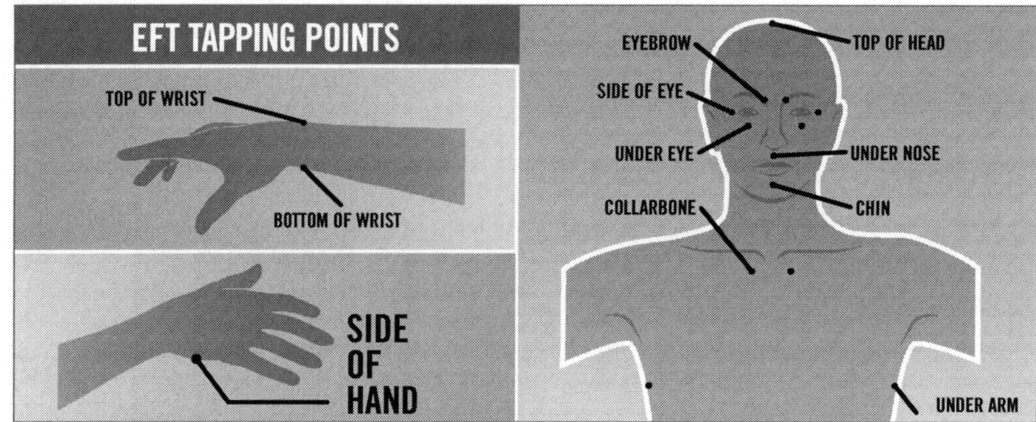

Extended Global Tapping Script: Let's begin tapping (see page 126)

Round 1

Setup:

Side of Hand: Even though I am really angry that my symptoms are back, I honor and respect my body.

Side of Hand: Even though I am lashing out at others in my anger, I am open to learning new ways.

Side of Hand: Even though my anger feels out of control, I honor and accept my feelings.

Top of Head: I am so angry that I still have Lyme disease!

Eyebrow: I am angry that I can't do what I used to do!

Side of Eye: I hurt others when I express my anger.

Under Eye: I am so angry for having (name your Lyme/TBD symptoms).

Under Nose: I am so angry at how unpredictable my life is.

Chin: I need to stuff my anger.

Collarbone: I am so angry that my life is controlled by Lyme disease!

Under Arm: I am so angry that I have had this so long and it doesn't seem to change!

Top of Wrists Together: I am so angry that I feel out of control!

Bottom of Wrists Together: I am so angry about how I've had to change my life!

Slowly complete a deep belly breath and then keep tapping.

Round 2

Top of Head: I am so angry that my life is out of my control!

Eyebrow: I feel so angry that life isn't the way I want it to be!

Side of Eye: I feel so angry that Lyme disease interferes with my family life!

Under Eye: I feel so angry at how my pain restricts my life!

Under Nose: I am expressing my anger in harmful ways.

Chin: I am angry with the bacteria for attacking my body!

Collarbone: My family doesn't deserve this!

Under Arm: I am so angry that I can't take care of my family the way I used to!

Top of Wrists Together: I feel so angry!

Bottom of Wrists Together: My life has changed because of Lyme/TBDs, and I am angry about that!

Take three slow, deep belly breaths as you complete another **Body Scan**. What do you notice now? Note changes to the Aspects and any new ones that may appear below:

Aspects	Description of Aspects	SUD #:
Global Issue	I'm so angry!	
Limiting Belief		
Thoughts		
Feelings		
Body Sensations		
Visual Image		

If your intensity level about this Global Issue, along with any of its Aspects, is still 3 or above on a SUD scale, continue tapping with the next round. (If you have a SUD scale of 0–2, skip down and finish by tapping through the positive statements and **Afformations**.)

Round 3

Setup:

Side of Hand: Even though I still feel angry, I accept all of my feelings.

Side of Hand: Even though I am still angry, I honor and accept myself.

Side of Hand: Even though there is still anger left, I am open to new possibilities.

Top of Head: This remaining anger.

Eyebrow: I don't know if my anger will ever fully go away.

Side of Eye: I might be angry forever.

Under Eye: Why is this happening to me?

Under Nose: I don't like how my life has changed!

Chin: I still don't feel safe expressing my anger. It's still unsafe for me to express my anger.

Collarbone: It's not fair!

Under Arm: All of this remaining anger.

Top of Wrists Together: My anger is no longer controlling me.

Bottom of Wrists Together: All of this anger that is still in my body has permission to leave now.

Take three slow, deep belly breaths as you complete another **Body Scan**. What do you notice now? Note changes to the Aspects and any new ones that may appear below:

Aspects	Description of Aspects	SUD #:
Global Issue	I'm so angry!	
Limiting Belief		
Thoughts		
Feelings		
Body Sensations		
Visual Image		

If your intensity level about this Global Issue, along with any of its Aspects, is still 3 or above on a SUD scale, keep tapping through what is in your awareness or move down to **Follow These Steps to Resolution**.

Once you reach a SUD level of 0–2 or when you just want to stop tapping for now and return at a later time, finish up by tapping through the positive statements and **Affornations**.

Round 4 – Now let's tap through some positive statements!

Top of Head: I honor all of my feelings.
Eyebrow: I give myself permission to feel angry.
Side of Eye: It is safe for me to feel anger.
Under Eye: I am no longer afraid of my anger.
Under Nose: I honor my anger.
Chin: I am able to move through my anger in constructive ways.
Collarbone: I am open to new possibilities for healing.
Under Arm: I invite myself to a new healing relationship with anger.
Top of Wrists Together: It is safe for me to be vulnerable.
Bottom of Wrists Together: I allow myself to process and release my anger in healthy ways.

Round 5 – Tapping with Afformations (see page 101)

Top of Head: Why is it safe for me to let go of my anger?

Eyebrow: Why is it acceptable for me to feel anger?

Side of Eye: Why is it easy for me to accept where I am right now?

Under Eye: How is it possible for me to listen to my anger and allow it to guide me to healing?

Under Nose: Why am I able to remain vulnerable and have courage?

Chin: Why is it easy for me to let go of what I can't control?

Collarbone: Why am I able to be with what is?

Under Arm: Why is it possible for me to be emotionally flexible and go with the flow in how I am feeling?

Top of Wrists Together: Why am I able to deeply accept how I feel?

Bottom of Wrists Together: Why is it easy for me to honor and accept all of my feelings?

Take three slow, deep belly breaths as you complete another **Body Scan**. What do you notice now? Note changes to the Aspects and any new ones that may appear below:

Aspects	Description of Aspects	SUD #:
Global Issue	I'm so angry!	
Limiting Belief		
Thoughts		
Feelings		
Body Sensations		
Visual Image		

If your intensity level about this Global Issue, along with any of its Aspects, is still 3 or above on a SUD scale, you need to explore them more in depth and follow the directives in **Follow These Steps to Resolution**, on the following page.

Exercise: Developing Self-Awareness

Describe your experience of tapping through this Global Issue.

Which Aspects resolved, decreased, increased, or stayed the same?

If you identified a Limiting Belief, state what (if anything) changed.

State any Empowering Beliefs (see page 119) that you notice now.

What Global Issues/Limiting Beliefs need to be resolved (if any)?

Follow These Steps to Resolution

- When you have the time and energy, move on to the next exercise, **Going Deeper with EFT.** Use this to help you identify Specific Events, along with their Aspects, that are contributing to not resolving this Global Issue/Limiting Belief or with any new ones that may have surfaced while tapping. You may identify many and this is to be expected.
- Just break down one Specific Event at a time and tap it until resolved. Title the rest of the Specific Events that you have identified and add them to the **List of Titled Specific Events** on page 156 so that you can return to them at a later time to tap. You can use the **Blank Tapping Script** on page 404 or the **Vent While You Tap** worksheet on page 409 to assist you while tapping through a Specific Event.

Exercise: Going Deeper with EFT

If you just completed tapping through the extended global tapping script, and you still feel that the issue is unresolved, it's time to go deeper. What is keeping it unresolved? Title your Global Issue in the space provided below. Answer the following questions so that you can discover, uncover, and recover from the unresolved Specific Events and related Aspects that created and support the Limiting Belief you wish to resolve.

Global Issue: ______________________________

1. What Limiting Beliefs do you have at the root of this Global Issue? Rate the level of intensity of how true they are for you between SUD 0 (not true at all) and 10 (completely true).

______________________________ • SUD # (0–10): ____

______________________________ • SUD # (0–10): ____

2. Title and list the Specific Events in which you learned the Limiting Belief(s) (you can also add them to your List of Titled Specific Events on page 156).

____

____

____

____

____

____

3. Choose one Specific Event to break down here. Title: ______________________________

____

4. Tune into your titled Specific Event and identify only those Aspects that apply to you, below:

What thoughts do you notice?

______________________________ • SUD # (0–10): ____

______________________________ • SUD # (0–10): ____

Do your thoughts have the quality of Small Mind or Large Mind (see page 90)?______________

Describe your Large Mind thoughts (if any):______________________________

____

Describe your Small Mind thoughts (if any): ______________________________

____

What emotions are you feeling?

______________________________ • SUD # (0–10): ____

______________________________ • SUD # (0–10): ____

______________________________ • SUD # (0–10): ____

What body sensation do you notice?

______________________________ • SUD # (0–10): ____

Where is the sensation located?______________________ • SUD # (0–10): ____

Does this sensation have a temperature?____ Describe:______________________

______________________________ • SUD # (0–10): ____

Texture?______________________________ • SUD # (0–10): ____

Color?______________________________ • SUD # (0–10): ____

Describe a visual image that you have (if any): ______________________

______________________________ • SUD # (0–10): ____

5. Use the Aspects you have just identified to create your Reminder Phrases.
6. Stay tuned into your titled Specific Event.
7. Start tapping using the Modified EFT Basic Recipe on page 121. You can use the Aspects you have identified here to fill in the Reminder Phrases on the **Blank Tapping Script** on page 404 or the **Vent While You Tap** worksheet on page 409 to assist you in creating your own tapping script.

REPEAT PROCESS IF UNRESOLVED

Be aware of any changes in the intensity of distress you feel in relation to the Aspects, along with any new ones that emerge as you tap through the Rounds of EFT. Continue to tap, repeating the EFT Basic Recipe until your Specific Event, along with its Aspects, is resolved at a SUD level of 0–2. Also be mindful of shifts in Limiting Beliefs and the emergence of any new Empowering ones. To get full resolution of a Global Issue, the Limiting Beliefs must be released by resolving other painful Specific Events that are validating them.

CHAPTER 22

I Feel So Sad and Depressed

Case Study

Note: *Limiting Beliefs are italicized* and **Empowering Beliefs are in bold.**

Louise, a 58-year-old artist never had a reason to believe she had Lyme disease, although she had gone on many hikes along the trails of her favorite state parks. Like many people who are bitten by ticks, Louise never developed the telltale bull's-eye rash that signals a tick bite or even remembered getting bitten. It was a while before she developed the debilitating fatigue, abdominal pain, and the strange burning sensations in her legs that led her to seek treatment.

For Louise, it was a long and difficult journey to being diagnosed with Lyme disease, but the search for an effective means of treatment was even more challenging. "I'm so tired of being tired. Some days it's as if the clouds are rolling in on me and *I can't do anything to stop the darkness from descending.* Sometimes I try to ignore it, but it doesn't work. Then there are times when I just feel like crying or I am so angry I could scream. I am worried because I'm so moody, and *I can't seem to get a grip.*"

There are a number of reasons that Lyme/TBDs can create depression. First, as we noted in Chapter 1 on page 17, Lyme/TBDs can cause a sufficient enough level of inflammation in the brain to create emotional imbalance and need effective treatment. Second, it is not unusual for a person to become depressed, sad, and/or angry in the midst of a prolonged and debilitating illness, especially when getting appropriate treatment is very difficult. There is also the fact that even with the best care, treatment failures are common because Lyme/TBDs are complex multisystem illnesses that have yet to be fully understood. Third, Lyme/TBD related changes and losses (Refer to the Lyme/TBDs-Related Change/Loss Inventory on page 57) often trigger unprocessed emotional pain from the past that can add to the intensity of present Lyme/TBDs-Related depression and other mood states.

At times, everything can feel so overwhelming that it seems as if there is nothing beyond the pain, fatigue, sadness, and depression that so often come with Lyme/TBDs. This is why Louise sought professional support. She knew she did not want to be overrun by her depression, but she also knew that she could not lift it on her own.

Louise wanted to address the losses she experienced that contributed to her sadness and depression. She identified Specific Events related to these issues and tapped on each of them until they lost their emotional charge. One day after tapping through many EFT sessions, Louise said, "**I believe the darkness of depression has lifted and I can see a way through for myself.** Tapping has helped me **see new possibilities for myself** I couldn't see before."

Louise continued using EFT and reported a reduction in her symptoms and an increase in her energy that made it possible for her to pursue new avenues of treatment.

For Louise, EFT proved to be an effective tool, and the same can be for you as well if you are experiencing sadness and/or depression. Depression is serious, and we encourage you to seek treatment and not to deal with it on your own. If it feels impossible or too intense for you to tap by yourself, ask a friend, partner, and/or a licensed mental-health practitioner certified in using EFT to support you through the process.

If the information presented here resonates with you, we invite you to begin with the extended global tapping script that follows. This is a gentle way to get you started and to decrease your overall intensity. Even though the scripted Reminder Phrases may not be reflective of your personal Aspects, we invite you to just go with it, track your progress, and see what happens!

Global Issue Title: I Feel So Sad and Depressed

- Focus your attention on this **Global Issue** (see page 119).
- Identify one **Limiting Belief** (see page 119) that may be at the root of this Global Issue.
- Take three slow, deep belly breaths as you do a **Body Scan** (see page 81).
- What **Aspects** (see page 123) do you notice?
- Using the **SUD scale** (see page 124), choose a number between 0 (no distress/peaceful) and 10 (highest intensity of distress) to **rate the intensity** of distress you feel about the **Global Issue and Limiting Belief**, along with only the **Aspects** (thoughts, feelings, body sensations, and visual image) that you notice that apply to you.

	Description	SUD #:
Global Issue	I Feel So Sad and Depressed	
Limiting Belief		
Thoughts		
Feelings		
Body Sensations		
Visual Image		

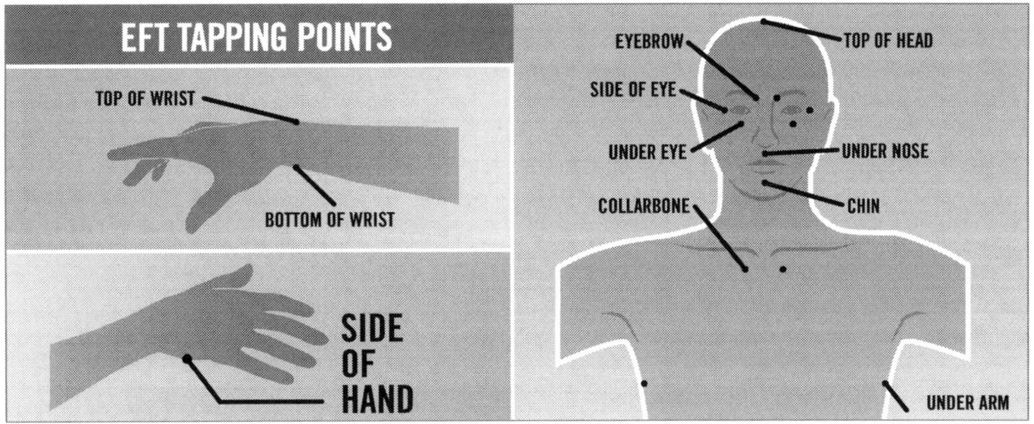

Extended Global Tapping Script: Let's begin tapping (see page 126)

Round 1

Setup:

Side of Hand: Even though I feel so sad and depressed, I accept all of my feelings.

Side of Hand: Even though I feel so sad, I accept how I feel right now.

Side of Hand: Even though I feel so depressed, I honor myself and my body.

Top of Head: Why am I feeling sad and depressed?

Eyebrow: I am so depressed because this has gone on for so long.

Side of Eye: I am so depressed because I am not getting well fast enough.

Under Eye: I am so tired of being tired.

Under Nose: I just feel so sad and depressed.

Chin: I don't even remember how to engage in life anymore.

Collarbone: I am so sad that I can't do anything I used to do.

Under Arm: I can't be with people I want to be with.

Top of Wrists Together: I am too depressed to care.

Bottom of Wrists Together: This dark cloud has overtaken me.

Slowly complete a deep belly breath and then keep tapping.

Round 2

Top of Head: Why am I feeling so sad and depressed?

Eyebrow: All I want to do is cry.

Side of Eye: This dark cloud won't leave me.

Under Eye: I miss my old life.

Under Nose: I miss my old body.

Chin: I feel so sad because I am stuck in a state of pain and fatigue.

Collarbone: I feel so much loss.

Under Arm: I feel stuck!

Top of Wrists Together: I feel so down.

Bottom of Wrists Together: There is no reason I should be feeling this bad.

Take three slow, deep belly breaths as you complete another **Body Scan**. What do you notice now? Note changes to the Aspects and any new ones that may appear below:

Aspects	Description of Aspects	SUD #:
Global Issue	I Feel So Sad and Depressed	
Limiting Belief		
Thoughts		
Feelings		
Body Sensations		
Visual Image		

If your intensity level about this Global Issue, along with any of its Aspects, is still 3 or above on a SUD scale, continue tapping with the next round. (If you have a SUD scale of 0–2, skip down and finish by tapping through the positive statements and **Affomations**.)

Round 3

Setup:

Side of Hand: Even though I still feel sad and depressed, I honor and respect myself.

Side of Hand: Even though I still have depression, I honor all of my feelings.

Side of Hand: Even though my sadness is still here, I accept where I am right now.

Top of Head: All of this remaining sadness.

Eyebrow: All these depressed feelings.

Side of Eye: My sadness feels like it will never end.

Under Eye: When will I feel like me again?

Under Nose: Will I ever be over this?

Chin: It feels so heavy. This dark cloud is still here.

Collarbone: I still feel dark.

Under Arm: I still feel like crying.

Top of Wrists Together: When will this sadness go away?

Bottom of Wrists Together: This remaining sadness and depression.

Take three slow, deep belly breaths as you complete another **Body Scan**. What do you notice now? Note changes to the Aspects and any new ones that may appear below:

Aspects	Description of Aspects	SUD #:
Global Issue	I Feel So Sad and Depressed	
Limiting Belief		
Thoughts		
Feelings		
Body Sensations		
Visual Image		

If your intensity level about this Global Issue, along with any of its Aspects, is still 3 or above on a SUD scale, keep tapping through what is in your awareness or move down to **Follow These Steps to Resolution**.

Once you reach a SUD level of 0–2 or when you just want to stop tapping for now and return at a later time, finish up by tapping through the positive statements and **Affoirmations**.

Round 4 – Now let's tap through some positive statements!

Top of Head: I've had this sadness before, and I can move through it again.

Eyebrow: I wonder if this sadness has another message for me.

Side of Eye: This sadness reminds me that I am human and that my emotions are okay.

Under Eye: I can tolerate all of my emotions.

Under Nose: This, too, will pass.

Chin: I am more than this sadness.

Collarbone: I feel better knowing that I can help myself by using EFT to process all of my feelings.

Under Arm: I feel empowered to help myself feel better.

Top of Wrists Together: I give my body permission to release this sadness now.

Bottom of Wrists Together: My sadness is lifting now.

Round 5 – Tapping with Affomations (see page 101)

Top of Head: Why am I able to experience and tolerate all of my emotions?
Eyebrow: Why is it so easy for me to use these tools to feel better?
Side of Eye: Why is it good for me to accept myself as I am?
Under Eye: Why is it easy for me to accept this as part of my healing journey?
Under Nose: Why is it easy for me to notice the improvements I am making?
Chin: How is it possible for me to see new possibilities for myself?
Collarbone: Why is it so easy for me to accept that I am healing?
Under Arm: Why is it possible for this dark cloud to move on?
Top of Wrists Together: Why am I feeling so much better?
Bottom of Wrists Together: Why is it so easy for me to remember that I am never alone in my healing?

Take three slow, deep belly breaths as you complete another **Body Scan**. What do you notice now? Note changes to the Aspects and any new ones that may appear below:

Aspects	Description of Aspects	SUD #:
Global Issue	I Feel So Sad and Depressed	
Limiting Belief		
Thoughts		
Feelings		
Body Sensations		
Visual Image		

If your intensity level about this Global Issue, along with any of its Aspects, is still 3 or above on a SUD scale, you need to explore them more in depth and follow the directives in **Follow These Steps to Resolution**, on the following page.

Exercise: Developing Self-Awareness

Describe your experience of tapping through this Global Issue.

Which Aspects resolved, decreased, increased, or stayed the same?

If you identified a Limiting Belief, state what (if anything) changed.

State any Empowering Beliefs (see page 119) that you notice now.

What Global Issues/Limiting Beliefs need to be resolved (if any)?

Follow These Steps to Resolution

- When you have the time and energy, move on to the next exercise, **Going Deeper with EFT.** Use this to help you identify Specific Events, along with their Aspects, that are contributing to not resolving this Global Issue/Limiting Belief or with any new ones that may have surfaced while tapping. You may identify many and this is to be expected.
- Just break down one Specific Event at a time and tap it until resolved. Title the rest of the Specific Events that you have identified and add them to the **List of Titled Specific Events** on page 156 so that you can return to them at a later time to tap. You can use the **Blank Tapping Script** on page 404 or the **Vent While You Tap** worksheet on page 409 to assist you while tapping through a Specific Event.

Exercise: Going Deeper with EFT

If you just completed tapping through the extended global tapping script, and you still feel that the issue is unresolved, it's time to go deeper. What is keeping it unresolved? Title your Global Issue in the space provided below. Answer the following questions so that you can discover, uncover, and recover from the unresolved Specific Events and related Aspects that created and support the Limiting Belief you wish to resolve.

Global Issue: ______________________________

1. What Limiting Beliefs do you have at the root of this Global Issue? Rate the level of intensity of how true they are for you between SUD 0 (not true at all) and 10 (completely true).

______________________________ • SUD # (0–10): ____

______________________________ • SUD # (0–10): ____

2. Title and list the Specific Events in which you learned the Limiting Belief(s) (you can also add them to your List of Titled Specific Events on page 156).

____

____

____

____

____

____

3. Choose one Specific Event to break down here. Title: ______________________________

____

4. Tune into your titled Specific Event and identify only those Aspects that apply to you, below:

What thoughts do you notice?

______________________________ • SUD # (0–10): ____

______________________________ • SUD # (0–10): ____

Do your thoughts have the quality of Small Mind or Large Mind (see page 90)?____________

Describe your Large Mind thoughts (if any):____________________

____

Describe your Small Mind thoughts (if any): ____________________

____

What emotions are you feeling?

______________________________ • SUD # (0–10): ____

______________________________ • SUD # (0–10): ____

______________________________ • SUD # (0–10): ____

What body sensation do you notice?

______________________________ • SUD # (0–10): ____

Where is the sensation located?____________________ • SUD # (0–10): ____

Does this sensation have a temperature?____ Describe:____________________

______________________________ • SUD # (0–10): ____

Texture?______________________________ • SUD # (0–10): ____

Color?______________________________ • SUD # (0–10): ____

Describe a visual image that you have (if any): ____________________

______________________________ • SUD # (0–10): ____

5. Use the Aspects you have just identified to create your Reminder Phrases.
6. Stay tuned into your titled Specific Event.
7. Start tapping using the Modified EFT Basic Recipe on page 121. You can use the Aspects you have identified here to fill in the Reminder Phrases on the **Blank Tapping Script** on page 404 or the **Vent While You Tap** worksheet on page 409 to assist you in creating your own tapping script.

REPEAT PROCESS IF UNRESOLVED

Be aware of any changes in the intensity of distress you feel in relation to the Aspects, along with any new ones that emerge as you tap through the Rounds of EFT. Continue to tap, repeating the EFT Basic Recipe until your Specific Event, along with its Aspects, is resolved at a SUD level of 0–2. Also be mindful of shifts in Limiting Beliefs and the emergence of any new Empowering ones. To get full resolution of a Global Issue, the Limiting Beliefs must be released by resolving other painful Specific Events that are validating them.

Personal Reflections

CHAPTER 23

I Feel Hopeless

Case Study

Note: *Limiting Beliefs are italicized* and **Empowering Beliefs are in bold**.

Jim was a tall athletic-looking man in his mid-thirties. He loved the outdoors and worked as a park ranger whose job included serving as a nature instructor for a summer youth program. He loved teaching kids about nature and how to survive in the woods. He spoke of how exciting it had been for him to see how much they learned as they hiked, camped, and kayaked together.

Being a park ranger was what Jim loved the most about his life. Having always had plenty of energy to do what he loved, he was puzzled when he noticed that he was becoming progressively more tired. Seeing no reason for his loss of energy, Jim kept on about his life, thinking his body would kick back into gear. When that didn't happen, he felt confused and worried, especially when he found that he didn't even have enough energy to take the kids into the woods. As his symptoms progressed, Jim became very concerned about what was happening to him and that he might "*really lose it.*" What began as a progressive loss of energy was now becoming a life-changing disability.

Over the course of the next five years, Jim saw six doctors before he found one who tested and diagnosed him with Lyme disease. While he was relieved to know the source of his illness, he felt overwhelmed by all the lifestyle changes he would have to make in order for his treatment to work. Even though it was challenging for him, Jim religiously followed all of his doctor's recommendations: maintaining a Lyme-aware diet, resting, and taking all the prescribed antibiotics and supplements. Still, his Lyme disease progressed to the point that he became too debilitated to work. This was a deep disappointment and a real hardship for him and his family. After four years of treatment, Jim was still sick and unable to work. Struggling to get by on disability insurance and believing *he would never get better*, Jim started feeling hopeless and having suicidal thoughts. This is when his wife encouraged him to seek therapy.

During his first session, Jim made it clear that he had come only to please his wife and that *he did not believe anything was going to help him.* "I really don't see the point of being here. But if it makes my wife feel better, I'll give it a shot."

When asked about the intensity level of his hopelessness, Jim reported that he felt it to be a 10 on the SUD scale. Because the intensity of Jim's hopelessness was so high, we began tapping through his hopelessness on a global level first to bring its intensity down before going deeper by tapping through the Specific Events and emotional Aspects underlying his despair. Halfway through the session, Jim reported a drop in intensity from 10 to 6 on the SUD scale for feeling hopeless, but he still *did not believe that he could be helped.* "*No one has the answer. I'm never going to get over this! I might as well just give up now! Nothing has helped me, and I doubt anything will.*"

Jim's doubt and frustration were among the first emotional layers to surface as he began using EFT to identify, process, and release the Specific Events underlying the hopelessness he felt. As Jim was tapping through the layers of his doubt and frustration, he said, "I did everything the doctor told me to do and more to try to get better, and I'm still sick! I'm lucky if I get one or two good days in, but then I'm back to square one with no solution. I've had a lot of challenges in my life, but I've never felt as helpless as I do now, and that makes me angry!"

Jim's shift from hopelessness to anger signaled that EFT was working, allowing a new emotional layer to surface. It also signaled an energizing shift in perspective that could be used to increase his hope and fuel his recovery. Jim was then led through global tapping on anger to reduce its overall intensity before going deeper and tapping through the specific treatment disappointments that validated the *Limiting Beliefs* at the root of his anger: "*Nobody has the answer and I am never going to get over this.*"

Applying EFT to each treatment disappointment created yet another shift in Jim's perspective so that he could now say, "**Maybe there is somebody or something out there that can help me. Other people have gotten better, why not me?**" This was for Jim a major cognitive shift into a **Large Mind** perspective filled with hope. Within the course of just a few sessions, Jim's state of mind shifted from one of complete hopelessness to believing that **there is hope for my recovery after all!**

Although Jim was beginning to feel hopeful about recovering from Lyme disease, he felt sad about losing the job that had given him so much joy. No longer able to hold back his tears he said, "I just feel so sad." Jim was experiencing yet another emotional layer relating to the impact Lyme disease had on him. He was holding deep sadness about losing his job as a park ranger and being an avid outdoorsman. As he tapped through his sadness, Jim began to realize that beneath the hopelessness and anger he felt were layers of unprocessed grief for all that he had lost due to Lyme disease.

Even though it took him many EFT sessions, Jim worked through his grief and gained a new, more hopeful perspective. "**I don't know why all of this happened to me, but I accept it. I will always love the outdoors. Nothing will change that for me.** But I can't go back out and risk reinfection. **I believe I got Lyme disease for a reason and that I am meant to walk a new path. I don't know what that is yet, but I believe that I will recover and that God will show me what it is I am meant to do.**"

Jim demonstrated a great amount of resilience and courage throughout his ordeal. Even in the midst of feeling hopeless and thinking that his life was over, Jim's heart remained open to his wife's suggestion to seek professional help. With the help of Anita, a licensed mental-health professional, who was also a certified EFT practitioner, Jim was able to safely peel away and process the many emotional layers at the root of his hopelessness. In so doing, he was able to fully grieve his losses and to begin cultivating a wellness state of mind rooted in compassion, acceptance, and hope for the future.

If you are having feelings of hopelessness, we strongly encourage you to reach out to your family and friends for support. Allow them to be with you just where you are and resist any temptations to push them away. We discourage the idea of isolating yourself even though you may believe that there is no way others can understand the depth of your pain. Some people may not fully understand what you're going through *and* they can be with you where you are.

The following global tapping script is not meant to take the place of professional help. You may find that some of the emotional layers that arise for you are quite intense. If that is the case, to ensure your safety, do not tap on this issue by yourself. It may be necessary to first receive professional mental-health treatment.

If you need assistance in tapping this issue, we encourage you to reach out to a certified EFT practitioner who can help to safely guide and support you in working through your hopelessness to gaining a new perspective.

If the information presented here resonates with you, we invite you to begin with the extended global tapping script that follows. This is a gentle way to get you started and to decrease your overall intensity. Even though the scripted Reminder Phrases may not be reflective of your personal Aspects, we invite you to just go with it, track your progress, and see what happens!

Global Issue Title: I Feel Hopeless

- Focus your attention on this **Global Issue** (see page 119).
- Identify one **Limiting Belief** (see page 119) that may be at the root of this Global Issue.
- Take three slow, deep belly breaths as you do a **Body Scan** (see page 81).
- What **Aspects** (see page 123) do you notice?
- Using the **SUD scale** (see page 124), choose a number between 0 (no distress/peaceful) and 10 (highest intensity of distress) to **rate the intensity** of distress you feel about the **Global Issue and Limiting Belief**, along with only the **Aspects** (thoughts, feelings, body sensations, and visual image) that you notice that apply to you.

	Description	SUD #:
Global Issue	I Feel Hopeless	
Limiting Belief		
Thoughts		
Feelings		
Body Sensations		
Visual Image		

If you ever feel suicidal and/or homicidal, get help right away! Call 911 or a suicide prevention hotline and/or go to the nearest hospital for help.

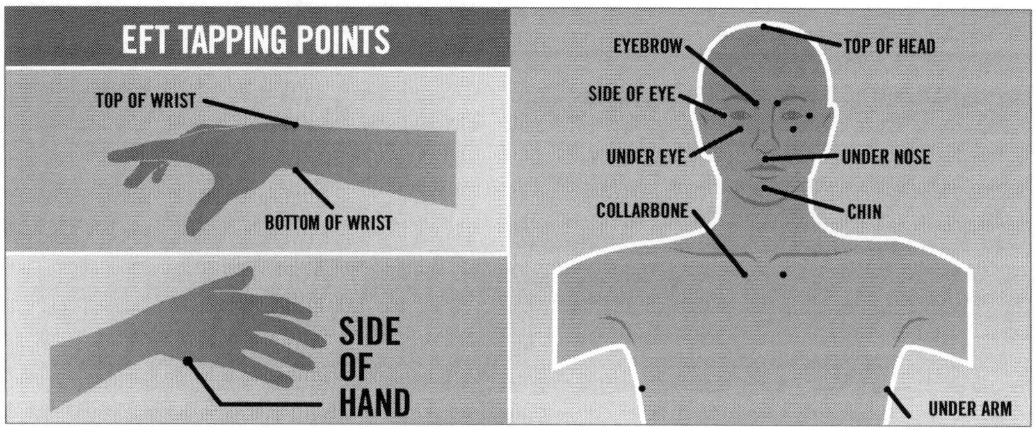

Extened Global Tapping Script: Let's begin tapping (see page 126)

Round 1

Setup:

Side of Hand: Even though I feel really hopeless right now, I accept all my feelings.

Side of Hand: Even though I don't believe I will ever get better, I honor and respect myself.

Side of Hand: Even though I don't believe anything will help me, I accept how I am feeling right now.

Top of Head: I am hopeless.

Eyebrow: Nobody knows how to help me.

Side of Eye: There's nothing that can help me.

Under Eye: I feel overwhelmed by this Lyme!

Under Nose: I just want my pain to stop.

Chin: Nobody understands the depth of my pain.

Collarbone: I can't see a way out of this!

Under Arm: I feel hopeless.

Top of Wrists Together: Why bother trying something new?

Bottom of Wrists Together: I just want to give up!

Slowly complete a deep belly breath and then keep tapping.

Round 2

Top of Head: I feel hopeless!

Eyebrow: This is too much for me to deal with.

Side of Eye: I have no one to turn to.

Under Eye: I am really scared.

Under Nose: I have no hope that things will change for the better.

Chin: I don't see a way out for me.

Collarbone: I've lost trust in the medical profession.

Under Arm: I just want to escape.

Top of Wrists Together: There's just no hope for me.

Bottom of Wrists Together: I am a hopeless case.

Take three slow, deep belly breaths as you complete another **Body Scan**. What do you notice now? Note changes to the Aspects and any new ones that may appear below:

Aspects	Description of Aspects	SUD #:
Global Issue	I Feel Hopeless	
Limiting Belief		
Thoughts		
Feelings		
Body Sensations		
Visual Image		

If your intensity level about this Global Issue, along with any of its Aspects, is still 3 or above on a SUD scale, continue tapping with the next round. (If you have a SUD scale of 0–2, skip down and finish by tapping through the positive statements and **Afformations**.)

Round 3

Setup:
Side of Hand: Even though I still feel hopeless, I honor and respect myself.
Side of Hand: Even though I still feel some hopelessness, I honor all of my feelings.
Side of Hand: Even though I still have this hopelessness, I am open to healing now.

Top of Head: This remaining hopelessness.
Eyebrow: This remaining hopelessness in my body.
Side of Eye: This remaining hopelessness in my chest.
Under Eye: This remaining hopelessness in my heart.
Under Nose: This remaining desire to just escape.
Chin: I still feel hopelessness in my body.
Collarbone: Maybe I will never get over this hopelessness.
Under Arm: This remaining hopelessness in my stomach.
Top of Wrists Together: This remaining desire to give up.
Bottom of Wrists Together: This remaining hopelessness is leaving my body now.

Take three slow, deep belly breaths as you complete another **Body Scan**. What do you notice now? Note changes to the Aspects and any new ones that may appear below:

Aspects	Description of Aspects	SUD #:
Global Issue	I Feel Hopeless	
Limiting Belief		
Thoughts		
Feelings		
Body Sensations		
Visual Image		

If your intensity level about this Global Issue, along with any of its Aspects, is still 3 or above on a SUD scale, keep tapping through what is in your awareness or move down to **Follow These Steps to Resolution**.

Once you reach a SUD level of 0–2 or when you just want to stop tapping for now and return at a later time, finish up by tapping through the positive statements and Affornations.

Round 4 – Now let's tap through some positive statements!

Top of Head: What if I can get over this?

Eyebrow: What if I can heal from this?

Side of Eye: Other people with Lyme must have the same feelings. Maybe I am not alone after all.

Under Eye: My body does want to heal.

Under Nose: I love how my body is working so hard to heal.

Chin: I am not this Lyme disease!

Collarbone: I am going to get better and find the help I need!

Under Arm: I do want to live.

Top of Wrists Together: I want to get back to feeling like myself again.

Bottom of Wrists Together: I do have hope that I will get better. I am determined to find the answer.

Round 5 – Tapping with Afformations (see page 101)

Top of Head: Why is it so easy to remember all the good people and things in my life?
Eyebrow: Why is it possible for me to find the treatment that will help me to fully heal?
Side of Eye: Why am I so grateful for the body God has given me?
Under Eye: Why does it feel so good to be hopeful?
Under Nose: Why does my body respond so well to these hopeful thoughts?
Chin: How do my positive thoughts help me heal?
Collarbone: Why is it possible for me to be hopeful?
Under Arm: Why do I know I deserve to heal?
Top of Wrists Together: Why is it possible for me to heal?
Bottom of Wrists Together: Why is it so easy for me to have hope today?

Take three slow, deep belly breaths as you complete another **Body Scan**. What do you notice now? Note changes to the Aspects and any new ones that may appear below:

Aspects	Description of Aspects	SUD #:
Global Issue	I Feel Hopeless	
Limiting Belief		
Thoughts		
Feelings		
Body Sensations		
Visual Image		

If your intensity level about this Global Issue, along with any of its Aspects, is still 3 or above on a SUD scale, you need to explore them more in depth and follow the directives in **Follow These Steps to Resolution**, on the following page.

Exercise: Developing Self-Awareness

Describe your experience of tapping through this Global Issue.

____

____

____

Which Aspects resolved, decreased, increased, or stayed the same?

____

____

If you identified a Limiting Belief, state what (if anything) changed.

____

____

State any Empowering Beliefs (see page 119) that you notice now.

____

____

What Global Issues/Limiting Beliefs need to be resolved (if any)?

____

____

Follow These Steps to Resolution

- When you have the time and energy, move on to the next exercise, **Going Deeper with EFT.** Use this to help you identify Specific Events, along with their Aspects, that are contributing to not resolving this Global Issue/Limiting Belief or with any new ones that may have surfaced while tapping. You may identify many and this is to be expected.
- Just break down one Specific Event at a time and tap it until resolved. Title the rest of the Specific Events that you have identified and add them to the **List of Titled Specific Events** on page 156 so that you can return to them at a later time to tap. You can use the **Blank Tapping Script** on page 404 or the **Vent While You Tap** worksheet on page 409 to assist you while tapping through a Specific Event.

Exercise: Going Deeper with EFT

If you just completed tapping through the extended global tapping script, and you still feel that the issue is unresolved, it's time to go deeper. What is keeping it unresolved? Title your Global Issue in the space provided below. Answer the following questions so that you can discover, uncover, and recover from the unresolved Specific Events and related Aspects that created and support the Limiting Belief you wish to resolve.

Global Issue: ______________________________

1. What Limiting Beliefs do you have at the root of this Global Issue? Rate the level of intensity of how true they are for you between SUD 0 (not true at all) and 10 (completely true).

______________________________ • SUD # (0–10): ____

______________________________ • SUD # (0–10): ____

2. Title and list the Specific Events in which you learned the Limiting Belief(s) (you can also add them to your List of Titled Specific Events on page 156).

____

____

____

____

____

____

3. Choose one Specific Event to break down here. Title: ______________________________

____

4. Tune into your titled Specific Event and identify only those Aspects that apply to you, below:

What thoughts do you notice?

______________________________ • SUD # (0–10): ____

______________________________ • SUD # (0–10): ____

Do your thoughts have the quality of Small Mind or Large Mind (see page 90)?______________

Describe your Large Mind thoughts (if any):____

____

Describe your Small Mind thoughts (if any): ____

____

What emotions are you feeling?

____ • SUD # (0–10): ____

____ • SUD # (0–10): ____

____ • SUD # (0–10): ____

What body sensation do you notice?

____ • SUD # (0–10): ____

Where is the sensation located?________________________ • SUD # (0–10): ____

Does this sensation have a temperature?____ Describe:________________________

____ • SUD # (0–10): ____

Texture?________________________________ • SUD # (0–10): ____

Color?__________________________________ • SUD # (0–10): ____

Describe a visual image that you have (if any): ______________________________

____ • SUD # (0–10): ____

5. Use the Aspects you have just identified to create your Reminder Phrases.
6. Stay tuned into your titled Specific Event.
7. Start tapping using the Modified EFT Basic Recipe on page 121. You can use the Aspects you have identified here to fill in the Reminder Phrases on the **Blank Tapping Script** on page 404 or the **Vent While You Tap** worksheet on page 409 to assist you in creating your own tapping script.

REPEAT PROCESS IF UNRESOLVED

Be aware of any changes in the intensity of distress you feel in relation to the Aspects, along with any new ones that emerge as you tap through the Rounds of EFT. Continue to tap, repeating the EFT Basic Recipe until your Specific Event, along with its Aspects, is resolved at a SUD level of 0–2. Also be mindful of shifts in Limiting Beliefs and the emergence of any new Empowering ones. To get full resolution of a Global Issue, the Limiting Beliefs must be released by resolving other painful Specific Events that are validating them.

CHAPTER

24 Filled with Guilt

Case Study

Note: *Limiting Beliefs are italicized* and **Empowering Beliefs are in bold.**

Dawn, casually dressed in a blouse and jeans, sat with her head slightly bowed, her long brown hair flowing like a veil around her face. She was flexing her fingers, saying, "I can't remember the last time I felt good. I don't even know what normal feels like." Now 48, Dawn was diagnosed with Lyme disease when she was 43, though she came to realize she had the disease since she was 18 when she returned from summer camp with the "flu." Having suffered for years with migrating joint pains, brain fog, lethargy, and insomnia, Dawn had to stop working at 45. She felt guilty about being *neither a "good" wife to her husband, Jake, nor a "good" mother to her two children, Evan and Julia.*

Guilt is a common and burdensome emotion for people who experience chronic bouts of debilitating Lyme/TBD symptoms. It often has its roots in what you believe you "should" or "should not" have done in response to particular events whether from the past or the present. You can become so preoccupied with *what you did "wrong,"* like "failing" to meet your responsibilities or not living up to the expectations of others, that you may come to believe that you are *a "bad" person.* To be consumed with guilt is to be caught in a constant barrage of self-criticism.

EFT is an excellent remedy for Lyme/TBDs-related guilt. It helps to release the burden of self-blame as expressed by such *Limiting Beliefs* as, *"I'm not pulling my weight," "I should be better, I don't do enough," or "I'm a failure."* Dawn was consumed with guilt: "*I let my husband down.* We haven't had the kind of life we planned. *I should be stronger. I'm a poor mom. I feel like a total failure.*" Her *Limiting Belief, "I had failed my children"* also distressed her and so she made that the target to start breaking down in the first EFT session.

Dawn began with the guilt she felt in relation to her son's disappointment when she could not attend his last soccer game. "I was so sick I couldn't get out of bed! Evan was counting on me, and I couldn't be there for him. Seeing how disappointed he was made me feel awful. I believe *I am a terrible mother* because I couldn't be there for my son."

Only after many rounds of tapping through the layers of guilt she felt in relation to *"failing" her son* when she was too sick to go to his soccer game, Dawn tearfully remembered a moment in time when her son said to her, "It's okay, Mom. I still love you. I know you don't feel good." She also became aware of the many times she was able to do things with her son and how happy they were to be together. Tapping uncovered the good memories of when she had been present for Evan. Prior to tapping, Dawn had been so consumed with guilt about what she could not do for her son that she had forgotten the many times she was able to be there for him.

The self-blame that comes with guilt can block the awareness of the good memories in your life. Using EFT to process and release her guilt, Dawn **believed she was truly a loving and present**

mother to her son even in the midst of her debilitating symptoms.

Dawn was now ready to address the guilt she felt about *"cheating"* her daughter out of the attention she needed and not doing things with her like going shopping. She recalled a Specific Event when she was too sick to take her daughter to the mall. "Julia was so angry with me, yelling about how her friends' moms could take them shopping and how I am always too sick or too busy to do things with her. At first I was furious with her, but then I felt awful about not having spent more time with her and not being there to help her through the changes that come with being a teenager."

Dawn tapped on her guilt and *beliefs of failure* about not being the mother she wanted to be to Julia. As Dawn vented and released the anger she felt toward her daughter for yelling at her, she remembered how restricted and frustrated she felt not being "allowed" to express any of her own anger with her mother when she herself was a teen. Now able to let that anger go, she realized that although hearing her daughter's anger toward her was hurtful, she was able to let her express it. In that moment, Dawn said, "**I am the mother I wanted to be**." Even so, she still had another layer of guilt to get through.

At the next session, Dawn recounted a Specific Event when her daughter accused her of caring more about her younger brother than herself. "I had no idea Julia felt that way until she said it. I know that both of my kids have missed out because I've been sick and have had to work and manage things at home, but I never thought about who was getting more attention."

After rounds of tapping, Dawn recalled that Julia was eight when her son Evan was born. "Julia had been the center of my attention until Evan came along. I had not been anticipating having another child and then there he was. Caring for a newborn and an eight-year-old while working was just exhausting, even with my husband's help. There were days, too, when I felt so sick that I could barely manage just taking care of Evan. He was five when Julia turned thirteen, and I just didn't have the energy to give them both what they needed, so I guess I did give him more attention. Poor Julia probably did feel neglected, and I didn't even know it!"

As Dawn tapped, long-held tears began to flow as her guilt was replaced with compassion for herself and her daughter. Where once her guilt *prevented her from believing that she could change things with her daughter*, Dawn now had the **Empowering Belief that they could work together to heal their relationship even as she was focused on recovering from Lyme disease.**

Dawn was now ready to address the guilt she felt about *"failing" her husband, Jake*. "We had so many plans when we got married, and then I started getting sicker and couldn't follow through. I believe *I've really let him down*. I haven't worked for the last three years, and even though I'm home, he still has to do most of the housework because I can't even manage that! Our sex life has suffered too because I just don't feel up to it. *My whole life feels like a failure.*"

After many sessions of tapping through each Specific Event, one day Dawn suddenly remembered the many times *she felt like a failure* when her parents criticized her for not living up to their expectations. "*I just couldn't do anything right*. No matter what I did, my parents criticized me. I believed *I was always letting them down*." This is when Dawn realized that the guilt she had been carrying about *"failing" her husband and her children* began long before her Lyme-related symptoms started to interfere with her functioning.

Choosing to address her present-day guilt about being too sick to be the wife and mother she wanted to be helped her realize that she had been operating out of *Limiting Beliefs* and guilt-related issues beginning in childhood. *Being sick with Lyme disease was one more failure to feel guilty about!* After several months with patient and compassionate application of EFT, Dawn was able to say with full conviction, "**I always did the best I could. I've made mistakes like anybody else, but I am NOT a failure! My husband and**

children still love me even though I can't always do things with them."

Dawn realized that the sense of failure she carried from childhood led her to the *Limiting Belief* that *she could not do anything right*. This belief, once activated by the debilitation that came with her Lyme disease symptoms, became a source of deep distressing guilt each time she could not perform "well" as a wife and mother. Having processed and released her *Limiting Beliefs*, Dawn reported a **greater sense of self-esteem and ability to engage with her family members even on days when her symptoms were more intense.**

Dawn now **valued herself** and made positive decisions in self-care. The result was that she began to feel better. "I'm actually having some good days when I have less pain and more energy to do things with my family." Dawn also began pursuing new treatment options for herself and including her family in her recovery process.

If the information presented here resonates with you, we invite you to begin with the extended global tapping script that follows. This is a gentle way to get you started and to decrease your overall intensity. Even though the scripted Reminder Phrases may not be reflective of your personal Aspects, we invite you to just go with it, track your progress, and see what happens!

Global Issue Title: Filled with Guilt

- Focus your attention on this **Global Issue** (see page 119).
- Identify one **Limiting Belief** (see page 119) that may be at the root of this Global Issue.
- Take three slow, deep belly breaths as you do a **Body Scan** (see page 81).
- What **Aspects** (see page 123) do you notice?
- Using the **SUD scale** (see page 124), choose a number between 0 (no distress/peaceful) and 10 (highest intensity of distress) to **rate the intensity** of distress you feel about the **Global Issue and Limiting Belief**, along with only the **Aspects** (thoughts, feelings, body sensations, and visual image) that you notice that apply to you.

	Description	SUD #:
Global Issue	Filled with Guilt	
Limiting Belief		
Thoughts		
Feelings		
Body Sensations		
Visual Image		

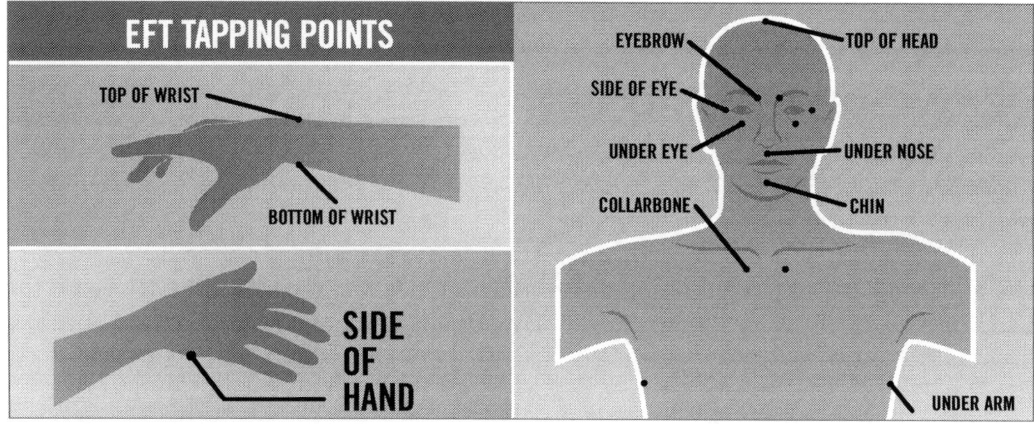

Extended Global Tapping Script: Let's begin tapping **(see page 126)**

Round 1

Setup:
Side of Hand: Even though I feel guilty, I accept all of my feelings about it.
Side of Hand: Even though my guilt overwhelms me, I honor and accept how I feel.
Side of Hand: Even though I am filled with guilt, I did the best I could.

Top of Head: I feel so guilty for not being able to do all that I did before getting sick.
Eyebrow: I am filled with guilt.
Side of Eye: I feel so guilty for not holding up my end of things.
Under Eye: I feel guilt flowing throughout my body!
Under Nose: All of this guilt.
Chin: I feel so guilty for failing my partner/kids.
Collarbone: I feel so bad for letting myself down!
Under Arm: I feel so guilty letting everyone down.
Top of Wrists: My guilt is overwhelming!
Bottom of Wrists: I feel so guilty I can't do anything right!

Slowly complete a deep belly breath and then keep tapping.

Round 2

Top of Head: I feel guilty for no longer being able to do the things I did before I got sick.
Eyebrow: All of this guilt.
Side of Eye: I feel so guilty for not living up to what is expected of me.
Under Eye: I can't get this guilt out of my mind.
Under Nose: I feel guilty for not being able to do what I used to do.
Chin: I feel so guilty.
Collarbone: I feel so bad about myself.
Under Arm: This guilt is such a heavy burden!
Top of Wrists Together: I feel so guilty.
Bottom of Wrists Together: I feel so guilty about how I've failed everyone.

Take three slow, deep belly breaths as you complete another **Body Scan**. What do you notice now? Note changes to the Aspects and any new ones that may appear below:

	Description	SUD #:
Global Issue	Filled with Guilt	
Limiting Belief		
Thoughts		
Feelings		
Body Sensations		
Visual Image		

If your intensity level about this Global Issue, along with any of its Aspects, is still 3 or above on a SUD scale, continue tapping with the next round. (If you have a SUD scale of 0–2, skip down and finish by tapping through the positive statements and Afformations.)

Round 3

Setup:

Side of Hand: Even though I still have some guilt, I give myself permission to heal.

Side of Hand: Even though I still blame myself, I accept what I am able to do.

Side of Hand: Even though I still feel guilty, I am doing the best that I can right now.

Top of Head: This remaining feeling of guilt.

Eyebrow: This remaining guilt about letting others down.

Side of Eye: This remaining guilt for letting myself down.

Under Eye: This remaining guilt in my body.

Under Nose: I still feel guilty.

Chin: This leftover guilt.

Collarbone: All this remaining guilt.

Under Arm: Am I ever going to be free of guilt?

Top of Wrists: This remaining sense of guilt.

Bottom of Wrists: I am doing the best I can.

Take three slow, deep belly breaths as you complete another **Body Scan**. What do you notice now? Note changes to the Aspects and any new ones that may appear below:

	Description	SUD #:
Global Issue	Filled with Guilt	
Limiting Belief		
Thoughts		
Feelings		
Body Sensations		
Visual Image		

If your intensity level about this Global Issue, along with any of its Aspects, is still 3 or above on a SUD scale, keep tapping through what is in your awareness or move down to **Follow These Steps to Resolution**.

Once you reach a SUD level of 0–2 or when you just want to stop tapping for now and return at a later time, finish up by tapping through the positive statements and Affirmations.

Round 4 – Now let's tap through some positive statements!

Top of Head: I feel so much compassion for myself.
Eyebrow: I accept myself even though I am doing less right now.
Side of Eye: I feel compassion for myself because I've been so sick.
Under Eye: I would have done things differently if I could have.
Under Nose: I am open to forgiving myself.
Chin: Tapping through my guilt is helping me to feel better about myself.
Collarbone: I am doing the best that I can right now and it is enough.
Top of Wrists: I am feeling better already.
Bottom of Wrists: I intend to release all this remaining guilt.

Round 5 – Tapping with Afformations (see page 101)

Top of Head: Why is it possible for me to accept my limitations for now, knowing it will not be forever?

Eyebrow: Why am I so grateful for who I am as a person?

Side of Eye: How is it possible for me to forgive myself?

Under Eye: Why is it easy for me to remember the good things in my life?

Under Nose: Why am I able to release my feelings of guilt and accept that I am doing the best I can?

Chin: Why is it possible for me to heal from my guilt and embrace self-acceptance?

Collarbone: Why is it easy to believe that I am a loving person?

Top of Wrists: Why does it feel so freeing to let go of guilt and be open to new possibilities for myself?

Bottom of Wrists: Why is it possible for me to release my guilt and know that I am doing the best I can right now?

Take three slow, deep belly breaths as you complete another **Body Scan**. What do you notice now? Note changes to the Aspects and any new ones that may appear below:

	Description	SUD #:
Global Issue	Filled with Guilt	
Limiting Belief		
Thoughts		
Feelings		
Body Sensations		
Visual Image		

If your intensity level about this Global Issue, along with any of its Aspects, is still 3 or above on a SUD scale, you need to explore them more in depth and follow the directives in **Follow These Steps to Resolution**, on the following page.

Exercise: Developing Self-Awareness

Describe your experience of tapping through this Global Issue.

Which Aspects resolved, decreased, increased, or stayed the same?

If you identified a Limiting Belief, state what (if anything) changed.

State any Empowering Beliefs (see page 119) that you notice now.

What Global Issues/Limiting Beliefs need to be resolved (if any)?

Follow These Steps to Resolution

- When you have the time and energy, move on to the next exercise, **Going Deeper with EFT.** Use this to help you identify Specific Events, along with their Aspects, that are contributing to not resolving this Global Issue/Limiting Belief or with any new ones that may have surfaced while tapping. You may identify many and this is to be expected.
- Just break down one Specific Event at a time and tap it until resolved. Title the rest of the Specific Events that you have identified and add them to the **List of Titled Specific Events** on page 156 so that you can return to them at a later time to tap. You can use the **Blank Tapping Script** on page 404 or the **Vent While You Tap** worksheet on page 409 to assist you while tapping through a Specific Event.

Exercise: Going Deeper with EFT

If you just completed tapping through the extended global tapping script, and you still feel that the issue is unresolved, it's time to go deeper. What is keeping it unresolved? Title your Global Issue in the space provided below. Answer the following questions so that you can discover, uncover, and recover from the unresolved Specific Events and related Aspects that created and support the Limiting Belief you wish to resolve.

Global Issue: ______________________________

1. What Limiting Beliefs do you have at the root of this Global Issue? Rate the level of intensity of how true they are for you between SUD 0 (not true at all) and 10 (completely true).

______________________________ • SUD # (0–10): ____

______________________________ • SUD # (0–10): ____

2. Title and list the Specific Events in which you learned the Limiting Belief(s) (you can also add them to your List of Titled Specific Events on page 156).

____

____

____

____

____

____

3. Choose one Specific Event to break down here. Title: ______________________________

____

4. Tune into your titled Specific Event and identify only those Aspects that apply to you, below:

What thoughts do you notice?

______________________________ • SUD # (0–10): ____

______________________________ • SUD # (0–10): ____

Do your thoughts have the quality of Small Mind or Large Mind (see page 90)?______________

Describe your Large Mind thoughts (if any):____________________________________

____

Describe your Small Mind thoughts (if any): ____________________________________

____

What emotions are you feeling?

____ • SUD # (0–10): ____

____ • SUD # (0–10): ____

____ • SUD # (0–10): ____

What body sensation do you notice?

____ • SUD # (0–10): ____

Where is the sensation located?____________________________ • SUD # (0–10): ____

Does this sensation have a temperature?____ Describe:____________________________

____ • SUD # (0–10): ____

Texture?____ • SUD # (0–10): ____

Color?____ • SUD # (0–10): ____

Describe a visual image that you have (if any): __________________________________

____ • SUD # (0–10): ____

5. Use the Aspects you have just identified to create your Reminder Phrases.
6. Stay tuned into your titled Specific Event.
7. Start tapping using the Modified EFT Basic Recipe on page 121. You can use the Aspects you have identified here to fill in the Reminder Phrases on the **Blank Tapping Script** on page 404 or the **Vent While You Tap** worksheet on page 409 to assist you in creating your own tapping script.

REPEAT PROCESS IF UNRESOLVED

Be aware of any changes in the intensity of distress you feel in relation to the Aspects, along with any new ones that emerge as you tap through the Rounds of EFT. Continue to tap, repeating the EFT Basic Recipe until your Specific Event, along with its Aspects, is resolved at a SUD level of 0–2. Also be mindful of shifts in Limiting Beliefs and the emergence of any new Empowering ones. To get full resolution of a Global Issue, the Limiting Beliefs must be released by resolving other painful Specific Events that are validating them.

CHAPTER

25 Unpredictability of My Lyme/TBD Symptoms

Case Study

Note: *Limiting Beliefs are italicized* and **Empowering Beliefs are in bold.**

Kathryn was a sociable and friendly woman in her mid thirties who loved her job as a teacher at a local elementary school. Although she had been experiencing Lyme-related symptoms off and on for years and believed that she did, in fact, have Lyme disease, she had only just been diagnosed before she came in for therapy to emotionally address recent episodes of unpredictable and intense migrating muscle pain, headaches, and fatigue. "I don't know what's going on. I haven't felt this bad and this worried in a long time. Things have been really hard over the last few months. Before that, I was doing okay. I would have some days when I wasn't feeling so hot, but I could manage. Now it's as if *everything has gone haywire,* and I never know what to expect."

Kathryn reported that she was worried about the impact of her symptoms on her performance as a teacher. She also felt anxious about making plans with family or friends for fear that she would have to cancel them at the last minute if her symptoms flared up. And even though she did have some good days without symptoms, *she had learned not to trust them.*

Having some sense of what's coming and how to manage it is critical to feeling safe in your body and your life. And so when Kathryn was suddenly struck with such painful and unpredictable symptoms, she felt as though she had been attacked out of nowhere. She felt anxious because of *not being able to trust her body.* "I never know what kind of day I'm going to have until I get up in the morning, and even then, I am not always so sure. Before all of this, I could make plans or just do whatever I wanted in the moment. I felt in charge of my life. Now *Lyme has taken control* and I never know what to expect from one moment to the next. And on the days when I do feel good, I'm so anxious about feeling sick again that I can't enjoy them. I am always on alert, anxiously waiting for the next *attack* as if I could be *ambushed* at any moment."

Kathryn agreed that it would be best to begin by using EFT to process her global feelings of anxiety in relation to the unpredictability of her symptoms. We began the first rounds of EFT tapping through, *"I could be ambushed at any moment."* Afterward, Kathryn stated that she was still anxious that her symptoms would return without warning. She then tapped on her emotional trigger for anxiety: "Having a good day and waiting to feel bad again." After rounds of tapping, Kathryn reported, "I feel calmer, but *I don't trust this feeling to last* because I know that I'm going to feel bad again."

The fact that Kathryn was able to feel calmer after tapping through the first layers of her anxiety demonstrates the initiation of a positive mind-body relaxation response. Even with that, however, there can be remaining issues. For example, Kathryn noticed that though she did feel calmer, *she still didn't trust that the peace she was feeling at the moment would last.* Kathryn continued to tap on this, and suddenly a new awareness emerged, *"I am trying so hard to protect myself that on good days, I can't let go of feeling anxious because I have to be ready for my symptoms to return."*

Kathryn was led through more tapping on this next emotional layer. Then Kathryn stopped and said, **"This anxiety is not protecting me at all! It's robbing me of enjoying my good days!** And on my bad days, feeling anxious makes my muscle pain, headaches, and fatigue worse!"

Kathryn agreed to also tap at home whenever she felt the need to *"go on alert."* She tapped through the anxiety that came up for her in the moment. While this process decreased her anxiety in the moment, she was still having difficulty creating a **Large Mind** perspective for herself that she could completely trust. Kathryn returned to therapy and chose to use EFT to go deeper into the underlying issues related to her anxiety about the unpredictability of her symptoms.

Tapping through the layers of anxiety, anger, and fear she felt in relation to the unpredictability of her symptoms, Kathryn discovered that she had, in many ways, been reliving the trauma she experienced growing up with an abusive alcoholic mother. "All of this reminds me of when I was abused as a child. My mom was an alcoholic, and I never knew when she was going to come home drunk and let me have it. All day at school I would feel anxious and worried about what was going to happen when I got home. There were so many days when I didn't want to go home because *I had to go on alert.* I had to stay on my toes and be ready for anything."

Kathryn made the connection that using anxiety to "protect" herself from the unpredictability of her Lyme disease symptoms was a continued strategy of protection that she used in childhood to cope with her mother's unpredictability. Where once her use of anxiety for protection helped her to survive childhood trauma, that same strategy was causing her Lyme symptoms to worsen and interfered with her ability to enjoy the good days.

With the supported use of EFT through a period of time, Kathryn was able to address and resolve many traumatic Specific Events from her childhood that were underlying her *belief that anxiety protected her.* She shared her new **Empowering Belief** saying, **"For the first time, I know I'm safe and can handle whatever happens.** I feel calm and no longer anxious."

With persistence and the successful use of EFT, Kathryn was able to stay present in the moment and felt more confident to make adjustments to life as it happened. She was also freed of the distrust about feeling good and allowed herself to enjoy her good days for as long as it lasted! Kathryn was now able to ride the waves of her symptoms rather than struggle against them.

When EFT didn't resolve Kathryn's anxiety by tapping on the initial emotional issues of the unpredictability of her Lyme symptoms, she returned to therapy to go deeper. She was able to identify and process through unresolved childhood trauma related to unpredictability that was at the root of how she anxiously perceived (interpreted) and experienced her current-day symptoms of Lyme. This is where her persistence with EFT led her to new **Empowering Beliefs** that supported a healthier way to cope and to enjoy the good days when they occurred.

If you do not get the results you want from EFT, you may also need to go deeper and address the underlying emotional root causes that may be keeping you from experiencing resolution.

If the information presented here resonates with you, we invite you to begin with the extended global tapping script that follows. This is a gentle way to get you started and to decrease your overall intensity. Even though the scripted Reminder Phrases may not be reflective of your personal Aspects, we invite you to just go with it, track your progress, and see what happens!

Global Issue Title: Unpredictability

- Focus your attention on this **Global Issue** (see page 119).
- Identify one **Limiting Belief** (see page 119) that may be at the root of this Global Issue.
- Take three slow, deep belly breaths as you do a **Body Scan** (see page 81).
- What **Aspects** (see page 123) do you notice?
- Using the **SUD scale** (see page 124), choose a number between 0 (no distress/peaceful) and 10 (highest intensity of distress) to **rate the intensity** of distress you feel about the **Global Issue and Limiting Belief**, along with only the **Aspects** (thoughts, feelings, body sensations, and visual image) that you notice that apply to you.

Aspects	Description of Aspects	SUD #:
Global Issue	Unpredictability	
Limiting Belief		
Thoughts		
Feelings		
Body Sensations		
Visual Image		

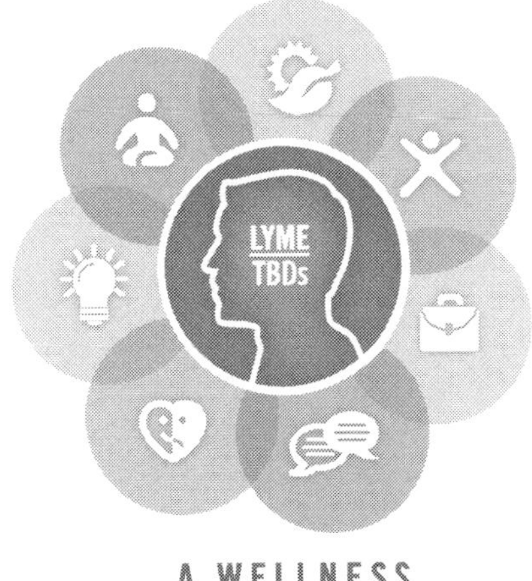

A WELLNESS
STATE OF MIND

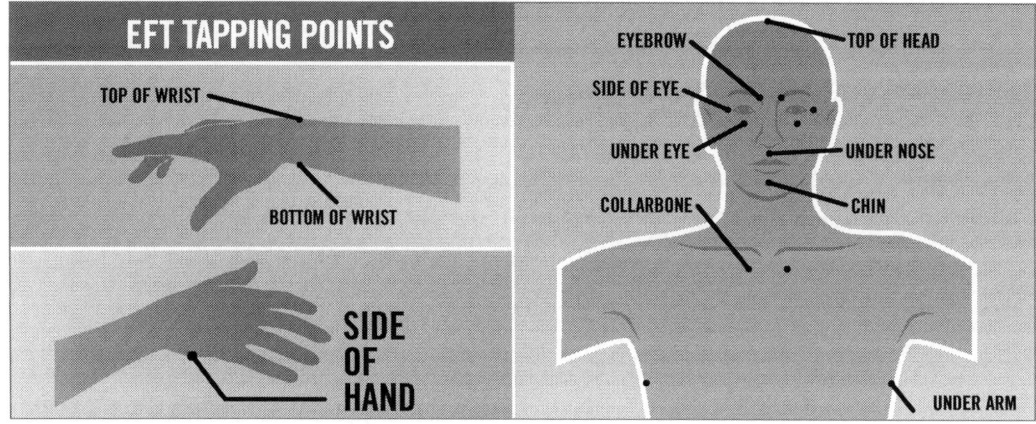

Extended Global Tapping Script: Let's begin tapping (see page 126)

Round 1

Setup:

Side of Hand: Even though I never know how I am going to feel, I accept all of my feelings about this.

Side of Hand: Even though my Lyme/TBD symptoms are unpredictable, I accept where I am right now.

Side of Hand: Even though I feel ambushed by my Lyme/TBD symptoms, I honor and respect my body.

Top of Head: Every day I wake up not knowing what to expect.

Eyebrow: Unpredictability makes me feel anxious.

Side of Eye: I feel ambushed by my symptoms!

Under Eye: I feel good, and then it changes. I can't trust feeling good!

Under Nose: I feel so anxious about the unpredictability of my body.

Chin: When I do feel good it doesn't last.

Collarbone: I feel so ambushed!

Under Arm: I feel out of control!

Top of Wrists Together: I am so anxious and stressed out!

Bottom of Wrists Together: My symptoms have control over me!

Slowly complete a deep belly breath and then keep tapping.

Round 2

Top of Head: These symptoms come out of nowhere!

Eyebrow: I don't have control!

Side of Eye: I feel so anxious not knowing what to expect.

Under Eye: I feel anxious when my body feels good.

Under Nose: Not being able to trust my body makes me feel both angry and anxious!

Chin: Sometimes I have to cancel plans and disappoint others.

Collarbone: Other people don't understand.

Under Arm: I feel so anxious not knowing what will happen next.

Top of Wrists Together: I have to stay hyper-vigilant and be ready for the next attack.

Bottom of Wrists Together: It is not safe for me to feel good.

Take three slow, deep belly breaths as you complete another **Body Scan**. What do you notice now? Note changes to the Aspects and any new ones that may appear below:

Aspects	Description of Aspects	SUD #:
Global Issue	Unpredictability	
Limiting Belief		
Thoughts		
Feelings		
Body Sensations		
Visual Image		

If your intensity level about this Global Issue, along with any of its Aspects, is still 3 or above on a SUD scale, continue tapping with the next round. (If you have a SUD scale of 0–2, skip down and finish by tapping through the positive statements and Afformations.)

Round 3

Setup:

Side of Hand: Even though I still feel anxious about my body being unpredictable, I honor all of my feelings about this.

Side of Hand: Even though I am still anxious about not knowing how I am going to feel, I accept where I am now.

Side of Hand: Even though I am still stressed about the unpredictability of my body, I honor and respect myself and my body.

Top of Head: I still feel angry at being ambushed by my body!

Eyebrow: I am still stressed about this!

Side of Eye: I still don't trust feeling good.

Under Eye: I am still angry at not having control!

Under Nose: I am still anxious about not knowing what will happen next.

Chin: I miss being spontaneous.

Collarbone: I am scared that I will never get better.

Under Arm: I get worried and anxious when I feel good.

Top of Wrists Together: My body is still unpredictable.

Bottom of Wrists Together: It is hard to trust feeling better.

Take three slow, deep belly breaths as you complete another **Body Scan**. What do you notice now? Note changes to the Aspects and any new ones that may appear below:

Aspects	Description of Aspects	SUD #:
Global Issue	Unpredictability	
Limiting Belief		
Thoughts		
Feelings		
Body Sensations		
Visual Image		

If your intensity level about this Global Issue, along with any of its Aspects, is still 3 or above on a SUD scale, keep tapping through what is in your awareness or move down to **Follow These Steps to Resolution**.

Once you reach a SUD level of 0–2 or when you just want to stop tapping for now and return at a later time, finish up by tapping through the positive statements and Affirmations.

Round 4 – Now let's tap through some positive statements!

Top of Head: My body is doing everything it can to heal.
Eyebrow: I honor my body and the strength it has.
Side of Eye: I let go of my control and live in the present moment.
Under Eye: I am able to adjust as life changes.
Under Nose: I am able to deal with whatever happens when it happens.
Chin: I accept this moment as it is.
Collarbone: I trust my body and know that it is doing everything it can to help me heal.
Under Arm: I no longer need to control the future. I have the strength to live now.
Top of Wrists Together: I accept that Lyme disease is unpredictable. It is what it is.
Bottom of Wrists Together: I am open to new possibilities for myself right here, right now.

Round 5 – Tapping with Afformations (see page 101)

Top of Head: How is it so easy for me to trust when I feel good?

Eyebrow: Why is it easy for me to notice new possibilities for healing?

Side of Eye: Why is it possible for me to honor my body and all that it is doing on my behalf to heal?

Under Eye: Why is it easy for me to give up being in control and just be?

Under Nose: Why is it so easy for me to live in the present moment with what is?

Chin: Why am I able to gently follow the rhythms and needs of my body even as they change?

Collarbone: Why is it easy for me to trust my body?

Under Arm: Why am I able to let go of the future and live now?

Top of Wrists Together: Why am I able to accept the ebbs and flow of my recovery?

Bottom of Wrists Together: Why is it so easy for me to honor what I need in this moment?

Take three slow, deep belly breaths as you complete another **Body Scan**. What do you notice now? Note changes to the Aspects and any new ones that may appear below:

Aspects	Description of Aspects	SUD #:
Global Issue	Unpredictability	
Limiting Belief		
Thoughts		
Feelings		
Body Sensations		
Visual Image		

If your intensity level about this Global Issue, along with any of its Aspects, is still 3 or above on a SUD scale, you need to explore them more in depth and follow the directives in **Follow These Steps to Resolution**, on the following page.

Exercise: Developing Self-Awareness

Describe your experience of tapping through this Global Issue.

Which Aspects resolved, decreased, increased, or stayed the same?

If you identified a Limiting Belief, state what (if anything) changed.

State any Empowering Beliefs (see page 119) that you notice now.

What Global Issues/Limiting Beliefs need to be resolved (if any)?

Follow These Steps to Resolution

- When you have the time and energy, move on to the next exercise, **Going Deeper with EFT.** Use this to help you identify Specific Events, along with their Aspects, that are contributing to not resolving this Global Issue/Limiting Belief or with any new ones that may have surfaced while tapping. You may identify many and this is to be expected.
- Just break down one Specific Event at a time and tap it until resolved. Title the rest of the Specific Events that you have identified and add them to the **List of Titled Specific Events** on page 156 so that you can return to them at a later time to tap. You can use the **Blank Tapping Script** on page 404 or the **Vent While You Tap** worksheet on page 409 to assist you while tapping through a Specific Event.

Exercise: Going Deeper with EFT

If you just completed tapping through the extended global tapping script, and you still feel that the issue is unresolved, it's time to go deeper. What is keeping it unresolved? Title your Global Issue in the space provided below. Answer the following questions so that you can discover, uncover, and recover from the unresolved Specific Events and related Aspects that created and support the Limiting Belief you wish to resolve.

Global Issue: ______________________________

1. What Limiting Beliefs do you have at the root of this Global Issue? Rate the level of intensity of how true they are for you between SUD 0 (not true at all) and 10 (completely true).

______________________________ • SUD # (0–10): ____

______________________________ • SUD # (0–10): ____

2. Title and list the Specific Events in which you learned the Limiting Belief(s) (you can also add them to your List of Titled Specific Events on page 156).

____

____

____

____

____

____

3. Choose one Specific Event to break down here. Title: ______________________________

____

4. Tune into your titled Specific Event and identify only those Aspects that apply to you, below:

What thoughts do you notice?

______________________________ • SUD # (0–10): ____

______________________________ • SUD # (0–10): ____

Do your thoughts have the quality of Small Mind or Large Mind (see page 90)?______________

Describe your Large Mind thoughts (if any):______________________________

____

Describe your Small Mind thoughts (if any): ______________________________

____

What emotions are you feeling?

____ • SUD # (0–10): ____

____ • SUD # (0–10): ____

____ • SUD # (0–10): ____

What body sensation do you notice?

____ • SUD # (0–10): ____

Where is the sensation located?________________________ • SUD # (0–10): ____

Does this sensation have a temperature?____ Describe:________________________

____ • SUD # (0–10): ____

Texture?______________________________________ • SUD # (0–10): ____

Color?____ • SUD # (0–10): ____

Describe a visual image that you have (if any): ____________________________

____ • SUD # (0–10): ____

5. Use the Aspects you have just identified to create your Reminder Phrases.
6. Stay tuned into your titled Specific Event.
7. Start tapping using the Modified EFT Basic Recipe on page 121. You can use the Aspects you have identified here to fill in the Reminder Phrases on the **Blank Tapping Script** on page 404 or the **Vent While You Tap** worksheet on page 409 to assist you in creating your own tapping script.

REPEAT PROCESS IF UNRESOLVED

Be aware of any changes in the intensity of distress you feel in relation to the Aspects, along with any new ones that emerge as you tap through the Rounds of EFT. Continue to tap, repeating the EFT Basic Recipe until your Specific Event, along with its Aspects, is resolved at a SUD level of 0–2. Also be mindful of shifts in Limiting Beliefs and the emergence of any new Empowering ones. To get full resolution of a Global Issue, the Limiting Beliefs must be released by resolving other painful Specific Events that are validating them.

CHAPTER 26

I'm Not Seen, Heard, or Understood

Case Study

Note: *Limiting Beliefs are italicized* and **Empowering Beliefs are in bold.**

Diane, an attractive soft-spoken woman in her early sixties, sat with her shoulders slightly hunched and her hands folded in her lap as she blinked back tears, saying, "I don't know where to begin. The life I had seems so far away now. We all used to be so close, my husband, Ken, the kids, and me. My kids are grown now, of course, but they live close enough that they used to visit us on the weekends and spend the holidays with us. But then I got Lyme disease and everything changed."

In sharing her story, Diane related that she had been diagnosed with Lyme disease six years prior. She had no idea how she got it and was confused and worried by the sudden onset of piercing headaches, pain, and swelling in her joints. Like so many others who have Lyme/TBDs, Diane went from one doctor to the next. Most of them told her that there was nothing wrong with her, while others added that perhaps she was experiencing some sort of nervous breakdown. Eventually, she found a doctor who tested and treated her for Lyme disease, but she continued to have long bouts of pain and fatigue that made it difficult for her to engage in too many activities.

After a while, Diane's husband and kids began to do things without her. She also noticed that, even when they were all together, they would talk about her as if she weren't there. Feeling frustrated and discouraged, Diane sought the help of a psychotherapist to learn how to better cope with the impact Lyme disease was having on her and her relationships with her family and friends. "At first I thought this person was going to give me support, and I was glad to have someone I could talk to about how difficult things were for me. But then I had to stop seeing her because she really hurt my feelings. She said that I was just going to have to deal with my symptoms, which would likely disappear anyway and that it's hard for others to believe that I'm sick because I look too healthy to be sick." Diane took a breath and said, "It's hard because nobody seems to understand what I am going through. *It's as if I'm all alone and that I just don't matter anymore."*

Diane then sought out a different kind of therapy with a therapist, Tracey, who used Emotional Freedom Techniques (EFT). She used EFT every session to tap through the pain of being misunderstood and the resulting loneliness of not being seen or heard in a meaningful way. Diane tapped through multiple Specific Events in which she felt misunderstood by her family, doctors, and former therapist. She cried through many of the tapping sessions as she processed her pain.

After many months of using EFT in therapy, Diane said, **"I never saw before how complicated this condition is for all of us.** I was so angry with myself and everyone else, and I was angry at Lyme disease for causing me so much pain. Now that I'm not angry anymore, I feel compassion toward my family and myself for all the confusion we've experienced. **It's not their fault, nor is it mine. This disease is just so confusing."**

Diane later reported that she had engaged in a different kind of conversation with her husband in which she was able to share more about what she was feeling and to listen and connect with how he was feeling. She said, "I really felt heard by Ken, and now **I believe that he really does want to understand.** We both accept that we don't have all the answers, and we are committed to going through this together. I am also in a better place with myself now. **I can accept and take responsibility for my needs,** and **I know that I can call on Ken and the children whenever I need their support.** I am so grateful to not have to do this on my own."

We all have a need to be seen, heard, and understood. These basic human needs (see page 410) are the foundation for our emotional health. When we are not seen, heard or understood, we suffer because our needs are going unmet. The feeling of isolation this causes can be extremely painful and destructive to the psyche and the heart. As Esther Sternberg and Phillip Gold put it in an article in *Scientific American*, "In humans, loneliness is associated with a 'threat,' or adrenalin-like pattern of activation of the stress response... ."[79] When healthcare professionals, family, and/or friends act as if "it's all in your head," they compound this problem.

When your symptoms are misdiagnosed or dismissed, it can be confusing and even isolating because it can feel as though no one understands you. It's really helpful to use EFT on the Specific Events when you have been left believing that you were not seen, heard, or understood. Unfortunately, these are all very common painful emotional issues for those who have Lyme/TBDs.

If the information presented here resonates with you, we invite you to begin with the extended global tapping script that follows. This is a gentle way to get you started and to decrease your overall intensity. Even though the scripted Reminder Phrases may not be reflective of your personal Aspects, we invite you to just go with it, track your progress, and see what happens!

Global Issue Title: I'm Not Seen, Heard, or Understood

- Focus your attention on this **Global Issue** (see page 119).
- Identify one **Limiting Belief** (see page 119) that may be at the root of this Global Issue.
- Take three slow, deep belly breaths as you do a **Body Scan** (see page 81).
- What **Aspects** (see page 123) do you notice?
- Using the **SUD scale** (see page 124), choose a number between 0 (no distress/peaceful) and 10 (highest intensity of distress) to **rate the intensity** of distress you feel about the **Global Issue and Limiting Belief**, along with only the **Aspects** (thoughts, feelings, body sensations, and visual image) that you notice that apply to you.

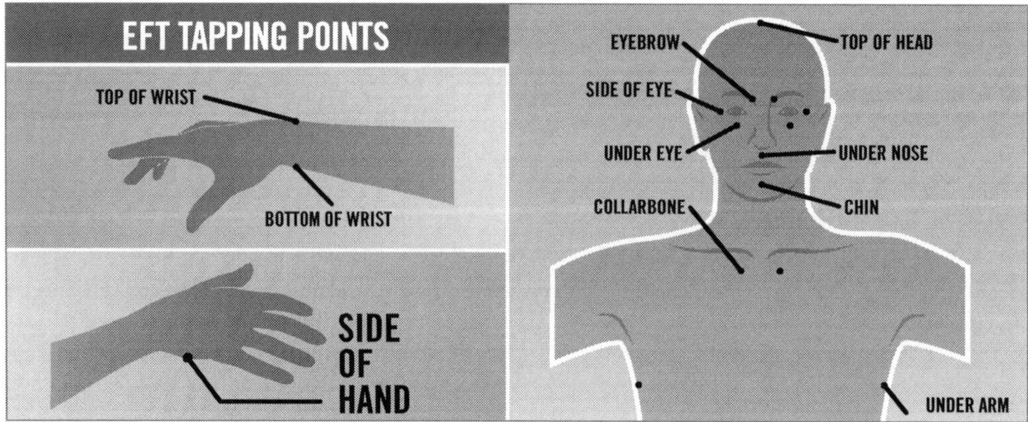

Aspects	Description of Aspects	SUD #:
Global Issue	I'm Not Seen, Heard, or Understood	
Limiting Belief		
Thoughts		
Feelings		
Body Sensations		
Visual Image		

Extended Global Tapping Script: Let's begin tapping (see page 126)

Round 1

Setup:

Side of Hand: Even though no one understands what I am going through, I honor all of my painful emotions.

Side of Hand: Even though I don't have anyone to talk to who understands what I am going through, I accept my feelings about this.

Side of Hand: Even though I don't feel seen or heard by (fill in appropriate names), I am open to the possibility of forgiving all those who have contributed to my pain.

Top of Head: I feel so (state the emotion) about not being understood.

Eyebrow: Nobody understands what I am going through.

Side of Eye: It is so painful to feel this isolated.

Under Eye: It is all in my head!

Under Nose: I feel so invisible!

Chin: I am so angry at people thinking it is all in my head!

Collarbone: My problems fall on deaf ears!

Underarm: Why am I so alone in this?

Top of Head: I feel so overwhelmed!

Top of Wrists Together: Nobody understands how deeply tired I feel.

Bottom of Wrists Together: It makes me so angry that some people think I am lazy!

Round 2

Top of Head: I just want people to understand how bad I feel.
Eyebrow: I feel so alone in my pain.
Side of Eye: I look healthy but feel like hell!
Under Eye: No one hears what I am saying! They just hear what they want to hear!
Under Nose: I feel invisible!
Under Chin: I am so isolated and alone in this!
Collarbone: They don't get me.
Underarm: I really do want to feel better!
Top of Wrists Together: I feel so misunderstood by (fill in appropriate names)!
Bottom of Wrists Together: I feel so alone in my exhaustion.

Take three slow, deep belly breaths as you complete another **Body Scan**. What do you notice now? Note changes to the Aspects and any new ones that may appear below:

Aspects	Description of Aspects	SUD #:
Global Issue	I'm Not Seen, Heard, or Understood	
Limiting Belief		
Thoughts		
Feelings		
Body Sensations		
Visual Image		

If your intensity level about this Global Issue, along with any of its Aspects, is still 3 or above on a SUD scale, continue tapping with the next round. (If you have a SUD scale of 0–2, skip down and finish by tapping through the positive statements and Afformations.)

Round 3

Setup:

Side of Hand: Even though I still feel alone, I honor all my feelings.

Side of Hand: Even though I still feel misunderstood, I accept how I feel.

Side of Hand: Even though I am still angry with people thinking this is "all in my head," I honor and respect how I feel.

Top of Head: I still feel so alone.

Eyebrow: Why don't they listen to me?

Side of Eye: Why don't they understand me?

Under Eye: I am not making all of this up!

Under Nose: I still feel so misunderstood!

Chin: I never thought it would be so hard to have someone listen to me.

Collarbone: I just want to get the help I need.

Underarm: I feel so alone.

Top of Wrists Together: No one truly understands what I am going through.

Bottom of Wrists Together: It is not all in my head!

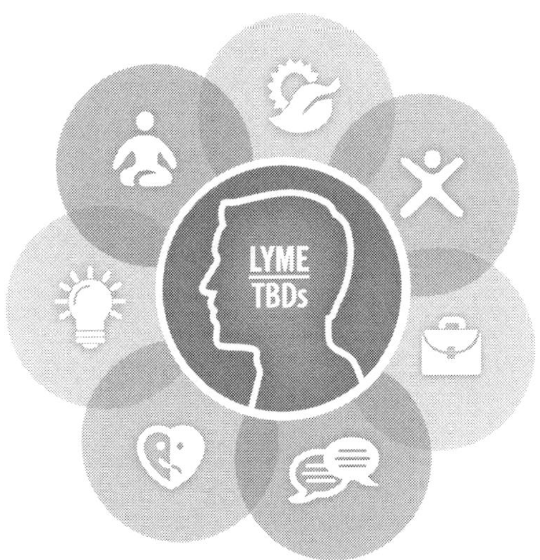

A WELLNESS
STATE OF MIND

Take three slow, deep belly breaths as you complete another **Body Scan**. What do you notice now? Note changes to the Aspects and any new ones that may appear below:

Aspects	Description of Aspects	SUD #:
Global Issue	I'm Not Seen, Heard, or Understood	
Limiting Belief		
Thoughts		
Feelings		
Body Sensations		
Visual Image		

If your intensity level about this Global Issue, along with any of its Aspects, is still 3 or above on a SUD scale, keep tapping through what is in your awareness or move down to **Follow These Steps to Resolution**.

Once you reach a SUD level of 0–2 or when you just want to stop tapping for now and return at a later time, finish up by tapping through the positive statements and Afformations.

Round 4 – Now let's tap through some positive statements!

Top of Head: I am so grateful for my body, and it telling me what it needs.

Eyebrow: I honor my body and its experiences.

Side of Eye: Anybody in my position would feel the way that I do!

Under Eye: I love how resourceful I am.

Under Nose: I am listening to myself and honor what I hear.

Chin: I love how resilient I am.

Collarbone: My body knows how to heal.

Underarm: Every cell in my body is being heard and honored by me.

Top of Wrists Together: I am doing the best I can where I am.

Bottom of Wrists Together: I am grateful for all of those in my life who hear, see, and want to understand what I am going through.

Round 5 – Tapping with Afformations (see page 101)

Top of Head: Why am I able to find practitioners who understand me?

Eyebrow: Why is it possible for me to reach out for support when I need it?

Side of Eye: How is it possible for me to forgive others who have hurt me?

Under Eye: Why is it so easy for me to accept my experiences and validate myself?

Under Nose: Why do I allow it to be easy for me to heal?

Chin: Why is it easy for me to know that I am healing now?

Collarbone: Why is it comforting to know I am healing from the inside out?

Underarm: Why is it possible for me to accept that I do have the need to be seen, heard, and understood?

Top of Wrists Together: Why is it possible for me to honor my experiences with patience, love, and compassion?

Take three slow, deep belly breaths as you complete another **Body Scan**. What do you notice now? Note changes to the Aspects and any new ones that may appear below:

Aspects	Description of Aspects	SUD #:
Global Issue	I'm Not Seen, Heard, or Understood	
Limiting Belief		
Thoughts		
Feelings		
Body Sensations		
Visual Image		

If your intensity level about this Global Issue, along with any of its Aspects, is still 3 or above on a SUD scale, you need to explore them more in depth and follow the directives in **Follow These Steps to Resolution**, on the following page.

Exercise: Developing Self-Awareness

Describe your experience of tapping through this Global Issue.

Which Aspects resolved, decreased, increased, or stayed the same?

If you identified a Limiting Belief, state what (if anything) changed.

State any Empowering Beliefs (see page 119) that you notice now.

What Global Issues/Limiting Beliefs need to be resolved (if any)?

Follow These Steps to Resolution

- When you have the time and energy, move on to the next exercise, **Going Deeper with EFT.** Use this to help you identify Specific Events, along with their Aspects, that are contributing to not resolving this Global Issue/Limiting Belief or with any new ones that may have surfaced while tapping. You may identify many and this is to be expected.
- Just break down one Specific Event at a time and tap it until resolved. Title the rest of the Specific Events that you have identified and add them to the **List of Titled Specific Events** on page 156 so that you can return to them at a later time to tap. You can use the **Blank Tapping Script** on page 404 or the **Vent While You Tap** worksheet on page 409 to assist you while tapping through a Specific Event.

Exercise: Going Deeper with EFT

If you just completed tapping through the extended global tapping script, and you still feel that the issue is unresolved, it's time to go deeper. What is keeping it unresolved? Title your Global Issue in the space provided below. Answer the following questions so that you can discover, uncover, and recover from the unresolved Specific Events and related Aspects that created and support the Limiting Belief you wish to resolve.

Global Issue: ______________________________

1. What Limiting Beliefs do you have at the root of this Global Issue? Rate the level of intensity of how true they are for you between SUD 0 (not true at all) and 10 (completely true).

______________________________ • SUD # (0–10): ____

______________________________ • SUD # (0–10): ____

2. Title and list the Specific Events in which you learned the Limiting Belief(s) (you can also add them to your List of Titled Specific Events on page 156).

____

____

____

____

____

____

3. Choose one Specific Event to break down here. Title: ______________________________

____

4. Tune into your titled Specific Event and identify only those Aspects that apply to you, below:

What thoughts do you notice?

______________________________ • SUD # (0–10): ____

______________________________ • SUD # (0–10): ____

Do your thoughts have the quality of Small Mind or Large Mind (see page 90)?____________

Describe your Large Mind thoughts (if any):________________________________

____

Describe your Small Mind thoughts (if any): ________________________________

____

What emotions are you feeling?

____ • SUD # (0–10): ____

____ • SUD # (0–10): ____

____ • SUD # (0–10): ____

What body sensation do you notice?

____ • SUD # (0–10): ____

Where is the sensation located?________________________ • SUD # (0–10): ____

Does this sensation have a temperature?____ Describe:______________________

____ • SUD # (0–10): ____

Texture?______________________________________ • SUD # (0–10): ____

Color?____ • SUD # (0–10): ____

Describe a visual image that you have (if any): ____________________________

____ • SUD # (0–10): ____

5. Use the Aspects you have just identified to create your Reminder Phrases.
6. Stay tuned into your titled Specific Event.
7. Start tapping using the Modified EFT Basic Recipe on page 121. You can use the Aspects you have identified here to fill in the Reminder Phrases on the **Blank Tapping Script** on page 404 or the **Vent While You Tap** worksheet on page 409 to assist you in creating your own tapping script.

REPEAT PROCESS IF UNRESOLVED

Be aware of any changes in the intensity of distress you feel in relation to the Aspects, along with any new ones that emerge as you tap through the Rounds of EFT. Continue to tap, repeating the EFT Basic Recipe until your Specific Event, along with its Aspects, is resolved at a SUD level of 0–2. Also be mindful of shifts in Limiting Beliefs and the emergence of any new Empowering ones. To get full resolution of a Global Issue, the Limiting Beliefs must be released by resolving other painful Specific Events that are validating them.

CHAPTER 27 Discouraged by Treatment Disappointments

Case Study

Note: *Limiting Beliefs are italicized* and **Empowering Beliefs are in bold**.

Susan was 24 years old and struggling to get by on a part-time job as an office assistant for a small business. She had been suffering with Lyme disease for more than ten years and was at a loss for where to turn for help. As she talked about her experiences, she said, "I've been to so many different doctors, but none of them have been able to help me. I've done everything they told me to do, and I still don't feel better. *I guess I'm just stuck with this.*"

Susan went on to say that she thought she contracted Lyme disease as a child while at summer camp. She recalled going to a camp counselor about a rash that a friend had noticed behind her knee. The counselor reported the rash to her mother, but it wasn't until Susan was home and came down with flu-like symptoms that her mother took her to the family doctor. He dismissed it as "nothing to worry about." Although Susan's initial symptoms cleared, she later developed migrating body pain, irritability, and fatigue. Her mother took her to several different doctors who said that her symptoms were nothing serious. Persisting in her effort to find out what was wrong with her daughter, Susan's mother finally found a doctor who listened but who misdiagnosed Susan with infectious mononucleosis, instructing her to rest.

As Susan's symptoms persisted and worsened, she struggled to get through high school. Not one to give up, she eventually graduated from college as well. Meanwhile, she continued seeking treatment for her symptoms. She saw many different doctors, none of whom helped her. Eventually, she found a doctor who diagnosed her with Lyme disease, but he prescribed no more than the standard protocol of antibiotics. Even though Susan did not feel better, and she continued to seek help.

Knowing that there was something wrong, Susan persisted in her search for help until she found a Lyme-literate physician who confirmed that she did, in fact, still have Lyme disease. This gave her tremendous hope, but the treatment she received did not yield the results she expected. She was quite disappointed and discouraged when she came in for therapy. "*It hurts too much now to believe anything will help me. There's just no point in getting my hopes up because I'll just be disappointed again.*"

Through many therapy sessions, Susan tapped through to resolution the specific treatment failures that had occurred up to that point in her process. She released her *Limiting Beliefs* and regained **hope for recovery**. Susan **believed again**

that she would find someone who could help her. Susan persisted in her quest for healing. It took great courage and resilience for her to keep looking for answers.

Susan was thrilled when she finally found a Lyme-literate doctor who took her seriously and was able to provide her with a proper diagnosis. It was a validation of her concerns and a reward for all the hard work she had done. But then, the treatments failed again and the recovery she had hoped for began to seem more like a mirage than a reality. "**I really believed that I had found a doctor who could help me. I believed that I was finally going to get better**, but none of his treatments worked for me. I feel so disappointed and discouraged again."

Tapping through her current treatment disappointments helped Susan release more Limiting Beliefs, along with her discouragement. She now acknowledged how resilient she had been through her ordeal. Susan noticed that she was feeling much calmer, **more hopeful,** and better able to manage and work through her challenges. "**I've gotten this far, and now I know I will find what I need for my recovery. It might take some time, but I'm really proud of myself for not giving up! I am stronger than I thought.** I also noticed the positive impact this work has made in my body. My pain level is down, and I am sleeping much better now." Susan continued to use EFT on current life stressors **and remained hopeful that she would find new treatments to help her recover**. She eventually did find treatment strategies that worked for her.

A mind state of distrust decreases the body's capacity to respond positively to treatment. It also closes a person to exploring other possibilities for recovery. The simple truth of the matter is that your mind is so powerful that if you believe *nothing will help you heal*, then nothing will.

If you, like Susan, have had too many treatment disappointments to trust that anything or anyone can help you now, we suggest that you make a list of the most painful ones you can remember. Give each one a title and then go through them one at a time at your own pace using EFT to facilitate resolution of painful emotions and *Limiting Beliefs*, thus fostering **Empowering Beliefs creating hope.**

If the information presented here resonates with you, we invite you to begin with the extended global tapping script that follows. This is a gentle way to get you started and to decrease your overall intensity. Even though the scripted Reminder Phrases may not be reflective of your personal Aspects, we invite you to just go with it, track your progress, and see what happens!

Global Issue Title: Discouraged by Treatment Disappointments

- Focus your attention on this **Global Issue** (see page 119).
- Identify one **Limiting Belief** (see page 119) that may be at the root of this Global Issue.
- Take three slow, deep belly breaths as you do a **Body Scan** (see page 81).
- What **Aspects** (see page 123) do you notice?
- Using the **SUD scale** (see page 124), choose a number between 0 (no distress/peaceful) and 10 (highest intensity of distress) to **rate the intensity** of distress you feel about the **Global Issue and Limiting Belief**, along with only the **Aspects** (thoughts, feelings, body sensations, and visual image) that you notice that apply to you.

Aspects	Description of Aspects	SUD #:
Global Issue	Treatment Disappointments	
Limiting Belief		
Thoughts		
Feelings		
Body Sensations		
Visual Image		

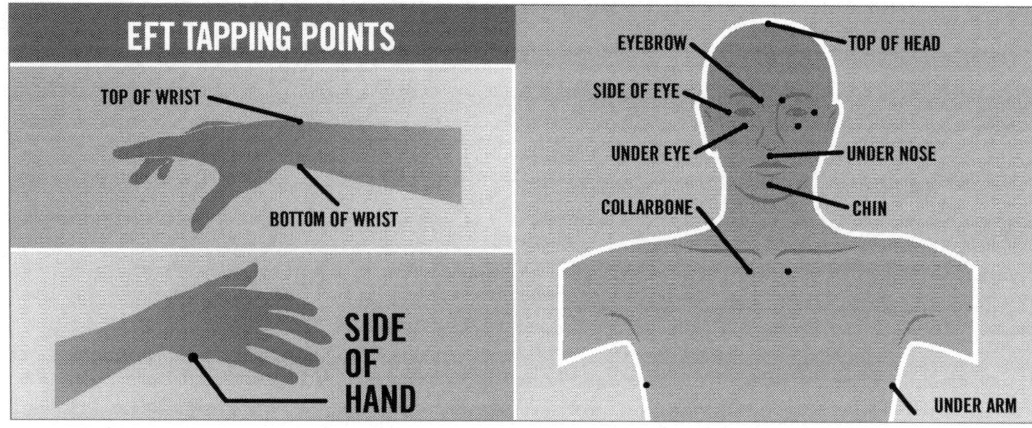

Extended Global Tapping Script: Let's begin tapping **(see page 126)**

Round 1

Setup:

Side of Hand: Even though I have not found a treatment that will help me, I am open and committed to finding it.

Side of Hand: Even though I have had so many disappointments with my treatments, I honor all of my feelings and experiences.

Side of Hand: Even though I have tried everything and nothing works, I am open to new possibilities.

Top of Head: I don't trust that any treatment will work for me, so why bother?

Eyebrow: It is my fate; I might as well accept it.

Side of Eye: Treatments didn't work for me in the past, so why would they now?

Under Eye: I've tried everything and nothing works.

Under Nose: I feel so disappointed!

Chin: I'll just get my hopes up and be disappointed again.

Collarbone: I really wanted this to work.

Under Arm: I trusted and was let down.

Top of Wrists Together: I've been disappointed every time; so why keep looking?

Bottom of Wrists Together: I don't have the energy to try something new.

Slowly complete a deep belly breath and then keep tapping.

Round 2

Top of Head: I feel so much disappointment.

Eyebrow: I really wanted it to work.

Side of Eye: My doctor(s) let me down.

Under Eye: I don't even know if I can trust doctors anymore.

Under Nose: I don't know whom to trust.

Chin: Nothing and no one can help me!

Collarbone: I might as well give up.

Under Arm: I feel so hopeless.

Top of Wrists Together: I feel so disappointed!

Bottom of Wrists Together: Why even bother?

Take three slow, deep belly breaths as you complete another **Body Scan**. What do you notice now? Note changes to the Aspects and any new ones that may appear below:

Aspects	Description of Aspects	SUD #:
Global Issue	Treatment Disappointments	
Limiting Belief		
Thoughts		
Feelings		
Body Sensations		
Visual Image		

If your intensity level about this Global Issue, along with any of its Aspects, is still 3 or above on a SUD scale, continue tapping with the next round. (If you have a SUD scale of 0–2, skip down and finish by tapping through the positive statements and Afformations.)

Round 3

Setup:

Side of Hand: Even though I am still disappointed, I honor and respect myself.

Side of Hand: Even though I still feel so much disappointment, I honor all of my feelings.

Side of Hand: Even though I still don't believe I can be helped, I am open to new possibilities for myself.

Top of Head: All of this remaining doubt.

Eyebrow: This remaining disappointment.

Side of Eye: Nothing will help me. Why bother?

Under Eye: So many doctors let me down. Whom can I trust?

Under Nose: It hurts too much to keep trying.

Chin: A part of me wants to keep trying new treatments, but another part wants to quit.

Collarbone: I don't know if I can trust like I used to.

Under Arm: It is still so painful to have believed and been let down.

Top of Wrists Together: All of this remaining disappointment.

Bottom of Wrists Together: I really do want to be open to new possibilities.

Take three slow, deep belly breaths as you complete another **Body Scan**. What do you notice now? Note changes to the Aspects and any new ones that may appear below:

Aspects	Description of Aspects	SUD #:
Global Issue	Treatment Disappointments	
Limiting Belief		
Thoughts		
Feelings		
Body Sensations		
Visual Image		

If your intensity level about this Global Issue, along with any of its Aspects, is still 3 or above on a SUD scale, keep tapping through what is in your awareness or move down to **Follow These Steps to Resolution**.

Once you reach a SUD level of 0–2 or when you just want to stop tapping for now and return at a later time, finish up by tapping through the positive statements and Afformations.

Round 4 – Now let's tap through some positive statements!

Top of Head: I am open to new possibilities for myself.

Eyebrow: Doctors did get it wrong in the past, but I am taking charge of my own healing now.

Side of Eye: I am eager to try new treatments to help myself heal.

Under Eye: I am in charge of my healing process and will not stop until I find what works for me.

Under Nose: I give my body permission to heal.

Chin: I know that I will find what I need to recover.

Collarbone: My body is capable of greatness, and I can overcome this.

Under Arm: I reclaim my power and direct my intention to fully recover.

Top of Wrists Together: I trust my intuition and my body to know what I need.

Bottom of Wrists Together: I will find what I need to recover.

Round 5 – Tapping with Afformations (see page 101)

Top of Head: How is it so easy for me to trust myself and go after what I need?

Eyebrow: Why is it possible for me to trust my healing process again?

Side of Eye: Why is it so easy to believe that I am being led to what I need to heal?

Under Eye: Why is it possible for my body to heal?

Under Nose: Why is it so easy to believe that my body is intelligent and is capable of healing?

Chin: Why am I able to have hope and trust today?

Collarbone: Why am I able to forgive those who've hurt me?

Under Arm: Why is it possible to find the treatments that work best for me?

Top of Wrists Together: Why is it so easy for me to trust a new treatment protocol?

Bottom of Wrists Together: Why is it possible for me to continue to take positive actions for my recovery?

Take three slow, deep belly breaths as you complete another **Body Scan**. What do you notice now? Note changes to the Aspects and any new ones that may appear below:

Aspects	Description of Aspects	SUD #:
Global Issue	Treatment Disappointments	
Limiting Belief		
Thoughts		
Feelings		
Body Sensations		
Visual Image		

If your intensity level about this Global Issue, along with any of its Aspects, is still 3 or above on a SUD scale, you need to explore them more in depth and follow the directives in **Follow These Steps to Resolution**, on the following page.

Exercise: Developing Self-Awareness

Describe your experience of tapping through this Global Issue.

Which Aspects resolved, decreased, increased, or stayed the same?

If you identified a Limiting Belief, state what (if anything) changed.

State any Empowering Beliefs (see page 119) that you notice now.

What Global Issues/Limiting Beliefs need to be resolved (if any)?

Follow These Steps to Resolution

- When you have the time and energy, move on to the next exercise, **Going Deeper with EFT.** Use this to help you identify Specific Events, along with their Aspects, that are contributing to not resolving this Global Issue/Limiting Belief or with any new ones that may have surfaced while tapping. You may identify many and this is to be expected.
- Just break down one Specific Event at a time and tap it until resolved. Title the rest of the Specific Events that you have identified and add them to the **List of Titled Specific Events** on page 156 so that you can return to them at a later time to tap. You can use the **Blank Tapping Script** on page 404 or the **Vent While You Tap** worksheet on page 409 to assist you while tapping through a Specific Event.

Exercise: Going Deeper with EFT

If you just completed tapping through the extended global tapping script, and you still feel that the issue is unresolved, it's time to go deeper. What is keeping it unresolved? Title your Global Issue in the space provided below. Answer the following questions so that you can discover, uncover, and recover from the unresolved Specific Events and related Aspects that created and support the Limiting Belief you wish to resolve.

Global Issue: ______________________________

1. What Limiting Beliefs do you have at the root of this Global Issue? Rate the level of intensity of how true they are for you between SUD 0 (not true at all) and 10 (completely true).

______________________________ • SUD # (0–10): ____

______________________________ • SUD # (0–10): ____

2. Title and list the Specific Events in which you learned the Limiting Belief(s) (you can also add them to your List of Titled Specific Events on page 156).

____

____

____

____

____

____

3. Choose one Specific Event to break down here. Title: ______________________________

____

4. Tune into your titled Specific Event and identify only those Aspects that apply to you, below:

What thoughts do you notice?

______________________________ • SUD # (0–10): ____

______________________________ • SUD # (0–10): ____

Do your thoughts have the quality of Small Mind or Large Mind (see page 90)?____________

Describe your Large Mind thoughts (if any):______________________________________

____

Describe your Small Mind thoughts (if any): ______________________________________

____

What emotions are you feeling?

____ • SUD # (0–10): ____

____ • SUD # (0–10): ____

____ • SUD # (0–10): ____

What body sensation do you notice?

____ • SUD # (0–10): ____

Where is the sensation located?________________________• SUD # (0–10): ____

Does this sensation have a temperature?____ Describe:______________________

____ • SUD # (0–10): ____

Texture?____ • SUD # (0–10): ____

Color?____ • SUD # (0–10): ____

Describe a visual image that you have (if any): ______________________________

____ • SUD # (0–10): ____

5. Use the Aspects you have just identified to create your Reminder Phrases.
6. Stay tuned into your titled Specific Event.
7. Start tapping using the Modified EFT Basic Recipe on page 121. You can use the Aspects you have identified here to fill in the Reminder Phrases on the **Blank Tapping Script** on page 404 or the **Vent While You Tap** worksheet on page 409 to assist you in creating your own tapping script.

REPEAT PROCESS IF UNRESOLVED

Be aware of any changes in the intensity of distress you feel in relation to the Aspects, along with any new ones that emerge as you tap through the Rounds of EFT. Continue to tap, repeating the EFT Basic Recipe until your Specific Event, along with its Aspects, is resolved at a SUD level of 0–2. Also be mindful of shifts in Limiting Beliefs and the emergence of any new Empowering ones. To get full resolution of a Global Issue, the Limiting Beliefs must be released by resolving other painful Specific Events that are validating them.

CHAPTER 28

Doctors Don't Always Know Best!

Case Study

Note: *Limiting Beliefs are italicized* and **Empowering Beliefs are in bold.**

Laura, a 40-year-old mother of three had unexplained pain for four months and went to ten different doctors and received ten different answers to her questions. She said, "I don't know who or what to believe. I learned to trust authority figures, especially doctors. I thought they would know how to help me, but no one is giving me answers! I've even had some doctors who were so condescending that they had the nerve to treat me like a child, standing there with their arms crossed looking down on me and telling me, 'There's nothing physically wrong with you. Maybe you should see a psychiatrist.' What! I just want someone to tell me what's wrong and to help me get better. I'm so angry and frustrated! I don't know what else to do, and I don't know where to turn!"

Laura tapped on her disappointments about her needs not being met by the medical professionals. She expressed regret that she relied on them for so many years without questioning her role in her own healing. Her "aha" moment came when she said, "I see now that I was expecting them to do all the work and to have all the answers for me. **I know now that I am the authority over my own body and that I need to take responsibility for it.** I feel so much better now that I believe this way!"

Laura's situation is very similar to many other people with undiagnosed Lyme/TBDs. They go from doctor to doctor looking for answers and are all too often met with negative judgments, nasty looks, and misdiagnoses. I, Tracey, had this happen to me, too! At the onset of my Lyme symptoms, I went to more than ten doctors over several years. I especially remember early in my process feeling horribly degraded after being hospitalized for a particularly severe episode of pain that seared through my body and prevented me from walking. A group of residents stood around my bed, shaking their heads because they did not know why I was so crippled. They then proposed that the cause could be a psychological issue.

As soon as they left the room, I started tapping through my anger and outrage at the doctors because I knew that I was not making it up! I tapped and cried out my outrage. I continued to seek out other doctors who chased my migrating joint pain and swelling with a scalpel. I had my gall bladder removed, a total knee replacement, neck fusion, and both shoulders repaired. Later on, I was diagnosed with bipolar disorder! I allowed them to convince me for a short time *that it was all in my head!*

I was also put on multiple psychiatric and neurological medications, and yet all of these interventions added up to nothing more than at best a temporary relief of my symptoms. And though I wasn't getting better, I accepted my doctors' explanations because I thought they had the answers, and because two of my Western Blot tests came back CDC-negative (Centers for Disease Control standards).

In the end and after many sessions of tapping, **I realized that it was going to be up to me to find the right people to help me recover.** I took my power back and decided not to return to my old doctors. I no longer had to rely on these "authorities" only to hear there was nothing wrong with me! **I felt empowered to act on the truth of what my body was telling me.**

Eventually, a Lyme-literate physician diagnosed me with Lyme disease. I received the proper treatment with compassionate care and eventually recovered. After being successfully treated, I no longer had any symptoms of bipolar disorder. It was determined that Lyme disease had, in fact, caused my unstable moods and that I had been misdiagnosed.

Many of us expect doctors to be nonjudgmental, compassionate, and caring professionals who either have the answers, will look for the answers, or will honestly tell us they don't know the answers. When these expectations are not met, it's very disappointing, confusing, and frustrating. Questions arise like, "Who can I trust with my healthcare needs?," "What's going to happen to me?," and "Am I ever going to get better?"

Unresolved disappointments can create a general mistrust of all doctors (authority figures), especially when dealing with those who lack awareness about Lyme disease. It's really important to take some time to tap through the Specific Events—past or present—when you have been discounted and/or disappointed by a doctor. Suppressed anger and disappointment can interfere with current treatment expectations, intentions, and faith in your current or future doctor. When a doctor shows a lack of empathy and compassion this may "induce negative expectations in the patient and may lead to clinical worsening." On the other hand, the expectation that a treatment will be helpful combined with consistent compassionate care can have "substantial therapeutic benefit."[80,81,82] It is also the case that patients with a history of treatment failures are less likely to trust that a new approach will work even if a Lyme-literate physician provides it.

EFT can help you to cultivate a wellness state of mind that will:

- Cultivate the hope needed to find the doctors and treatments needed to recover
- Help you to build trust and rapport with the doctors/treatment team of your choosing
- Open you to new possibilities for healing and recovery
- Increase your body's responsiveness to treatment

To resolve this Global Issue, identify the painful Specific Events that you have had with doctor(s) that are impeding your ability to find and trust the doctors, along with the treatments, that are needed to help you recover. If you still do not experience resolution, you may need to go deeper and ask yourself when in the past have you also been let down by someone in "authority" such as a caregiver, teacher, or mentor. This is important because it may be that the unresolved emotional pain of those Specific Events are at the root to your current distrust of doctors and treatment options.

If the information presented here resonates with you, we invite you to begin with the extended global tapping script that follows. This is a gentle way to get you started and to decrease your overall intensity. Even though the scripted Reminder Phrases may not be reflective of your personal Aspects, we invite you to just go with it, track your progress, and see what happens!

Global Issue Title: Doctors Don't Always Know Best!

- Focus your attention on this **Global Issue** (see page 119).
- Identify one **Limiting Belief** (see page 119) that may be at the root of this Global Issue.
- Take three slow, deep belly breaths as you do a **Body Scan** (see page 81).
- What **Aspects** (see page 123) do you notice?
- Using the **SUD scale** (see page 124), choose a number between 0 (no distress/peaceful) and 10 (highest intensity of distress) to **rate the intensity** of distress you feel about the **Global Issue and Limiting Belief**, along with only the **Aspects** (thoughts, feelings, body sensations, and visual image) that you notice that apply to you.

Aspects	Description of Aspects	SUD #:
Global Issue	Doctors Don't Always Know Best!	
Limiting Belief		
Thoughts		
Feelings		
Body Sensations		
Visual Image		

A WELLNESS
STATE OF MIND

Extended Global Tapping Script: Let's begin tapping (see page 126)

Round 1

Setup:

Side of Hand: Even though doctors don't know best, I honor my body and all that it is telling me about what I need.

Side of Hand: Even though he/she said there's no such thing as chronic Lyme disease, I know what I am experiencing.

Side of Hand: Even though my doctor(s) were wrong in their assessment of me, I know something isn't right and I have to keep looking.

Top of Head: I feel so judged and let down!

Eyebrow: It is all in my head!

Side of Eye: I feel so disappointed!

Under Eye: I feel so angry!

Under Nose: I went to (X number of) doctors and no one believed me!

Chin: I was laughed at!

Collarbone: They said I don't look sick!

Under Arm: I am so angry with them!

Top of Wrists Together: It is all psychological!

Bottom of Wrists Together: I feel so misunderstood and let down by those I trusted.

Slowly complete a deep belly breath and then keep tapping.

Round 2

Top of Head: I am so disappointed with the medical profession. It failed me!

Eyebrow: I feel alone in my pain. No doctor believes me.

Side of Eye: They didn't hear or believe my experiences of my pain!

Under Eye: I was misdiagnosed with a mental illness!

Under Nose: They were rude and condescending to me!

Chin: Who do they think they are?!

Collarbone: I am so angry!

Under Arm: Doctors don't know everything!

Top of Wrists Together: My insurance company doesn't even believe in chronic Lyme and won't cover my treatment!

Bottom of Wrists Together: I can't even get my antibiotics covered because they say I don't need them!

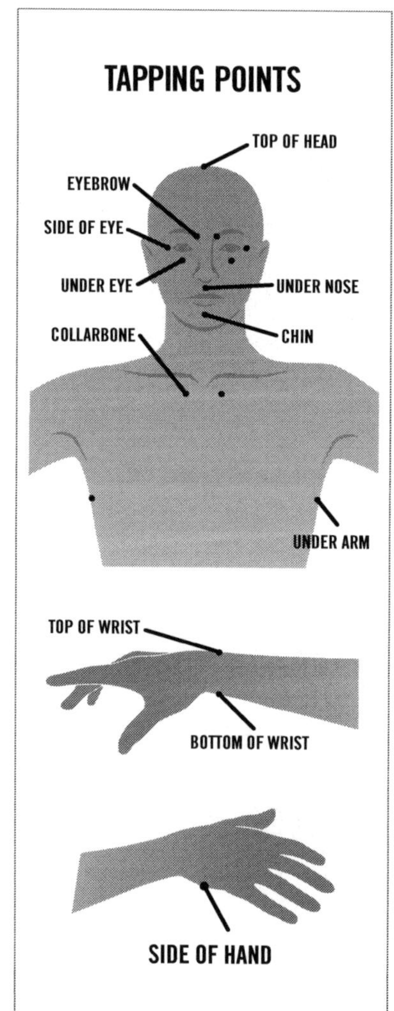

Take three slow, deep belly breaths as you complete another **Body Scan**. What do you notice now? Note changes to the Aspects and any new ones that may appear below:

Aspects	Description of Aspects	SUD #:
Global Issue	Doctors Don't Always Know Best!	
Limiting Belief		
Thoughts		
Feelings		
Body Sensations		
Visual Image		

If your intensity level about this Global Issue, along with any of its Aspects, is still 3 or above on a SUD scale, continue tapping with the next round. (If you have a SUD scale of 0–2, skip down and finish by tapping through the positive statements and Affornations.)

Round 3

Setup:

Side of Hand: Even though I still feel (state the emotion) about my doctor(s), I honor all of my feelings.

Side of Hand: Even though I still feel (state the emotion) about my insurance company for not covering my treatment, I will find a way to persevere.

Side of Hand: Even though I still feel distrusting of doctors, I am open to the possibility that I will find the right doctor and treatment to help me recover.

Top of Head: I still feel so let down.

Eyebrow: I continue to feel invisible to my doctors!

Side of Eye: I am still frustrated with my insurance company!

Under Eye: I feel so dismissed by everyone!

Under Nose: My doctors let me down.

Chin: Why didn't they just listen to me and believe what I was experiencing?

Collarbone: It is not all in my head!

Under Arm: I was misdiagnosed so many times! I trusted them!

Top of Wrists Together: How can chronic Lyme disease not exist when I am suffering from it?

Bottom of Wrists Together: So much time was wasted because nobody believed me!

Take three slow, deep belly breaths as you complete another **Body Scan**. What do you notice now? Note changes to the Aspects and any new ones that may appear below:

Aspects	Description of Aspects	SUD #:
Global Issue	Doctors Don't Always Know Best!	
Limiting Belief		
Thoughts		
Feelings		
Body Sensations		
Visual Image		

If your intensity level about this Global Issue, along with any of its Aspects, is still 3 or above on a SUD scale, keep tapping through what is in your awareness or move down to **Follow These Steps to Resolution**.

Once you reach a SUD level of 0–2 or when you just want to stop tapping for now and return at a later time, finish up by tapping through the positive statements and Afformations.

Round 4 – Now let's tap through some positive statements!

Top of Head: I am the authority of my body, and I will not stop until I find what is going to help me.

Eyebrow: I honor all of my feelings about this. Anybody in my situation would feel the same way!

Side of Eye: I am so grateful for my body's intelligence. It was right all along.

Under Eye: My body knows what it needs, and I am listening.

Under Nose: I am my own advocate, and I will find what I need to recover.

Chin: I am power-filled to make the decisions I need to create a full recovery.

Collarbone: I believe in what my body is saying.

Under Arm: I will advocate for myself and find who I need to get well.

Top of Wrists Together: I am my authority figure.

Bottom of Wrists Together: I am open to forgiving those who let me down in the past and moving forward with an open mind.

Round 5 – Tapping with Afformations (see page 101)

Top of Head: Why is it so easy for me to find the doctor who values my best and highest good?

Eyebrow: How is it so easy for me to be open to abundance in all forms?

Side of Eye: Why am I able to advocate for myself and keep speaking my truth?

Under Eye: Why is it so easy for me to be my own authority figure and find what I need to recover?

Under Nose: Why is it so easy for me to believe that my best and highest good is being served?

Chin: Why is it so easy for me to release the past so I may move forward now?

Collarbone: Why is it so easy for me to follow the guidance of my Higher Self?

Under Arm: Why is it possible for me to trust the doctor I have and the treatment I have chosen?

Top of Wrists Together: Why is it so easy for me to be grateful for what I do have?

Bottom of Wrists Together: Why is it possible for me to be a partner with my doctor, who sees, hears, and understands me?

Take three slow, deep belly breaths as you complete another **Body Scan**. What do you notice now? Note changes to the Aspects and any new ones that may appear below:

Aspects	Description of Aspects	SUD #:
Global Issue	Doctors Don't Always Know Best!	
Limiting Belief		
Thoughts		
Feelings		
Body Sensations		
Visual Image		

If your intensity level about this Global Issue, along with any of its Aspects, is still 3 or above on a SUD scale, you need to explore them more in depth and follow the directives in **Follow These Steps to Resolution**, on the following page.

Exercise: Developing Self-Awareness

Describe your experience of tapping through this Global Issue.

Which Aspects resolved, decreased, increased, or stayed the same?

If you identified a Limiting Belief, state what (if anything) changed.

State any Empowering Beliefs (see page 119) that you notice now.

What Global Issues/Limiting Beliefs need to be resolved (if any)?

Follow These Steps to Resolution

- When you have the time and energy, move on to the next exercise, **Going Deeper with EFT.** Use this to help you identify Specific Events, along with their Aspects, that are contributing to not resolving this Global Issue/Limiting Belief or with any new ones that may have surfaced while tapping. You may identify many and this is to be expected.
- Just break down one Specific Event at a time and tap it until resolved. Title the rest of the Specific Events that you have identified and add them to the **List of Titled Specific Events** on page 156 so that you can return to them at a later time to tap. You can use the **Blank Tapping Script** on page 404 or the **Vent While You Tap** worksheet on page 409 to assist you while tapping through a Specific Event.

Exercise: Going Deeper with EFT

If you just completed tapping through the extended global tapping script, and you still feel that the issue is unresolved, it's time to go deeper. What is keeping it unresolved? Title your Global Issue in the space provided below. Answer the following questions so that you can discover, uncover, and recover from the unresolved Specific Events and related Aspects that created and support the Limiting Belief you wish to resolve.

Global Issue: ______________________________

1. What Limiting Beliefs do you have at the root of this Global Issue? Rate the level of intensity of how true they are for you between SUD 0 (not true at all) and 10 (completely true).

______________________________ • SUD # (0–10): ____

______________________________ • SUD # (0–10): ____

2. Title and list the Specific Events in which you learned the Limiting Belief(s) (you can also add them to your List of Titled Specific Events on page 156).

____

____

____

____

____

____

3. Choose one Specific Event to break down here. Title: ______________________________

____

4. Tune into your titled Specific Event and identify only those Aspects that apply to you, below:

What thoughts do you notice?

______________________________ • SUD # (0–10): ____

______________________________ • SUD # (0–10): ____

Do your thoughts have the quality of Small Mind or Large Mind (see page 90)?______________

Describe your Large Mind thoughts (if any):______________________________

____

Describe your Small Mind thoughts (if any): ______________________________

____

What emotions are you feeling?

____ • SUD # (0–10): ____

____ • SUD # (0–10): ____

____ • SUD # (0–10): ____

What body sensation do you notice?

____ • SUD # (0–10): ____

Where is the sensation located?_______________________ • SUD # (0–10): ____

Does this sensation have a temperature?____ Describe:________________________

____ • SUD # (0–10): ____

Texture?_____________________________________ • SUD # (0–10): ____

Color?______________________________________ • SUD # (0–10): ____

Describe a visual image that you have (if any): ___________________________

____ • SUD # (0–10): ____

5. Use the Aspects you have just identified to create your Reminder Phrases.
6. Stay tuned into your titled Specific Event.
7. Start tapping using the Modified EFT Basic Recipe on page 121. You can use the Aspects you have identified here to fill in the Reminder Phrases on the **Blank Tapping Script** on page 404 or the **Vent While You Tap** worksheet on page 409 to assist you in creating your own tapping script.

REPEAT PROCESS IF UNRESOLVED

Be aware of any changes in the intensity of distress you feel in relation to the Aspects, along with any new ones that emerge as you tap through the Rounds of EFT. Continue to tap, repeating the EFT Basic Recipe until your Specific Event, along with its Aspects, is resolved at a SUD level of 0–2. Also be mindful of shifts in Limiting Beliefs and the emergence of any new Empowering ones. To get full resolution of a Global Issue, the Limiting Beliefs must be released by resolving other painful Specific Events that are validating them.

CHAPTER 29

Am I Ever Going to Get Better?

Case Study

 **Note:** *Limiting Beliefs are italicized* and **Empowering Beliefs are in bold.**

Anyone who has a chronic disease, especially one as taxing and complicated to treat as Lyme/TBDs, has periods when their hope for recovery is challenged by the longevity of the illness. As months slip into years and the pain and exhaustion continue, hope can gradually slip away with doubt creeping in. This can create the Global issue, *"I'm never going to get better."*

As I, Tracey, was in the midst of my own Lyme disease recovery process, I had many periods when I became so discouraged and depressed. I knew that maintaining a wellness state of mind was critical to my healing and recovery, but there were some days when I was so overcome by exhaustion and apathy, that I just couldn't get myself there. I sat in my recliner and stared blankly at the TV. I watched commercial after commercial and wondered, "Am I ever going to get better?" Believe it or not, moments like these are the perfect time to tap, but honestly it was the last thing I wanted to do!

I admit it. Despite all that I knew I just didn't want to tap! I was in what I called the *"forgetting fog"*—not the brain fog we can get, but rather *forgetting that recovery was possible* and justified not taking any positive action steps to help myself feel better. During these times, one part of me wanted to use EFT to remove the *forgetting fog* and **be hopeful that I can feel better**, while *another part of me was resigned to remaining stuck in it.* I was in an internal conflict between *my* Empowering Beliefs *wanting to take action and my Limiting Beliefs in the "forgetting fog"* justifying that no action be taken. *I believed that the hardest thing for me to do right at that moment was to tap.* The only way through was to force myself to take some kind of positive action, even if I did not want to.

Either I could stay there in limbo with my pain and exhaustion getting the better of me or I could use EFT or TAB (see page 411) to help myself feel better. As hard as it was to do anything at all, I chose to tap through the inner conflict I was in. It took no more than about 10 to 15 minutes of tapping for me to experience a positive cognitive and emotional shift.

Whenever I found myself back in the *"forgetting fog,"* I would push myself to tap, and I always experienced a positive emotional shift. I will never forget the day when, having finished many rounds of tapping, I just got up out of my recliner, picked up around the house, and took a shower! It was as if I had suddenly come back to life! I had energy again: energy to **have hope that I can recover**, energy **to care**, and energy **to make positive choices** and **to take positive action**. It wasn't easy, but on those days when I felt myself becoming ensnared in the *"forgetting fog,"* I forced myself to tap.

The more I tapped, the more the *Limiting Beliefs* in the *"forgetting fog"* lost its grip on me until it finally lifted. My Empowering Beliefs shifted my perception to remembering, **"I can help myself feel better** and that **my recovery was happening."** I then **believed** that, **"it is what it is for now and it will not be forever. I am getting better and I will recover."** And I did!

It may be that you have experienced other times in your recovery when you felt conflicted about taking positive action to help yourself. There is no judgment here, but rather honoring yourself in these moments on the healing journey and moving through them as gently and compassionately as possible. If you are in an internal conflict between Limiting Beliefs that support no action and Empowering Beliefs that enable you to take positive action, this global tapping script is a great place to start. Stay tuned in to the feelings and body sensations you are having now and follow along with the tapping script. Even though the scripted Reminder Phrases may not be reflective of your personal Aspects, we invite you to just go with it, track your progress, and see what happens!

Global Issue Title: Am I Ever Going to Get Better?

- Focus your attention on this **Global Issue** (see page 119).
- Identify one **Limiting Belief** (see page 119) that may be at the root of this Global Issue.
- Take three slow, deep belly breaths as you do a **Body Scan** (see page 81).
- What **Aspects** (see page 123) do you notice?
- Using the **SUD scale** (see page 124), choose a number between 0 (no distress/peaceful) and 10 (highest intensity of distress) to **rate the intensity** of distress you feel about the **Global Issue and Limiting Belief**, along with only the **Aspects** (thoughts, feelings, body sensations, and visual image) that you notice that apply to you.

Aspects	Description of Aspects	SUD #:
Global Issue	Am I ever going to get better?	
Limiting Belief		
Thoughts		
Feelings		
Body Sensations		
Visual Image		

Extended Global Tapping Script: Let's begin tapping (see page 126)

Round 1

Setup:

Side of Hand: Even though I don't believe I'll ever get better and I question why I should bother to do things to help myself, I honor and respect myself.

Side of Hand: Even though I am stuck in a "forgetting fog," I am still able to take positive action to help myself.

Side of Hand: Even though I don't even want to tap this right now, I honor how I am feeling and still choose to help myself.

Top of Head: A part of me wants to take positive action to help myself and a part of me doesn't.

Eyebrow: I don't even want to bother, but I don't want to stay where I am!

Side of Eye: I am not ever going to get better, so why tap now? But I need to do something.

Under Eye: This is the last thing I want to do right now, but I do want to feel better!

Under Nose: This awful disease is never going to go away, so why bother?!

Chin: One part of me wants to stay hopeful that new techniques will work, but another part of me doesn't believe anything will work.

Collarbone: I am too tired to care today, and I am struggling to take positive action to help myself.

Under Arm: I am stuck in the "forgetting fog" and feel paralyzed to create positive change.

Top of Wrists Together: Nothing will help, so why bother?

Bottom of Wrists Together: It hurts too much to care.

Slowly complete a deep belly breath and then keep tapping.

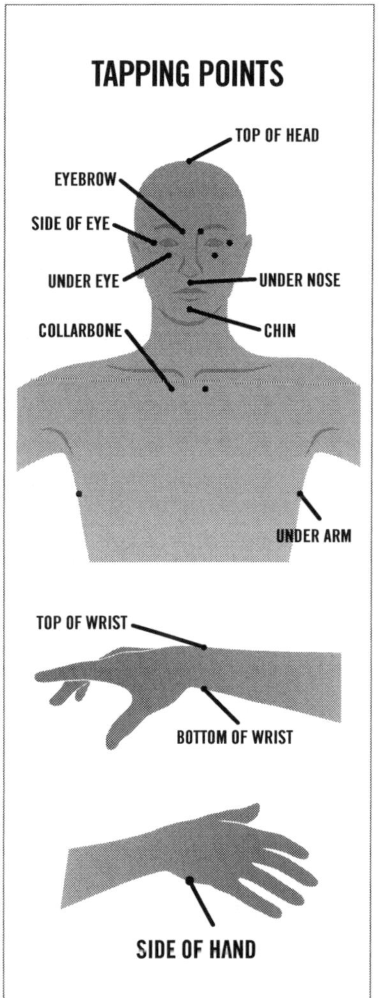

Round 2

Top of Head: Am I ever going to get better?

Eyebrow: I am really scared.

Side of Eye: How long is this suffering going to last?

Under Eye: I am too tired to help myself, but I need to.

Under Nose: What if this lasts forever?

Chin: Is this how my life will be from now on?

Collarbone: I feel like giving up!

Under Arm: I know I should take positive actions to help myself, but why bother?

Top of Wrists Together: I am scared.

Bottom of Wrists Together: Am I ever going to get better?

Take three slow, deep belly breaths as you complete another **Body Scan**. What do you notice now? Note changes to the Aspects and any new ones that may appear below:

Aspects	Description of Aspects	SUD #:
Global Issue	Am I ever going to get better?	
Limiting Belief		
Thoughts		
Feelings		
Body Sensations		
Visual Image		

If your intensity level about this Global Issue, along with any of its Aspects, is still 3 or above on a SUD scale, continue tapping with the next round. (If you have a SUD scale of 0–2, skip down and finish by tapping through the positive statements and Afformations.)

Round 3

Setup:

Side of Hand: Even though I am still struggling to have hope of recovery, I honor all of my feelings.

Side of Hand: Even though I still struggle to take positive action to help myself, I honor and accept myself.

Side of Hand: Even though I still wonder if I am ever going to get better, I honor and accept my body.

Top of Head: I still feel torn between taking positive action and no action.

Eyebrow: I am still wondering if I am ever going to get better.

Side of Eye: I still struggle with having hope for recovery.

Under Eye: I am still stuck in the forgetting fog.

Under Nose: I still don't believe that I can do anything to help myself.

Chin: I am still afraid that I will be sick forever.

Collarbone: Why bother to use new techniques if I believe I will be sick forever?

Under Arm: It is still too painful today to have hope.

Top of Wrists Together: I am still feeling (state the emotion) about this.

Bottom of Wrists Together: Why bother? Because I choose to heal!

Take three slow, deep belly breaths as you complete another **Body Scan**. What do you notice now? Note changes to the Aspects and any new ones that may appear below:

Aspects	Description of Aspects	SUD #:
Global Issue	Am I ever going to get better?	
Limiting Belief		
Thoughts		
Feelings		
Body Sensations		
Visual Image		

If your intensity level about this Global Issue, along with any of its Aspects, is still 3 or above on a SUD scale, keep tapping through what is in your awareness or move down to **Follow These Steps to Resolution**.

Once you reach a SUD level of 0–2 or when you just want to stop tapping for now and return at a later time, finish up by tapping through the positive statements and Afformations.

Round 4 – Now let's tap through some positive statements!

Top of Head: I choose to use EFT or TAB to help myself even when it is most challenging to do so.

Eyebrow: I feel so much empathy for myself for going through this really hard time.

Side of Eye: My body is doing so much healing on my behalf, and I am grateful.

Under Eye: I give myself permission today to feel the way I do.

Under Nose: I am so grateful that my body is not giving up on me.

Chin: My body is so loyal to me and is doing everything to help me heal!

Collarbone: I choose to take positive action steps to help myself.

Under Arm: I commit to using the self-help tools in my toolkit to help me cope in positive ways.

Top of Wrists Together: I know that I will recover and will do what it takes to make that happen.

Bottom of Wrists Together: It is what it is for now, and it is temporary.

Round 5 – Tapping with Afformations (see page 101)

Top of Head: Why is it possible for me to use the tools in this workbook to help myself?

Eyebrow: Why is it safe for me to have hope of recovery and take positive actions to help create it?

Side of Eye: How is it possible for me to recover?

Under Eye: Why is it possible for me to cultivate a wellness state of mind?

Under Nose: Why am I able to have hope that I am healing?

Chin: Why is it possible for me to accept myself right where I am?

Collarbone: Why is it so easy for me to remain optimistic and hopeful?

Under Arm: Why is it possible to believe that I am doing the best that I can?

Top of Wrists Together: Why is it so easy for me to remember that every cell in my body is in full alignment with healing?

Bottom of Wrists Together: Why is it possible for me to believe that it is what it is for now, and it is temporary?

Take three slow, deep belly breaths as you complete another **Body Scan**. What do you notice now? Note changes to the Aspects and any new ones that may appear below:

Aspects	Description of Aspects	SUD #:
Global Issue	Am I ever going to get better?	
Limiting Belief		
Thoughts		
Feelings		
Body Sensations		
Visual Image		

If your intensity level about this Global Issue, along with any of its Aspects, is still 3 or above on a SUD scale, you need to explore them more in depth and follow the directives in **Follow These Steps to Resolution**, on the following page.

Exercise: Developing Self-Awareness

Describe your experience of tapping through this Global Issue.

____

____

____

Which Aspects resolved, decreased, increased, or stayed the same?

____

____

If you identified a Limiting Belief, state what (if anything) changed.

____

____

State any Empowering Beliefs (see page 119) that you notice now.

____

____

What Global Issues/Limiting Beliefs need to be resolved (if any)?

____

____

Follow These Steps to Resolution

- When you have the time and energy, move on to the next exercise, **Going Deeper with EFT.** Use this to help you identify Specific Events, along with their Aspects, that are contributing to not resolving this Global Issue/Limiting Belief or with any new ones that may have surfaced while tapping. You may identify many and this is to be expected.
- Just break down one Specific Event at a time and tap it until resolved. Title the rest of the Specific Events that you have identified and add them to the **List of Titled Specific Events** on page 156 so that you can return to them at a later time to tap. You can use the **Blank Tapping Script** on page 404 or the **Vent While You Tap** worksheet on page 409 to assist you while tapping through a Specific Event.

Exercise: Going Deeper with EFT

If you just completed tapping through the extended global tapping script, and you still feel that the issue is unresolved, it's time to go deeper. What is keeping it unresolved? Title your Global Issue in the space provided below. Answer the following questions so that you can discover, uncover, and recover from the unresolved Specific Events and related Aspects that created and support the Limiting Belief you wish to resolve.

Global Issue: ______________________________

1. What Limiting Beliefs do you have at the root of this Global Issue? Rate the level of intensity of how true they are for you between SUD 0 (not true at all) and 10 (completely true).

______________________________ • SUD # (0–10): ____

______________________________ • SUD # (0–10): ____

2. Title and list the Specific Events in which you learned the Limiting Belief(s) (you can also add them to your List of Titled Specific Events on page 156).

____

____

____

____

____

____

3. Choose one Specific Event to break down here. Title: ______________________________

____

4. Tune into your titled Specific Event and identify only those Aspects that apply to you, below:

What thoughts do you notice?

______________________________ • SUD # (0–10): ____

______________________________ • SUD # (0–10): ____

Do your thoughts have the quality of Small Mind or Large Mind (see page 90)?____________

Describe your Large Mind thoughts (if any):____

____

Describe your Small Mind thoughts (if any): _______________________________________

____

What emotions are you feeling?

____ • SUD # (0–10): ____

____ • SUD # (0–10): ____

____ • SUD # (0–10): ____

What body sensation do you notice?

____ • SUD # (0–10): ____

Where is the sensation located?______________________________ • SUD # (0–10): ____

Does this sensation have a temperature?____ Describe:______________________________

____ • SUD # (0–10): ____

Texture?____ • SUD # (0–10): ____

Color?____ • SUD # (0–10): ____

Describe a visual image that you have (if any): ____________________________________

____ • SUD # (0–10): ____

5. Use the Aspects you have just identified to create your Reminder Phrases.
6. Stay tuned into your titled Specific Event.
7. Start tapping using the Modified EFT Basic Recipe on page 121. You can use the Aspects you have identified here to fill in the Reminder Phrases on the **Blank Tapping Script** on page 404 or the **Vent While You Tap** worksheet on page 409 to assist you in creating your own tapping script.

REPEAT PROCESS IF UNRESOLVED

Be aware of any changes in the intensity of distress you feel in relation to the Aspects, along with any new ones that emerge as you tap through the Rounds of EFT. Continue to tap, repeating the EFT Basic Recipe until your Specific Event, along with its Aspects, is resolved at a SUD level of 0–2. Also be mindful of shifts in Limiting Beliefs and the emergence of any new Empowering ones. To get full resolution of a Global Issue, the Limiting Beliefs must be released by resolving other painful Specific Events that are validating them.

Personal Reflections

CHAPTER 30

Pain, Pain, and More Pain

Case Study

Note: *Limiting Beliefs are italicized* and **Empowering Beliefs are in bold.**

Cathy was a marketing professional working in a fast-paced environment when she was diagnosed with Lyme disease. By the time she received her diagnoses, the disease had taken hold, and she was no longer able to function as she once did. She reported that in addition to becoming extremely fatigued and not being able to concentrate, she was always in pain. Being a self-professed "overachiever," Cathy continued to push herself until the day came when her body said, "no." When she came in for therapy, Cathy said, *I don't believe that I am able to deal with all of this stress!* Cathy could no longer keep up the pace at her job and was facing unemployment.

Like many people who have Lyme disease, Cathy noticed that her pain would migrate from one place in her body to another but that she rarely had a moment when she wasn't hurting in some way. "Sometimes the pain is so bad, I can barely move, and now it's worse than ever." As we discussed her pain, Cathy confirmed that the frequency and intensity of her pain was much worse when she was stressed, and she stated that her current pain level was a 9, on a scale of 0 (none) to 10 (most severe).

After many rounds of tapping, Cathy stated, "Oh, **I have so much more clarity** and the pain is about a 3/10!" As we continued tapping, she said, "**I believe that I am able reduce my stress**," and her physical pain decreased to a 1/10. "This EFT is really helping me to decrease my stress and pain. **I now think more clearly and feel more empowered to deal with my issues.**"

Cathy was able to notice that when she was stressed, her pain level increased. It's important to pay attention to what happens in your body when you become emotionally distressed. Increased stress can increase inflammation, thus increasing pain (see page 396). You may also find that when you experience both emotional and physical pain, you may hurt too much to tap. If that is true for you, try the other self-help tools in the toolkit. Use 4/8 belly breathing (see page 86), TAB (see page 411), and **meditation** (see page 105). You may be surprised at the relief you can create.

Using pain as the focus of your tapping session is a great place to start. Be aware that there may be deeper issues underlying your pain, which may be triggered and brought to the surface as you tap. Our own experience has taught us that these issues are often an underlying force that can influence the frequency and intensity of pain. It is common while using EFT that pain can migrate to other parts of the body. Follow it while tapping!

If the information presented here resonates with you, we invite you to begin with the extended global tapping script that follows. This is a gentle way to get you started and to decrease your overall intensity. Even though the scripted Reminder Phrases may not be reflective of your personal Aspects, we invite you to just go with it, track your progress, and see what happens!

Global Issue Title: Overall Pain

- Focus your attention on this **Global Issue** (see page 119).
- Identify one **Limiting Belief** (see page 119) that may be at the root of this Global Issue.
- Take three slow, deep belly breaths as you do a **Body Scan** (see page 81).
- What **Aspects** (see page 123) do you notice in relation to your experience of pain? For this script, also tune in to its specific location(s), describe it, and identify its intensity with a SUD scale rating.
- Using the **SUD scale** (see page 124), choose a number between 0 (no distress/peaceful) and 10 (highest intensity of distress) to **rate the intensity** of distress you feel about the **Global Issue and Limiting Belief**, along with only the **Aspects** (thoughts, feelings, body sensations, and visual image) that you notice that apply to you.

Aspects	Description of Aspects	SUD #:
Global Issue	Overall Pain	
Limiting Belief		
Thoughts		
Feelings		
Body Sensations:		
Pain in my _______ feels like:		
Pain in my _______ feels like:		
Pain in my _______ feels like:		
Visual Image		

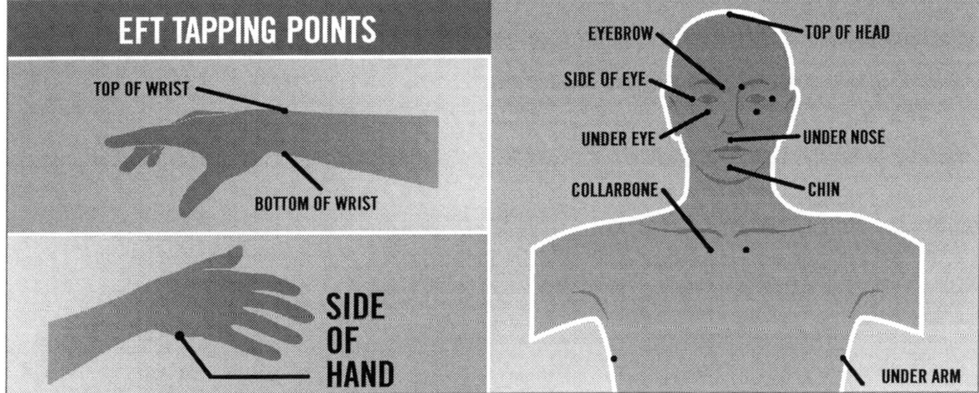

Extended Global Tapping Script: Let's begin tapping (see page 126)

Round 1

Setup:

Side of Hand: Even though I have pain in (name areas of the body), I honor and accept my body.

Side of Hand: Even though this pain has taken over my body, I honor and accept all of my feelings about it.

Side of Hand: Even though I do not want to pay attention to my body because of this pain, I am open to embracing all parts of myself.

Top of Head: This pain in my (name areas of the body).

Eyebrow: I hate this pain!

Side of Eye: It is never going to go away.

Under Eye: Everyone says I look so healthy, but I am in agonizing pain!

Under Nose: I can't stand to be touched!

Chin: My pain won't leave me alone! It just moves from one part of my body to the next.

Collarbone: This pain in my (name areas of the body) is making me so mad!

Under Arm: I am so angry at my body for causing me this pain!

Top of Wrists Together: How can my body do this to me?

Bottom of Wrists Together: I feel so attacked by my body.

Slowly complete a deep belly breath and then keep tapping.

Round 2

Top of Head: My pain ambushes me, attacking different parts of my body.

Eyebrow: This constant, searing pain in my (name areas of the body).

Side of Eye: I can't even let anybody touch me!

Under Eye: My pain shows up in one place and then moves to another!

Under Nose: I never know what to expect.

Chin: I am so tired of hurting.

Collarbone: I just want it to stop. GIVE ME A BREAK!

Under Arm: My pain is exhausting!

Top of Wrists Together: I feel so ambushed by my body!

Bottom of Wrists Together: My pain is interfering with my life.

Take three slow, deep belly breaths as you complete another **Body Scan**. What do you notice now? Note changes to the Aspects and any new ones that may appear below:

Aspects	Description of Aspects	SUD #:
Global Issue	Overall Pain	
Limiting Belief		
Thoughts		
Feelings		
Body Sensations:		
Pain in my _______ feels like:		
Pain in my _______ feels like:		
Pain in my _______ feels like:		
Visual Image		

If your rounds of tapping have led you to awareness about unresolved Specific Events that are being triggered and thus enhancing your pain, title each one and add it to the **List of Titled Specific Events** on page 156 to tap through at another time. If your intensity level about this Global Issue, along with any of its Aspects, is still 3 or above on a SUD scale, continue tapping with the next round. (If you have a SUD scale of 0–2, skip down and finish by tapping through the positive statements and Affomations.)

Round 3

Setup:

Side of Hand: Even though I still have pain in my (name areas of the body), I forgive my body for having it.

Side of Hand: Even though my pain is still intense, I am open to the possibility of reducing it.

Side of Hand: Even though I don't believe my pain will ever stop, anything is possible and miracles are happening now.

Top of Head: This remaining pain is taking over my body!

Eyebrow: I still have pain!

Side of Eye: I am so frustrated that nothing is changing, and I still have so much pain!

Under Eye: I still have migrating pain!

Under Nose: I still hurt all over!

Chin: This remaining pain in my (name areas of the body).

Collarbone: This migrating pain really stresses me out!

Under Arm: All I do is hurt!

Top of Wrists Together: I am in too much pain to be tapping!

Bottom of Wrists Together: I am so angry at my body for this remaining pain!

Take three slow, deep belly breaths as you complete another **Body Scan**. What do you notice now? Note changes to the Aspects and any new ones that may appear below:

Aspects	Description of Aspects	SUD #:
Global Issue	Overall Pain	
Limiting Belief		
Thoughts		
Feelings		
Body Sensations:		
Pain in my _______ feels like:		
Pain in my _______ feels like:		
Pain in my _______ feels like:		
Visual Image		

If your intensity of pain in any location is still 3 or above on a SUD scale, keep tapping through what is in your awareness. (Remember, pain often migrates to different locations in the body, so follow the pain and use the words that fit your experience.) If you feel as though you have decreased your pain enough and/or want to stop tapping, finish with these last two rounds.

Round 4 – Now let's tap through some positive statements!

Top of Head: Using EFT relaxes me and reduces my pain.
Eyebrow: My body is healing even if I feel pain.
Side of Eye: I am open to the possibility of finding relief.
Under Eye: I know my body is healing right now.
Under Nose: My pain is what it is for now.
Chin: My body is loyal to me and is doing everything it can to heal.
Collarbone: I accept my body even while feeling pain.
Under Arm: It is possible for me to let go of this pain and relax now.
Top of Wrists Together: I accept myself even while feeling pain.
Bottom of Wrists Together: My body is so loyal to me.

Round 5 – Tapping with Afformations (see page 101)

Top of Head: Why is it possible for me to forgive my body?

Eyebrow: How is it possible for my body to forgive me?

Side of Eye: Why is it possible for me to use EFT to stimulate pain reduction?

Under Eye: Why does every cell in my body know exactly what needs to heal?

Under Nose: Why is it possible for me to remember that my body is intelligent and is doing everything possible to help me heal?

Chin: Why do I love my body and am grateful for its service to me?

Collarbone: Why is it possible for my body and me to be on the same team?

Under Arm: Why is it possible for me to give my body permission to let go of this pain and relax now?

Top of Wrists Together: Why do I know it is safe for me to relax now?

Bottom of Wrists Together: Why am I able to reduce my pain now?

Take three slow, deep belly breaths as you complete another **Body Scan**. What do you notice now? Note changes to the Aspects and any new ones that may appear below:

Aspects	Description of Aspects	SUD #:
Global Issue	Overall Pain	
Limiting Belief		
Thoughts		
Feelings		
Body Sensations:		
Pain in my ________ feels like:		
Pain in my ________ feels like:		
Pain in my ________ feels like:		
Visual Image		

EFT helps to release painful emotions, resolve Specific Events, and decrease the stress response that could be contributing to your pain. When these issues have been addressed, and you are still experiencing pain over a SUD scale of 3, your intensity level may be reflecting the direct effect that Lyme/TBDs are having on your body, without the added emotional impact. This is expected even with the proper and thorough use of EFT.

Exercise: Developing Self-Awareness

Describe your experience of tapping through this Global Issue.

Which Aspects resolved, decreased, increased, or stayed the same?

If you identified a Limiting Belief, state what (if anything) changed.

State any Empowering Beliefs (see page 119) that you notice now.

What Global Issues/Limiting Beliefs need to be resolved (if any)?

Follow These Steps to Resolution

- When you have the time and energy, move on to the next exercise, **Going Deeper with EFT.** Use this to help you identify Specific Events, along with their Aspects, that are contributing to not resolving this Global Issue/Limiting Belief or with any new ones that may have surfaced while tapping. You may identify many and this is to be expected.
- Just break down one Specific Event at a time and tap it until resolved. Title the rest of the Specific Events that you have identified and add them to the **List of Titled Specific Events** on page 156 so that you can return to them at a later time to tap. You can use the **Blank Tapping Script** on page 404 or the **Vent While You Tap** worksheet on page 409 to assist you while tapping through a Specific Event.

Exercise: Going Deeper with EFT

If you just completed tapping through the extended global tapping script, and you still feel that the issue is unresolved, it's time to go deeper. What is keeping it unresolved? Title your Global Issue in the space provided below. Answer the following questions so that you can discover, uncover, and recover from the unresolved Specific Events and related Aspects that created and support the Limiting Belief you wish to resolve.

Global Issue: ____

1. What Limiting Beliefs do you have at the root of this Global Issue? Rate the level of intensity of how true they are for you between SUD 0 (not true at all) and 10 (completely true).

________________________________ • SUD # (0–10): ____

________________________________ • SUD # (0–10): ____

2. Title and list the Specific Events in which you learned the Limiting Belief(s) (you can also add them to your List of Titled Specific Events on page 156).

____

____

____

____

____

____

3. Choose one Specific Event to break down here. Title: ____________________

____

4. Tune into your titled Specific Event and identify only those Aspects that apply to you, below:

What thoughts do you notice?

________________________________ • SUD # (0–10): ____

________________________________ • SUD # (0–10): ____

Do your thoughts have the quality of Small Mind or Large Mind (see page 90)?____________

Describe your Large Mind thoughts (if any):____

____

Describe your Small Mind thoughts (if any): ____

____

What emotions are you feeling?

____ • SUD # (0–10): ____

____ • SUD # (0–10): ____

____ • SUD # (0–10): ____

What body sensation do you notice?

____ • SUD # (0–10): ____

Where is the sensation located?________________________ • SUD # (0–10): ____

Does this sensation have a temperature?____ Describe:________________________

____ • SUD # (0–10): ____

Texture?____ • SUD # (0–10): ____

Color?____ • SUD # (0–10): ____

Describe a visual image that you have (if any): ______________________________

____ • SUD # (0–10): ____

5. Use the Aspects you have just identified to create your Reminder Phrases.
6. Stay tuned into your titled Specific Event.
7. Start tapping using the Modified EFT Basic Recipe on page 121. You can use the Aspects you have identified here to fill in the Reminder Phrases on the **Blank Tapping Script** on page 404 or the **Vent While You Tap** worksheet on page 409 to assist you in creating your own tapping script.

REPEAT PROCESS IF UNRESOLVED

Be aware of any changes in the intensity of distress you feel in relation to the Aspects, along with any new ones that emerge as you tap through the Rounds of EFT. Continue to tap, repeating the EFT Basic Recipe until your Specific Event, along with its Aspects, is resolved at a SUD level of 0–2. Also be mindful of shifts in Limiting Beliefs and the emergence of any new Empowering ones. To get full resolution of a Global Issue, the Limiting Beliefs must be released by resolving other painful Specific Events that are validating them.

Personal Reflections

CHAPTER

31 Chasing the Pain with EFT

Case Study

Note: *Limiting Beliefs are italicized* and **Empowering Beliefs are in bold**.

Sandra was diagnosed with Lyme four years ago. In addition to having difficulty thinking, she had muscle fatigue, stiff hips, and sore heels. She could put up with the pain, but when she was stressed, it got worse. Her major stressor was dealing with the breakup of a long-term relationship. Sandra said, "I came to therapy to get help with letting this relationship go! I feel so sad and *can't get him out of my mind!* I am stressing myself out and it just makes my pain worse!"

Before the first round of tapping, Sandra rated the pain in her heels (did not notice any pain in other parts of her body) with a SUD scale of 7 out of 10. After rounds of tapping that started with Sandra's feelings of sadness about the breakup, she noted that her pain moved to her right hip with a SUD of 5 and decreased in intensity in her heels to a SUD of 3. Sandra continued to tap through the painful emotional layers of her breakup. After doing another **Body Scan**, she said that the pain in her heels was gone, the pain in her hips decreased to a 2, and now the back of her neck was aching with a SUD of 8. "Now I have a pain in the neck! See, I told you my symptoms increase with stress! *I don't believe this is working.*"

At this point in the tapping rounds, Sandra had dropped down into deep anger (SUD of 8) at her former partner about specific things that really hurt her feelings. Sandra was reassured and encouraged to keep tapping through her anger and pain. Sandra chose to continue to tap while she vented her anger, at times crying. After many more rounds of EFT through the layers of anger, Sandra let out a big sigh and said, "I am letting him go. I'm not even thinking about him. I just feel so peaceful and calm. It feels so good to get that out. My goodness, I feel as though I could just go to bed now and sleep."

Sandra then was asked about the pain in her neck. She replied, "What pain? I forgot that I even had that! I am overcome right now by deep peace (SUD for sadness 2, SUD for anger 0)." After completing another **Body Scan**, Sandra noticed that the pain in her heels and hip was gone and noted a SUD of 2 in her neck. "I hardly even notice it. I do believe EFT is working!"

This is a very common experience while using EFT with somebody who has physical pain. You can chase the pain like Sandra did by noting between rounds the intensity of your pain at each location and how it has changed, while focusing your tapping on processing and resolving painful emotional issues. Note that even though Sandra did not focus on her pain directly, it was still affected by her emotional state. Some pain started in a new location, while other locations decreased or even increased in pain. Notice that, as Sandra resolved her emotional issues, her pain naturally decreased. The relaxation response of her body was ignited by her emotional releases into feelings of "peaceful and calm."

You can also chase the pain by just focusing on the specifics of your pain as reminder phrases while tapping, then noting between rounds through a **Body Scan** the intensity and descriptions (noting changes) of pain at each location in your body. Be aware if and how your pain changes and moves. Then, for the next round of tapping, shift your focus to any new areas of pain that emerged and keep tapping. The goal is to keep tapping through Aspects and sensations that come into your awareness until the pain reduces and/or resolves. (You can also go back to "Pain, Pain and More Pain" on page 281 to use the global tapping script to guide you through this process.)

Many people who are new to EFT become concerned that it's not working because their pain moves and shifts from one part of the body to another as they tap. Pain increases stress, and stress increases pain, especially with Lyme/TBDs. They are in direct relationship with each other, and you can see this dynamic with Sandra's story. Persistence, persistence, and more persistence is the best way to get results with tapping while chasing your pain. Since pain is such a common problem with Lyme/TBDs, we provided two case examples and scripts (this one and the one in the previous chapter) to help you effectively reduce your pain and possibly the underlying unresolved emotions.

If the information presented here resonates with you, we invite you to begin with the extended global tapping script that follows. This is a gentle way to get you started and to decrease your overall intensity. Even though the scripted Reminder Phrases may not be reflective of your personal Aspects, we invite you to just go with it, track your progress, and see what happens!

A WELLNESS STATE OF MIND

Global Issue Title: Migrating Pain

- Focus your attention on this **Global Issue** (see page 119).
- Identify one **Limiting Belief** (see page 119) that may be at the root of this Global Issue.
- Take three slow, deep belly breaths as you do a **Body Scan** (see page 81).
- What **Aspects** (see page 123) do you notice in relation to your experience of pain? For this script, also tune in to its specific location(s), describe it, and identify its intensity with a SUD scale rating. Use this to notice if you are chasing your pain.
- Using the **SUD scale** (see page 124), choose a number between 0 (no distress/peaceful) and 10 (highest intensity of distress) to **rate the intensity** of distress you feel about the **Global Issue and Limiting Belief**, along with only the **Aspects** (thoughts, feelings, body sensations, and visual image) that you notice that apply to you.

	Description	SUD #:
Global Issue	Migrating Pain	
Limiting Belief		
Thoughts		
Feelings		
Body Sensations:		
Pain in my _______ feels like:		
Pain in my _______ feels like:		
Pain in my _______ feels like:		
Visual Image		

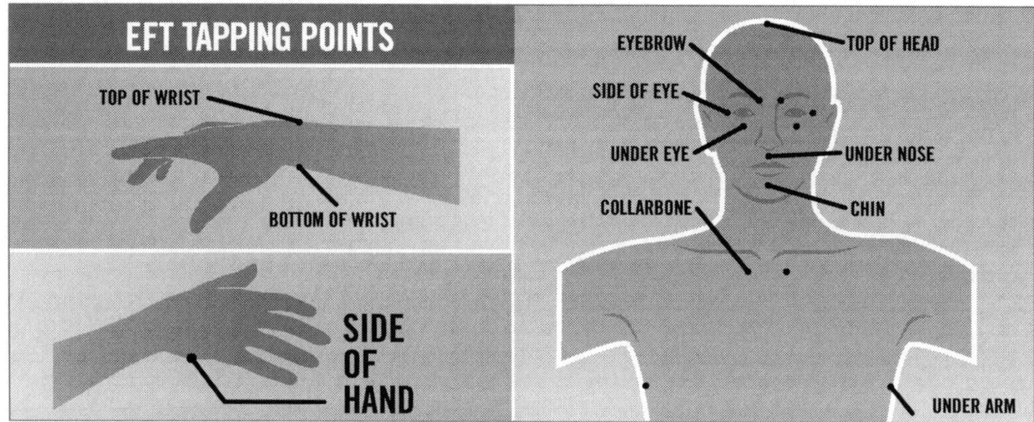

Extended Global Tapping Script: Let's begin tapping **(see page 126)**

Round 1

Setup:

Side of Hand: Even though I have pain in my (name areas of the body), I honor and accept my body.

Side of Hand: Even though this pain comes and goes, I honor how I feel about this.

Side of Hand: Even though I sometimes feel like rejecting my painful body, I am open to the possibility of embracing it.

Top of Head: This pain in my (name areas of the body).

Eyebrow: I hate this pain! It's so unpredictable!

Side of Eye: I feel frustrated about the pain in my (name areas of the body).

Under Eye: My pain keeps migrating through my body, coming and going.

Under Nose: I don't know what to expect.

Chin: This pain is stressing me out!

Collarbone: This pain in my (name areas of the body) is making me feel (state the emotion).

Under Arm: I am so angry with my body for causing me this pain!

Top of Wrists Together: My stress is making my pain worse!

Bottom of Wrists Together: I just don't know what to expect next!

Slowly complete a deep belly breath and then keep tapping.

Round 2

Top of Head: I just can't deal with this unpredictable pain!

Eyebrow: This constant, searing pain in my (name areas of the body).

Side of Eye: My pain changes and moves throughout my body.

Under Eye: Chasing my pain with EFT is tiring.

Under Nose: I don't know what to expect in regard to my body pain.

Chin: Why can't I just be stressed and not feel more pain?

Collarbone: My pain migrates, and it is unpredictable.

Under Arm: It is hard to notice how my pain changes.

Top of Wrists Together: I feel so ambushed at times by my body!

Bottom of Wrists Together: I am going to keep chasing my pain with EFT.

Take three slow, deep belly breaths as you complete another **Body Scan**. What do you notice now? Note changes to the Aspects and any new ones that may appear below:

	Description	SUD #:
Global Issue	Migrating Pain	
Limiting Belief		
Thoughts		
Feelings		
Body Sensations:		
Pain in my _______ feels like:		
Pain in my _______ feels like:		
Pain in my _______ feels like:		
Visual Image		

If your rounds of tapping have led you to awareness about unresolved Specific Events that are being triggered and thus enhancing your pain, title each one and add it to the **List of Titled Specific Events** on page 156 to tap through at another time. If your intensity level about this Global Issue, along with any of its Aspects, is still 3 or above on a SUD scale, continue tapping with the next round. (If you have a SUD scale of 0–2, skip down and finish by tapping through the positive statements and Afformations.)

Round 3

Setup:

Side of Hand: Even though I still have this migrating pain.

Side of Hand: Even though my pain is still intense, I honor and accept myself.

Side of Hand: Even though I believe my pain will never stop, I choose to heal.

Top of Head: This remaining pain!

Eyebrow: I am still chasing my pain.

Side of Eye: I feel (fill in emotion) about my pain.

Under Eye: I can't live like this!

Under Nose: My pain is now more intense in one area and less in another.

Chin: This remaining pain in my (name areas of the body).

Collarbone: I still feel so much stress about this.

Under Arm: My pain keeps changing. I never know what to expect.

Top of Wrists Together: I feel powerless over my pain!

Bottom of Wrists Together: I am so angry at my body for this remaining pain!

Take three slow, deep belly breaths as you complete another **Body Scan**. What do you notice now? Note changes to the Aspects and any new ones that may appear below:

	Description	SUD #:
Global Issue	Migrating Pain	
Limiting Belief		
Thoughts		
Feelings		
Body Sensations:		
Pain in my _______ feels like:		
Pain in my _______ feels like:		
Pain in my _______ feels like:		
Visual Image		

If your intensity of pain in any location is still 3 or above on a SUD scale, keep tapping through what is in your awareness. (Remember, pain often migrates to different locations in the body, so follow the pain and use the words that fit your experience.) If you feel as though you have decreased your pain enough and/or want to stop tapping, finish with these last two rounds.

Round 4 – Now let's tap through some positive statements!

Top of Head: My body loves how I am helping it reduce stress with these simple techniques.

Eyebrow: My body is healing even if I feel pain.

Side of Eye: I am open to the possibility of finding relief.

Under Eye: I accept that my pain is unpredictable.

Under Nose: It is possible that chasing my pain with EFT will help me to feel better.

Chin: My body is loyal to me and is doing everything it can to help me heal.

Collarbone: My pain is what it is for now.

Under Arm: It is possible for me to let go of this stress and relax now.

Top of Wrists Together: I forgive my body for being in pain.

Bottom of Wrists Together: My body is so loyal to me.

Round 5 – Tapping with Afformations (see page 101)

Top of Head: Why is it okay for me to forgive my body for being in pain?

Eyebrow: Why is it possible for me to reduce my stress and pain with EFT?

Side of Eye: Why am I able to remember that healing energy surrounds every cell in my body?

Under Eye: Why is it so easy for me to accept the unpredictability of my pain?

Under Nose: Why do I know that my body is intelligent and is doing everything possible to help me heal?

Chin: Why am I able to accept my body just as it is for today?

Collarbone: Why is it okay for me to release my pain now?

Under Arm: How is it possible for me to give my body permission to let go of this pain and relax now?

Top of Wrists Together: Why do I know it is safe for me to relax and let go of this pain now?

Bottom of Wrists Together: Why am I letting go of this pain now?

Take three slow, deep belly breaths as you complete another **Body Scan**. What do you notice now? Note changes to the Aspects and any new ones that may appear below:

	Description	SUD #:
Global Issue	Migrating Pain	
Limiting Belief		
Thoughts		
Feelings		
Body Sensations:		
Pain in my _______ feels like:		
Pain in my _______ feels like:		
Pain in my _______ feels like:		
Visual Image		

EFT helps to release painful emotions, resolve Specific Events, and decrease the stress response that could be contributing to your pain. When these issues have been addressed, and you are still experiencing pain over a SUD scale of 3, your intensity level may be reflecting the direct effect that Lyme/TBDs are having on your body, without the added emotional impact. This is expected even with the proper and thorough use of EFT.

Exercise: Developing Self-Awareness

Describe your experience of tapping through this Global Issue.

Which Aspects resolved, decreased, increased, or stayed the same?

If you identified a Limiting Belief, state what (if anything) changed.

State any Empowering Beliefs (see page 119) that you notice now.

What Global Issues/Limiting Beliefs need to be resolved (if any)?

Follow These Steps to Resolution

- When you have the time and energy, move on to the next exercise, **Going Deeper with EFT.** Use this to help you identify Specific Events, along with their Aspects, that are contributing to not resolving this Global Issue/Limiting Belief or with any new ones that may have surfaced while tapping. You may identify many and this is to be expected.
- Just break down one Specific Event at a time and tap it until resolved. Title the rest of the Specific Events that you have identified and add them to the **List of Titled Specific Events** on page 156 so that you can return to them at a later time to tap. You can use the **Blank Tapping Script** on page 404 or the **Vent While You Tap** worksheet on page 409 to assist you while tapping through a Specific Event.

Exercise: Going Deeper with EFT

If you just completed tapping through the extended global tapping script, and you still feel that the issue is unresolved, it's time to go deeper. What is keeping it unresolved? Title your Global Issue in the space provided below. Answer the following questions so that you can discover, uncover, and recover from the unresolved Specific Events and related Aspects that created and support the Limiting Belief you wish to resolve.

Global Issue: ______________________________

1. What Limiting Beliefs do you have at the root of this Global Issue? Rate the level of intensity of how true they are for you between SUD 0 (not true at all) and 10 (completely true).

______________________________ • SUD # (0–10): ____

______________________________ • SUD # (0–10): ____

2. Title and list the Specific Events in which you learned the Limiting Belief(s) (you can also add them to your List of Titled Specific Events on page 156).

____

____

____

____

____

____

3. Choose one Specific Event to break down here. Title: ______________________________

____

4. Tune into your titled Specific Event and identify only those Aspects that apply to you, below:

What thoughts do you notice?

______________________________ • SUD # (0–10): ____

______________________________ • SUD # (0–10): ____

Do your thoughts have the quality of Small Mind or Large Mind (see page 90)?______________

Describe your Large Mind thoughts (if any):____

____

Describe your Small Mind thoughts (if any): ____

____

What emotions are you feeling?

____ • SUD # (0–10): ____

____ • SUD # (0–10): ____

____ • SUD # (0–10): ____

What body sensation do you notice?

____ • SUD # (0–10): ____

Where is the sensation located?_________________________ • SUD # (0–10): ____

Does this sensation have a temperature?____ Describe:______________________

____ • SUD # (0–10): ____

Texture?______________________________________ • SUD # (0–10): ____

Color?____ • SUD # (0–10): ____

Describe a visual image that you have (if any): ______________________________

____ • SUD # (0–10): ____

5. Use the Aspects you have just identified to create your Reminder Phrases.
6. Stay tuned into your titled Specific Event.
7. Start tapping using the Modified EFT Basic Recipe on page 121. You can use the Aspects you have identified here to fill in the Reminder Phrases on the **Blank Tapping Script** on page 404 or the **Vent While You Tap** worksheet on page 409 to assist you in creating your own tapping script.

REPEAT PROCESS IF UNRESOLVED

Be aware of any changes in the intensity of distress you feel in relation to the Aspects, along with any new ones that emerge as you tap through the Rounds of EFT. Continue to tap, repeating the EFT Basic Recipe until your Specific Event, along with its Aspects, is resolved at a SUD level of 0–2. Also be mindful of shifts in Limiting Beliefs and the emergence of any new Empowering ones. To get full resolution of a Global Issue, the Limiting Beliefs must be released by resolving other painful Specific Events that are validating them.

CHAPTER 32

I'm on Empty!

Case Study

Note: *Limiting Beliefs are italicized* and **Empowering Beliefs are in bold**.

Exhaustion and fatigue were the biggest challenges for me, Tracey, with Lyme disease. I could gut out what I needed to do for the day even with severe migrating joint and muscle pains, but when the fatigue set in and I was on empty, I believed *that I couldn't do anything more.* The most I could get out of myself on those bad "on empty" days was to sit in front of the TV and get lost in commercials because they were the only stimulation I could handle.

There were many days when I would just go to bed. I never would have thought that a former collegiate athlete with almost three master's degrees and a successful professional career could be so exhaustedly on empty! Looking back on my experience of feeling on empty, I realize that I couldn't tell the difference between depression and exhaustion. Maybe there is no real difference or maybe one influences the other, but either way, there is a risk for becoming completely apathetic.

I have to be honest here, on my lowest of low days, I couldn't even find it in myself to tap! I believed *that I couldn't do it* because I was too tired. It was in some of those times that my roommate would come sit by me in my recliner and encourage me to tap with her. I would follow her tapping while she vented for me because I was too tired to even vent! Other times tapping took more energy than I had at the moment, so I would lie down in bed and use TAB (see page 411). Both of these techniques worked to shift my exhaustion and fatigue to something more manageable. Every time I worked through an episode of exhaustion with these techniques and found relief, I learned that **I can do it**!

I found that the biggest challenge for me in using any of the self-help tools and mindfulness-based techniques was just getting started! Once I forced myself to begin, it would get easier because I felt the benefits. The more I used the tools, the better I felt and the **more confident** I became. The first 5 minutes of deciding to take positive action were the hardest for me. I realized that it was in those first 5 minutes that my fate for the day would be determined, that either I was going to do nothing or I could take a positive action that supported me to push through "my wall of stagnation" and start to feel lighter and more energized.

I reasoned with myself, "Heck, my wall of stagnation is only in the first five minutes, **surely I can do something.**" Once I made the decision to go through the wall and address the *Limiting Belief, I can't do it,* and started using EFT or TAB, I was able to push through it. I soon learned that the wall inside me (*I can't do it*), which seemed impossible and intimidating to get through, would disappear like a thin cloud when using EFT or TAB.

Wow, I realized for myself that the wall was not actually a wall (which is what it felt like), but a mirage of one made up of the *Limiting Belief, I can't do it!* Before I knew it, I was on the other side feeling better because I learned that **I could take positive action to help myself!** Once I learned how I responded, it got easier and less intimidating to move through the first 5 minutes of the mirage of my wall of stagnation.

You really can make a choice to take positive action to help yourself even when you are on empty if you **believe you can**. If you believe *you can't do it*, use EFT or TAB to support shifting it, to decrease the intensity of exhaustion, and to allow for you to take positive actions to help yourself. Other positive actions that you can take to boost your energy and clear your mind is to eat foods that do not add to inflammation (for more on these foods, check out **Eat to Live or Live to Eat?** on page 321) while getting plenty of sleep and rest. Listening to your body and doing what you need to do to get well demonstrates the flexibility of a wellness state of mind that sees and responds to what is needed at any given time for recovery.

If the information presented here resonates with you, we invite you to begin with the extended global tapping script that follows. This is a gentle way to get you started and to decrease your overall intensity. Even though the scripted Reminder Phrases may not be reflective of your personal Aspects, we invite you to just go with it, track your progress, and see what happens!

Global Issue Title: Exhaustion

- Focus your attention on this **Global Issue** (see page 119).
- Identify one **Limiting Belief** (see page 119) that may be at the root of this Global Issue.
- Take three slow, deep belly breaths as you do a **Body Scan** (see page 81).
- What **Aspects** (see page 123) do you notice?
- Using the **SUD scale** (see page 124), choose a number between 0 (no distress/peaceful) and 10 (highest intensity of distress) to **rate the intensity** of distress you feel about the **Global Issue and Limiting Belief**, along with only the **Aspects** (thoughts, feelings, body sensations, and visual image) that you notice that apply to you.

Aspects	Description of Aspects	SUD #:
Global Issue	Exhaustion	
Limiting Belief		
Thoughts		
Feelings		
Overall Body Sensations of Exhaustion		
Describe if It Has a Temperature		

Extended Global Tapping Script: Let's begin tapping (see page 126)

Round 1

Setup:

Side of Hand: Even though I feel too exhausted to take positive action to help myself, I honor myself.

Side of Hand: Even though I am on empty and don't even want to tap, I am open to new possibilities for helping myself.

Side of Hand: Even though I don't have enough energy to tap, I honor and respect my body so much that I will use TAB instead.

Top of Head: I can't do anything to help myself today!

Eyebrow: I have no energy!

Side of Eye: I feel paralyzed by exhaustion!

Under Eye: I am on empty.

Under Nose: All of this exhaustion located in my (name location) and (name location).

Chin: I have no energy left.

Collarbone: A wall of stagnation blocks me.

Under Arm: I feel helpless to change how I feel.

Top of Wrists Together: I am on empty, why bother?

Bottom of Wrists Together: I don't have enough energy to care.

Slowly complete a deep belly breath and then keep tapping.

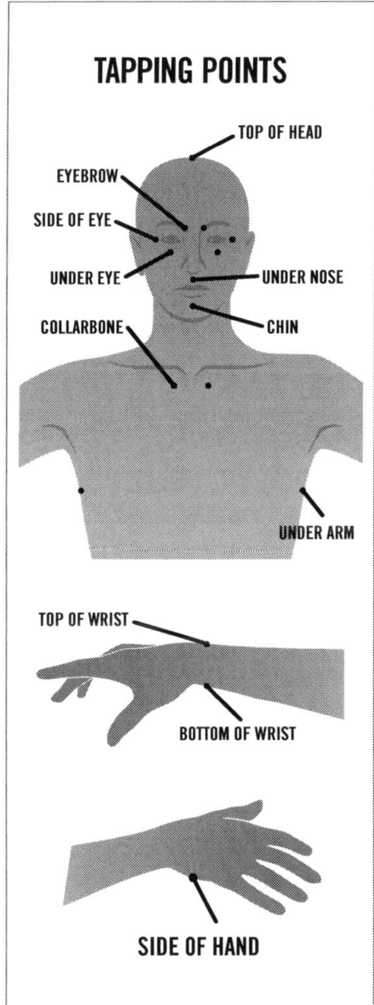

Round 2

Top of Head: I am stagnant.

Eyebrow: I feel like my body weighs (fill in number) pounds.

Side of Eye: I feel (fill in emotion) about this.

Under Nose: I feel too heavy to move or care.

Under Eye: My tank is empty.

Under Nose: This won't help me feel better.

Chin: This wall of stagnation is too thick to get through.

Collarbone: I am so exhausted.

Under Arm: I won't be able to move through this.

Top of Wrists Together: I feel stuck.

Bottom of Wrists Together: I feel too exhausted to help myself.

Take three slow, deep belly breaths as you complete another **Body Scan**. What do you notice now? Note changes to the Aspects and any new ones that may appear below:

Aspects	Description of Aspects	SUD #:
Global Issue	Exhaustion	
Limiting Belief		
Thoughts		
Feelings		
Overall Body Sensations of Exhaustion		
Describe if It Has a Temperature		

If your rounds of tapping have led you to awareness about unresolved Specific Events that are being triggered and thus enhancing your exhaustion, title each one and add it to the **List of Titled Specific Events** on page 156 to tap through at another time.) If your intensity level about this Global Issue, along with any of its Aspects, is still 3 or above on a SUD scale, continue tapping with the next round. (If you have a SUD scale of 0–2, skip down and finish by tapping through the positive statements and Affomations.)

Round 3

Setup:

Side of Hand: Even though I still have this fatigue and exhaustion, I honor and respect myself.

Side of Hand: Even though I still feel like I am on empty, I honor all of my feelings about it.

Side of Hand: Even though I still feel stagnant, I am open to new possibilities for helping myself.

Top of Head: This remaining fatigue.

Eyebrow: This remaining exhaustion.

Side of Eye: I am still on empty.

Under Eye: It is hard to care when I am on empty.

Under Nose: I still feel too exhausted to do anything.

Chin: This remaining fatigue.

Collarbone: I give my body permission to move through this wall of stagnation.

Under Arm: I am tired of feeling tired.

Top of Wrists Together: Maybe it is possible to shift how I feel.

Bottom of Wrists Together: I am open to new possibilities for helping myself.

Take three slow, deep belly breaths as you complete another **Body Scan**. What do you notice now? Note changes to the Aspects and any new ones that may appear below:

Aspects	Description of Aspects	SUD #:
Global Issue	Exhaustion	
Limiting Belief		
Thoughts		
Feelings		
Overall Body Sensations of Exhaustion		
Describe if It Has a Temperature		

If your intensity of exhaustion is still 3 or above on a SUD scale, keep tapping through what is in your awareness. If you feel as though you have decreased the intensity of your exhaustion enough and/or want to stop tapping, finish with these last two rounds.

Round 4 – Now let's tap through some positive statements!

Top of Head: I choose to take positive action steps to help myself feel better.
Eyebrow: I am able to help myself even though I feel exhausted.
Side of Eye: My body is filling up with energy as I tap.
Under Eye: My body is responding to EFT, and I am waking up.
Under Nose: I am taking my power back.
Chin: I am taking positive action right now by tapping.
Collarbone: I have the tools that I need to help myself.
Under Arm: I can now take deep breaths to bring in more oxygen and energy.
Top of Wrists Together: I am open to new possibilities for myself today!
Bottom of Wrists Together: I am back in my body and embrace it.

Round 5 – Tapping with Afformations (see page 101)

Top of Head: How is it so easy for me to take positive action to help myself?

Eyebrow: Why is my body so wise and knows what it needs?

Side of Eye: Why is it possible for me to use the self-help tools in the toolkit to shift my energy?

Under Eye: Why is it so easy for me to rest when I need to?

Under Nose: Why is it possible for me to do what I can and let go of the rest?

Chin: Why is it possible for me to give my body permission to rest and heal?

Collarbone: Why is my energy increasing as I tap?

Under Arm: Why do I now have the power to take positive actions to help myself?

Top of Wrists Together: Why am I now open to new possibilities?

Bottom of Wrists Together: Why is it possible for my body to fill up with energy now?

Take three slow, deep belly breaths as you complete another **Body Scan**. What do you notice now? Note changes to the Aspects and any new ones that may appear below:

Aspects	Description of Aspects	SUD #:
Global Issue	Exhaustion	
Limiting Belief		
Thoughts		
Feelings		
Overall Body Sensations of Exhaustion		
Describe if It Has a Temperature		

EFT helps to release painful emotions, resolve Specific Events, and decrease the stress response that could be contributing to your exhaustion. When these issues have been addressed and you are still experiencing exhaustion over a SUD scale of 3, your intensity level may be reflecting the direct effect that Lyme/TBDs are having on your body, without the added emotional impact. This is expected even with the proper and thorough use of EFT.

Exercise: Developing Self-Awareness

Describe your experience of tapping through this Global Issue.

Which Aspects resolved, decreased, increased, or stayed the same?

If you identified a Limiting Belief, state what (if anything) changed.

State any Empowering Beliefs (see page 119) that you notice now.

What Global Issues/Limiting Beliefs need to be resolved (if any)?

Follow These Steps to Resolution

- When you have the time and energy, move on to the next exercise, **Going Deeper with EFT.** Use this to help you identify Specific Events, along with their Aspects, that are contributing to not resolving this Global Issue/Limiting Belief or with any new ones that may have surfaced while tapping. You may identify many and this is to be expected.
- Just break down one Specific Event at a time and tap it until resolved. Title the rest of the Specific Events that you have identified and add them to the **List of Titled Specific Events** on page 156 so that you can return to them at a later time to tap. You can use the **Blank Tapping Script** on page 404 or the **Vent While You Tap** worksheet on page 409 to assist you while tapping through a Specific Event.

Exercise: Going Deeper with EFT

If you just completed tapping through the extended global tapping script, and you still feel that the issue is unresolved, it's time to go deeper. What is keeping it unresolved? Title your Global Issue in the space provided below. Answer the following questions so that you can discover, uncover, and recover from the unresolved Specific Events and related Aspects that created and support the Limiting Belief you wish to resolve.

Global Issue: ______________________________

1. What Limiting Beliefs do you have at the root of this Global Issue? Rate the level of intensity of how true they are for you between SUD 0 (not true at all) and 10 (completely true).

______________________________ • SUD # (0–10): ____

______________________________ • SUD # (0–10): ____

2. Title and list the Specific Events in which you learned the Limiting Belief(s) (you can also add them to your List of Titled Specific Events on page 156).

____

____

____

____

____

____

3. Choose one Specific Event to break down here. Title: ______________________________

____

4. Tune into your titled Specific Event and identify only those Aspects that apply to you, below:

What thoughts do you notice?

______________________________ • SUD # (0–10): ____

______________________________ • SUD # (0–10): ____

Do your thoughts have the quality of Small Mind or Large Mind (see page 90)?____________

Describe your Large Mind thoughts (if any):____

____

Describe your Small Mind thoughts (if any): ____

____

What emotions are you feeling?

____ • SUD # (0–10): ____

____ • SUD # (0–10): ____

____ • SUD # (0–10): ____

What body sensation do you notice?

____ • SUD # (0–10): ____

Where is the sensation located?________________________ • SUD # (0–10): ____

Does this sensation have a temperature?____ Describe:________________________

____ • SUD # (0–10): ____

Texture?____ • SUD # (0–10): ____

Color?____ • SUD # (0–10): ____

Describe a visual image that you have (if any): ______________________________

____ • SUD # (0–10): ____

5. Use the Aspects you have just identified to create your Reminder Phrases.
6. Stay tuned into your titled Specific Event.
7. Start tapping using the Modified EFT Basic Recipe on page 121. You can use the Aspects you have identified here to fill in the Reminder Phrases on the **Blank Tapping Script** on page 404 or the **Vent While You Tap** worksheet on page 409 to assist you in creating your own tapping script.

REPEAT PROCESS IF UNRESOLVED

Be aware of any changes in the intensity of distress you feel in relation to the Aspects, along with any new ones that emerge as you tap through the Rounds of EFT. Continue to tap, repeating the EFT Basic Recipe until your Specific Event, along with its Aspects, is resolved at a SUD level of 0–2. Also be mindful of shifts in Limiting Beliefs and the emergence of any new Empowering ones. To get full resolution of a Global Issue, the Limiting Beliefs must be released by resolving other painful Specific Events that are validating them

Personal Reflections

CHAPTER 33

My Head Is in the Clouds (Brain Fog)

Case Study

Note: *Limiting Beliefs are italicized* and **Empowering Beliefs are in bold.**

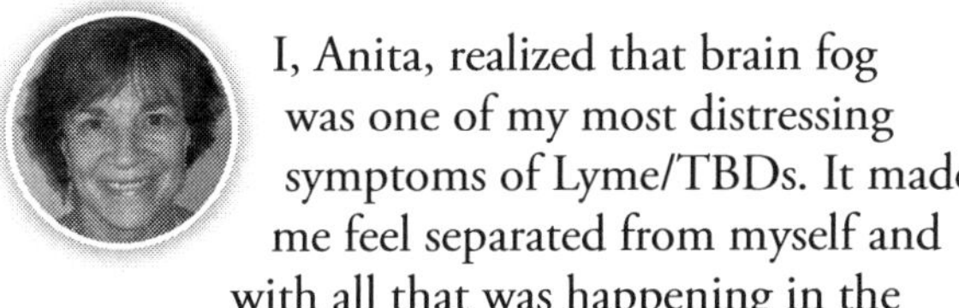

I, Anita, realized that brain fog was one of my most distressing symptoms of Lyme/TBDs. It made me feel separated from myself and with all that was happening in the outside world. I felt as though my head was in the clouds and I could not process what was happening within and around me. There were many mornings when I awoke with my head feeling heavy. I believed that *I was trapped* in a dense, thick cloud. My thinking was muddled; information just didn't stick. I had trouble retrieving the appropriate words and solving basic problems. Sometimes I would even have a moment of feeling lost while driving, even though I was in a familiar area. This was really scary!

During these episodes of brain fog, the kind of question I asked myself about it determined the kind of answer I would get. This depended on the state of mind I was in at the time. When I allowed *Limiting Beliefs* to create Small Mind (see page 90) based on fear, I panicked while asking myself, "What's happening to me?" The answers I got were made up of triggered *Limiting Beliefs* based on my fears like: *I am developing dementia! I'm not ever going to be able to function again! I will be like this forever! I am trapped!*

I learned that when I allowed *fear-based Limiting Beliefs* to dictate my perspective, I resisted my experience and as a result, stimulated my stress response. I was then caught in an emotional downward spiral that increased my fear and anxiety, which made my brain fog worse. I remembered the acronym FEAR—False Evidence Appearing Real—and during those times, I operated from a Small Mind made up of *Limiting Beliefs* that increased my unnecessary suffering.

While in Small Mind, I was able to choose to use EFT and TAB (see page 411) to help clear the fear-based *Limiting Beliefs* that brain fog triggered in me and shifted my perspective to **Large Mind** (see page 90), along with its **Empowering Beliefs**. I was also able to ask myself an Afformation (see page 101) such as, "**How is it possible for me to remember that this is brain fog and it will pass?**" The **Empowering Beliefs** that came to me sounded like, "**This is brain fog and it will pass. I am going through another Herxheimer reaction and this is just part of my healing process. It is what it is for now and it is temporary.**" This allowed me to be compassionately present and patient with myself even while experiencing brain fog.

Through the daily use of EFT and/or TAB, I was able to release my *Limiting Beliefs* that were triggered by my brain fog and refocused to a **Large Mind** perspective made up of **Empowering Beliefs**. Also after tapping, I often experienced a decrease in the intensity of my brain fog and on some occasions, it disappeared altogether!

I learned to **believe that my episodes of brain fog were temporary** and I no longer panicked when they came. I used **Afformations** to stay focused on my **Empowering Beliefs** that cultivated self-compassion and patience during an episode of brain fog. I encourage you also to take these positive action steps to help yourself maintain a **Large Mind** perspective while experiencing brain fog and to possibly even reduce its intenisity.

If the information presented here resonates with you, we invite you to begin with the extended global tapping script that follows. This is a gentle way to get you started and to decrease your overall intensity. Even though the scripted Reminder Phrases may not be reflective of your personal Aspects, we invite you to just go with it, track your progress, and see what happens!

Global Issue Title: Brain Fog

- Focus your attention on this **Global Issue** (see page 119).
- Identify one **Limiting Belief** (see page 119) that may be at the root of this Global Issue.
- Take three slow, deep belly breaths as you do a **Body Scan** (see page 81).
- What **Aspects** (see page 123) do you notice?
- Using the **SUD scale** (see page 124), choose a number between 0 (no distress/peaceful) and 10 (highest intensity of distress) to **rate the intensity** of distress you feel about the **Global Issue and Limiting Belief**, along with only the **Aspects** (thoughts, feelings, body sensations, and visual image) that you notice that apply to you.

	Description	SUD #:
Global Issue	Brain Fog	
Limiting Belief		
Thoughts		
Feelings		
Body Sensations		
Visual Image		

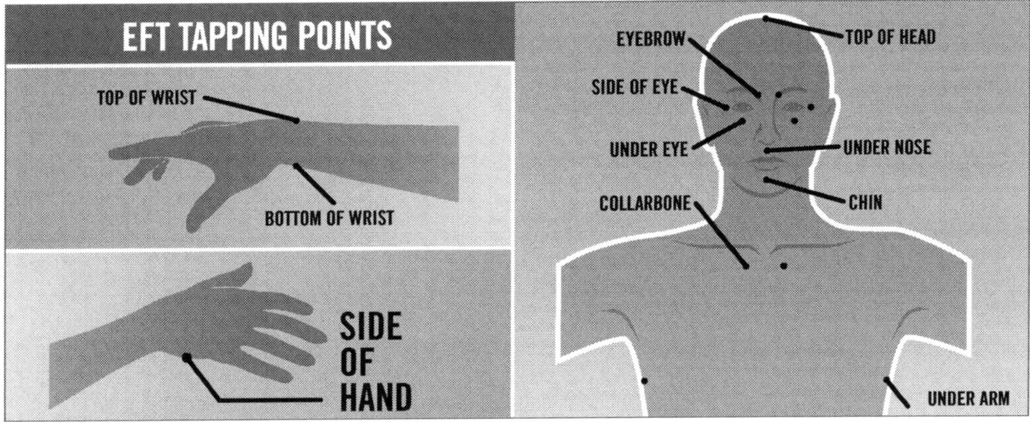

Extended Global Tapping Script: Let's begin tapping **(see page 126)**

Round 1

Setup:

Side of Hand: Even though my head is in the clouds, I accept that this is what I am experiencing now.

Side of Hand: Even though I am experiencing brain fog, I compassionately accept how I feel.

Side of Hand: Even though I can't think clearly, I honor and accept my body.

Top of Head: My head is in the clouds!

Eyebrow: What's happening to me?

Side of Eye: I can't find the right words to use.

Under Eye: I have brain fog!

Under Nose: I am scared I won't get my brain back!

Chin: I am scared this will lead to dementia!

Collarbone: I feel so disconnected.

Under Arm: I can't focus on anything.

Top of Wrists Together: How am I going to function with all that I have to do today?

Bottom of Wrists Together: I am scared of forgetting something important.

Slowly complete a deep belly breath and then keep tapping.

Round 2

Top of Head: I am so forgetful!

Eyebrows: Will I ever get over this?

Side of Eye: I want my brain back!

Under Eye: I am living in a fog.

Under Nose: I feel separated from others.

Chin: I feel separated from myself.

Collarbone: What's happening in my brain?

Under Arm: I am frightened this will last forever!

Top of Wrists Together: What if I never get my memory back?

Bottom of Wrists Together: I can't even think my way out of a paper bag!

Take three slow, deep belly breaths as you complete another **Body Scan**. What do you notice now? Note changes to the Aspects and any new ones that may appear below:

	Description	SUD #:
Global Issue	Brain Fog	
Limiting Belief		
Thoughts		
Feelings		
Body Sensations		
Visual Image		

If your rounds of tapping have led you to awareness about unresolved Specific Events that are being triggered and thus enhancing your experience of brain fog, title each one and add it to the **List of Titled Specific Events** on page 156 to tap through at another time. If your intensity level about this Global Issue, along with any of its Aspects, is still 3 or above on a SUD scale, continue tapping with the next round. (If you have a SUD scale of 0–2, skip down and finish by tapping through the positive statements and Afformations.)

Round 3

Setup:

Side of Hand: Even though I still have this brain fog, I honor and accept my brain.

Side of Hand: Even though I still feel disconnected, I honor and respect myself.

Side of Hand: Even though my brain fog is still here, I am hopeful it will pass.

Top of Head: This remaining brain fog.

Eyebrow: I am still fearful that I will be like this forever.

Side of Eye: I am afraid it is going to get worse.

Under Eye: Will I ever get over this?

Under Nose: If it goes, I know it will just come back.

Chin: This remaining brain fog.

Collarbone: I still feel disconnected.

Underarm: My head is still in the clouds.

Top of Wrists Together: This remaining brain fog.

Bottom of Wrists Together: I give it permission to leave now.

Take three slow, deep belly breaths as you complete another **Body Scan**. What do you notice now? Note changes to the Aspects and any new ones that may appear below:

	Description	SUD #:
Global Issue	Brain Fog	
Limiting Belief		
Thoughts		
Feelings		
Body Sensations		
Visual Image		

If your intensity of brain fog is still 3 or above on a SUD scale, keep tapping through what is in your awareness. If you feel as though you have decreased the intensity of your brain fog enough and/or want to stop tapping, finish with these last two rounds.

Round 4 – Now let's tap through some positive statements!

Top of Head: My brain fog is decreasing now.
Eyebrow: My brain fog is temporary.
Side of Eye: I choose to be compassionate and patient with myself.
Under Eye: I am open to new possibilities.
Under Nose: I feel more connected to myself.
Chin: Brain fog is what it is for now, and it is temporary.
Collarbone: My best and highest good is happening now.
Under Arm: My feet are on the ground, and my head is in the clouds.
Top of Wrists Together: I found my way through the fog.
Bottom of Wrists Together: I am healing in my own way and in my own time.

Round 5 – Tapping with Afformations (see page 101)

Top of Head: Why is it easy for me to think in Large Mind?

Eyebrow: How is it possible that my brain fog is clearing now?

Side of Eye: Why is it so easy for me to connect with myself and others?

Under Eye: Why is it so easy to remember that brain fog is temporary?

Under Nose: Why is it possible for me to decrease my brain fog with EFT?

Chin: Why is it so easy for me to remember what I need?

Collarbone: Why is it easy for me to allow my body to heal in its own time?

Under Arm: Why is it possible to shift my focus with Afformations?

Top of Wrists Together: Why is it possible for me to take positive action using EFT or TAB for my brain fog?

Bottom of Wrists together: Why is it okay for me to be mindfully present right here, right now?

Take three slow, deep belly breaths as you complete another **Body Scan**. What do you notice now? Note changes to the Aspects and any new ones that may appear below:

	Description	SUD #:
Global Issue	Brain Fog	
Limiting Belief		
Thoughts		
Feelings		
Body Sensations		
Visual Image		

EFT helps to release painful emotions, resolve Specific Events, and decrease the stress response that could be contributing to your brain fog. When these issues have been addressed and you are still experiencing brain fog over a SUD scale of 3, your intensity level may be reflecting the direct effect that Lyme/TBDs are having on your body, without the added emotional impact. This is expected even with the proper and thorough use of EFT.

Exercise: Developing Self-Awareness

Describe your experience of tapping through this Global Issue.

Which Aspects resolved, decreased, increased, or stayed the same?

If you identified a Limiting Belief, state what (if anything) changed.

State any Empowering Beliefs (see page 119) that you notice now.

What Global Issues/Limiting Beliefs need to be resolved (if any)?

Follow These Steps to Resolution

- When you have the time and energy, move on to the next exercise, **Going Deeper with EFT.** Use this to help you identify Specific Events, along with their Aspects, that are contributing to not resolving this Global Issue/Limiting Belief or with any new ones that may have surfaced while tapping. You may identify many and this is to be expected.
- Just break down one Specific Event at a time and tap it until resolved. Title the rest of the Specific Events that you have identified and add them to the **List of Titled Specific Events** on page 156 so that you can return to them at a later time to tap. You can use the **Blank Tapping Script** on page 404 or the **Vent While You Tap** worksheet on page 409 to assist you while tapping through a Specific Event.

Exercise: Going Deeper with EFT

If you just completed tapping through the extended global tapping script, and you still feel that the issue is unresolved, it's time to go deeper. What is keeping it unresolved? Title your Global Issue in the space provided below. Answer the following questions so that you can discover, uncover, and recover from the unresolved Specific Events and related Aspects that created and support the Limiting Belief you wish to resolve.

Global Issue: ______________________________

1. What Limiting Beliefs do you have at the root of this Global Issue? Rate the level of intensity of how true they are for you between SUD 0 (not true at all) and 10 (completely true).

______________________________ • SUD # (0–10): ____

______________________________ • SUD # (0–10): ____

2. Title and list the Specific Events in which you learned the Limiting Belief(s) (you can also add them to your List of Titled Specific Events on page 156).

____

____

____

____

____

____

3. Choose one Specific Event to break down here. Title: ______________________________

____

4. Tune into your titled Specific Event and identify only those Aspects that apply to you, below:

What thoughts do you notice?

______________________________ • SUD # (0–10): ____

______________________________ • SUD # (0–10): ____

Do your thoughts have the quality of Small Mind or Large Mind (see page 90)?____________

Describe your Large Mind thoughts (if any):______________________________

____

Describe your Small Mind thoughts (if any): ______________________________

____

What emotions are you feeling?

______________________________ • SUD # (0–10): ____

______________________________ • SUD # (0–10): ____

______________________________ • SUD # (0–10): ____

What body sensation do you notice?

______________________________ • SUD # (0–10): ____

Where is the sensation located?__________________• SUD # (0–10): ____

Does this sensation have a temperature?____ Describe:__________________

______________________________ • SUD # (0–10): ____

Texture?__________________________ • SUD # (0–10): ____

Color?__________________________ • SUD # (0–10): ____

Describe a visual image that you have (if any): __________________

______________________________ • SUD # (0–10): ____

5. Use the Aspects you have just identified to create your Reminder Phrases.
6. Stay tuned into your titled Specific Event.
7. Start tapping using the Modified EFT Basic Recipe on page 121. You can use the Aspects you have identified here to fill in the Reminder Phrases on the **Blank Tapping Script** on page 404 or the **Vent While You Tap** worksheet on page 409 to assist you in creating your own tapping script.

REPEAT PROCESS IF UNRESOLVED

Be aware of any changes in the intensity of distress you feel in relation to the Aspects, along with any new ones that emerge as you tap through the Rounds of EFT. Continue to tap, repeating the EFT Basic Recipe until your Specific Event, along with its Aspects, is resolved at a SUD level of 0–2. Also be mindful of shifts in Limiting Beliefs and the emergence of any new Empowering ones. To get full resolution of a Global Issue, the Limiting Beliefs must be released by resolving other painful Specific Events that are validating them.

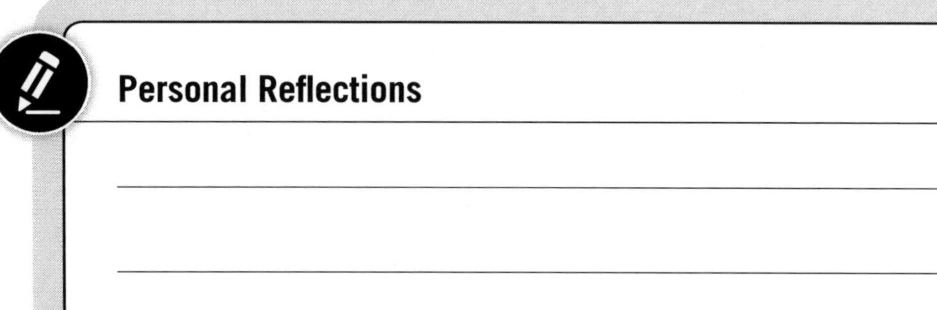

Personal Reflections

CHAPTER 34

Eat to Live or Live to Eat?

Note: *Limiting Beliefs are italicized* and **Empowering Beliefs are in bold**.

Recovery from Lyme/TBDs is more likely to be achieved when there is a comprehensive plan that includes the proper nutrition needed to reduce symptoms and to enhance the immune system to promote healing. Did you know, for example, that there are a number of foods that cause inflammation? Gluten, which is found in wheat products, is a major culprit. There are also many others including fried foods, dairy products, and sugar. As you may know with Lyme/TBDs, an increase of inflammation can increase symptoms.

Learning which foods aggravate your symptoms and which foods promote your healing will help you to optimize your body's capacity for self-repair. Not only is it necessary to be mindful of foods that can increase your inflammation, but also it is important to know that developing food allergies/sensitivities are common symptoms of Lyme/TBDs. People who never had food allergies/sensitivities before getting Lyme/TBDs have often been surprised by negative reactions to foods that they could once eat without any problem.

Getting a handle on proper nutrition is tough even without having an illness like Lyme/TBDs. Everywhere we turn, there is another "expert" telling us what we should and shouldn't eat, and sometimes they contradict each other. Fortunately, there are some solid and reliable resources for developing wellness-based nutrition. One very useful source for doing this is Dr. Kenneth B. Singleton's book, The Lyme Disease Solution. In his book, Dr. Singleton provides detailed information about his Lyme Inflammation Diet® (LID). The LID consists of four phases, beginning with a one-week period of detox. Dr. Singleton states:

> The goal is to quickly help your body shut down the mechanisms of chronic inflammation and begin detoxifying the body. This is accomplished by a primarily vegetarian diet that consists of eating safe foods that are low in what I call Universal Negative Inflammation Triggers (UNITs). Examples of UNIT foods include trans-fatty acids, AGEs (foods with glucose, fructose, poor quality carbohydrates, fried meats, and refined sugar).[83]

Dr. Singleton goes on to discuss how obesity and environmental toxins such as molds, pollutants, and tobacco smoke are also high UNITs. Dr. Singleton explains, "The degree to which chronic low-grade inflammation exists in the body is directly related to the severity of symptoms."[84] By choosing to be mindful about your nutrition and environmental factors, you can drastically reduce inflammation. The goal of Phase 1 in the LID is a one-week detox while shutting down the mechanisms of chronic inflammation. As a person moves through the remaining Phases 2–4, certain foods are slowly added back into the diet to observe their effect on the body. If eating a particular food makes a person feel worse, then the message is to stay away from it!

A dynamic mother-daughter team, Gail and Laura Piazza, wrote a fantastic cookbook called Recipes for Repair that features Dr. Singleton's LID. In it they describe each Phase and include for each an extensive list of healthy foods and delicious recipes with instructions that are easy to follow (total of 150). Throughout the book's layout are 50 stunning full-colored photographed pictures of completed recipes brought to life with an artistic flare! It also provides readers with a list of those foods to be avoided because of their high content of (UNITs). Best of all, the recipes are easy to make and taste yummy![85]

The Lyme Disease Solution and Recipes for Repair educated us and facilitated our implementation of a wellness-based nutritional plan. Their work has been instrumental in our own recovery. Choosing the right foods actually made us feel better. We had much less pain and way more energy than we thought was possible! It was amazing! Still, maintaining this nutritional lifestyle did take discipline. On days when we ate the UNIT foods just to "treat" ourselves, we paid big time with increased Lyme/TBD symptoms. We could feel the difference! We had more pain and less energy. Even so, we learned that **we had the ability to make healthy lifestyle choices** and that **we are active agents in our own healing process**.

As you can see, we know just how challenging it can be to give up our favorite UNIT foods even when they cause us pain. It also doesn't help that we live in a culture that promotes a literal smorgasbord of over-the-counter products for masking the heartburn and other painful results of eating foods that don't agree with us. The myth is that you can eat whatever you want because "we've got a pill for that." The truth is that if you have Lyme/TBDs, eating whatever you want whenever you want could be a recipe for increased symptoms and ongoing illness. What you can do is learn to change your emotional relationship to food and how you think about it, so that you can develop the discipline you need to be an active agent in making food choices that help promote your healing and recovery.

Case Study: But I LOVE Bread!

Ann really struggled with giving up gluten. She admitted, "*I'm addicted to flour!* I love bread! *I have to have bread! I am not able to give up bread!* Lyme disease has already taken so much from me, and now *it's taking away* my favorite foods! I am very angry about *having to do this*! *I can't do this!*"

Ann started to use EFT on her anger about "*having*" to give up bread.

As we tapped, Ann vented her anger and *disbelief about being able to make the changes that she knew would help her.* When she finished tapping through her anger and resistance, Ann said, "I don't feel angry anymore, but I am going to miss my favorite sandwich." I asked her if she wanted to do an experiment to see if she could make herself not want the sandwich anymore. Ann *didn't believe it was possible*, but she was willing to try it. I asked her to buy the sandwich, hold it in her lap, and just start tapping. I instructed her to allow herself to really smell it, see it, and even taste it while she tapped. She was to keep tapping until she didn't want it anymore.

The next week Ann came back into the office with a huge smile on her face, proclaiming the success of her experiment. Ann said, "I did what you said. I got my favorite sandwich, took a bite, and tapped. I smelled it and kept tapping. I couldn't take my eyes off it and my mouth was watering, but I still kept tapping like you said. After about twenty minutes of tapping, I was tired of looking at it! For some reason it didn't even smell good anymore. I got up and threw it into the trash! A part of me was ecstatic that **it worked** and another part of me was in *disbelief*! Was I really doing this? Then I wondered how long it would last. It's been a week and **I have no problem choosing not to eat bread**. I do know that **I am able to tap again if the urge comes back**."

It was exciting to see Ann become **empowered** to help herself with EFT to make **Large Mind** choices to support her recovery. Notice how Ann went from "*having*" to make these changes to "**choosing**" to make them. "*Having*" to do something can feel victimizing, while "**choosing**" to do something feels **empowering**.

Did You Know?

Many stores now stock a variety of delicious gluten-free breads, pastas, cereals, flours, and desserts? Being on a gluten-free diet doesn't mean you have to give up all of your favorite foods. You can find lots of different and tasty products and recipes in stores and online. We highly recommend Recipes for Repair by Gail and Laura Piazza because the recipes are easy to make and taste great!

As you think about what you've read so far, you might want to ask yourself, "Do I eat to live or do I live to eat?" There is a huge difference between these two mindsets. "Eat to live" reflects a mindful-approach to eating that allows for tailoring your habits to the unique needs of your body. "Live to eat" allows you to slip easily into emotional eating or overindulging in a way that not only adds to inflammation and pain but also can create new illnesses. The important thing is to be mindful of what you are eating and why you are eating it.

Changing how you eat can be most challenging. Like Ann, you may find that the invitation to follow a wellness-based plan of nutrition sparks anger, anxiety, and even sadness. There may be some foods you consider your "comfort" foods, the ones you usually go to when you are feeling down in the hopes of feeling better. Other times, you may treat yourself to certain types of food to celebrate a success or just because you want to feel good about something. No matter what those foods might be in your particular case, they usually share the common ingredients of fat, salt, and sugar.

Did you know that these ingredients—fat, salt, and sugar—trigger the same pleasure centers in the brain that addictive drugs like alcohol, opiates, and stimulants trigger? It's true! That's why they can be so addictive. The food industry knows this, which is why fast-food businesses, restaurants, and food manufacturers fill their products with these ingredients. They know you'll keep coming back for your fix.

The foods you choose to eat can also be an expression of how you experience family, friends, and community in general. What you eat can be reflective of your cultural and ethnic identity and include many happy memories of eating them with loved ones. It's a big deal! That's why changing what and how you eat can be so emotionally tough for some people. Still, it's necessary when the foods you love don't love you or support your recovery.

Using EFT to Get to the Emotional Roots of Food-Related Issues

Food-related issues often have deep emotional roots that can influence your choices regarding what, why, and when you eat certain foods. They vary from person to person, and it is not unusual for medically needed changes in eating habits to trigger an array of unresolved emotional issues. If you are feeling challenged by the need to change your eating habits, complete the following exercise **Identifying the Emotional Roots of Eating for Comfort** to identify some possible unresolved emotional issues at the root of your food cravings and your resistance to trading them in for recovery-based foods.

Following the exercise, we will teach how you can use EFT to go deeper into the emotional roots of your cravings and address any resistance that you may feel to help you resolve them. Resolving these emotional issues with EFT can help empower you to choose the foods your body needs to heal and recover.

Food-related issues can be very emotionally complex. If using EFT to work through your particular issues does not give you the benefits you desire, we suggest that you work with a certified EFT practitioner who can support you through the process of going even deeper to resolve your emotional issues with food.

Exercise: Identifying the Emotional Roots of Eating for Comfort

Make a list of your top-10 favorite comfort foods. Pay particular attention to the foods you most LOVE to eat.

1.____________________ 2.____________________

3.____________________ 4.____________________

5.____________________ 6.____________________

7.____________________ 8.____________________

9.____________________ 10.____________________

Check off the ones that contain **Universal Negative Inflammation Triggers (UNITs),** such as refined sugar, glucose, fructose, salt, and fat. Choose four foods from your list that contain UNITs. Answer the following questions in relation to each of the foods you have chosen, reflecting your experience with each one in as much detail as possible.

UNITs Favorite Food:	
What do you like about this food?	
When do you eat this food?	
How often do you eat it?	
What emotions trigger you to eat this food?	
How do you feel physically after eating it?	
How do you feel emotionally after eating it?	
What Specific Events (see page 122) in your past do you remember enjoying this food with others? (You may need to use EFT on positive memories where you have experienced happiness and a feeling of connection with others while eating it. Make a list of titled Specific Events to use with EFT.)	
How often do you eat it with others?	
How often do you eat it alone?	
How does this food serve your well-being?	
How could this food interfere with your Lyme/TBD recovery?	
What Limiting Beliefs (if any) do you have about letting this food go?	
Do you notice any resistance in your mind-body about the thought of letting this food go?	

UNITs Favorite Food:	
What do you like about this food?	
When do you eat this food?	
How often do you eat it?	
What emotions trigger you to eat this food?	
How do you feel physically after eating it?	
How do you feel emotionally after eating it?	
What Specific Events (see page 122) in your past do you remember enjoying this food with others? (You may need to use EFT on positive memories where you have experienced happiness and a feeling of connection with others while eating it. Make a list of titled Specific Events to use with EFT.)	
How often do you eat it with others?	
How often do you eat it alone?	
How does this food serve your well-being?	
How could this food interfere with your Lyme/TBD recovery?	
What Limiting Beliefs (if any) do you have about letting this food go?	
Do you notice any resistance in your mind-body about the thought of letting this food go?	

UNITs Favorite Food:	
What do you like about this food?	
When do you eat this food?	
How often do you eat it?	
What emotions trigger you to eat this food?	
How do you feel physically after eating it?	
How do you feel emotionally after eating it?	
What Specific Events (see page 122) in your past do you remember enjoying this food with others? (You may need to use EFT on positive memories where you have experienced happiness and a feeling of connection with others while eating it. Make a list of titled Specific Events to use with EFT.)	
How often do you eat it with others?	
How often do you eat it alone?	
How does this food serve your well-being?	
How could this food interfere with your Lyme/TBD recovery?	
What Limiting Beliefs (if any) do you have about letting this food go?	
Do you notice any resistance in your mind-body about the thought of letting this food go?	

UNITs Favorite Food:	
What do you like about this food?	
When do you eat this food?	
How often do you eat it?	
What emotions trigger you to eat this food?	
How do you feel physically after eating it?	
How do you feel emotionally after eating it?	
What Specific Events (see page 122) in your past do you remember enjoying this food with others? (You may need to use EFT on positive memories where you have experienced happiness and a feeling of connection with others while eating it. Make a list of titled Specific Events to use with EFT.)	
How often do you eat it with others?	
How often do you eat it alone?	
How does this food serve your well-being?	
How could this food interfere with your Lyme/TBD recovery?	
What Limiting Beliefs (if any) do you have about letting this food go?	
Do you notice any resistance in your mind-body about the thought of letting this food go?	

Exercise: Pulling Out the Emotional Roots with EFT

There are many different ways to tap through emotional issues related to food. Here are a few of them:

1. **Tap through your resistance.** If you feel resistance to changing your eating habits and letting go of your favorite UNITs food to develop a food plan that will support your Lyme/TBD recovery, tap through your resistance! The global tapping script offered later in this chapter is on resistance. This is a gentle place to start. To fully resolve this Global issue, you need to release any underlying Limiting Beliefs that are validating it by using the **Going Deeper with EFT** exercise at the end of this chapter. This can also be applied to numbers 2 and 3 below.
2. **Tap through cravings.** If you are craving one of your favorite, but harmful, UNITs foods, start tapping! As you tap, focus your attention on the specific emotions that are triggering your cravings for the particular food you desire. Continue tapping until the craving subsides. If your craving does not subside, go to number 3 below. (This is a way to start globally on this issue and gently ease yourself into the more deeply rooted issues underlying your craving. If your craving returns, it may be because you need to go deeper to the root cause of your craving—both the positive and negative Specific Events that created and support how you feel emotionally about eating that particular food.)
3. **Tap through Specific Events.** The best way to resolve emotional issues related to food is by using EFT on the Specific Events that created and support it. Remember, the

foods that you eat are connected to your emotions. You may find that when you feel sad, angry, hurt, or anxious, you want to reach for a favorite comfort food, which has a good chance of being high in UNITs. Many people eat comfort food as a way of either protecting themselves from emotional pain or reliving positive experiences from the past.

Either way, comfort food is most often attached to Specific Events from the past when food was used to either make you feel better or join with family and friends in a pleasant meal or celebration. Perhaps you remember times in your childhood when you were offered food as an attempt to make you feel better when something went wrong. You may also have positive memories of holidays, celebrations, and good times spent with loved ones that involved a variety of sweet and savory foods that now bring back feelings of joy, love, and connection that are associated with those pleasant experiences. Eating these foods now is a way of stimulating the emotions from those times when you felt happy, loved, and connected.

List one of your favorite UNITs foods and answer the following two questions:

UNITs Favorite Food: ______________________________

1. What positive memories do you connect with while eating this food? (List and title Specific Events for future tapping sessions.)

____

____

____

____

2. What negative/painful memories do you have in relation to eating this food? (List and title Specific Events for future tapping sessions.)

____

____

____

____

The most important thing to keep in mind is to start where you feel comfortable. If food is an emotionally charged topic for you, we suggest that you start tapping globally and then move gently into the underlying root causes (Refer back to number 3 on page 326).

If the information presented here resonates with you, we invite you to begin with the extended global tapping script that follows. This is a gentle way to get you started and to decrease your overall intensity. Even though the scripted Reminder Phrases may not be reflective of your personal Aspects, we invite you to just go with it, track your progress, and see what happens!

Global Issue Title: Resistance to Changing Eating Habits

- Focus your attention on this **Global Issue** (see page 119).
- Identify one **Limiting Belief** (see page 119) that may be at the root of this Global Issue.
- Take three slow, deep belly breaths as you do a **Body Scan** (see page 81).
- What **Aspects** (see page 123) do you notice?
- Using the **SUD scale** (see page 124), choose a number between 0 (no distress/peaceful) and 10 (highest intensity of distress) to **rate the intensity** of distress you feel about the **Global Issue and Limiting Belief**, along with only the **Aspects** (thoughts, feelings, body sensations, and visual image) that you notice that apply to you.

	Description	SUD #:
Global Issue	Resistance to Changing Eating Habits	
Limiting Belief		
Thoughts		
Feelings		
Body Sensations		
Visual Image		

Extended Global Tapping Script: Let's begin tapping (see page 126)

Round 1

Setup:

Side of Hand: Even though I don't want to give up my favorite food, I honor and respect myself.

Side of Hand: Even though there is no way I will ever be able to give up these foods, I will do whatever it takes to recover.

Side of Hand: Even though I am angry at the thought of giving up my favorite foods, I honor and respect myself.

Top of Head: I am so angry that Lyme/TBDs are now taking away some of my favorite foods!

Eyebrow: There is no way that I can do this!

Side of Eye: I am an emotional eater.

Under Eye: I can't do this right now; I am in too much pain.

Under Nose: Lyme/TBDs have taken everything else, and now they're taking away my favorite foods.

Chin: I am so angry about learning that the food I enjoy is bad for me!

Collarbone: This seems like too big of a change.

Under Arm: I will start to eat healthier once I am feeling better.

Top of Wrists Together: I am too fatigued to even think about doing this now.

Bottom of Wrists Together: I am not going to give up one more thing!

Slowly complete a deep belly breath and then keep tapping.

Round 2

Top of Head: This recommended dietary change is too overwhelming!

Eyebrow: I just can't do this. It is too much!

Side of Eye: It is too expensive to eat healthy.

Under Eye: I don't have enough time to plan my meals.

Under Nose: I will have to pack my food every day. It is not convenient.

Chin: What will I enjoy now?

Collarbone: I am so angry that I might need to do this to support my recovery.

Under Arm: I will have to throw away a lot of food, and I don't want to waste it.

Top of Wrists Together: This will be too hard to stick to.

Bottom of Wrists Together: My family won't want to eat what I eat!

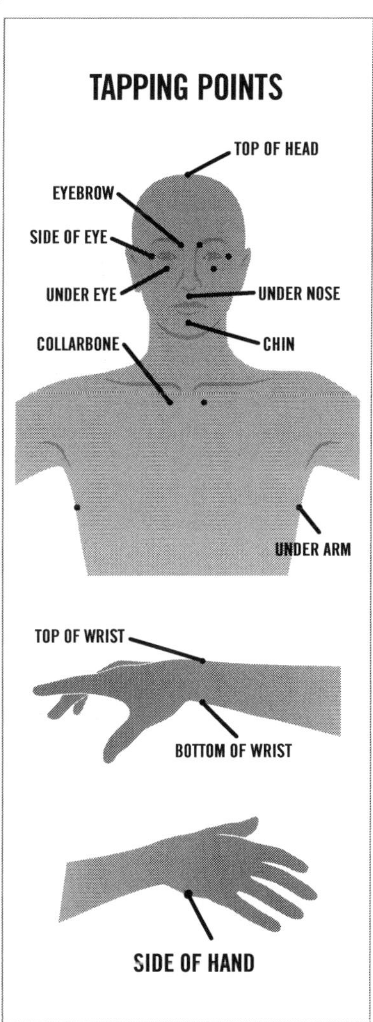

Take three slow, deep belly breaths as you complete another **Body Scan**. What do you notice now? Note changes to the Aspects and any new ones that may appear below:

	Description	SUD #:
Global Issue	Resistance to Changing Eating Habits	
Limiting Belief		
Thoughts		
Feelings		
Body Sensations		
Visual Image		

If your intensity level about this Global Issue, along with any of its Aspects, is still 3 or above on a SUD scale, continue tapping with the next round. (If you have a SUD scale of 0–2, skip down and finish by tapping through the positive statements and Afformations.)

Round 3

Setup:

Side of Hand: Even though I still feel resistant to this new way of eating, I honor and respect myself.

Side of Hand: Even though I still feel overwhelmed about this, I accept all of my feelings.

Side of Hand: Even though I still have some doubt that I can do this successfully, I am willing to do whatever it takes to recover.

Top of Head: I am still overwhelmed!

Eyebrow: This remaining resistance!

Side of Eye: I still don't want to start this now!

Under Eye: I still doubt that I can do this successfully.

Under Nose: I am still angry that Lyme/TBDs have now taken away my favorite foods.

Chin: I still believe this is too much to do now.

Collarbone: I don't know if I will ever be ready.

Under Arm: I might as well live with the pain that UNITs cause me.

Top of Wrists Together: Maybe it will be worth it to commit to the Lyme Inflammation Diet.

Bottom of Wrists Together: Maybe the Lyme Inflammation Diet will make me feel better.

Take three slow, deep belly breaths as you complete another **Body Scan**. What do you notice now? Note changes to the Aspects and any new ones that may appear below:

	Description	SUD #:
Global Issue	Resistance to Changing Eating Habits	
Limiting Belief		
Thoughts		
Feelings		
Body Sensations		
Visual Image		

If your intensity level about this Global Issue, along with any of its Aspects, is still 3 or above on a SUD scale, keep tapping through what is in your awareness or move down to **Follow These Steps to Resolution**.

Once you reach a SUD level of 0–2 or when you just want to stop tapping for now and return at a later time, finish up by tapping through the positive statements and Afformations.

Round 4 – Now let's tap through some positive statements!

Top of Head: I am so glad there is something I can do to help myself!
Eyebrow: I feel empowered to make these changes!
Side of Eye: There is no better time than the present!
Under Eye: I will do everything I can to feel better and recover.
Under Nose: What do I have to lose but pain?
Chin: Lyme/TBDs are actually calling me to a healthier lifestyle.
Collarbone: I know that I can do this!
Under Arm: The time is now!
Top of Wrists Together: I choose to take an active role in my recovery.
Bottom of Wrists Together: I am excited to learn that the Lyme Inflammation Diet can help me feel better!

Round 5 – Tapping with Afformations (see page 101)

Top of Head: Why is it so easy for me to follow the Lyme Inflammation Diet?
Eyebrow: Why is it possible for me to change my food plan to support my recovery?
Side of Eye: Why do I feel good knowing that I am helping my body heal?
Under Eye: Why is it possible that eliminating UNITs could reduce my pain and fatigue?
Under Nose: Why is it so easy for me to make these changes?
Chin: Why am I enjoying this new way of eating?
Collarbone: Why is this easier than I first thought?
Under Arm: Why is it easy for me to imagine that I will feel better if I eliminate UNITs?
Top of Wrists Together: Why is it so easy to choose foods that support my recovery?
Bottom of Wrists Together: Why am I able to take positive actions to support my recovery?

Take three slow, deep belly breaths as you complete another **Body Scan**. What do you notice now? Note changes to the Aspects and any new ones that may appear below:

	Description	SUD #:
Global Issue	Resistance to Changing Eating Habits	
Limiting Belief		
Thoughts		
Feelings		
Body Sensations		
Visual Image		

If your intensity level about this Global Issue, along with any of its Aspects, is still 3 or above on a SUD scale, you need to explore them more in depth and follow the directives in **Follow These Steps to Resolution**, on the following page.

Exercise: Developing Self-Awareness

Describe your experience of tapping through this Global Issue.

____

____

____

Which Aspects resolved, decreased, increased, or stayed the same?

____

____

If you identified a Limiting Belief, state what (if anything) changed.

____

____

State any Empowering Beliefs (see page 119) that you notice now.

____

____

What Global Issues/Limiting Beliefs need to be resolved (if any)?

____

____

Follow These Steps to Resolution

- When you have the time and energy, move on to the next exercise, **Going Deeper with EFT.** Use this to help you identify Specific Events, along with their Aspects, that are contributing to not resolving this Global Issue/Limiting Belief or with any new ones that may have surfaced while tapping. You may identify many and this is to be expected.
- Just break down one Specific Event at a time and tap it until resolved. Title the rest of the Specific Events that you have identified and add them to the **List of Titled Specific Events** on page 156 so that you can return to them at a later time to tap. You can use the **Blank Tapping Script** on page 404 or the **Vent While You Tap** worksheet on page 409 to assist you while tapping through a Specific Event.

Exercise: Going Deeper with EFT

If you just completed tapping through the extended global tapping script, and you still feel that the issue is unresolved, it's time to go deeper. What is keeping it unresolved? Title your Global Issue in the space provided below. Answer the following questions so that you can discover, uncover, and recover from the unresolved Specific Events and related Aspects that created and support the Limiting Belief you wish to resolve.

Global Issue: ______________________________

1. What Limiting Beliefs do you have at the root of this Global Issue? Rate the level of intensity of how true they are for you between SUD 0 (not true at all) and 10 (completely true).

______________________________ • SUD # (0–10): ____

______________________________ • SUD # (0–10): ____

2. Title and list the Specific Events in which you learned the Limiting Belief(s) (you can also add them to your List of Titled Specific Events on page 156).

____

____

____

____

____

____

3. Choose one Specific Event to break down here. Title: ______________________________

____

4. Tune into your titled Specific Event and identify only those Aspects that apply to you, below:

What thoughts do you notice?

______________________________ • SUD # (0–10): ____

______________________________ • SUD # (0–10): ____

Do your thoughts have the quality of Small Mind or Large Mind (see page 90)?____________

Describe your Large Mind thoughts (if any):____

____

Describe your Small Mind thoughts (if any): ____

____

What emotions are you feeling?

____ • SUD # (0–10): ____

____ • SUD # (0–10): ____

____ • SUD # (0–10): ____

What body sensation do you notice?

____ • SUD # (0–10): ____

Where is the sensation located?___________________________ • SUD # (0–10): ____

Does this sensation have a temperature?____ Describe:___________________________

____ • SUD # (0–10): ____

Texture?_______________________________________ • SUD # (0–10): ____

Color?____ • SUD # (0–10): ____

Describe a visual image that you have (if any): ________________________________

____ • SUD # (0–10): ____

5. Use the Aspects you have just identified to create your Reminder Phrases.
6. Stay tuned into your titled Specific Event.
7. Start tapping using the Modified EFT Basic Recipe on page 121. You can use the Aspects you have identified here to fill in the Reminder Phrases on the **Blank Tapping Script** on page 404 or the **Vent While You Tap** worksheet on page 409 to assist you in creating your own tapping script.

REPEAT PROCESS IF UNRESOLVED

Be aware of any changes in the intensity of distress you feel in relation to the Aspects, along with any new ones that emerge as you tap through the Rounds of EFT. Continue to tap, repeating the EFT Basic Recipe until your Specific Event, along with its Aspects, is resolved at a SUD level of 0–2. Also be mindful of shifts in Limiting Beliefs and the emergence of any new Empowering ones. To get full resolution of a Global Issue, the Limiting Beliefs must be released by resolving other painful Specific Events that are validating them

Personal Reflections

CHAPTER 35

Ly"me" Is Not ME!

Case Study

Note: *Limiting Beliefs are italicized* and **Empowering Beliefs are in bold**.

Mary, a 53-year-old business woman, was diagnosed with Lyme disease seven years ago and has been in treatment with different practitioners who have not been able to help her return to her previous state of health. She reported occasionally getting some relief from her migrating body pain, brain fog, and fatigue, but that her symptoms always returned with much more intensity than before.

"Eventually I went on short-term disability, and after using up my sick time, I was asked to leave my job. I gave up on my dreams and now I can barely remember what day it is. I have difficulty focusing, remembering things, and keeping up with the bare essentials. **My husband is supportive** and has taken over most of the household tasks. I am grateful to him for doing that, but I enjoyed doing those things, and now I can't. *I guess this is my life and I don't see any way of changing it* because I've tried everything I know. I did everything the doctors told me to do, but I still don't feel any better. They told me I might never get over this. I just have to accept that I have a chronic illness that will probably never go away. I've been so depressed. I can't even remember what life was like before all the pain, fatigue, and brain fog set in. My whole life now is about how I'm feeling. It's as if who I was and what I used to do just disappeared. Sometimes I even *believe* that, "*I am Lyme disease!*"

It can be very easy for some people to lose touch with themselves after years, sometimes even decades, of experiencing the debilitating symptoms that are the hallmarks of having chronic Lyme/TBDs. Survival itself becomes so all-consuming that there seems to be little room for anything else. Life roles that were once performed with relative ease and provided a "sense of self" are now redefined in relation to symptoms. In the midst of so much change and loss (Refer to the Lyme/TBDs-Related Change/Loss Inventory on page 57), it is no wonder that so many people have difficulty maintaining a connection with their sense of self, the "I am." Mary reflected this dynamic in one of her sessions. "My life as it was once experienced is no longer. *I don't know who I am anymore.*"

Mary's story brings out the most challenging aspects of chronic Lyme/TBDs: adjusting to changes and losses. This disease makes it almost impossible to carry out the usual roles and lifestyle habits that were experienced before getting sick. This may cause you to question everything you believed about yourself. This can happen if your identity is so closely tied in with what you do and the roles you play.

These role changes can bring about a slow unconscious process in which your identity can become enmeshed with your symptoms (i.e., identifying with Lyme disease). You may not even realize it is happening. This can be a common way of adapting to many changes that occur over a long period of time that affect how you relate to yourself and how that is expressed in every dimension of your life. This is what happened to Mary. After seven years of living with chronic Lyme disease, she didn't know who she was anymore stating, "I am Lyme disease."

Mary's identity crisis ultimately prompted her to seek help. During the next several months, she used EFT to peel away and process the many layers of grief, anger, and sadness she felt from all the changes and losses chronic Lyme disease brought into her life. With time and persistent tapping, Mary developed the patience, self-compassion, and hope that allowed her to reconnect with her core self.

"You know, I am more than my Lyme disease. Lyme disease is not me! Chronic Lyme disease took over my life, and somewhere I lost myself. This whole process has opened me up to a part of myself that I never knew before. I have new priorities now and interests I want to explore in the future when I am feeling better. I am looking at what really matters to me, like renewing my relationship with my husband and doing things that bring joy back into my life. I still have some very bad days and I don't know when I will be able to work again, yet I am no longer going to allow my symptoms to define who I am. It seems weird to say, but I think if it weren't for Lyme disease, I might never have gone deeper into myself to see who I really am and redefine what is most important to me. I also know that I could not have gotten here by myself."

We have been deeply inspired by clients like Mary, who have the courage to walk through their despair to meet the challenges of Lyme/TBDs and to allow those challenges to be their own catalyst for personal growth and transformation. It is not an easy road, and the resilience and courage that are shown every day, in every breath, by people like Mary are truly inspiring.

We have been to rallies and Lyme/TBDs support groups where we have heard people say, "I am a Lymie." We absolutely understand that the term "Lymie" is being used in this context as a way to identify with and belong to the Lyme/TBDs community, a group where we have met some of the most courageous and inspirational people we have ever encountered. We are grateful to be members of this community for so many life-giving reasons! Belonging to a group of people who truly understand what we have gone through, unlike anybody else, is a transformative experience. We merely offer this one invitation: Be aware of what follows an "I am" statement and why you are using it. If you use the term "Lymie," we invite you to check in with yourself to make sure you are identifying with the Lyme/TBDs community and not unconsciously with the disease. You will know immediately where you are coming from. If a part of you identifies with your symptoms, tap through this Global Issue to get your focus back on the community.

If the information presented here resonates with you, we invite you to begin with the extended global tapping script that follows. This is a gentle way to get you started and to decrease your overall intensity. Even though the scripted Reminder Phrases may not be reflective of your personal Aspects, we invite you to just go with it, track your progress, and see what happens!

Global Issue Title: "I Am Not Sure Who I Am Anymore!"

- Focus your attention on this **Global Issue** (see page 119).
- Identify one **Limiting Belief** (see page 119) that may be at the root of this Global Issue.
- Take three slow, deep belly breaths as you do a **Body Scan** (see page 81).
- What **Aspects** (see page 123) do you notice?
- Using the **SUD scale** (see page 124), choose a number between 0 (no distress/peaceful) and 10 (highest intensity of distress) to **rate the intensity** of distress you feel about the **Global Issue and Limiting Belief**, along with only the **Aspects** (thoughts, feelings, body sensations, and visual image) that you notice that apply to you.

	Description	SUD #:
Global Issue	"I Am Not Sure Who I Am Anymore!"	
Limiting Belief		
Thoughts		
Feelings		
Body Sensations		
Visual Image		

A WELLNESS
STATE OF MIND

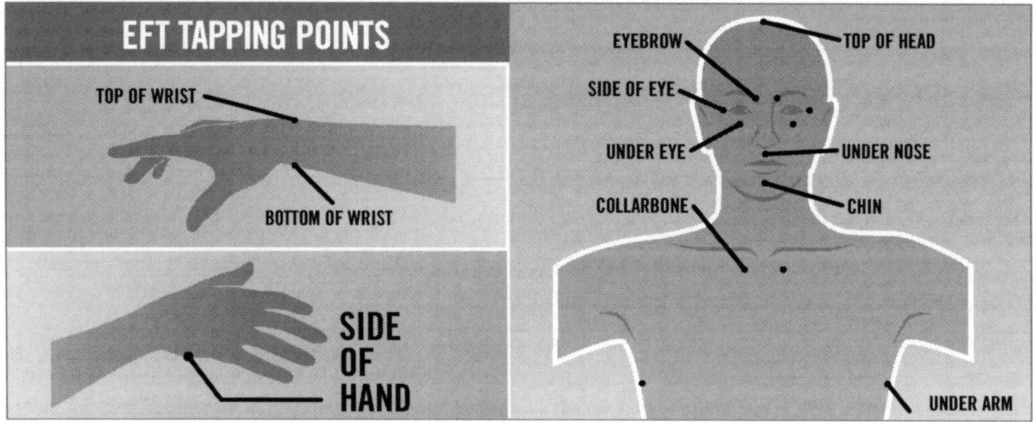

Extended Global Tapping Script: Let's begin tapping **(see page 126)**

Round 1

Setup:

Side of Hand: Even though I feel so confused about who *I am* now, I honor and respect myself.

Side of Hand: Even though I feel so lost in my Lyme/TBD symptoms, I accept all my feelings.

Side of Hand: Even though I am not sure who *I am* anymore, I am open to new possibilities about myself.

Top of Head: I am really confused about who *I am* now since having chronic Lyme/TBDs.

Eyebrow: What has happened to me?

Side of Eye: Who *am* I now?

Under Eye: Where did I go?

Under Nose: I feel so lost!

Chin: I don't know who *I am* anymore!

Collarbone: I feel so confused!

Under Arm: I feel so (state the emotion).

Top of Wrists Together: I am starting to believe that Lyme/TBDs are me!

Bottom of Wrists Together: Who *am I* really?

Slowly complete a deep belly breath and then keep tapping.

Round 2

Top of Head: *I am* really confused!

Eyebrow: I miss the person I used to be.

Side of Eye: If I can't beat this Lyme/TBD, I might as well join it.

Under Eye: I feel so sad about what I have lost.

Under Nose: Who *am I* now?

Chin: I just have to accept that *I am* my symptoms.

Collarbone: Who *am I* really?

Under Arm: Is this all that *I am*?

Top of Wrists Together: I feel so lost in my pain.

Bottom of Wrists Together: I miss who I used to be.

Take three slow, deep belly breaths as you complete another **Body Scan**. What do you notice now? Note changes to the Aspects and any new ones that may appear below:

	Description	SUD #:
Global Issue	"I Am Not Sure Who I Am Anymore!"	
Limiting Belief		
Thoughts		
Feelings		
Body Sensations		
Visual Image		

If your intensity level about this Global Issue, along with any of its Aspects, is still 3 or above on a SUD scale, continue tapping with the next round. (If you have a SUD scale of 0–2, skip down and finish by tapping through the positive statements and Afformations.)

Round 3

Setup:

Side of Hand: Even though I still feel lost, I honor and accept myself.

Side of Hand: Even though I am still confused about who *I am* now, I am open to new possibilities in self-awareness.

Side of Hand: Even though I still feel out of touch with myself, I accept that's where I am for now.

Top of Head: This remaining confusion.

Eyebrow: This remaining anger.

Side of Eye: I still feel lost.

Under Eye: I still don't know who *I am* other than a Lyme patient.

Under Nose: I still don't remember who *I am* under all of this pain.

Chin: All of my feelings of (state the emotion).

Collarbone: This remaining sadness.

Under Arm: I miss my old self so much!

Top of Wrists Together: *I am* still lost.

Bottom of Wrists Together: All these remaining emotions about this.

Take three slow, deep belly breaths as you complete another **Body Scan**. What do you notice now? Note changes to the Aspects and any new ones that may appear below:

	Description	SUD #:
Global Issue	"I Am Not Sure Who I Am Anymore!"	
Limiting Belief		
Thoughts		
Feelings		
Body Sensations		
Visual Image		

If your intensity level about this Global Issue, along with any of its Aspects, is still 3 or above on a SUD scale, keep tapping through what is in your awareness or move down to **Follow These Steps to Resolution**.

Once you reach a SUD level of 0–2 or when you just want to stop tapping for now and return at a later time, finish up by tapping through the positive statements and Afformations.

Round 4 – Now let's tap through some positive statements!

Top of Head: *I am* more than my Lyme/TBD symptoms.
Eyebrow: *I am* more than my thoughts.
Side of Eye: *I am* more than my feelings.
Under Eye: *I am* more than my emotions.
Under Nose: *I am* more than my actions.
Chin: *I am* more than how my body feels.
Collarbone: *I am* more than a chronic Lyme patient.
Under Arm: *I am* more than this brain fog and fatigue.
Top of Wrists Together: *I am* more than what I have done.
Bottom of Wrists Together: I am learning more each day about *who I am* outside of what I do.

Round 5 – Tapping with Afformations (see page 101)

Top of Head: Why is it possible for me to remember who *I really am*?

Eyebrow: Why is it possible to find and reconnect with myself again?

Side of Eye: Why is it so easy for me to know that *I am* more than my symptoms?

Under Eye: Why is it possible for me know that *I am* more than what I used to be able to do?

Under Nose: Why is it possible for me to connect deeply with my true self?

Chin: Why does it bring me joy to reconnect with myself?

Collarbone: Why is it so easy for me to be grateful for knowing *I am* more powerful than I thought?

Under Arm: Why is possible for me to remember that *I am* more than what I do?

Top of Wrists Together: Why is it possible for me to separate my symptoms from my identity?

Bottom of Wrists Together: Why is it possible for me to know that Lyme disease is a catalyst for personal transformation?

Take three slow, deep belly breaths as you complete another **Body Scan**. What do you notice now? Note changes to the Aspects and any new ones that may appear below:

	Description	SUD #:
Global Issue	"I Am Not Sure Who I Am Anymore!"	
Limiting Belief		
Thoughts		
Feelings		
Body Sensations		
Visual Image		

If your intensity level about this Global Issue, along with any of its Aspects, is still 3 or above on a SUD scale, you need to explore them more in depth and follow the directives in **Follow These Steps to Resolution**, on the following page.

Exercise: Developing Self-Awareness

Describe your experience of tapping through this Global Issue.

___

___

___

Which Aspects resolved, decreased, increased, or stayed the same?

___

___

If you identified a Limiting Belief, state what (if anything) changed.

___

___

State any Empowering Beliefs (see page 119) that you notice now.

___

___

What Global Issues/Limiting Beliefs need to be resolved (if any)?

___

___

Follow These Steps to Resolution

- When you have the time and energy, move on to the next exercise, **Going Deeper with EFT.** Use this to help you identify Specific Events, along with their Aspects, that are contributing to not resolving this Global Issue/Limiting Belief or with any new ones that may have surfaced while tapping. You may identify many and this is to be expected.
- Just break down one Specific Event at a time and tap it until resolved. Title the rest of the Specific Events that you have identified and add them to the **List of Titled Specific Events** on page 156 so that you can return to them at a later time to tap. You can use the **Blank Tapping Script** on page 404 or the **Vent While You Tap** worksheet on page 409 to assist you while tapping through a Specific Event.

Exercise: Going Deeper with EFT

If you just completed tapping through the extended global tapping script, and you still feel that the issue is unresolved, it's time to go deeper. What is keeping it unresolved? Title your Global Issue in the space provided below. Answer the following questions so that you can discover, uncover, and recover from the unresolved Specific Events and related Aspects that created and support the Limiting Belief you wish to resolve.

Global Issue: ______________________________

1. What Limiting Beliefs do you have at the root of this Global Issue? Rate the level of intensity of how true they are for you between SUD 0 (not true at all) and 10 (completely true).

______________________________ • SUD # (0–10): ____

______________________________ • SUD # (0–10): ____

2. Title and list the Specific Events in which you learned the Limiting Belief(s) (you can also add them to your List of Titled Specific Events on page 156).

____

____

____

____

____

____

3. Choose one Specific Event to break down here. Title: ______________________________

____

4. Tune into your titled Specific Event and identify only those Aspects that apply to you, below:

What thoughts do you notice?

______________________________ • SUD # (0–10): ____

______________________________ • SUD # (0–10): ____

Do your thoughts have the quality of Small Mind or Large Mind (see page 90)?______________

Describe your Large Mind thoughts (if any):______________________________

____

Describe your Small Mind thoughts (if any): ______________________________

____

What emotions are you feeling?

____ • SUD # (0–10): ____

____ • SUD # (0–10): ____

____ • SUD # (0–10): ____

What body sensation do you notice?

____ • SUD # (0–10): ____

Where is the sensation located?________________________ • SUD # (0–10): ____

Does this sensation have a temperature?____ Describe:____________________

____ • SUD # (0–10): ____

Texture?_______________________________________ • SUD # (0–10): ____

Color?____ • SUD # (0–10): ____

Describe a visual image that you have (if any): ________________________

____ • SUD # (0–10): ____

5. Use the Aspects you have just identified to create your Reminder Phrases.
6. Stay tuned into your titled Specific Event.
7. Start tapping using the Modified EFT Basic Recipe on page 121. You can use the Aspects you have identified here to fill in the Reminder Phrases on the **Blank Tapping Script** on page 404 or the **Vent While You Tap** worksheet on page 409 to assist you in creating your own tapping script.

REPEAT PROCESS IF UNRESOLVED

Be aware of any changes in the intensity of distress you feel in relation to the Aspects, along with any new ones that emerge as you tap through the Rounds of EFT. Continue to tap, repeating the EFT Basic Recipe until your Specific Event, along with its Aspects, is resolved at a SUD level of 0–2. Also be mindful of shifts in Limiting Beliefs and the emergence of any new Empowering ones. To get full resolution of a Global Issue, the Limiting Beliefs must be released by resolving other painful Specific Events that are validating them.

CHAPTER 36

My Body Betrayed Me!

Case Study

Note: *Limiting Beliefs are italicized* and **Empowering Beliefs are in bold**.

Alex, a 32-year-old computer programmer who once enjoyed cycling and rock climbing, was suffering with particularly serious complications related to Lyme disease. Where once he enjoyed being in his body and the freedom he felt as he rode his bike or climbed a rock face, he now felt a bitter resentment about not being able to do the things he loved to do.

During his first few therapy sessions, Alex repeatedly stated, *"I hate my body now.* I don't know the last time I could even walk across the room without feeling pain. And the treatment I've been getting isn't doing anything to help me, so I'm not going back to the doctor! I used to be able to get on my bike and ride thirty miles. I could climb a two-hundred-foot cliff, and now I'm lucky if I can even get on my bike, let alone ride it. *This isn't fair! I can't even trust my legs!* And the treatments I get hardly make a difference. Well, *I don't care! One way or another, I'm going to beat my body,* and **it's not going to get the best of me!** I'm not going to let this disease turn me into some kind of *loser*!"

Alex was consumed with resentment about the impact Lyme disease was having on his body and the limitations it placed on him. He had come to reject his body because he *believed that it had betrayed him.* Alex was angry at not having control over what Lyme disease was doing to his body and then blamed his body for failing to overcome it.

Prior to being infected with Lyme disease, he had been healthy and athletic; now he was experiencing how debilitating Lyme disease can be. This experience stirred up old memories and feelings about having grown up with a controlling father who demanded perfection in all areas of life and who rejected Alex when he did not achieve success. Alex began tapping through his current hatred and *betrayal of his body for not beating Lyme disease.*

After tapping through the current layers of *believing that his body had betrayed him*, he started to have more self-compassion: **"I am doing the best that I can right now. I see that it is not my body's fault that I have Lyme disease,** *but I should be successful at beating it."* Notice that Alex was starting to develop **Empowering Beliefs** through tapping. Even so, he still had unresolved feelings of rejection from his father.

"All this stuff with my body reminds me of a time in middle school when I felt the same way. I was benched in a soccer game for not playing well, and my dad went nuts! He criticized me for making mistakes and playing poorly. He said I ran too slowly and had bad passing skills. I can hear him now, 'You need to practice harder and get better!' I believed he didn't love me unless I performed well. I remember hating myself for letting him down. *I hated my body for not being more athletic so that I could be worthy of his love."*

Tapping through this memory of self-hatred opened the door to processing and clearing many other experiences that, for Alex, validated the *Limiting Belief* that *his body betrayed him* and was a disappointment to his father. Alex internalized his father's harsh criticism as evidence that *his body was not good enough* and, as a result, *believed he was not lovable.* Notice that rather than expressing his anger to his father, Alex turned his anger onto himself and rejected his body.

Over time, Alex compensated for *"not being good enough"* by becoming an overachiever to impress his father and feel worthy as a person. "I decided then that I would train as hard as I could to be stronger, faster, and better than other people no matter what sport I did."

With continued support in therapy through tapping, Alex was able to go deeper to process and release how resentful he felt toward his father. Alex first tapped through the resentment he felt about having Lyme disease for the way it triggered him to feel like *"a loser"* when he couldn't "beat it." Tapping through his resentment about having Lyme disease helped Alex realize that this experience was triggering the resentment he had carried toward his father long after he became an adult.

"I accept my body now and I feel more resentful toward my father! He is the one who always made me feel like a *loser.*" Alex continued to tap through the emotional layers. He came to realize that in the same way his father had betrayed him by not providing him the love and acceptance he needed as a child, he was betraying himself by rejecting, rather than caring, for his body when it did not perform the way he expected. Through further tapping sessions, Alex was able to release his anger and sadness and to begin to forgive his father. This in turn helped him heal his relationship with his body.

He said, "I never realized I was judging myself just like my father judged me. **My body did not betray me.** By tapping through all of this, I now see that my experience with Lyme disease really brought to my attention how I was relating to my body and all the things I was doing just to feel worthy. I didn't even realize I was living my life in this way. Wow, it all makes sense! I realize now that the more *I hated my body***,** the sicker I got, but I just couldn't see that before."

With this critically important shift in beliefs, Alex was able to develop compassion for himself and **to forgive his body** for getting sick and not meeting his expectations. He said, **"I accept my body and believe that I can recover."** He committed to finding and receiving the treatment he needed to help his body heal and to move toward recovery.

We have encountered other clients who, like Alex, believed that their *body betrayed and victimized* them as a result of having Lyme/TBDs. If these kinds of *Limiting Beliefs* remain unresolved, they can create a vicious cycle of elevated stress, which can compromise the immune system and increase inflammation. This can lead to worsening symptoms and interfere with the effectiveness of treatment. Using EFT on these issues supported Alex in cultivating a wellness state of mind rooted in self-compassion, self-acceptance, and a renewed and hopeful commitment to his treatment and recovery.

Exercise: Body-Image Belief Inventory

In the presence and experience of Lyme/TBDs, what *Limiting Beliefs* (see page 119) do you have that support a negative body image? Check all that apply.

- My body betrayed me! ❑
- My body is not strong enough to recover. ❑
- My body can't do anything right. ❑
- My body keeps attacking me! ❑
- My body is against me. ❑
- I can't accept my body with all of its pain and limitations. ❑
- I don't like my body. ❑
- I hate my body! ❑
- I reject my body. ❑
- I don't love my body. ❑
- My body is too weak to recover! ❑
- My body should be over this by now. ❑
- Lyme/TBDs are more powerful than my body. ❑
- Add your own: ________ ❑
- ________ ❑
- ________ ❑
- ________ ❑

How do these *Limiting Beliefs* make you feel? ________

____

In the presence and experience of Lyme/TBDs, what **Empowering Beliefs** (see page 119) do you have that support a positive body image? Check all that apply.

- My body is doing all that it can to help me recover. ❑
- My body is strong. ❑
- My body is resilient and is healing. ❑
- I am so grateful for what my body is doing on my behalf to recover. ❑
- My body and I are a team. ❑
- My body is full of brilliant mechanisms that aid in my healing. ❑
- My body is wise and gives me feedback on the effectiveness of my treatments. ❑
- I honor my body no matter how I am feeling. ❑
- I trust that my body knows how to heal. ❑
- I accept my body no matter what. ❑
- I love my body. ❑
- Add your own: ________ ❑
- ________ ❑
- ________ ❑
- ________ ❑

How do these **Empowering Beliefs** make you feel? ________

____

If you do have Limiting Beliefs that result in a negative body image:

- Title and list the Specific Events that happened from the past that taught you these Limiting Beliefs about your body. Add them to the **List of Titled Specific Events** on page 156 to use with EFT at a later time.
- Title and list the Specific Events that happened while having Lyme disease that validated these Limiting Beliefs about your body. Add the to the **List of Titled Specific Events** on page 156 to use with EFT at a later time.

If the information presented here resonates with you, we invite you to begin with the extended global tapping script that follows. This is a gentle way to get you started and to decrease your overall intensity. Even though the scripted Reminder Phrases may not be reflective of your personal Aspects, we invite you to just go with it, track your progress, and see what happens!

Global Issue Title: My Body Betrayed Me!

- Focus your attention on this **Global Issue/Limiting Belief** (at times Global Issues and Limiting Beliefs are the same, see page 121).
- Take three slow, deep belly breaths as you do a **Body Scan** (see page 81).
- What **Aspects** (see page 123) do you notice?
- Using the **SUD scale** (see page 124), choose a number between 0 (no distress/peaceful) and 10 (highest intensity of distress) to **rate the intensity** of distress you feel about the **Global Issue/Limiting Belief**, along with only the **Aspects** (thoughts, feelings, body sensations, and visual image) that you notice that apply to you.

	Description	SUD #:
Global Issue	My Body Betrayed Me!	
Limiting Belief	My Body Betrayed Me!	
Thoughts		
Feelings		
Body Sensations		
Visual Image		

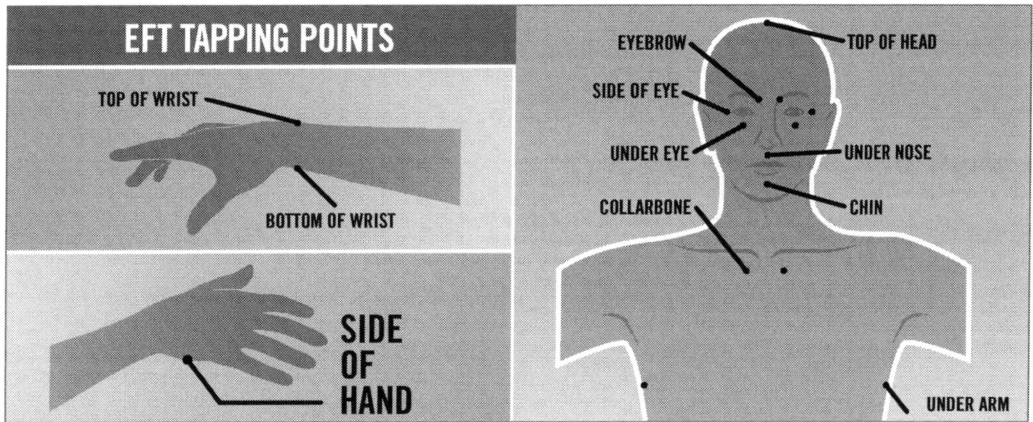

Extended Global Tapping Script: Let's begin tapping (see page 126)

Round 1

Setup:

Side of Hand: Even though I do believe my body betrayed me because I still have Lyme/TBDs, I am open to forgiving it.

Side of Hand: Even though there may be times that I hate my body because of how badly I feel, I am open to accepting it.

Side of Hand: Even though I feel angry that my body betrayed me, I am open to the possibility of embracing it no matter what.

Top of Head: I feel so betrayed by my body!

Eyebrow: It is my body's fault that I have not recovered from Lyme/TBDs!

Side of Eye: I am so angry at my body!

Under Eye: How could my body do this to me!

Under Nose: I reject my body!

Chin: I hate my body!

Collarbone: My body is too painful to be liked.

Under Arm: I feel so betrayed!

Top of Wrists Together: My body is unpredictable! I can't trust it!

Bottom of Wrists Together: My body should have prevented me from getting Lyme disease!

Slowly complete a deep belly breath and then keep tapping.

Round 2

Top of Head: My body let me down!

Eyebrow: I am so angry with my body!

Side of Eye: I wish I could just step out of this pain and move on with my life.

Under Eye: I feel so betrayed by my body!

Under Nose: My body is too painful to be acceptable.

Chin: I want a new body!

Collarbone: I am so angry at my body for not being able to do what I used to do.

Under Arm: My body failed me!

Top of Wrists Together: I am not going to let my body get the best of me!

Bottom of Wrists Together: I wish I could get a new body and leave this one behind!

Take three slow, deep belly breaths as you complete another **Body Scan**. What do you notice now? Note changes to the Aspects and any new ones that may appear below:

	Description	SUD #:
Global Issue	My Body Betrayed Me!	
Limiting Belief	My Body Betrayed Me!	
Thoughts		
Feelings		
Body Sensations		
Visual Image		

If your intensity level about this Global Issue/Limiting Belief, along with any of its Aspects, is still 3 or above on a SUD scale, continue tapping with the next round. (If you have a SUD scale of 0–2, skip down and finish by tapping through the positive statements and Affirmations.)

Round 3

Setup:

Side of Hand: Even though I still believe my body betrayed me, I am open to accepting my body one day.

Side of Hand: Even though I still have some feelings of anger at my body, I honor all of my feelings.

Side of Hand: Even though I still feel betrayed, I am open to new possibilities of becoming a team again.

Top of Head: These remaining feelings of betrayal.

Eyebrow: All of this remaining anger at my body.

Side of Eye: I am still feeling (state the emotion) about my body.

Under Eye: I think my body should be healing faster from Lyme disease!

Under Nose: What is taking it so long? My body is weak!

Chin: I am still angry that my body hasn't recovered yet!

Collarbone: I still feel so betrayed by my body that I can't do the things I used to do.

Under Arm: I still want out of this body. It is too painful to stay.

Top of Wrists Together: I still want my old body back.

Bottom of Wrists Together: Why do I still feel attacked by my body?

Take three slow, deep belly breaths as you complete another **Body Scan**. What do you notice now? Note changes to the Aspects and any new ones that may appear below:

	Description	SUD #:
Global Issue	My Body Betrayed Me!	
Limiting Belief	My Body Betrayed Me!	
Thoughts		
Feelings		
Body Sensations		
Visual Image		

If your intensity level about this Global Issue/Limiting Belief, along with any of its Aspects, is still 3 or above on a SUD scale, keep tapping through what is in your awareness or move down to **Follow These Steps to Resolution**.

Once you reach a SUD level of 0–2 or when you just want to stop tapping for now and return at a later time, finish up by tapping through the positive statements and Afformations.

Round 4 – Now let's tap through some positive statements!

Top of Head: I accept my body now. It is doing everything it can to help me heal.
Eyebrow: It is not my body's fault I got Lyme disease.
Side of Eye: My body is doing everything in its power to heal from Lyme disease.
Under Eye: My body is working 24/7 on my behalf and is doing the best it can.
Under Nose: My body wants to get rid of these bacteria.
Chin: My body and I are a team in healing.
Collarbone: My body is strong and resilient and is healing now.
Under Arm: I give my body permission to do whatever it needs to do to heal.
Top of Wrists Together: My body is working hard to be healthy again.
Bottom of Wrists Together: I commit to being a partner with my body in the healing process.

Round 5 – Tapping with Afformations (see page 101)

Top of Head: Why is it so easy for me to accept my body as it is?
Eyebrow: Why is it so easy for me to forgive my body?
Side of Eye: Why is it so easy for me to activate my body's innate abilities to heal?
Under Eye: Why is it so easy for me to trust that my body knows how to heal?
Under Nose: Why is it possible for me to accept my body just as it is?
Chin: Why is it possible for me to believe that my body is healing now?
Collarbone: Why is it possible for me to be vulnerable in my healing process?
Under Arm: Why is it possible for me to join with my body and create healing?
Top of Wrists Together: Why is it safe for me to remain in this body?
Bottom of Wrists Together: Why is it so easy for me to remember my body and I are one?

Take three slow, deep belly breaths as you complete another **Body Scan**. What do you notice now? Note changes to the Aspects and any new ones that may appear below:

	Description	SUD #:
Global Issue	My Body Betrayed Me!	
Limiting Belief	My Body Betrayed Me!	
Thoughts		
Feelings		
Body Sensations		
Visual Image		

If your intensity level about this Global Issue/Limiting Belief, along with any of its Aspects, is still 3 or above on a SUD scale, you need to explore them more in depth and follow the directives in **Follow These Steps to Resolution**, on the following page.

Exercise: Developing Self-Awareness

Describe your experience of tapping through this Global Issue/Limiting Belief.

____

____

____

Which Aspects resolved, decreased, increased, or stayed the same?

____

____

In the identified Limiting Belief, state what (if anything) changed or any new ones that emerged.

____

____

State any Empowering Beliefs (see page 119) that you notice now.

____

____

What Global Issues/Limiting Beliefs need to be resolved (if any)?

____

____

Follow These Steps to Resolution

- When you have the time and energy, move on to the next exercise, **"Going Deeper with EFT."** Use this to help you identify Specific Events, along with its Aspects, that are contributing to not resolving this Global Issue/Limiting Belief or with any new ones that may have surfaced while tapping. You may identify many and this is to be expected.
- Just break down one Specific Event at a time and tap it until resolved. Title the rest of the Specific Events that you have identified and add them to the **List of Titled Specific Events** on page 156 so that you can return to them at a later time to tap. You can use the **Blank Tapping Script** on page 404 or the **Vent While You Tap** worksheet on page 409 to assist you while tapping through a Specific Event.

Exercise: Going Deeper with EFT

If you just completed tapping through the extended global tapping script, and you still feel that the issue is unresolved, it's time to go deeper. What is keeping it unresolved? Title your Global Issue in the space provided below. Answer the following questions so that you can discover, uncover, and recover from the unresolved Specific Events and related Aspects that created and support the Limiting Belief you wish to resolve.

Global Issue: ______________________________

1. What Limiting Beliefs do you have at the root of this Global Issue? Rate the level of intensity of how true they are for you between SUD 0 (not true at all) and 10 (completely true).

______________________________ • SUD # (0–10): ____

______________________________ • SUD # (0–10): ____

2. Title and list the Specific Events in which you learned the Limiting Belief(s) (you can also add them to your List of Titled Specific Events on page 156).

____

____

____

____

____

____

3. Choose one Specific Event to break down here. Title: ______________________________

____

4. Tune into your titled Specific Event and identify only those Aspects that apply to you, below:

What thoughts do you notice?

______________________________ • SUD # (0–10): ____

______________________________ • SUD # (0–10): ____

Do your thoughts have the quality of Small Mind or Large Mind (see page 90)?____________

Describe your Large Mind thoughts (if any):____________________________

____

Describe your Small Mind thoughts (if any): ____________________________

____

What emotions are you feeling?

______________________________ • SUD # (0–10): ____

______________________________ • SUD # (0–10): ____

______________________________ • SUD # (0–10): ____

What body sensation do you notice?

______________________________ • SUD # (0–10): ____

Where is the sensation located?____________________ • SUD # (0–10): ____

Does this sensation have a temperature?____ Describe:____________________

______________________________ • SUD # (0–10): ____

Texture?__________________________ • SUD # (0–10): ____

Color?____________________________ • SUD # (0–10): ____

Describe a visual image that you have (if any): ________________________

______________________________ • SUD # (0–10): ____

5. Use the Aspects you have just identified to create your Reminder Phrases.
6. Stay tuned into your titled Specific Event.
7. Start tapping using the Modified EFT Basic Recipe on page 121. You can use the Aspects you have identified here to fill in the Reminder Phrases on the **Blank Tapping Script** on page 404 or the **Vent While You Tap** worksheet on page 409 to assist you in creating your own tapping script.

REPEAT PROCESS IF UNRESOLVED

Be aware of any changes in the intensity of distress you feel in relation to the Aspects, along with any new ones that emerge as you tap through the Rounds of EFT. Continue to tap, repeating the EFT Basic Recipe until your Specific Event, along with its Aspects, is resolved at a SUD level of 0–2. Also be mindful of shifts in Limiting Beliefs and the emergence of any new Empowering ones. To get full resolution of a Global Issue, the Limiting Beliefs must be released by resolving other painful Specific Events that are validating them.

Personal Reflections

CHAPTER

37 There's Something Wrong with Me!

Case Study

Note: *Limiting Beliefs are italicized* and **Empowering Beliefs are in bold**.

Martha was a 40-year-old woman who had chronic Lyme disease for twenty years before coming to therapy. The years of struggle and disappointment in treatment outcomes left her feeling overwhelmed with fear, anxiety, sadness, and anger that increased her exhaustion. They had also taken their toll on her relationship with her husband and children, as well as on her ability to work.

In therapy, after one of the initial tapping rounds addressing her general overwhelm, Martha recalled memories from when she was young and her parents constantly criticized her for being "too emotional" and "irresponsible." Over time, Martha came to truly believe that *she was "defective" and that "there is something wrong with me."* Each time she faced a challenge like doing poorly in high-school algebra or feeling pressured to pull "all-nighters" in college but was unable to, this validated Martha's *Limiting Belief* that *she was defective.* Still, she made efforts to ignore this belief and focused on moving herself forward.

After being told by ten different doctors that there was nothing wrong with her and experiencing the frustration of not getting better throughout her twenty-year struggle with Lyme disease, Martha was in an emotional crisis. She could no longer ignore the *Limiting Beliefs* she had about herself that started in childhood and that were validated by not recovering from chronic Lyme disease. She realized that she had to face and heal the unresolved emotional pain from these beliefs that made her *doubt her ability to recover.*

Martha, like many of our clients, knew that something was interfering with her ability to recover from Lyme disease. She just did not know how to name it. There is a conscious sense that something isn't right, but the need to avoid pain and survive overrides it. However, the subconscious mind remembers everything (refer to page 118). Martha's medical experiences validated for her that old deep-seated *Limiting Belief that she was defective* and triggered the painful memories from childhood that supported it.

When Martha first came for therapy, she was mentally, emotionally, and physically exhausted. There were also times when she was so sick she could not engage in even the simplest activities with her children. The emotional pain she was experiencing was not only making her physical pain worse, but it was also sapping her entire system of the energy it needed to repair itself.

Martha committed to several more months of therapy in which she used EFT to tap through the multiple complex emotional layers beneath *her Liming Beliefs, "I am defective" and "there's something wrong with me."* The process included tapping to resolution the many Specific Events from her childhood and the treatment failures that supported these *beliefs*. As a result, she came to **believe that she was resilient and able to recover.** Compassion emerged and continued to grow for the little girl who was repeatedly told there was *something wrong with her* and for the woman who had struggled for so long under the burden of that *Limiting Belief*. She was now able to put her emotional energy toward developing a new plan of recovery for herself.

If the information presented here resonates with you, we invite you to begin with the extended global tapping script that follows. This is a gentle way to get you started and to decrease your overall intensity. Even though the scripted Reminder Phrases may not be reflective of your personal Aspects, we invite you to just go with it, track your progress, and see what happens!

Global Issue Title: There's Something Wrong with Me!

- Focus your attention on this **Global Issue/Limiting Belief** (at times Global Issues and Limiting Beliefs are the same, see page 121).
- Take three slow, deep belly breaths as you do a **Body Scan** (see page 81).
- What **Aspects** (see page 123) do you notice?
- Using the **SUD scale** (see page 124), choose a number between 0 (no distress/peaceful) and 10 (highest intensity of distress) to **rate the intensity** of distress you feel about the **Global Issue/Limiting Belief**, along with only the **Aspects** (thoughts, feelings, body sensations, and visual image) that you notice that apply to you.

	Description	SUD #:
Global Issue	There's Something Wrong with Me!	
Limiting Belief	There's Something Wrong with Me!	
Thoughts		
Feelings		
Body Sensations		
Visual Image		

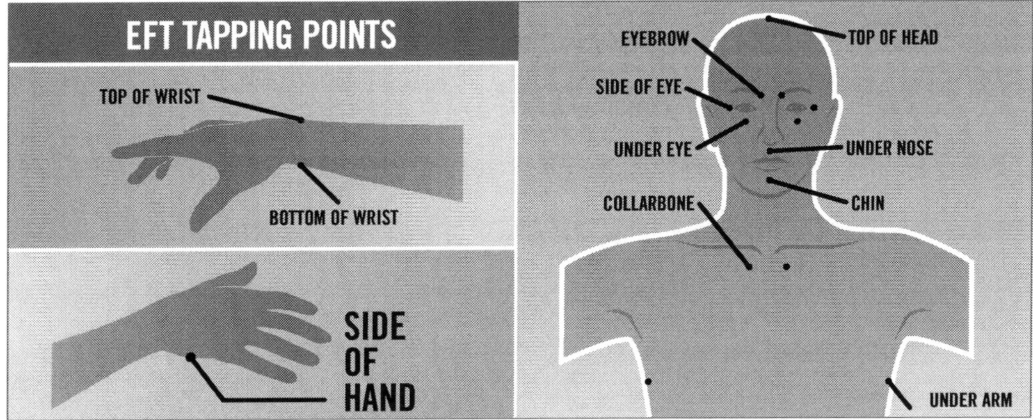

Extended Global Tapping Script: Let's begin tapping **(see page 126)**

Round 1

Setup:

Side of Hand: Even though I believe that I am defective, I honor and accept myself.

Side of Hand: Even though chronic Lyme validates that there is something wrong with me, I accept myself anyway.

Side of Hand: Even though I have this false belief that something is wrong with me, I am open to accepting myself as I am now.

Top of Head: There is something wrong with me!

Eyebrow: It's all my fault!

Side of Eye: Lyme disease validates this for me!

Under Eye: I am defective!

Under Nose: My body has failed me!

Chin: I feel defeated at times.

Collarbone: I feel so (state the emotion).

Under Arm: My body is defective!

Top of Wrists Together: I am so tired of not getting better!

Bottom of Wrists Together: There is something wrong with me if I can't get better!

Slowly complete a deep belly breath and then keep tapping.

Round 2

Top of Head: I am scared.

Eyebrow: I hate not having control of my body!

Side of Eye: I am defective.

Under Eye: Lyme disease has taught me that there is something wrong with me.

Under Nose: Some of my doctors validated that it is "all in my head."

Chin: There is something wrong with me!

Collarbone: Sometimes I wish I had a different body!

Under Arm: I feel so confused!

Top of Wrists Together: I am defective.

Bottom of Wrists Together: There is something wrong with me!

Take three slow, deep belly breaths as you complete another **Body Scan**. What do you notice now? Note changes to the Aspects and any new ones that may appear below:

	Description	SUD #:
Global Issue	There's Something Wrong with Me!	
Limiting Belief	There's Something Wrong with Me!	
Thoughts		
Feelings		
Body Sensations		
Visual Image		

If your intensity level about this Global Issue/Limiting Belief, along with any of its Aspects, is still 3 or above on a SUD scale, continue tapping with the next round. (If you have a SUD scale of 0–2, skip down and finish by tapping through the positive statements and Affirmations.)

Round 3

Setup:

Side of Hand: Even though I still believe something is wrong with me, I am open to accepting myself.

Side of Hand: Even though I still believe I am defective in some way, I choose to honor and respect myself now.

Side of Hand: Even though I still believe that there is something wrong with me, I am open to the possibility of accepting myself.

Top of Head: This remaining self-criticism.

Eyebrow: This remaining blame for not getting better.

Side of Eye: This remaining belief that my body just isn't strong enough to overcome this disease.

Under Eye: This remaining belief that I am defective.

Under Nose: I still feel like some of my illness is my fault.

Chin: This remaining false belief that my body does not know how to heal.

Collarbone: This remaining disappointment with my body.

Under Arm: I am so tired of not feeling enough!

Top of Wrists Together: I still feel (state the emotion) about this issue.

Bottom of Wrists Together: This remaining self-blame and judgment.

Take three slow, deep belly breaths as you complete another **Body Scan**. What do you notice now? Note changes to the Aspects and any new ones that may appear below:

	Description	SUD #:
Global Issue	There's Something Wrong with Me!	
Limiting Belief	There's Something Wrong with Me!	
Thoughts		
Feelings		
Body Sensations		
Visual Image		

If your intensity level about this Global Issue/Limiting Belief, along with any of its Aspects, is still 3 or above on a SUD scale, keep tapping through what is in your awareness or move down to **Follow These Steps to Resolution**.

Once you reach a SUD level of 0–2 or when you just want to stop tapping for now and return at a later time, finish up by tapping through the positive statements and Afformations.

Round 4 – Now let's tap through some positive statements!

Top of Head: I honor my body and all that it's doing to recover!
Eyebrow: My body is doing the best that it can to heal.
Side of Eye: I accept my body.
Under Eye: I am more than Lyme disease.
Under Nose: I love my body.
Chin: I am doing the best I can right now to recover.
Collarbone: My body is resilient and is doing everything it can to heal.
Under Arm: I am enough.
Top of Wrists Together: I accept myself and honor my body.
Bottom of Wrists Together: I am so proud of my body for being so resilient.

Round 5 – Tapping with Afformations (see page 101)

Top of Head: Why is it easy for me to accept myself right where I am now?

Eyebrow: What is right with me?

Side of Eye: Why is it so easy to give myself permission to feel what I need to feel?

Under Eye: Why is it easy for me to forgive my body for being sick?

Under Nose: Why do I know there is nothing my body and I can't do when we put our love into it?

Chin: Why do I know that every cell in my body is healing right now?

Collarbone: Why is it possible to love and accept myself?

Under Arm: Why is it easy and natural for me to accept that my body is enough?

Top of Wrists Together: Why do I love and honor my body and celebrate its magnificence?

Bottom of Wrists Together: Why am I deeply grateful for all that my body is doing for me to heal?

Take three slow, deep belly breaths as you complete another **Body Scan**. What do you notice now? Note changes to the Aspects and any new ones that may appear below:

	Description	SUD #:
Global Issue	There's Something Wrong with Me!	
Limiting Belief	There's Something Wrong with Me!	
Thoughts		
Feelings		
Body Sensations		
Visual Image		

If your intensity level about this Global Issue/Limiting Belief, along with any of its Aspects, is still 3 or above on a SUD scale, you need to explore them more in depth and follow the directives in **Follow These Steps to Resolution**, on the following page.

Exercise: Developing Self-Awareness

Describe your experience of tapping through this Global Issue/Limiting Belief.

___

___

___

Which Aspects resolved, decreased, increased, or stayed the same?

___

___

In the identified Limiting Belief, state what (if anything) changed or any new ones that emerged.

___

___

State any Empowering Beliefs (see page 119) that you notice now.

___

___

What Global Issues/Limiting Beliefs need to be resolved (if any)?

___

___

Follow These Steps to Resolution

- When you have the time and energy, move on to the next exercise, **"Going Deeper with EFT."** Use this to help you identify Specific Events, along with its Aspects, that are contributing to not resolving this Global Issue/Limiting Belief or with any new ones that may have surfaced while tapping. You may identify many and this is to be expected.
- Just break down one Specific Event at a time and tap it until resolved. Title the rest of the Specific Events that you have identified and add them to the **List of Titled Specific Events** on page 156 so that you can return to them at a later time to tap. You can use the **Blank Tapping Script** on page 404 or the **Vent While You Tap** worksheet on page 409 to assist you while tapping through a Specific Event.

Exercise: Going Deeper with EFT

If you just completed tapping through the extended global tapping script, and you still feel that the issue is unresolved, it's time to go deeper. What is keeping it unresolved? Title your Global Issue in the space provided below. Answer the following questions so that you can discover, uncover, and recover from the unresolved Specific Events and related Aspects that created and support the Limiting Belief you wish to resolve.

Global Issue: ____

1. What Limiting Beliefs do you have at the root of this Global Issue? Rate the level of intensity of how true they are for you between SUD 0 (not true at all) and 10 (completely true).

____ • SUD # (0–10): ____

____ • SUD # (0–10): ____

2. Title and list the Specific Events in which you learned the Limiting Belief(s) (you can also add them to your List of Titled Specific Events on page 156).

____

____

____

____

____

____

3. Choose one Specific Event to break down here. Title: ____________________

____

4. Tune into your titled Specific Event and identify only those Aspects that apply to you, below:

What thoughts do you notice?

____ • SUD # (0–10): ____

____ • SUD # (0–10): ____

Do your thoughts have the quality of Small Mind or Large Mind (see page 90)?____________

Describe your Large Mind thoughts (if any):____

____

Describe your Small Mind thoughts (if any): ____

____

What emotions are you feeling?

____ • SUD # (0–10): ____

____ • SUD # (0–10): ____

____ • SUD # (0–10): ____

What body sensation do you notice?

____ • SUD # (0–10): ____

Where is the sensation located?____________________________________ • SUD # (0–10): ____

Does this sensation have a temperature?____ Describe:________________________________

____ • SUD # (0–10): ____

Texture?____ • SUD # (0–10): ____

Color?____ • SUD # (0–10): ____

Describe a visual image that you have (if any): ____________________________________

____ • SUD # (0–10): ____

5. Use the Aspects you have just identified to create your Reminder Phrases.
6. Stay tuned into your titled Specific Event.
7. Start tapping using the Modified EFT Basic Recipe on page 121. You can use the Aspects you have identified here to fill in the Reminder Phrases on the **Blank Tapping Script** on page 404 or the **Vent While You Tap** worksheet on page 409 to assist you in creating your own tapping script.

REPEAT PROCESS IF UNRESOLVED

Be aware of any changes in the intensity of distress you feel in relation to the Aspects, along with any new ones that emerge as you tap through the Rounds of EFT. Continue to tap, repeating the EFT Basic Recipe until your Specific Event, along with its Aspects, is resolved at a SUD level of 0–2. Also be mindful of shifts in Limiting Beliefs and the emergence of any new Empowering ones. To get full resolution of a Global Issue, the Limiting Beliefs must be released by resolving other painful Specific Events that are validating them.

Personal Reflections

CHAPTER 38 I Am at War with Lyme/TBDs!

Do you believe you are "*at war*" with the Lyme/TBD bacteria in your body? If so, do you experience a disconnection with your body and/or an increase in stress as a result? If you answered yes to both of these questions, this chapter is for you. This Global Issue was addressed in Chapter 4: **Spirochetes, Crisis, and Transformation** on page 41. If you have not read that chapter yet, we suggest you do that first.

Chapter 4 also includes a transformative imagery used by Anita while tapping called, **Making Peace with the Spirochetes**. "I desired peace and harmony within and about my body and noticed that being 'at war' with the spirochetes interfered with that. I tapped through a lot of fear and anger to create the peace I desired and much more!"

This global tapping script focuses on making peace with the Lyme/TBD bacteria in your body to cultivate a wellness state of mind that can enhance connection with your body, reduce stress, and promote healing. A question to ponder: Is it possible to consider that when the spirochetes go dormant, that they are in a state of peaceful coexistence?

Global Issue Title: I Am at War with Lyme/TBDs!

If the information presented here resonates with you, we invite you to begin with the extended global tapping script that follows. This is a gentle way to get you started and to decrease your overall intensity. Even though the scripted Reminder Phrases may not be reflective of your personal Aspects, we invite you to just go with it, track your progress, and see what happens!

- Focus your attention on this **Global Issue** (see page 119).
- Identify one **Limiting Belief** (see page 119) that may be at the root of this Global Issue.
- Take three slow, deep belly breaths as you do a **Body Scan** (see page 81).
- What **Aspects** (see page 123) do you notice?
- Using the **SUD scale** (see page 124), choose a number between 0 (no distress/peaceful) and 10 (highest intensity of distress) to **rate the intensity** of distress you feel about the **Global Issue and Limiting Belief**, along with only the **Aspects** (thoughts, feelings, body sensations, and visual image) that you notice that apply to you.

	Description	SUD #:
Global Issue	I Am at War with Lyme/TBDs!	
Limiting Belief		
Thoughts		
Feelings		
Body Sensations		
Visual Image		

Extended Global Tapping Script: Let's begin tapping (see page 126)

Round 1

Setup:

Side of Hand: Even though I am scared to be in harmony with the Lyme/TBD bacteria, I honor all of my feelings about this.

Side of Hand: Even though I don't believe it is possible for me, I honor and respect myself.

Side of Hand: Even though I think this a weird idea, I am open to new possibilities.

Top of Head: I am scared of Lyme/TBD bacteria!

Eyebrow: Lyme/TBD hurt me!

Side of Eye: They lie dormant waiting to surprise attack me!

Under Eye: Joining with Lyme/TBDs is the dumbest thing I have ever heard!

Under Nose: This can't possibly work for me!

Chin: I don't want to make peace with the bacteria!

Collarbone: I'm so angry at these Lyme/TBDs!

Under Arm: I want to be free of this bacteria!

Top of Wrists Together: There is no way I will be in harmony with THEM!

Bottom of Wrists Together: Lyme/TBDs are my enemy!

Slowly complete a deep belly breath and then keep tapping.

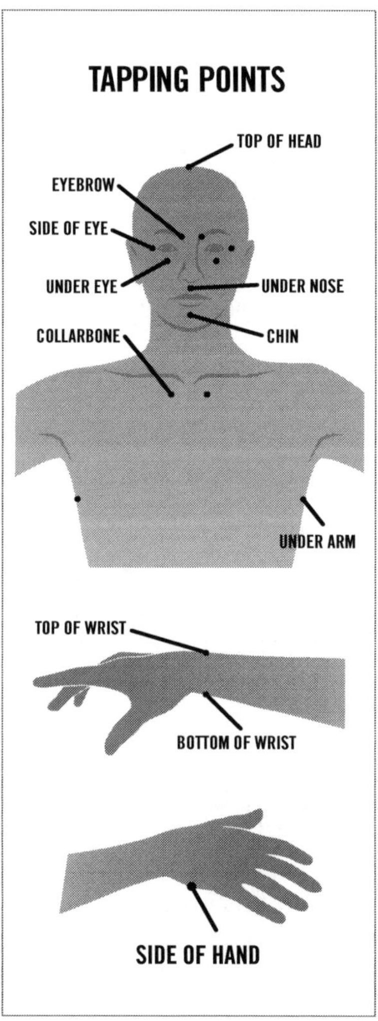

Round 2

Top of Head: It is me against them!

Eyebrow: I am scared I will never feel better.

Side of Eye: They were dormant, and now they're hurting me!

Under Eye: I just want them out of my body!

Under Nose: I don't believe this will work for me.

Chin: This is too silly to work!

Collarbone: I can't trust that this Lyme/TBD bacteria can be dormant.

Under Arm: I feel attacked by this bacteria!

Top of Wrists Together: They're hiding in every cell of my body!

Bottom of Wrists Together: I feel ambushed by these bacteria!

Take three slow, deep belly breaths as you complete another **Body Scan**. What do you notice now? Note changes to the Aspects and any new ones that may appear below:

	Description	SUD #:
Global Issue	I Am at War with Lyme/TBDs!	
Limiting Belief		
Thoughts		
Feelings		
Body Sensations		
Visual Image		

If your intensity level about this Global Issue, along with any of its Aspects, is still 3 or above on a SUD scale, continue tapping with the next round. (If you have a SUD scale of 0–2, skip down and finish by tapping through the positive statements and Afformations.)

Round 3

Setup:

Side of Hand: Even though I still can't imagine being in harmony with the Lyme/TBD bacteria, I honor and respect myself.

Side of Hand: Even though I doubt this will make me feel better, I am still open to new possibilities.

Side of Hand: Even though I can't imagine I can live in harmony with these bacteria, I honor and accept myself.

Top of Head: I still can't imagine being in harmony with them!

Eyebrow: I doubt this will help me!

Side of Eye: I still believe I need to be totally free of Lyme/TBDs!

Under Eye: It is just too much of a stretch to believe we can live in harmony and still remain in treatment.

Under Nose: I still think this is a silly idea.

Chin: A part of me wants to believe this will work, but the other part thinks it is impossible.

Collarbone: What are they doing when they go dormant?

Under Arm: I may never be totally free of Lyme bacteria.

Top of Wrists Together: I am living in harmony with a lot of other bacteria, so why not them?

Bottom of Wrists Together: I would love to live in harmony with what's happening in my body.

Take three slow, deep belly breaths as you complete another **Body Scan**. What do you notice now? Note changes to the Aspects and any new ones that may appear below:

	Description	SUD #:
Global Issue	I Am at War with Lyme/TBDs!	
Limiting Belief		
Thoughts		
Feelings		
Body Sensations		
Visual Image		

If your intensity level about this Global Issue, along with any of its Aspects, is still 3 or above on a SUD scale, keep tapping through what is in your awareness or move down to **Follow These Steps to Resolution**.

Once you reach a SUD level of 0–2 or when you just want to stop tapping for now and return at a later time, finish up by tapping through the positive statements and Afformations.

Round 4 – Now let's tap through some positive statements!

Top of Head: I am open to this new idea of living in peace with my whole body, including Lyme/TBD bacteria.

Eyebrow: I accept my body and believe in its ability to heal.

Side of Eye: I am open to the possibility of creating harmony with the bacteria.

Under Eye: The bacteria and I can be in harmony with each other.

Under Nose: I no longer have to fight against myself.

Chin: I live peacefully with many other bacteria in my body.

Collarbone: I am open to doing anything that will support my recovery.

Under Arm: I choose to be at peace with my body.

Top of Wrists Together: Dormancy is peaceful.

Bottom of Wrists Together: I choose peace.

Round 5 – Tapping with Afformations (see page 101)

Top of Head: Why is it so easy for me to be in harmony with Lyme/TBD bacteria and create peace and wellness?

Eyebrow: Why is it possible for the Lyme/TBD bacteria to be dormant and peaceful?

Side of Eye: Why does it feel so good to know I am creating a peaceful state of mind and body?

Under Eye: Why is it easy for me to cultivate a Large Mind story about the bacteria?

Under Nose: Why is it possible for Lyme/TBD bacteria and I to work together toward harmony?

Chin: Why does it feel so good to be at peace with my body?

Collarbone: Why is it so easy for my bacteria to be quiet and peaceful?

Under Arm: Why is it possible for me to create a wellness state of mind?

Top of Wrists Together: Why is it possible to be at peace with the bacteria while still being active in treatment to recover?

Bottom of Wrists Together: Why does being in harmony with the Lyme/TBD bacteria help me to decrease stress in my body?

Take three slow, deep belly breaths as you complete another **Body Scan**. What do you notice now? Note changes to the Aspects and any new ones that may appear below:

	Description	SUD #:
Global Issue	I Am at War with Lyme/TBDs!	
Limiting Belief		
Thoughts		
Feelings		
Body Sensations		
Visual Image		

If your intensity level about this Global Issue, along with any of its Aspects, is still 3 or above on a SUD scale, you need to explore them more in depth and follow the directives in **Follow These Steps to Resolution**, on the following page.

Exercise: Developing Self-Awareness

Describe your experience of tapping through this Global Issue.

Which Aspects resolved, decreased, increased, or stayed the same?

If you identified a Limiting Belief, state what (if anything) changed.

State any Empowering Beliefs (see page 119) that you notice now.

What Global Issues/Limiting Beliefs need to be resolved (if any)?

Follow These Steps to Resolution

- When you have the time and energy, move on to the next exercise, **Going Deeper with EFT.** Use this to help you identify Specific Events, along with their Aspects, that are contributing to not resolving this Global Issue/Limiting Belief or with any new ones that may have surfaced while tapping. You may identify many and this is to be expected.
- Just break down one Specific Event at a time and tap it until resolved. Title the rest of the Specific Events that you have identified and add them to the **List of Titled Specific Events** on page 156 so that you can return to them at a later time to tap. You can use the **Blank Tapping Script** on page 404 or the **Vent While You Tap** worksheet on page 409 to assist you while tapping through a Specific Event.

Exercise: Going Deeper with EFT

If you just completed tapping through the extended global tapping script, and you still feel that the issue is unresolved, it's time to go deeper. What is keeping it unresolved? Title your Global Issue in the space provided below. Answer the following questions so that you can discover, uncover, and recover from the unresolved Specific Events and related Aspects that created and support the Limiting Belief you wish to resolve.

Global Issue: ____________________

1. What Limiting Beliefs do you have at the root of this Global Issue? Rate the level of intensity of how true they are for you between SUD 0 (not true at all) and 10 (completely true).

____________________ • SUD # (0–10): ____

____________________ • SUD # (0–10): ____

2. Title and list the Specific Events in which you learned the Limiting Belief(s) (you can also add them to your List of Titled Specific Events on page 156).

____

____

____

____

____

____

3. Choose one Specific Event to break down here. Title: ____________________

____

4. Tune into your titled Specific Event and identify only those Aspects that apply to you, below:

What thoughts do you notice?

____________________ • SUD # (0–10): ____

____________________ • SUD # (0–10): ____

Do your thoughts have the quality of Small Mind or Large Mind (see page 90)?____________

Describe your Large Mind thoughts (if any):____________________

____

Describe your Small Mind thoughts (if any): ____________________

____

What emotions are you feeling?

____________________ • SUD # (0–10): ____

____________________ • SUD # (0–10): ____

____________________ • SUD # (0–10): ____

What body sensation do you notice?

____________________ • SUD # (0–10): ____

Where is the sensation located?____________________ • SUD # (0–10): ____

Does this sensation have a temperature?____ Describe:____________________

____________________ • SUD # (0–10): ____

Texture?____________________ • SUD # (0–10): ____

Color?____________________ • SUD # (0–10): ____

Describe a visual image that you have (if any): ____________________

____________________ • SUD # (0–10): ____

5. Use the Aspects you have just identified to create your Reminder Phrases.
6. Stay tuned into your titled Specific Event.
7. Start tapping using the Modified EFT Basic Recipe on page 121. You can use the Aspects you have identified here to fill in the Reminder Phrases on the **Blank Tapping Script** on page 404 or the **Vent While You Tap** worksheet on page 409 to assist you in creating your own tapping script.

REPEAT PROCESS IF UNRESOLVED

Be aware of any changes in the intensity of distress you feel in relation to the Aspects, along with any new ones that emerge as you tap through the Rounds of EFT. Continue to tap, repeating the EFT Basic Recipe until your Specific Event, along with its Aspects, is resolved at a SUD level of 0–2. Also be mindful of shifts in Limiting Beliefs and the emergence of any new Empowering ones. To get full resolution of a Global Issue, the Limiting Beliefs must be released by resolving other painful Specific Events that are validating them.

CHAPTER

39 I Can't Afford to Be Sick!

Case Study

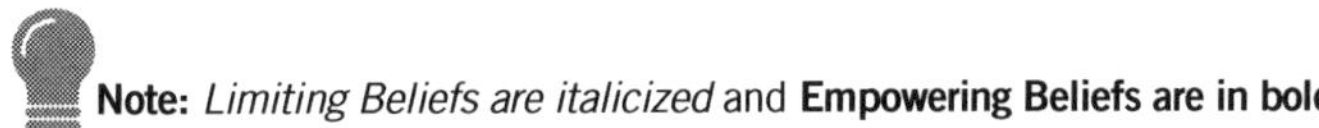
Note: *Limiting Beliefs are italicized* and **Empowering Beliefs are in bold**.

Cindy was a 47-year-old wife and mother of two grown children and had been working at a job she loved for more than thirty years. Her husband was nearing his retirement, and both of their incomes were necessary to maintain a middle-class lifestyle. After a hiking trip seven years earlier, Cindy began to feel sick. She did not remember getting bit by a tick and did not have the telltale bull's-eye rash. After several trips to many different doctors, she was finally diagnosed with Lyme disease. Her doctor treated her with a two-week round of antibiotics and said he could do nothing more for her. Initially she felt better, but her symptoms returned and gradually worsened.

After learning more about chronic Lyme disease, Cindy sought a Lyme-literate physician. The treatment was not covered by insurance, and these out-of-pocket medical expenses took a toll on her and her husband's savings. She was able to continue working, but she had to take a lot of sick time off from work. She was very worried about depleting their savings and not being able to put money away for their retirement. Cindy's worry about not having enough money kept her awake at night, which added to her anxiety, because she knew how important sleep was to her recovery.

Cindy said that not having enough money was always a concern for her, even though she and her husband had the financial means to meet their needs. Her beliefs and concerns about money began in childhood. She said her family struggled to make enough money just to get by. She had learned not to ask for things because there was not enough money for extras. When she did ask for money, she was told, *"Do you think money grows on trees? There's not enough to go around.* Why should you have it when your sister will want it, too? Your dad has to work hard for it. We can't waste it on nonessentials! We are poor folk, not like some of your friends. Wait until you get a job, *you'll see how hard life is. Life is a struggle.* Wait, you'll see!"

Cindy said that her current worries about money reminded her of her parents' money struggles. She had many childhood experiences that created *Limiting Beliefs* about money and knew her anxiety was interfering with her recovery process. She decided to seek help to resolve these beliefs. Her first step was to become aware of her own *Limiting Beliefs* about money and the fears and worry they caused. She knew they made it more difficult to think clearly about how to resolve her problems. She also noticed that they increased her stress and sometimes triggered painful episodes of her symptoms.

Cindy realized that the source of her *Limiting Beliefs* about money came from her mother. As young children, all of us absorb the beliefs of our family/caregivers until they become our own. Most of the time we don't even question them;

we believe this is just the way life is. As adults, we continue to live out the beliefs we learned earlier in life. We may even hear ourselves saying some of the same things we heard from our parents. Cindy reflected, "Oh my goodness, I grew up to be just like mom! I am worrying about money just the way she did!"

Unfortunately, the beliefs Cindy learned were based in fear and interfered with her ability to heal due to increased stress and were a barrier to thinking more creatively about how to deal with her finances. Cindy recalled Specific Events from the past when she learned her *Limiting Beliefs* about money and used EFT to resolve and reduce the stress they caused. Weeks later, she came into the office and said, **"There is nothing my husband and I can't do when we put our minds together. We'll figure it out.** Right now, I need to get well so that I can enjoy my retirement. I have stopped beating myself up for spending money on my treatment. I'm doing this for my family and me. I'm not fixing anything by worrying about it. **It is what it is right now."**

EFT helped Cindy release her *Limiting Beliefs* about money and to embrace **Empowering Beliefs** based on sufficiency, trust, and partnership with her husband. She now felt much calmer about money and was able to think more clearly. Cindy's **Empowering Beliefs** opened her to the **new possibility that she and her husband could manage together to find creative ways to resolve their financial concerns, while they invested in her recovery.**

Money can invoke a sense of power and security when there is enough to connect resources with need. Yet, when there are more needs than resources, it can trigger a person into feeling fearful, unsafe, and powerless. With the current issue of most insurance companies only covering treatment short-term, many people do not have the financial resources needed to fully recover. Others just opt-out and don't get any treatment at all due to the high out-of-pocket costs. Financial concerns are an inherent and a valid psychosocial stressor for the majority of people with chronic Lyme/TBDs.

When sufficient financial resources are unavailable to cover the costs of complex treatments needed to recover, it can cause major stress. Unfortunately, this is the current reality for many who want to obtain adequate Lyme treatment. This is what it is for now. However, dealing with this major life stressor can also trigger any *Limiting Beliefs* you may have concerning money, adding to the inherently present stress and thus intensifying your fears, worry and symptoms. This high stress level can then block your ability to creatively solve problems. For example, some people have challenged their insurance companies and won payment for their extensive treatments! This requires a lot of hope, energy, and persistence.

It may be helpful for you to explore any *Limiting Beliefs* about money that could be adding stress to an already highly stressful situation. If you do identify any, break them down in the **Going Deeper with EFT** exercise at the end of this chapter.

Exercise: Developing Self-Awareness About Money

What are your beliefs about money? Read the following questions and record your responses. This is an exercise in self-discovery—not in criticism, judgment, or blame toward yourself or your parents/caregivers. Everyone has done the best they could, and that includes you and your parents. The purpose is to uncover, discover, and recover from a way of believing and behaving that no longer serves you. The intention is to be in **Large Mind** so that you can be open to the abundance and unlimited possibilities that already exist.

Is your Lyme/TBDs treatment causing you financial stress? If so, what is being triggered?

Limiting Beliefs: ____________________

Thoughts: ____________________

Feelings: ____________________

Body Sensations: ____________________

Images: ____________________

What did you learn about money when you were growing up?

____

____

Did your parents/caregivers model financial success or failure? ____________________

What messages did you get about money growing up?

____

____

Did your parents/caregivers just get by, "pinch pennies," or make fun of people who had money? ____________________

Did your parents/caregivers spend irresponsibly? ____________________

Did your parents/caregivers avoid buying "nice" things even if they could afford it? ________

Did your parents/caregivers think money was "dirty"? ____________________

Did you learn that you have to work hard to get ahead because nothing comes easy? ________

Did your parents/caregivers have a balance between spending and saving? ____________

Do you have a hidden belief that you can't rise above your parents/caregivers' financial status? ____________________

How are your beliefs about money similar to those of your parents/caregivers'?

____

____

How does your life reflect your money beliefs?

____

____

Do you believe you're worthy or deserving of having the money you need or desire? _______

Now, in the table below, identify each common limiting belief about money that pertains to you, if any; add your own if necessary. Then, identify where you may have learned that belief. Do this for your Empowering Beliefs about money as well.

Limiting Beliefs	**Where did you learn this belief?**
I'll never have enough.	
I have to work hard to get money.	
Money doesn't grow on trees.	
People who have money are greedy/selfish.	
I'm not worthy or deserving of having the money I desire/need.	
I'm not good with money.	
I'm in debt and I'll never get out.	
No one in my family is rich, so how can I earn more than they do?	
It's not spiritual to be wealthy.	
Add your own:	
Empowering Beliefs	**Where did you learn this belief?**
I am worthy/I deserve to have the money I need.	
I can call my congressman about the injustice of the insurance system.	
I have faith that I will find a way.	
Money is an aspect of my spirituality.	
I will attend a Lyme support group where others may have suggestions.	
I am open to learning how to manage my resources effectively.	
I will get advice about how to deal with my debt.	
I will reevaluate what is really important to me.	
Add your own:	

Global Issue Title: I Can't Afford to Be Sick!

If the information presented here resonates with you, we invite you to begin with the extended global tapping script that follows. This is a gentle way to get you started and to decrease your overall intensity. Even though the scripted Reminder Phrases may not be reflective of your personal Aspects, we invite you to just go with it, track your progress, and see what happens!

- Focus your attention on this **Global Issue** (see page 119).
- Identify one **Limiting Belief** (see page 119) that may be at the root of this Global Issue.
- Take three slow, deep belly breaths as you do a **Body Scan** (see page 81).
- What **Aspects** (see page 123) do you notice?
- Using the **SUD scale** (see page 124), choose a number between 0 (no distress/peaceful) and 10 (highest intensity of distress) to **rate the intensity** of distress you feel about the **Global Issue and Limiting Belief**, along with only the **Aspects** (thoughts, feelings, body sensations, and visual image) that you notice that apply to you.

	Description	SUD #:
Global Issue	I Can't Afford to Be Sick!	
Limiting Belief		
Thoughts		
Feelings		
Body Sensations		
Visual Image		

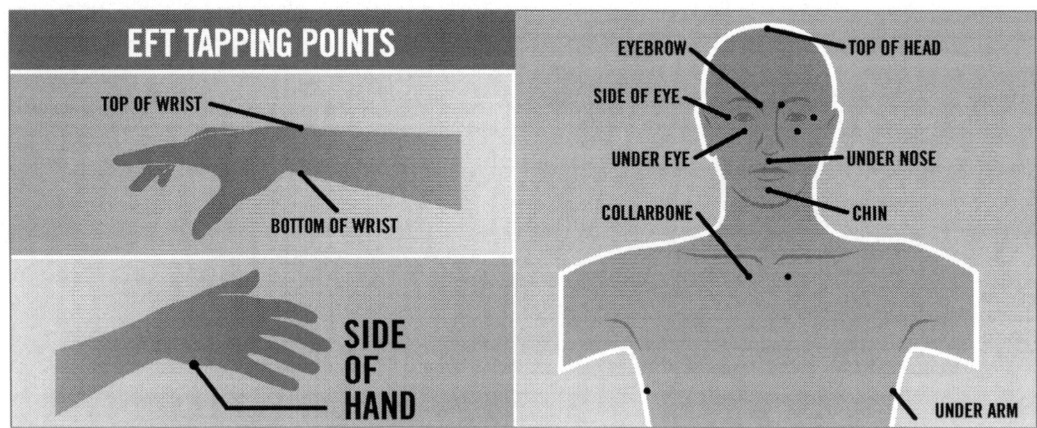

Extended Global Tapping Script: Let's begin tapping (see page 126)

Round 1

Setup:

Side of Hand: Even though I am scared about not having enough money to pay my bills, I honor all of my feelings.

Side of Hand: Even though I am so angry that my insurance won't pay for my treatment, I honor and accept myself.

Side of Hand: Even though I am afraid I'll never get out of this financial hole, I am open to new possibilities and creative solutions.

Top of Head: I am so angry I have all of these bills!

Eyebrow: How am I going to pay them?

Side of Eye: I am scared!

Under Eye: It is not fair!

Under Nose: It is just too hard!

Chin: I can't afford to go to the doctor.

Collarbone: Money doesn't grow on trees!

Under Arm: There's just not enough!

Top of Wrists Together: I've worked hard all my life; this just isn't fair!

Bottom of Wrists Together: What am I going to do?

Round 2

Top of Head: I have every right to feel as I do!

Eyebrow: I don't know what to do!

Side of Eye: I've worked hard all of my life, and now I could lose my savings!

Under Eye: Money worries are always in the back of my mind.

Under Nose: Life is just too hard!

Chin: I don't know how I can resolve this.

Collarbone: I am so scared!

Under Arm: I am so worried.

Top of Wrists Together: I can't afford Lyme/TBD treatment!

Bottom of Wrists Together: I am so worried about using all of my savings.

Take three slow, deep belly breaths as you complete another **Body Scan**. What do you notice now? Note changes to the Aspects and any new ones that may appear below:

Aspects	Description of Aspects	SUD #:
Global Issue	I Can't Afford to Be Sick!	
Limiting Belief		
Thoughts		
Feelings		
Body Sensations		
Visual Image		

If your intensity level about this Global Issue, along with any of its Aspects, is still 3 or above on a SUD scale, continue tapping with the next round. (If you have a SUD scale of 0–2, skip down and finish by tapping through the positive statements and Affornations.)

Round 3

Setup:

Side of Hand: Even though I still have fears about money, I honor and respect myself.

Side of Hand: Even though I am still worried about money, I am open to creative solutions.

Side of Hand: Even though I still feel stressed about this, I accept my feelings about it.

Top of Head: This remaining worry about money.

Eyebrow: This remaining anger about my money situation.

Side of Eye: This remaining worry about money that keeps me awake.

Under Eye: This remaining fear that I will not have enough.

Under Nose: This remaining anxiety that I will not get the treatment I need.

Chin: This remaining anger that I am in this situation.

Collarbone: This remaining anger at the injustice of insurance companies not to pay for the treatment I need.

Under Arm: All of these remaining fears about not having enough.

Top of Wrists Together: My worry is still here.

Bottom of Wrists Together: I am open to a new relationship with money!

Take three slow, deep belly breaths as you complete another **Body Scan**. What do you notice now? Note changes to the Aspects and any new ones that may appear below:

Aspects	Description of Aspects	SUD #:
Global Issue	I Can't Afford to Be Sick!	
Limiting Belief		
Thoughts		
Feelings		
Body Sensations		
Visual Image		

If your intensity level about this Global Issue, along with any of its Aspects, is still 3 or above on a SUD scale, keep tapping through what is in your awareness or move down to **Follow These Steps to Resolution**.

Once you reach a SUD level of 0–2 or when you just want to stop tapping for now and return at a later time, finish up by tapping through the positive statements and Afformations.

Round 4 – Now let's tap through some positive statements!

Top of Head: I will find a way to pay for the treatment I need.
Eyebrow: It is what it is for now, and I will find and create solutions.
Side of Eye: I am grateful for what I have.
Under Eye: Money is a resource that I deserve.
Under Nose: I am worthy and deserving, and I invite money into my life.
Chin: I am able to advocate for what I need.
Collarbone: I am doing the best I can right now.
Under Arm: I am releasing my Limiting Beliefs about money.
Top of Wrists Together: I am able to create new ways for money to come to me.
Bottom of Wrists Together: I can develop creative solutions for my financial problems.

Round 5 – Tapping with Afformations (see page 101)

Top of Head: Why does money come to me easily?

Eyebrow: Why am I able to creatively manifest solutions?

Side of Eye: Why is it easy to talk about money with my spouse/partner?

Under Eye: Why am I able to find the Lyme treatments I need and to challenge the insurance company to pay for them?

Under Nose: Why is it possible for me to have what I need?

Chin: Why is it easy for me to feel good about money?

Collarbone: Why is easy for me to be open to new financial possibilities?

Under Arm: Why is it possible to ask others for help?

Top of Wrists Together: Why am I able to manage my money effectively?

Bottom of Wrists Together: Why is it possible to remain hopeful that I will get the treatment that I need?

Take three slow, deep belly breaths as you complete another **Body Scan**. What do you notice now? Note changes to the Aspects and any new ones that may appear below:

Aspects	Description of Aspects	SUD #:
Global Issue	I Can't Afford to Be Sick!	
Limiting Belief		
Thoughts		
Feelings		
Body Sensations		
Visual Image		

If your intensity level about this Global Issue, along with any of its Aspects, is still 3 or above on a SUD scale, you need to explore them more in depth and follow the directives in **Follow These Steps to Resolution**, on the following page.

Exercise: Developing Self-Awareness

Describe your experience of tapping through this Global Issue.

___

___

___

Which Aspects resolved, decreased, increased, or stayed the same?

___

___

If you identified a Limiting Belief, state what (if anything) changed.

___

___

State any Empowering Beliefs (see page 119) that you notice now.

___

___

What Global Issues/Limiting Beliefs need to be resolved (if any)?

___

___

Follow These Steps to Resolution

- When you have the time and energy, move on to the next exercise, **Going Deeper with EFT.** Use this to help you identify Specific Events, along with their Aspects, that are contributing to not resolving this Global Issue/Limiting Belief or with any new ones that may have surfaced while tapping. You may identify many and this is to be expected.
- Just break down one Specific Event at a time and tap it until resolved. Title the rest of the Specific Events that you have identified and add them to the **List of Titled Specific Events** on page 156 so that you can return to them at a later time to tap. You can use the **Blank Tapping Script** on page 404 or the **Vent While You Tap** worksheet on page 409 to assist you while tapping through a Specific Event.

Exercise: Going Deeper with EFT

If you just completed tapping through the extended global tapping script, and you still feel that the issue is unresolved, it's time to go deeper. What is keeping it unresolved? Title your Global Issue in the space provided below. Answer the following questions so that you can discover, uncover, and recover from the unresolved Specific Events and related Aspects that created and support the Limiting Belief you wish to resolve.

Global Issue: ____________________

1. What Limiting Beliefs do you have at the root of this Global Issue? Rate the level of intensity of how true they are for you between SUD 0 (not true at all) and 10 (completely true).

____________________ • SUD # (0–10): ____

____________________ • SUD # (0–10): ____

2. Title and list the Specific Events in which you learned the Limiting Belief(s) (you can also add them to your List of Titled Specific Events on page 156).

____

____

____

____

____

____

3. Choose one Specific Event to break down here. Title: ____________________

____

4. Tune into your titled Specific Event and identify only those Aspects that apply to you, below:

What thoughts do you notice?

____________________ • SUD # (0–10): ____

____________________ • SUD # (0–10): ____

Do your thoughts have the quality of Small Mind or Large Mind (see page 90)?____________

Describe your Large Mind thoughts (if any):______________________________

____

Describe your Small Mind thoughts (if any): ______________________________

____

What emotions are you feeling?

____ • SUD # (0–10): ____

____ • SUD # (0–10): ____

____ • SUD # (0–10): ____

What body sensation do you notice?

____ • SUD # (0–10): ____

Where is the sensation located?______________________ • SUD # (0–10): ____

Does this sensation have a temperature?____ Describe:______________________

____ • SUD # (0–10): ____

Texture?____________________________________ • SUD # (0–10): ____

Color?______________________________________ • SUD # (0–10): ____

Describe a visual image that you have (if any): __________________________

____ • SUD # (0–10): ____

5. Use the Aspects you have just identified to create your Reminder Phrases.
6. Stay tuned into your titled Specific Event.
7. Start tapping using the Modified EFT Basic Recipe on page 121. You can use the Aspects you have identified here to fill in the Reminder Phrases on the **Blank Tapping Script** on page 404 or the **Vent While You Tap** worksheet on page 409 to assist you in creating your own tapping script.

REPEAT PROCESS IF UNRESOLVED

Be aware of any changes in the intensity of distress you feel in relation to the Aspects, along with any new ones that emerge as you tap through the Rounds of EFT. Continue to tap, repeating the EFT Basic Recipe until your Specific Event, along with its Aspects, is resolved at a SUD level of 0–2. Also be mindful of shifts in Limiting Beliefs and the emergence of any new Empowering ones. To get full resolution of a Global Issue, the Limiting Beliefs must be released by resolving other painful Specific Events that are validating them.

PART 5
An Introduction to the Science

CHAPTER 40

The Mind-Body Communication Network

As we've discussed throughout this workbook, a person's state of mind plays a critical role in healing and recovering from Lyme disease and other TBDs. Beliefs, perceptions, thoughts, and emotions can either facilitate or hinder the healing process. This is why it is important to have a basic understanding of the mind-body communication network.

According to Dr. Richard Horowitz, author of *Why Can't I Get Better? Solving the Mystery of Lyme and Chronic Disease*, "Pain and suffering associated with Lyme disease and MSIDS (multiple systemic infection disease syndrome) not only manifests as physical symptoms but has a strong emotional component."[86] Patients, he notes, have a wide range of emotional experiences spanning from "mild sadness to severe depression, with elements of anxiety, shame, anger, guilt, fear, and grief," all of which can make people who have Lyme disease "more vulnerable to the worst ravages of the disease. Early trauma can damage the immune system."[87] Understanding how the mind-body communication system works can help you to optimize your own healing process.

Although we've made reference to the "mind-body system" and the "mind-body connection" in the earlier parts of this workbook, you may be interested in learning more. This chapter will review our earlier discussions while further clarifying what these terms mean, how they work, and what impact mind-body system coherence has on the treatment of Lyme/TBDs.

How It Works

Interest in mind-body communication dates back many centuries, and there is now a wealth of research demonstrating how the mind and body influence each other. For our purposes, "mind" refers to the beliefs, perceptions, thoughts, and emotions that determine the meaning and quality of our experiences. Studies from the emerging field of psychoneuroimmunology (the study of how mind-body communication affects our health) point to a sophisticated mind-body communication system that is largely responsible for all of the body's neurobiological functions.

The mind and the brain are in constant communication with each other. Every belief, perception, thought, and emotion a person experiences is immediately passed from the mind to the brain. The brain then quickly processes and transmits that information to the rest of the system by firing off neurons that serve as the brain's messenger service. Within just milliseconds of being fired off, those little chemical messengers are traveling at top speed along the complex network of nerve pathways that make up the body's "information superhighway." Information flows from one system to another and back again. For example, the management of important regulatory functions occurs via interaction between the brain, endocrine, and immune system.[88,89,90] Even the cells are "listening" and responding (receptor cells) to the information coming from the mind and brain.[91]

It is important to keep in mind that the mind-body communication system is a literal network linking all of our systems together so that each system functions in relation to the other. Everything the mind conceptualizes, therefore, has a direct impact on the body, and vice versa.

Let's revisit Martha's story from Chapter 37 on page 359 as an example of what this can look like for a person who has Lyme/TBDs: Martha's belief that "there is something wrong with me" was significantly interfering with her healing and recovery, but you might still be wondering how it could possibly be that even that one belief could be so powerful as to produce negative results in her physical body.

> *In thinking about these matters, then, it might make more sense to emphasize the perspective of psychology rather than of neuroscience, for the term, psycho, clearly conveys the study of the brain. I like to speculate that the mind is the flow of information as it moves among the cells, organs and systems of the body. And since one of the qualities of information flow is that it can be unconscious, occurring below the level of awareness, we see it in operation at the autonomic, or involuntary, level of our physiology. The mind, then, is that which holds the network together, often acting below consciousness, linking and coordinating the major systems and their organs and cells in an intelligently orchestrated symphony of life.*
>
> —*Candace Pert,* Molecules of Emotion[92]

In *Molecules of Emotion*, neuroscientist and pharmacologist Candace Pert explains that the mind is responsible for the flow of information exchanged between the brain and the body. "The neuropeptides and receptors, the biochemicals of emotion are the messengers carrying information to link the major systems of the body into one unit that we call the body-mind. Emotions are the nexus between matter and mind, going back and forth between the two and influencing both."[93] This means that our body absorbs and responds to all of our thoughts and emotions. In fact, the mind-body communication network is so intricately designed that the immune, endocrine, and gastrointestinal systems contain "information chemicals" that can regulate emotion, and these chemicals (neuropeptides) can pass directly into the brain. It's as if we have our own biological form of instant messaging, or, as Pert puts it, a "multidirectional network of communication" linking all of our systems together.[94]

Pert emphasizes the relationship between the mind and emotions on health. "The neuropeptides and their receptors are the substrates of the emotions, and they are in constant communication with the immune system, the mechanism through which health and disease are created."[95] Lipton states, an "inappropriate unconscious control of emotions can easily make a healthy body diseased."[96] This is the reason our mental and emotional well-being is so important to our physical well-being.

Increased conscious awareness of Limiting Beliefs and painful emotions related to Lyme/TBDs allow for what Lipton calls the "proper use of consciousness" that can bring health to an ailing body.[97] We think of it as being a lot like noticing weeds in a garden. The weeds need to be identified before they can be properly uprooted, and the same is true for those "psychological weeds" that make Lyme/TBD symptoms worse and prevent healing. It's not until you become consciously aware of these weeds (Limiting Beliefs and painful emotions) that you can properly identify them and clear them from your system.

As Lipton explains, "Our responses to environmental stimuli are indeed controlled by perceptions, but not all of our learned perceptions are accurate. Perception controls biology, but perceptions can be true or false. Therefore, we would be more accurate to refer to these controlling perceptions as beliefs. Beliefs control biology!"[98] Your beliefs act like corrective glasses, changing how you see and respond. Beliefs create thoughts and emotions, which directly affect how your body responds. Lipton adds, "Thoughts, the mind's energy, directly influence how the physical brain controls the body's physiology. Thought energy can activate or inhibit the cell's functions-producing proteins via the mechanics of constructive and destructive interference."[99]

Unfortunately, just thinking positive thoughts alone will not have a lasting effect on the mind-body system due to the impact of the subconscious mind. The subconscious mind, or unconscious mind as some refer to it, describes a dynamic that is active in the mind beyond our conscious awareness, yet still impacts it. The subconscious and conscious parts of the mind both hold beliefs, empowering and limiting, with stored memory, thoughts, emotions, and behavioral responses. The conscious mind is the creative one, the one that holds our aspirations and goals. In contrast, the subconscious mind is like a tape player. It plays back stimulus-response recordings that were made starting in the third trimester and throughout life. It is merely habitual—yet, when triggered, it is a "million times more powerful than the conscious mind."[100]

Internal conflicts can arise when the subconscious mind and the conscious mind hold opposing beliefs. In these times, the subconscious mind frequently overrides the conscious mind. If limiting beliefs, unresolved traumatic memories, and/or unprocessed emotional pain is triggered from the subconscious mind, destructive and reactive behaviors can be seen. These are the times when you may have self-sabotaged a goal, relived a past trauma, done something out of character, or felt ambushed by emotional responses coming from out of what feels like nowhere.

Since there is no way to reason with the subconscious mind, using energy psychology techniques like EFT are proving beneficial. EFT involves the body and mind in the process of releasing unresolved issues in the subconscious mind, which directly impacts perception on the conscious level, thus throughout the whole person. This is still a limited view of the new biology because it does not include the influence of receptor cells and a person's spirit on being human. We highly recommend that you read more about this in Bruce Lipton's book *The Biology of Belief.*

Understanding how the mind-body communication network works can empower you to take a more conscious and active role in your own healing process. Tapping into a wellness state of mind involves releasing the Limiting Beliefs, along with its destructive thoughts and painful emotional states that can lead to damaging bodily responses. It also involves sustaining and developing new Empowering Beliefs with its restorative responses that can stimulate your body's innate ability to heal.

Mind-Body Communication and the Treatment Experience

Let's consider now how Martha's story illustrates the critical intersection between mind-body communication and treatment experiences. Martha related that during the past twenty years of her life she had seen ten different doctors, each of whom had repeated the same message to her: "There's nothing wrong with you." Each time a doctor repeated that message, Martha's subconscious mind received it as a validation of her belief that she was "defective" and that she was always overreacting to things. And, in fact, Martha blamed herself for having Lyme disease and for not being able to keep pace with her peers and the needs of her husband and children.

How could she believe that she would ever get better when the doctors and other authority figures continued to tell her that there was nothing wrong with her? Hearing that message reminded Martha of being constantly chastised by her parents for overreacting to things and being irresponsible. For Martha then, the implication from the doctors validated that she was, in fact, "overreacting" and behaving "irresponsibly" by insisting that her symptoms were real when "there was nothing wrong with her."

Martha's treatment experiences are all too common among people who have Lyme/TBDs. A person's Limiting Beliefs and related unresolved emotions about themselves require a knowledgeable, compassionate practitioner who not only understands Lyme/TBDs but also has training in the important role that emotional intelligence plays in optimizing the effectiveness of treatment.

A number of researchers who have been studying the role of patient expectations and emotions in relation to the doctor-patient relationship and the overall treatment environment emphasize that the meaning patients attach to a particular aspect of their health care creates a "genuine psychobiological event" that can contribute to either a beneficial or nonbeneficial effect.[101,102,103] The interaction then between a patient's mental and emotional state and the treatment environment can have a significant impact on the body's response to treatment.

When a doctor shows a lack of empathy and compassion, it may "induce negative expectations in the patient and may lead to clinical worsening.[104] On the other hand, the expectation that a treatment will be helpful, combined with consistent compassionate care, can have "substantial therapeutic benefit."[105,106,107]

The following is a list of the psychosocial factors researchers found to be most critical to the development of a supportive doctor-patient relationship and the overall effectiveness of treatment:

- Beliefs and expectations of both the patient and the clinician
- Previous treatment experiences (includes successes and failures)
- The relationship between the patient and the clinician
- Clinician's approach to the patient (words, attitude, gestures, behavior)
- Treatment methods used (drug delivery, devices used, procedures)
- Experience of treatment methods (color, taste, smell, touch, pain/no pain)
- The overall treatment environment (location, atmosphere, staff interactions, encounters with other patients)

If these factors are all expressed and received in a positive, affirming, uplifting manner, they can facilitate a supportive doctor-patient relationship. By the same token, if the patient and the doctor are unable to see eye to eye, or if the physician is dismissive of the patient's emotional needs, the opposite effect is achieved.

The development of a supportive doctor-patient relationship and overall treatment environment can contribute significantly to creating a mind-body state that promotes healing and recovery from Lyme/TBDs. Given the large number of individuals who encounter less than adequate support from the medical system, strides should be taken to ensure that physicians and other healthcare professionals are educated regarding the impact that both the doctor-patient relationship and the treatment environment have on a patient's response to any treatment intervention.

CHAPTER 41

The Stress Response in Action

As discussed in the previous chapter, every perception, belief, thought, and emotion we have in response to an event immediately pass from the mind to the brain, where the information is quickly processed and transmitted to the rest of the body via the neurons through neurochemical messengers.

As soon as they are released, these neurons speed along the complex network of nerve pathways that make up the body's own information superhighway. Within fractions of a second, all parts of the mind-body system are in communication with each other about how to respond to a particular event. If the mind is relaxed, then the message is, "All is well." If the mind perceives the event as threatening, then the brain sends out messages like, "We're in trouble. Red alert! Prepare for defense!" This activates the stress response.

Researchers often use the term "perceived threat" when referring to the event that initiates the stress response. This is an important term because it acknowledges that it isn't the event in and of itself that activates the stress response, but rather how the event is perceived and interpreted by the mind. For example, the level of anxiety a person may have about getting a medical exam is not determined by the eventuality of the exam, but by the memories, thoughts, and emotions the person associates with seeing a doctor and getting a checkup. When such an event is perceived as a threat and interpreted as scary or painful, this activates the body's stress response.

The process of assessing whether or not an event is a threat happens, more often than not, below our conscious awareness. This is because the brain is equipped with its own automatic threat-detection device called the amygdala. (We briefly discussed this part of the brain, which is located in the limbic system.) The amygdala's job is to be on guard for any potential threats to the emotional system. It is important to understand that the amygdala does not distinguish between an internal threat based on an internal perception (such as the belief that "medical exams are scary") and an external, physical threat (such as being chased by a rabid dog) and thus responds to both of these types of threats in the same manner.

Emotional distress signals the amygdala and the rest of the brain to activate the sympathetic nervous system and the fight-flight-freeze response that keeps us focused and alert through stressful situations. During the stress response, both the HPA axis (the hypothalamus-pituitary-adrenal gland circuit) and the immune system work together to produce just the right amount of pro-inflammatory protein molecules (cytokines) that serve to protect the body from illness or injury. (See **Cytokines and "Sickness Behavior"** in Chapter 1 on page 19.) The HPA axis, for example, releases hormones called glucocorticoids that work to both activate and deactivate cytokine production by the immune system. Their job then is to regulate the amount of cytokine production throughout the stress response so that the body does not develop too much inflammation.

Problems arise, however, when the mind-body system is inundated with more stressors than it can handle. When this happens, chronic stress can set in and throw the whole system off balance, thus creating increased inflammation. The neuroendocrine and immune systems become impaired, making the system vulnerable to a variety of illnesses. (See the illustration below.)

Dysregulation of the neuroendocrine and immune response to stress has lasting damaging effects. According to researchers Silverman and Heim, et al.:

> *Dysregulation of any of these stress systems can lead to dysregulation of multiple physiological and behavioral systems, which leads to a maladaptive response to stress. Indeed, dysregulation of neural-immune interactions is described in many stress-related disorders, including inflammatory, autoimmune, metabolic, and cardiovascular disease, as well as psychiatric and somatic disorders.*[108]

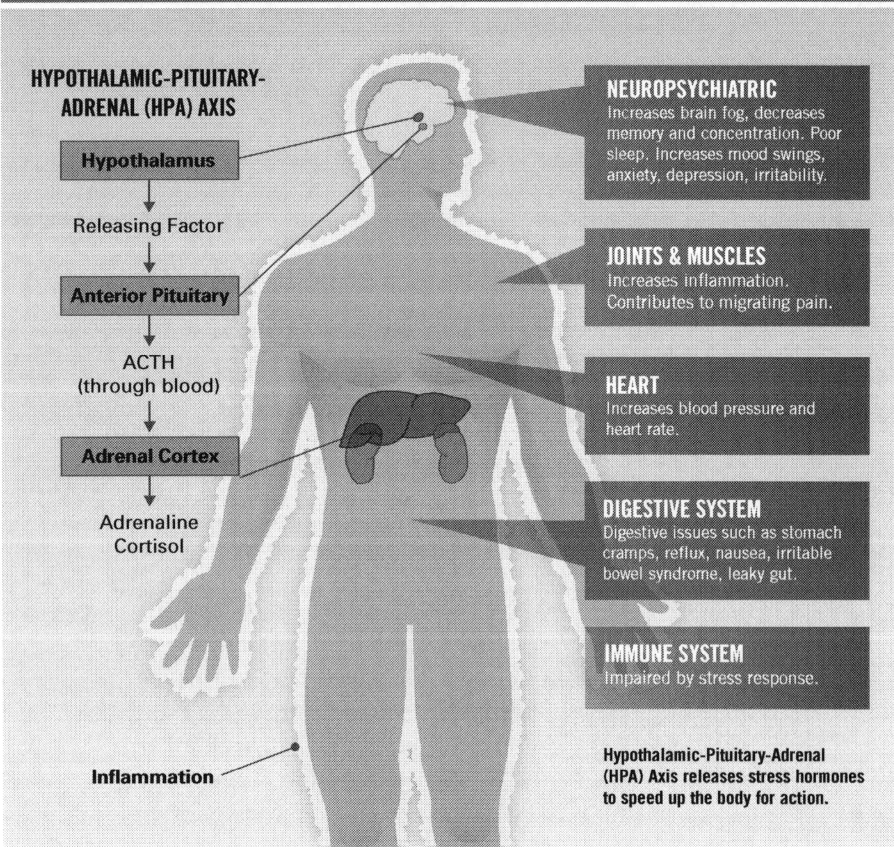

How striking that most of these conditions are implicated in Lyme/TBDs! In fact, chronic Lyme/TBDs and chronic stress often occur together because chronic illness and the psychosocial stressors that can come with it create a continuous cycle of stress without resolution. The results are chemical imbalances in the neuroendocrine and immune systems that lead to:

- Increased pain and inflammation
- Increased fatigue
- Sleep disturbances
- Vulnerability to relapse and new illnesses
- Memory impairment
- Difficulty concentrating and retaining information
- Increased anxiety and depression (feeds back into above conditions)

As Dr. Margo De Kooker explains, the good news is that "the research to date is as compelling concerning immunoenhancement and recovery as it is concerning immunosuppression and stress."[109] She goes on to state that, "coping, continued life involvement, emotional processing, social support, doctor-patient relationship, and spirituality are all variables that influence healthy survival."

These are all things you can choose for yourself to enhance your resilience and promote your healing and recovery from Lyme/TBDs. How? By tapping into a wellness state of mind.

CHAPTER

42 EFT: An Effective Tool for Stress Reduction

We have known for some time now that EFT, the process of tapping on specific acupoints while focusing on, venting, and releasing an identified stressor (which is referred to as a Specific Event throughout this workbook) is an extremely effective tool for stress reduction. One reason for this is that it creates a form of electrical stimulation (much like that experienced in acupuncture) that, with repeated practice, leads to profound and lasting improvements in neurological, physiological, and mental states.[110,111,112]

When you experience chronic stress, as is most often the case with chronic Lyme/TBDs, the stress response—fight, flight, or freeze—begins to work overtime. Rather than shutting off, as it would typically do, it stays "on" for a prolonged period, taxing and draining your immune, endocrine, organ, and cellular functions. Not only does this hinder your body's ability to heal from an existing illness, but it also impairs its ability to fight off new infections, and this can lead to relapses. Energy psychology techniques such as EFT disrupt this damaging process and deactivate the stress signals so that the body can relax and begin to repair itself.

As mentioned in the introduction to this book, many people have referred to EFT as "acupuncture for the emotions without the needles." That's how we think of it, too. You get all the benefits, and you can use it on yourself anytime, anywhere, whenever you need to! Dr. Richard Horowitz, author of *Why Can't I Get Better: Solving the Mystery of Lyme Disease,* includes EFT in his list of recommended psychotherapeutic techniques for "shifting frozen emotional memories that are stuck in the body, affecting our mood and immunity."[113] Once these memories and the accompanying Limiting Beliefs are released, all of the energy used to contain them becomes available for healing.

EFT can best be described as:

- A novel treatment that combines three essential ingredients: exposure (focusing on a Specific Event), cognitive self-acceptance (included in the Setup statements), and somatic stimulation (tapping on acupoints, also called EFT Tapping Points).
- A form of energy psychology (EP) that engages both the body and mind in identifying, processing, and releasing distressing thoughts and emotions to significantly reduce stress and restore the balance and flow of energy needed by the body for optimal function and repair.
- An effective form of exposure therapy for treating anxiety and posttraumatic stress disorder (PTSD) that works to reduce the production of distressing emotions such as fear, anger, and panic triggered by the arousal of the amygdala during the stress response.

Personal Reflections

CHAPTER 43

The Early EFT Research Findings

As mentioned earlier in this workbook, Emotional Freedom Techniques (EFT) is a form of energy psychology (EP), which refers to a number of techniques that "combine physical interventions for regulating electrical signals or energy fields with mental involvement in a feeling, cognition or behavior that is a target for change." The EP approach is rooted in both well-grounded psychological principles and non-Western systems for healing and spiritual development.[114]

Traditional Chinese medicine views disturbances of the mind and body as resulting from disruptions in energy flow.[115] Western psychology tends to explore mental and behavioral difficulties in terms of affect and cognition. Both Traditional Chinese medicine and Western psychotherapeutic approaches are now widely accepted practices in many arenas. According to clinical psychologist Dr. David Feinstein, there are over two dozen variations of EP, all of which contain practices and concepts derived from acupuncture.[116]

Since 1997, the National Institutes of Health (NIH) has acknowledged acupuncture as a legitimate treatment for a variety of conditions.[117] EP is distinctive in its use of acupressure points (acupoints) to quickly reduce emotional distress. The manual stimulation of these points creates neurochemical messages that are passed through the cortical and subcortical areas of the brain to the amygdala through which emotion passes into expression.[118,119] Using modern neuroimaging technology to measure the response of the cerebro-cerebellar and limbic systems to acupuncture, one study collected data that supports the analgesic effect of acupuncture on the limbic system through which cognition and affect are processed.[120]

Though not the same process as acupuncture, EFT uses the tactile manipulation of acupoints to significantly reduce and, in many cases, neutralize elevated states of fear, anger, and anxiety.[121] As noted earlier (and indeed, pharmacologically based treatments recognize this), neurochemistry plays a significant role in the development and expression of emotional arousal.[122,123] The amygdala, as the last pathway through which emotion becomes expression, plays a large part in the arousal of anger.[124,125] With its ability to alter the neurochemical process by which the amygdala produces an emotional response,[126,127] EFT shows promise as an effective intervention for minimizing emotional distress.

Research on EFT is still in the early phase, and it is not without controversy.[128,129,130] Even so, it has demonstrated much promise as a treatment modality.[131,132,133,134] For example, the use of EFT has demonstrated some rather impressive results in therapeutic work with veterans suffering from posttraumatic stress disorder.[135] Studying the effects of EFT on a group of forty-nine veterans diagnosed with PTSD, Dawson Church and colleagues found that, following six one-hour sessions of EFT, 86 percent of the participants no longer met the diagnostic criteria for PTSD—a result that remained stable as of a three-month follow-up.[136]

As you've learned, the somatic element of EFT involves tapping acupoints.[137] The cognitive element of EFT consists of assessing distress levels by using the Subjective Units of Distress (SUD) scale—where 0 represents absolutely no distress, and 10 represents the maximum distress possible—and by providing a "Setup Statement" that emphasizes the identified problem combined with a statement of self-acceptance.[138] An example of such a statement is, "Even though I lost my temper, I honor and accept myself." The statement is paired with the tapping, and the SUD is reassessed after the second round. If the level of distress has not decreased, then one or more rounds may be repeated.[139]

Essentially, EFT neutralizes damaging subconscious core beliefs by engaging the mind and body in sending new information to the subconscious with physical stimulation. "Hard-wired behavioral programs"[140] are changed so that the neurological and physiological signals that once called forth an emotionally intense response are deactivated. Previously triggering environmental cues no longer set off a chain reaction of painful emotions, distressing thoughts, and destructive behaviors. In discussing the impact of tapping through a variety of disorders, Ruden states that "the mind is what the brain produces," and he argues that tapping has an effect on "the brain's electrical activity, the concentration of neurochemicals, the threshold to neuronal activation and the neural connections that are available." Bringing forth the target emotion and disrupting the neural circuits that initially encoded it creates a lasting change in perception.[141]

Lipton, Ruden, and Feinstein all agree that tapping creates electrical impulses that profoundly change neurological, physiological, and mental states while reprogramming original encoding to eradicate maladaptive core beliefs. Over time, and with repetition, perceptions change, and EFT users develop the skills to enhance the quality of their thoughts, feelings, and behaviors.[142,143,144]

There are some important advantages to using EFT. One is that it accesses and stimulates acupoints without the intrusion of needles, an aspect of acupuncture that can be off-putting for many people who have not yet tried it. Another is that EFT is a self-help tool that can be learned and self-administered. A third is that EFT does not require any particular equipment or setup. It can be done at any time and in any environment where the person feels comfortable tapping.

If you are interested in learning more about the emerging research done on EFT, the following is a list of helpful articles from the Association for Comprehensive Energy Psychology (ACEP). You can visit the ACEP website at www.energypsych.org. Many of these articles and much more information can be found on www.eftuniverse.com.

"A Feasibility Study: Emotional Freedom Techniques for Depression in Australian Adults."
Stapleton, P., Devine, S., Chatwin, H., Porter, B., and Sheldon, T. 2014. *Curr. Res. Psychol., 5:* 19–33. http://thescipub.com/abstract/10.3844/crpsp.2014.19.33.

"Acupoint Stimulation in Treating Psychological Disorders: Evidence of Efficacy. Review of General Psychology."
Feinstein, D. (2012). Advance online publication. doi: 10.1037/a0028602

"Application of Emotional Freedom Techniques."
Church, D., & Brooks, A. (2010b). *Integrative Medicine: A Clinician's Journal,* 2010, August/September 2010.

"Brief Group Intervention Using EFT (Emotional Freedom Techniques) for Depression in College Students: A Randomized Controlled Trial."
Church, D., De Asis, M., & Brooks, A. J. (2012). *Depression Research & Treatment,* 2012. doi:10.1155/2012/257172

"Clinical Benefits of Emotional Freedom Techniques on Food Cravings."
Stapleton, P., Sheldon, T., & Porter, B. (2012). At 12-months follow-up: A randomized controlled trial. *Energy Psychology Journal, 4*(1), 13–24.

"Clinical EFT as an Evidence-Based Practice for the Treatment of Psychological and Physiological Conditions."
Church, D. (2013). *Psychology, 4*(8). http://www.scirp.org/journal/PaperInformation.aspx?PaperID=35751.

"The Effect of a Brief EFT (Emotional Freedom Techniques) Self-Intervention on Anxiety, Depression, Pain and Cravings in Healthcare Workers."
Church, D., & Brooks, A. (2010a). *Integrative Medicine: A Clinician's Journal,* Oct/Nov.

"Effect of the Emotional Freedom Technique on Perceived Stress, Quality of Life, and Cortisol Salivary Levels in Tension-Type Headache Sufferers: A Randomized Controlled Trial."
Bougea, A. M., Spandideas, N., Alexopoulos, E. C., Thomaides, T., Chrousos, G. P., & Darviri, C. (2013). *EXPLORE: The Journal of Science and Healing, 9*(2), 91–99. doi:10.1016/j.explore.2012.12.005

"The Effect of Emotional Freedom Technique (EFT) on Stress Biochemistry: A Randomized Controlled Trial."
Church, D., Yount, G., & Brooks, A. (2012). *Journal of Nervous and Mental Disease, 200*(10), 891–896.

"The Effects of EFT on Long-Term Psychological Symptoms."
Rowe, J. (2005). *Counseling and Clinical Psychology Journal, 2*(3):104.
Previous research (Salas, 2000; Wells et al., 2003), theoretical writings (Arenson, 2001, Callahan, 1985, Durlacher, 1994, Flint, 1999, Gallo, 2002, Hover-Kramer, 2002, Lake & Wells, 2003, Lambrou & Pratt, 2000, and Rowe, 2003).

"The Neurochemistry of Counterconditioning: Acupressure Desensitization in Psychotherapy."
Lane, J. (2009). *Energy Psychology: Theory, Research, & Treatment, 1*(1), 31–44.

"Preliminary Report of the First Large-Scale Study of Energy Psychology."
Andrade, J. & Feinstein, D. (2004). Energy Psychology Interactive: Rapid Interventions for Lasting Change. Ashland, OR: Innersource.

"The Psychobiology and Clinical Principles of Energy Psychology Treatments for PTSD: A Review."
Church, D., & Feinstein, D. (2012). In T. Van Leeuwen and M. Brouwer, editors, *Psychology of Trauma.* Hauppage, NY: Nova Publishers.

"Psychological Trauma Symptom Improvement in Veterans Using EFT (Emotional Freedom Techniques): A Randomized Controlled Trial."
Church, D., Hawk, C, Brooks, A., Toukolehto, O., Wren, M., Dinter, I., & Stein, P. (2013). *Journal of Nervous & Mental Disease, 201*(2), 153–160.

"Self-Administered EFT (Emotional Freedom Techniques) in Individuals with Fibromyalgia: a Randomized Trial."
Brattberg, G. (2008). *Integrative Medicine: A Clinician's Journal,* August/September 2008.

"Your DNA Is Not Your Destiny: Behavioral Epigenetics and the Role of Emotions in Health."
Church, D. (2010). *Anti-Aging Medical Therapeutics, 13.*

Appendix A
EFT Tapping Points

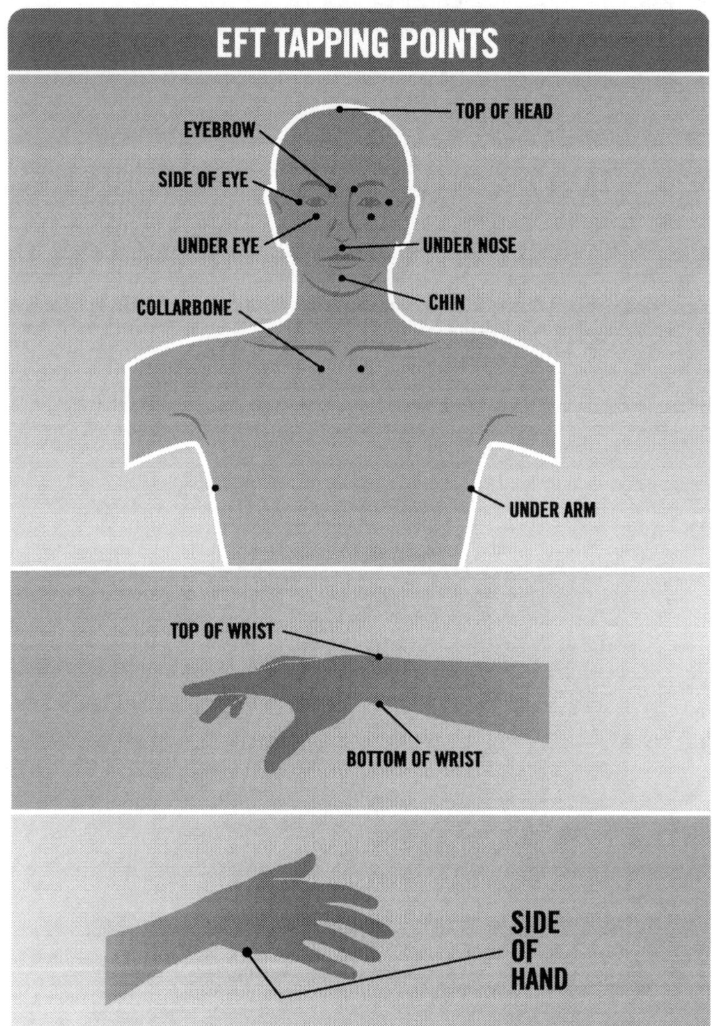

Appendix B
The Modified EFT Basic Recipe

Preparation: Identify a Limiting Belief/Global Issue you desire to resolve using EFT.

Step 1: Identify a Specific Event and give it a title. BE SPECIFIC.

Step 2: Subjective Units of Distress (SUD) #1: Rate the intensity of distress that you feel.

Step 3: Setup Statement: State the problem combined with a statement of acceptance, repeating three times while tapping on the Side of Hand.

Step 4: Two rounds of tapping with Reminder Phrases to keep you focused on your Issue.

Step 5: Subjective Units of Distress (SUD) #2: Rate the intensity of distress that you feel now.

Appendix C
Sample EFT Setup Statements

Repeat the Setup Statement three times while tapping the Side of Hand (see page 125).

Setup Statement: State your problem (Even though . . .) and connect it to a positive statement.

Even though ______________________________, I love and accept myself.

Even though ______________________________, I honor and respect myself.

Even though ______________________________, I accept all of my feelings about this.

Even though ______________________________, I accept my body and all that it is doing to help me heal.

Even though ______________________________, I am open to forgiving my body.

Even though ______________________________, I am open to loving and accepting myself.

Even though ______________________________, I am open to new possibilities for myself.

Even though ______________________________, I am open to the possibility of forgiving myself and all those who have contributed to my pain.

Even though ______________________________, anything is possible and miracles are happening now.

Even though ______________________________, it is what it is right now and it is not forever.

Even though ______________________________, I choose to (state what you desire; keep it positive, specific, and present).

Even though ______________________________, I choose to surprise myself by allowing it to be easy.

Even though ______________________________, what if I (state what you desire; keep it positive, specific, and present)?

Even though ______________________________, I give myself permission to (state what you desire; keep it positive, specific, and present).

Even though ______________________________, it is now time to (state what you desire; keep it positive, specific, and present).

Have fun creating your own!

Appendix D
Blank Tapping Script

Date:______________ Specific Event Title:____

- Focus your attention on your titled **Specific Event** (see page 122).
- Identify one **Limiting Belief** (see page 119) that may be at the root.
- Take three slow, deep belly breaths as you do a **Body Scan** (see page 81).
- What **Aspects** (see page 123) do you notice?
- Using the **SUD scale** (see page 124), choose a number between 0 (no distress/peaceful) and 10 (highest intensity of distress) to **rate the intensity** of distress you feel about the **Specific Event and Limiting Belief**, along with only the **Aspects** (thoughts, feelings, body sensations, and visual image) that you notice that apply to you.

	Description	SUD #:
Specific Event		
Limiting Belief		
Thoughts		
Feelings		
Body Sensations		
Visual Image		

Extended Global Tapping Script: Let's begin tapping (see page 126)

Round 1

Setup:

Side of Hand: ____

Side of Hand: ____

Side of Hand: ____

Top of Head: ____

Eyebrow: ____

Side of Eye: ____

Under Eye: ____

Under Nose: ____

Chin: ______________________________

Collarbone: ______________________________

Under Arm: ______________________________

Top of Wrists Together: ______________________________

Bottom of Wrists Together: ______________________________

Slowly complete a deep belly breath and then keep tapping.

Round 2

Top of Head: ______________________________

Eyebrow: ______________________________

Side of Eye: ______________________________

Under Eye: ______________________________

Under Nose: ______________________________

Chin: ______________________________

Collarbone: ______________________________

Under Arm: ______________________________

Top of Wrists Together: ______________________________

Bottom of Wrists Together: ______________________________

Take three slow, deep belly breaths as you complete another **Body Scan**. What do you notice now? Note changes to the Aspects and any new ones that may appear below:

	Description	SUD #:
Specific Event		
Limiting Belief		
Thoughts		
Feelings		
Body Sensations		
Visual Image		

If your intensity level about this Specific Event, along with any of its Aspects, is still 3 or above on a SUD scale, continue tapping with the next round. (If you have a SUD scale of 0–2, skip down and finish by tapping through the positive statements and **Afformations**.)

Round 3

Setup:

Side of Hand: Even though ______________________________

Side of Hand: Even though ______________________________

Side of Hand: Even though ______________________________

Top of Head: ______________________________

Eyebrow: ______________________________

Side of Eye: ______________________________

Under Eye: ______________________________

Under Nose: ______________________________

Chin: ______________________________

Collarbone: ______________________________

Under Arm: ______________________________

Top of Wrists Together: ______________________________

Bottom of Wrists Together: ______________________________

Take three slow, deep belly breaths as you complete another **Body Scan**. What do you notice now? Note changes to the Aspects and any new ones that may appear below:

	Description	SUD #:
Specific Event		
Limiting Belief		
Thoughts		
Feelings		
Body Sensations		
Visual Image		

If your intensity level about this Specific Event, along with any of its Aspects, is still 3 or above on a SUD scale, keep tapping through what is in your awareness or move down to **Follow These Steps to Resolution**.

Once you reach a SUD level of 0–2 or when you just want to stop tapping for now and return at a later time, finish up by tapping through the positive statements and **Affirmations**.

Round 4 – Now let's tap through some positive statements!

Top of Head: ______

Eyebrow: ______

Side of Eye: ______

Under Eye: ______

Under Nose: ______

Chin: ______

Collarbone: ______

Under Arm: ______

Top of Wrists Together: ______

Bottom of Wrists Together: ______

Round 5 – Tapping with Afformations (see page 101)

Top of Head: How is it possible for ______

Eyebrow: Why am I able to ______

Side of Eye: Why is it so easy ______

Under Eye: Why is it possible ______

Under Nose: Why am I grateful for ______

Chin: How am I able to ______

Collarbone: Why is it so easy for me to ______

Under Arm: How am I able to ______

Top of Wrists Together: What is right about ______

Bottom of Wrists Together: Why is it possible for ______

Take three slow, deep belly breaths as you complete another **Body Scan**. What do you notice now? Note changes to the Aspects and any new ones that may appear below:

	Description	SUD #:
Specific Event		
Limiting Belief		
Thoughts		
Feelings		
Body Sensations		
Visual Image		

If your intensity level about this Specific Event, along with any of its Aspects, is still 3 or above on a SUD scale, you need to explore them more in depth and follow the directives in **Follow These Steps to Resolution,** on the following page.

Exercise: Developing Self-Awareness

Describe your experience of tapping through this Specific Event.

___

___

___

Which Aspects resolved, decreased, increased, or stayed the same?

___

___

___

If you identified a Limiting Belief, state what (if anything) changed.

___

___

State any Empowering Beliefs (see page 119) that you notice now.

___

___

What Global Issues/Limiting Beliefs need to be resolved (if any)?

___

___

Follow These Steps to Resolution

- When you have the time and energy, use the exercise, **Going Deeper with EFT** that can be found at the end of every chapter in Part 4 (Chapters 19–39). Use this to help you identify any additional Specific Events, along with their Aspects, that are contributing to not resolving your Global Issue/Limiting Belief or with any new ones that may have surfaced while tapping. You may identify many and this is to be expected.
- Just break down one Specific Event at a time and tap it until resolved. Title the rest of the Specific Events that you have identified and add them to the **List of Titled Specific Events** on page 156 so that you can return to them at a later time to tap. You can also use the **Vent While You Tap** worksheet on the next page to assist you while tapping through a Specific Event.

Appendix E
Vent While You Tap Worksheet

Specific Event title:______________________________ Date:____________

Fill in the Aspects that apply to you below and Vent while you tap!

Give your Event a Voice!

VENT Limiting Beliefs about self/world:

1.____________________

2.____________________

3.____________________

4.____________________

5.____________________

VENT destructive thoughts/fears:

1.____________________

2.____________________

3.____________________

4.____________________

5.____________________

VENT feelings:

1.____________________

2.____________________

3.____________________

4.____________________

5.____________________

VENT destructive behaviors:

1.____________________

2.____________________

3.____________________

4.____________________

5.____________________

VENT

Alternate pros/cons while tapping

Reasons why to let go:

1.____________________

2.____________________

Reasons why not to let go:

1.____________________

2.____________________

VENT Body sensations and specific pain:

1.____________________

2.____________________

3.____________________

VENT compassionate understanding statements:

1.____________________

2.____________________

3.____________________

VENT what you desire:

4.____________________

5.____________________

6.____________________

TAP TAP TAP ANY ORDER & COMBO TAP TAP TAP

Appendix F
List of Needs and Feelings

These are some basic needs we all have:

Autonomy
- Choosing dreams/goals/values
- Choosing plans for fulfilling one's dreams, goals, values

Celebration
- Celebrate the creation of life and dreams fulfilled
- Celebrate losses: loved ones, dreams, etc, (mourning)

Integrity
- Authenticity
- Creativity
- Meaning
- Self-worth

Interdependence
- Acceptance
- Appreciation
- Closeness
- Community
- Consideration
- Contribute to the enrichment of life
- Emotional Safety
- Empathy: To be seen, heard, and understood

Physical Nurturance
- Air
- Food
- Movement, exercise
- Protection from life-threatening forms of life: viruses, bacteria insects, predatory animals
- Rest
- Sexual expression
- Shelter
- Touch
- Water

Play
- Fun
- Laughter

Spiritual Communion
- Beauty
- Harmony
- Inspiration
- Order
- Peace
- Honesty (the empowering honesty that enables us to learn from our limitations)
- Love
- Reassurance
- Respect
- Support
- Trust
- Understanding

These are some basic feelings we all have:

Feelings when needs "are" fulfilled:
- Amazed
- Comfortable
- Confident
- Eager
- Energetic
- Fulfilled
- Glad
- Hopeful
- Inspired
- Intrigued
- Joyous
- Moved
- Optimistic
- Proud
- Relieved
- Stimulated
- Surprised
- Thankful
- Touched
- Trustful

Feelings when needs "are not" fulfilled:
- Angry
- Annoyed
- Concerned
- Confused
- Disappointed
- Discouraged
- Distressed
- Embarrassed
- Frustrated
- Helpless
- Hopeless
- Impatient
- Irritated
- Lonely
- Nervous
- Overwhelmed
- Puzzled
- Reluctant
- Sad
- Uncomfortable

Adapted from Speak Peace in a World of Conflict: What You Say Next Will Change Your World *by Marshall B. Rosenberg, PhD. (2005).*

Appendix G
Touch and Breathe (TAB)

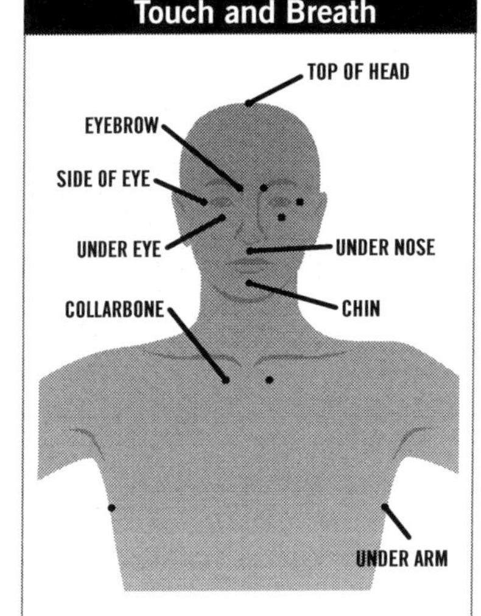

Step 1: Identify a **Specific Event** and give it a title (see page 122).

Focus your attention on your titled **Specific Event**.

Take three slow, deep belly breaths as you do a **Body Scan** (see page 81).

Identify only those **Aspects** (see page 123) that apply to you and describe them in the table below.

Step 2: SUD #1—Using the **SUD scale** (see page 124), choose a number between 0 (no distress/peaceful) and 10 (highest intensity of distress) to **rate the intensity** of distress you feel about the Specific Event, along with only the **Aspects** (thoughts, feelings, body sensations, and visual image) that apply to you and write them in the table below in the "Start SUD" column.

Step 3: Gently touch and hold with the first two fingers on an EFT acupoint while doing one set of **4/8 Diaphragmatic Breathing**/deep belly breath (see page 86). TAB through each of the EFT acupoints for Round 1.

Step 4: Stop and take three slow, deep belly breaths as you do a **Body Scan**.

What **Aspects** do you notice now?

Step 5: SUD #2—Using the **SUD scale** again, choose a number between 0 (no distress/peaceful) and 10 (highest intensity of distress) to **rate the intensity** of distress you now feel about the **Specific Event**, along with only the **Aspects** (thoughts, feelings, body sensations, and visual image) that apply to you and write them in the table below in the Round 1 SUD column.

If your SUD scale is 3 or above on the **Specific Event**, along with any of its **Aspects**, continue **TAB** by repeating Steps 2–5 for additional rounds until you have resolution with a SUD of 2 or below.

	Description	Start SUD #:	Round 1 SUD #:	Round 2 SUD #:	Round 3 SUD #:
Specific Event					
Limiting Belief					
Thoughts					
Feelings					
Body Sensations					
Visual Image					

Touch and Breathe has been adapted from the work of John Diepold, PhD.

Appendix H
Lyme/TBDs-Related Belief Inventory

Place a checkmark next to each statement that applies to you. (Refer to Chapter 6 on page 55).

Limiting Beliefs		Empowering Beliefs	
Self-help tools won't work for me.	☐	Self-help tools will work for me.	☐
There are no Lyme treatments that work for me.	☐	I will find the Lyme treatments that work for me.	☐
I don't trust the medical system to help me recover.	☐	I will find the people in the medical system to help me recover.	☐
I can't get the help I need.	☐	I will continue to seek the help I need.	☐
If doctors can't help me, no one can.	☐	I believe there are doctors and people out there who can help me.	☐
It must be all in my head.	☐	I know my body and acknowledge something is wrong.	☐
There is no future for me.	☐	My future is full of new possibilities.	☐
My life is out of control.	☐	I am emotionally flexible and able to move through the changes in my life.	☐
I'll never get better.	☐	I do believe I will recover. It is what it is for now, and it is temporary.	☐
I am useless and/or defective.	☐	I am useful and have value.	☐
Life will always be a struggle.	☐	Life is full of change and new possibility.	☐
It's all my fault that I'm still sick.	☐	I have Lyme/TBDs.	☐
I am filled with guilt.	☐	I am not to blame for this.	☐
I do not believe medications will help me.	☐	I am open to the possibility that medications will help me.	☐
This treatment protocol is too much for me.	☐	I have the resilience needed to heal through this treatment protocol.	☐
My body betrayed me.	☐	My body is doing everything it can to help me heal, and I am grateful.	☐
I don't know who I am anymore.	☐	I am gaining a deeper understanding of myself as a result of going through this.	☐
I'll never get my energy back.	☐	This fatigue is what it is, and it is temporary.	☐
I will be in pain forever.	☐	This pain is what it is, and it is temporary.	☐
I am disconnected from everybody.	☐	I am able to connect with others, even though I am in pain.	☐
There is no way that I can give up my favorite high-inflammatory foods.	☐	I am able to choose foods that support my healing and recovery.	☐
Nobody understands what I am going through.	☐	I am able to find people who can understand what I am going through.	☐
I'll never be able to work again.	☐	I believe I will be able to work again in the future. It is what it is for now, and it is not forever.	☐

(continued on the next page)

Limiting Beliefs	Empowering Beliefs
Lyme/TBDs are taking everything away from me. ☐	I accept the loss I experience and believe new possibilities surround me. ☐
I don't have any friends I can count on. ☐	I am able to and will find friends I can count on. ☐
My family doesn't understand what's happening to me. ☐	My family understands what is happening to me to the level that they are capable. ☐
I have failed my spouse/partner and/or kids. ☐	I am doing the best I can for my spouse/partner/kids based on where I am and how I feel. ☐
I am not carrying my weight.	I can only do so much and accept that it's okay for now.
I can't cope with the stress of Lyme/TBDs. ☐	I am able to cope with the stress related to Lyme/TBDs by using the self-help tools suggested in this workbook. ☐
I'll never enjoy being in the outdoors again. ☐	With the right precautions, I can enjoy the outdoors. ☐
I will never get out of this depression. ☐	My depression is what it is for now, and it is temporary. ☐
I don't have enough money to make it. ☐	I am capable of figuring out my finances, and I am open to creative solutions. ☐
Life will always be a struggle. ☐	I accept where I am now, learning what I need to learn for my best and highest good. ☐
There's no hope for me. ☐	There are always new possibilities for me. ☐
Add any additional Limiting Beliefs you may have:	Add any additional Empowering Beliefs you may have:

My Top-Five Limiting Beliefs (if any):	**My Top-Five Empowering Beliefs (if any):**
1.	1.
2.	2.
3.	3.
4.	4.
5.	5.
How do you **FEEL** right now while reflecting on the Limiting Beliefs you have identified?	How do you **FEEL** right now while reflecting on the Empowering Beliefs you have identified?
Do you believe that it is possible that the Limiting Beliefs you have identified could be inhibiting your recovery from Lyme/TBDs? If yes or no, describe in what ways.	Do you believe that it is possible that the Empowering Beliefs you have identified could be enhancing your recovery from Lyme/TBDs? If yes or no, describe in what ways.

Appendix I
Coping with Emotional Stress Scale • Introduction and Directions

Maintaining your emotional wellness is critical in living a stress-free life. Emotional wellness includes awareness of your emotions at any given time, the ability to maintain an even emotional state regardless of what is happening around you, and the ability to control your emotions.

This assessment contains 20 statements related to your emotional wellness. Read each statement and decide whether or not the statement describes you. If the statement *does* describe you, circle the number under the TRUE column next to that item. If the statement *does not* describe you, circle the number under the FALSE column next to that item.

In the following example, the circled number under "TRUE" indicates the statement is descriptive of the person completing the inventory.

	TRUE	FALSE
I have difficulty identifying my feelings	①	2

This is not a test. Since there are no right or wrong answers, do not spend too much time thinking about your answers. Be sure to respond to every statement.

Coping with Emotional Stress Scale

	TRUE	FALSE
I have difficulty identifying my feelings	1	2
I have fairly consistent emotional states	2	1
I usually understand how others are feeling	2	1
I am able to maintain intimate relationships with others	2	1
I often am unable to express my emotions clearly	1	2
I adjust to change and cope with the stress of daily life	2	1
I tend to be positive most of the time	2	1
I have inner peace and contentment	2	1
Minor setbacks cause me stress	1	2
I don't waste time or energy dwelling on the past	2	1
I am unable to stay focused on the present	1	2
I am aware of my personal limitations	2	1
I have a hard time valuing and accepting myself	1	2
I manage my emotions well	2	1
I am aware of how my negative emotions affect others	2	1
I worry a lot about failure	1	2
I find it easy to forgive others	2	1
I am not able to laugh at myself	1	2
I can appropriately express my feelings	2	1
I have a hard time accepting constructive criticism	1	2

Scoring Directions

The *Coping with Emotional Stress Scale* is designed to help you explore how you are managing your emotions in this stress-filled society.

Add the numbers that you circled on the scale. This will allow you to get your Emotional Wellness score. You will get a total in the range from 20 to 40. Then, transfer this total to the space below:

EMOTIONAL WELLNESS TOTAL = ______

Profile Interpretation

Scale Score	Result	Indications
20 to 26	Low	Low scores indicate that you are rarely able to manage your emotions well. Complete the following exercise to develop greater emotional wellness.
27 to 33	Moderate	Moderate scores indicate that you sometimes are able to manage your emotions well. Complete the following exercises to develop greater emotional wellness.
34 to 40	High	High scores indicate that you are pretty effective in managing your emotions.

Appendix J
Exercise: Cultivate Large Mind

Specific Event Title (see page 122) ____________________

As a specific life event is happening and you notice yourself *starting* to feel negatively defensive or reactive, **STOP! Ask yourself:**

1. *What is happening?* (State just the facts. No interpretation.) ____________________

   ____

2. *How am I relating to it?*

   My perception/interpretation of the facts (my story) is: ____________________

   ____

   As a result, **my** strategies for responding/behaving are: ____________________

   In this situation, **am I** in Small Mind or Large Mind (see page 90)? ____________________

3. *Do* I *want to continue to believe, think, feel, and respond the way that* I am *doing?* __________

Self-Inventory to Develop Mindfulness About Small Mind

If you are in Small Mind and answered "NO" to question number 3:
BE CURIOUS and EXPLORE the impact of your choices by completing this self-inventory with compassionate understanding.

A (if any) Limiting Belief (see page 119) that may be supporting **my** Small Mind interpretation is:

____

____

My Limiting Belief (if any) makes **me** feel: ____________________

As a result of **me** believing in this Small Mind way, **my** Small Mind thoughts are: __________

____

____

As a result of having **my** Small Mind thoughts:

I am making **myself** feel: ____________________

____

I am making **my** body feel (body sensations): ____________________

____

The visual image (if any) that **I am** creating for **myself** is: ______________________________

____

My visual image is making **me** feel: ______________________________

My strategies for responding/behaving are: ______________________________

The needs (see page 410) that **I am** not honoring **in myself** by using these strategies for responding/behaving are: ______________________________

These **make me** feel: ______________________________

The needs (see page 410) that **I am** not honoring **in others** by using these strategies for responding/behaving are: ______________________________

These **make me** feel: ______________________________

Now that you are more self-aware of the impact of Small Mind, you are ready and ABLE to make a CHOICE! Ask yourself a new question: *Do* I choose *to continue to believe, think, feel, and respond the way that* I am *doing?* ______If NO: ______________________________

Choose Large Mind!

Self-Inventory to Develop Mindfulness to Cultivate Large Mind

Choose mindfulness to reframe and/or use EFT in the present moment to cultivate Large Mind, which is a wellness state of mind.

1. Use Mindfulness to Reframe

Restate what is happening. (State just the facts. No interpretation.)______________________________

____

How am I relating to it now? ______________________________

My Large Mind perception/interpretation of the facts is: ______________________________

____

As a result, **my** Large Mind strategies for responding/behaving are: ______________________________

____

An (if any) Empowering Belief (see page 119) that supports **my** Large Mind interpretation is: ______

____

My Empowering Belief (if any) makes **me** feel: ______________________________

As a result of **me** believing in this Large Mind way, **my** Large Mind thoughts are: ____________________

____

As a result of my choosing Large Mind thoughts:

I am making **myself** feel: ____

I am making **my** body feel (body sensations): ______________________________

____

The visual image (if any) that **I am** creating for myself is: ______________________

____

My visual image is making **me** feel: ____

____

My strategies for responding/behaving are: ____________________________________

The needs (see page 410) that **I am** honoring **in myself** by choosing these strategies for responding/behaving are: ______________________

These choices **make me** feel: ____

The needs (see page 410) that **I am** honoring **in others** by choosing these strategies for responding/behaving are: ______________________

These choices **make me** feel: ____

2. Use Emotional Freedom Techniques (EFT)

You can use EFT to tap just on your Small Mind thoughts, feelings, and behaviors in the present moment for a quicker reframe to Large Mind.

You can also use EFT to resolve the Limiting Belief(s) within unresolved painful Specific Events to naturally cultivate a Large wellness state of mind (see Chapter 15 on page 137). By doing this, reframing is no longer needed since you will have resolved the underlying issues that originally created Small Mind.

Appendix K
I. Effect of Biocharger™ on Chronically Ill Individuals

JANUARY 2015 **EFFECT OF BIOCHARGER ON CHRONICALLY ILL INDIVIDUALS**

Overview

Lyme disease patients and chronically ill individuals participated in a market research study using BioCharger, a high voltage multi-frequency, resonant transformer/modified Tesla Coil that wirelessly transmits pulsed waves of electromagnetic and photonic energy. The goal of the study was to assess if BioCharger improved the health and general well-being of the participants.

Eleven individuals with chronic health issues participated in the study. One underage participant was excluded from the final analysis. Participants used the BioCharger at least four times a week for four consecutive weeks.

The participants were asked to fill out a self-assessment of their symptoms and well-being at the beginning of the study, and on a weekly basis for four consecutive weeks.

Participant Demographic

The average participant was 57 years old, retired and/or disabled due to chronic health issues and was actively taking medications. The average participant listed at least four health issues. Most of the participants listed Lyme disease as one of their ongoing health issues. Seventy percent of the participants were women.

Overall Results

The results below reflect participants self-assessments in week 4 in comparison to their self-assessments prior to using the BioCharger (baseline period). All participants noticed at least some improvement in their health and well-being four weeks after using the BioCharger. When asked whether their overall quality of life had improved, 90% said yes.

Significantly Less Pain

The average participant experienced 40% less pain than the baseline period.

All the participants experienced some level of pain in the baseline period. 80% of the participants experienced significant, chronic pain or discomfort that interfered with their general activity and mood prior to using the BioCharger.

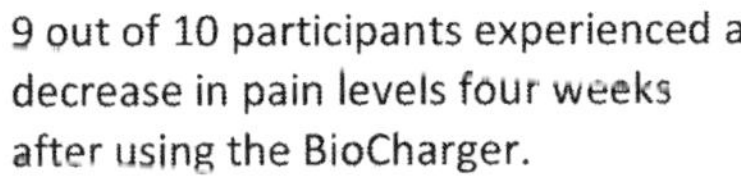

9 out of 10 participants experienced a decrease in pain levels four weeks after using the BioCharger.

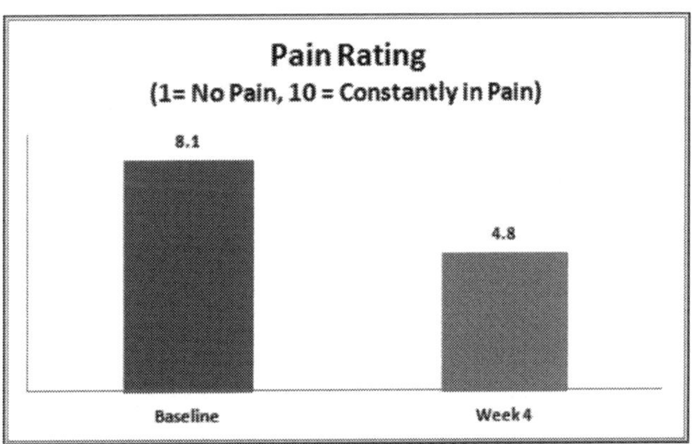

JANUARY 2015 **EFFECT OF BIOCHARGER ON CHRONICALLY ILL INDIVIDUALS**

Better Sleep Quality

Participants reported a **39% increase** in their sleep quality.

Sleep Quality Measurements:

1. Fall asleep easily
2. Sleep soundly
3. Wake up in the morning feeling refreshed

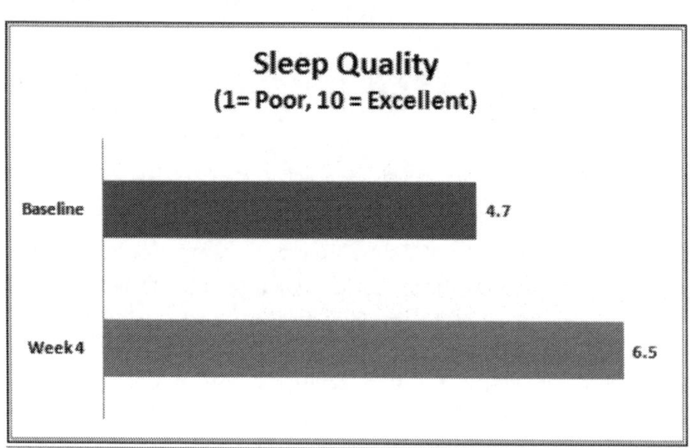

Mental Alertness and Concentration
(1 = Poor, 10 = Excellent)

	Mental Alertness	Concentration
Baseline	4.3	4.6
Week4	6.0	5.8

Increased Ability to Focus and Concentrate

The majority of participants saw an increase in their mental clarity and ability to concentrate.

1. The average participant was **38% more mentally alert**.
2. Their **ability to focus and concentrate increased 26%**.

More Energy

Participants felt **35% more energetic and healthy**.

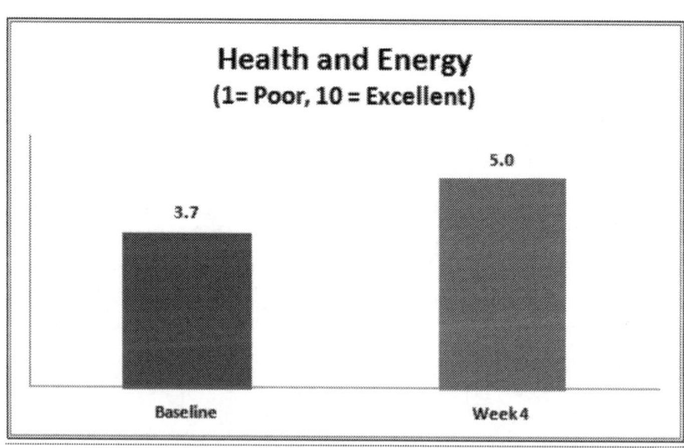

www.BioCharger.com Page 2

JANUARY 2015 **EFFECT OF BIOCHARGER ON CHRONICALLY ILL INDIVIDUALS**

Lyme Participants

Participants with Lyme disease were also asked to fill out an additional questionnaire containing 71 questions assessing typical Lyme related symptoms on a weekly basis.

Results

Participants experienced a **21% reduction in the severity and frequency of their symptoms** four weeks after using the BioCharger.

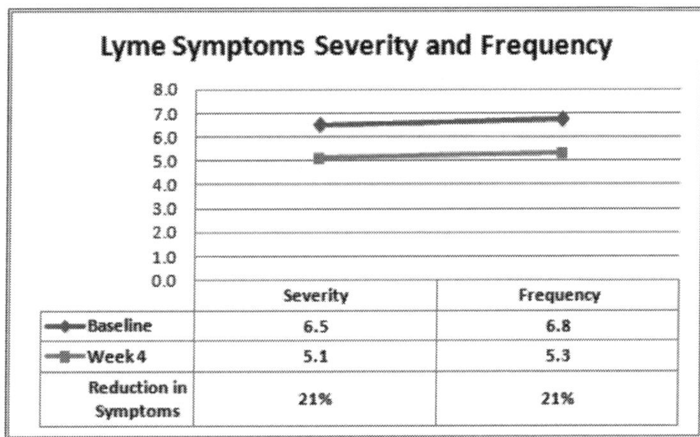

	Severity	Frequency
Baseline	6.5	6.8
Week4	5.1	5.3
Reduction in Symptoms	21%	21%

Reduction in Lyme Symptoms - Results By Category

Categories	Description	Severity	Frequency
Eyes/Vision	*Light sensitivity, double vision/blurry floaters*	33%	21%
Respiratory and Circulatory Systems	*Heart murmur, palpitations, heart block, chest pain/sore ribs, breathlessness/chronic cough, night sweats*	31%	20%
Head/Face/Neck	*Sore throat, seizures, headaches, facial paralysis (Bell's palsy), dental pain, neck creaks, unexplained hair loss, head congestion*	29%	14%
Musculoskeletal System	*Joint pain, joint swelling, back pain, stiffness of the joints, muscle pain/cramps, muscle weakness, face/muscle twitching*	25%	29%
Ears/Hearing	*Sound sensitivity, ear pain, buzzing/ringing/decreased hearing*	24%	17%
Reproduction and Sexuality	*Genital pain, menstrual irregularity, milk production, erectile disfunction, loss of libido*	20%	15%
General Well-Being - Other	*Persistent swollen glands, unexplained weight gain/loss, Exaggerated symptoms/ worse hangover from alcohol, symptom flares every 4 weeks, degree of disability*	16%	16%
Neurologic System	*Tremors, motion sickness/vertigo/spinning, light-headedness/wooziness, tingling/numbing/burning sensation/shooting pains/skin hypersensitivity, fatigue/poor stamina*	13%	15%
Psychological well-being	*Confusion/difficulty thinking, mood swings/irritability/ depression, anxiety/panic attacks, psychosis, Insomnia/fractionated sleep/early awakening, excessive night time sleep, napping*	18%	34%
Mental Capability	*Difficulty with concentration/ reading/problem absorbing new information, Word search/name block, Forgetfulness/poor short term memory poor attention, disorientation, speech errors*	8%	23%

Appendix J
Recommended Reading

Brecker, Helene. *Living with Lyme Disease:* 2015.

Dweck, Carol S. *Mindset: The New Psychology of Success.* New York: Random House, Inc., 2007.

Church, Dawson. *The Genie in your Genes: Epigenetic Medicine and the New Biology of Intention.* Santa Rosa, CA: Energy Psychology Press, 2008.

Dispenza, Joe. *You Are the Placebo: Making your Mind Matter.* Carlsbad, CA: Hay House, Inc., 2014.

Doyle, III, Bruce I. *How to Think Your Way to the Life You Want: A Guide to Understanding How Your Thoughts and Beliefs Create Your Life.* Charlottesville, VA: Hampton Roads, 2011.

Foster, Suzette Faith. *Calling Back Your Power: Your Catalyst for Personal and Spiritual Transformation.* Choose 2 Survive Publishing, 2011.

Lipton, Bruce. *The Biology of Belief: Unleashing the Power of Consciousness, Matter & Miracles.* Santa Rosa, CA: Mountain of Love/Elite Books, 2005.

Mate, Gabor. *When the Body Says No: Understanding the Stress-Disease Connection.* Hoboken, New Jersey: John Wiley & Sons, Inc., 2003.

Nakazawa Jackson, Donna. *Childhood Disrupted: How Your Biography Becomes Your Biology, and How You Can Heal.* New York, NY: Atria Books, An Imprint of Simon & Schuster, Inc., 2015.

Nakazawa Jackson, Donna. *The Last Best Cure: My Quest to Awaken the Healing Parts of My Brain and Get Back My Body, My Joy, My Life.* USA: Hudson Street Press, 2013.

Seibert, Al. *The Resiliency Advantage: Master Change, Thrive Under Pressure, and Bounce Back from Setbacks.* Oakland, CA: Berrett-Koehler Publishers, Inc., 2005.

Acknowledgments

First and foremost, we honor God (the Divine, Higher Power, All That Is) with deep gratitude for helping us to recover from Lyme/TBDs and giving us the Grace and vision that created this book. It is our belief in God—a Divine Force greater than ourselves—that directed our healing and led us on a path of deeper personal growth. We are forever humbled by the experience of contracting Lyme disease, for it has been a catalyst for transformation in ways we, at first, did not know was possible.

We send deep love to our families and friends who remained hopeful for our recovery from Lyme/TBDs, were our greatest cheerleaders on days when we struggled the most, and stayed by our side through the unknowns, always holding the belief in new possibility. We thank them for encouraging us to share our stories of struggle, hope, and recovery in this workbook.

We thank all the people we met personally through our private integrative psychotherapy practices, at Lyme rallies, Lyme support groups, and Lyme conferences. Listening to their stories inspired us to heal by witnessing their relentless efforts to do all that is possible, not only to recover, but also to transform their lives as a result of the challenges they faced living with Lyme/TBDs. Some of these people used the tools offered in this workbook and have entrusted us to share their inspirational stories of hope and transformation with you out of love, solidarity, and the calling to serve others, as they have been served. May their offerings inspire you as they have us.

We send out our deepest gratitude to all those who advocate for people with Lyme/TBDs. Those who treat, educate, lead rallies, challenge insurance companies for coverage, conduct research, offer comprehensive Lyme-related resources on their websites, lead support groups, and formulate and get congressional bills passed in support of valid Lyme/TBD treatments with legal coverage for doctors. To the Microbes and Mental Illness (MMI) listserv, for being such a prophetic group of people who gather to explore this topic, and to Dr. Robert Bransfield, who created this forum to provide a safe space where people can be heard and ideas can be shared. Gratitude to International Lyme and Associated Diseases Society (ILADS) for leading the way in advocating Lyme/TBD literate treatment guidelines at all levels and training doctors on the complexities of issues and on integrative comprehensive treatment options.

Our sincere thanks to Kenneth B. Singleton, MD, MPH, the author of *the Lyme Disease Solution,* for believing in our work and for giving us the encouragement to write this workbook to help others. We thank him for his wise counsel and his patient support of us as we found our voice. He took this journey along with us for the past four years, offering guidance, advice, and positive emotional support. His dedication to the treatment and healing of his patients with Lyme/TBDs is heart-centered, compassionate, and Lyme-informed. You can find him on his website, www.lymedoctor.com.

Our deep gratitude goes out to Laura Piazza for sharing her immense creative talents as this book's graphic designer. Laura shared her vision of a workbook that is reader friendly, creatively expressed, and professionally crafted. Laura's positive attitude, endless dedication to producing a quality product, and passion for serving the Lyme/TBD community made her a joy to work with. Laura is a top-notch, incredibly talented professional who maintained a positive attitude, met all deadlines, and succeeded in creating our vision in the design, format, and layout. Laura and her mother, Gail, are the authors of *Recipes for Repair* (www.recipesforrepair.com). Laura also has a freelance design and photography business. You can learn more about her at www.piazzacreative.com.

We have deep gratitude for Carol Killman Rosenberg, editorial specialist, who performed the final edit. Carol exhibited comprehensive skills in editing that blew our minds and opened our hearts wider. She was dedicated to learning and understanding our vision for this workbook and used her skills as our copyeditor to help us clarify and sharpen our message to aid in serving our readers. Her attention to detail and making the material consistent throughout the manuscript was superb! Carol was available to us when needed, was positively engaged, and worked as a collaborative team member. She not only met her deadlines, but she also finished ahead of schedule! We recommend her to anybody who needs a highly qualified, talented, hardworking, and collaborative editor. We learned that no matter how big this project was, Carol was up to the task with a positive attitude, tremendous writing and editorial skills, and a determination to help create a quality product. You can learn more about her at carolkillmanrosenberg.com.

We are deeply grateful to Lori J. Lewis for an exceptional job proofreading. She was meticulous in her craft, a joy to work with and always made her deadlines. Lori has been freelance proofreading for more than thirteen years. She loves her work and has experience proofreading both fiction and nonfiction. She can be reached at ljlewis126@aol.com.

Very special thanks to Liz O'Donnell, who participated with us on the formulation of the first draft of this workbook. Liz is a gifted writer and a diligent researcher. She has the skills to navigate the complexities of Lyme/TBDs issues, science, and neuropsychiatric factors. She has a master's degree in psychology and English.

To Kathy Repass who offered continuous positive support and was integral in guiding some of our creative brainstorming sessions. We consider Kathy a member of our family, and it has been fun having her support on this project.

We would like to honor David Terry, our graphic designer. He designed the cover for this book and the interior graphics. David is a very talented professional who ably transformed our complex ideas into graphic form through patient listening and artistic skill. David met his deadlines and was a pleasure to work with. You can check him out on his website at www.dterry.net.

We also want to share our gratitude for the hours spent by the proofreaders who offered their ideas, encouragement, and feedback to help ensure the integrity and quality of this book: Gary Bains, Sr. Ellen McCarth-FCJ, Susan Hetherington, Susan Myers, and Kandice Dickover.

We offer a special thank-you to Katina Makris for sharing some of her personal recovery story. She inspired us with a message that is grounded in hope and transcends into personal transformation through Lyme/TBD recovery. Katina Makris, CCH, CIH, has worked in natural health care for thirty years. Award-winning author of *Out of the Woods: Healing Lyme Disease—Body, Mind & Spirit*. Her latest book, *Autoimmune Illness and Lyme Disease Recovery: Mending the Body, Mind, and Spirit,* was released in 2015. She can be reached through her website at www.katinamakris.com.

To Vir McCoy, who contributed the "Fire-Love" exercise, which he used in his own recovery process from Lyme disease. This exercise, which incorporates meditation and transformative imagery, was excerpted from his book *Liberating Lyme*. Vir's dedication to helping others to recover from Lyme through his writings and educational talks is an inspiration to us all. Vir can be reached through his website at virmccoy.com. We also want to thank Lia Gaertner for connecting us with Vir and for her advocacy work in supporting people with Lyme/TBDs.

We offer our gratitude to Dr. Kathy Spreen, who generously spent an afternoon sharing her wisdom and book-writing skills about Lyme/TBDs. She was a great resource in educating us in the process of writing, editing, and publishing.

We offer love and gratitude to our close friend Daniel Donovan. He was a constant loving support to us throughout the years of writing this workbook. His financial donations to support the publication of this workbook are deeply appreciated.

To Barbara Rookard: we are so grateful for her counsel, emotional support, and friendship, and for offering great resource ideas.

As you can see, creating this workbook involved a community of people who contributed, guided, and encouraged its manifestation in the hope of serving and helping others. We hold everybody in our hearts in gratitude, even the people whom we did not get to mention by name here. For it is within community that all things are possible.

Notes

1. Horowitz, R. (2013). *Why Can't I Get Better? Solving the Mystery of Lyme and Chronic Disease.* New York, NY: St. Martin's Press, page 445.
2. Ruden, R. (2005). Why tapping works: Speculations from the observable brain. Retrieved from www.lifescriptcounseling.com/research/whyitworks.pdf.
3. Feinstein, D. (2008). Energy Psychology: A review of the preliminary evidence. *Psychotherapy: Theory, Research, Practice, Training,* 45 (2), 199–213. Retrieved from http://innersource.net/ep/images/stories/downloads/Research_in_EP.pdf.
4. Ibid.
5. Lubin, H., & Schneider, T. (2009). Change is possible: EFT (emotional freedom techniques) with life-sentence and veteran prisoners at San Quentin State Prison. *Energy Psychology,* 1 (1), 1–6. Retrieved from http://www.stressproject.org/documents/lubin-pdf.
6. Ruden, R. (2005). Why tapping works: Speculations from the observable brain. Retrieved from http://www.lifescriptcounseling.com/research/whyitworks.pdf.
7. Hover-Kramer, D. (2011). *Creating Healing Relationships*: Professional Standards for Energy Therapy Practitioners. Santa Rosa, CA; page 230.
8. Omitted in text.
9. Omitted in text.
10. Omitted in text.
11. Singleton, K. (2008). *The Lyme Disease Solution.* Dallas, TX: Brown Books Publishing Group.
12. Ibid.
13. www.multiwaveoscillator.org.
14. Horowitz, R. (2013). *Why Can't I Get Better? Solving the Mystery of Lyme and Chronic Disease.* New York, NY: St. Martin's Press, page 445.
15. Ruden, R. (2005). Why tapping works: Speculations from the observable brain. Retrieved from http://www.lifescriptcounseling.com/research/whyitworks.pdf.
16. Horowitz, R. (2013). *Why Can't I Get Better? Solving the Mystery of Lyme and Chronic Disease.* New York, NY: St. Martin's Press, page 445.
17. Ibid. page 332.
18. Schaller, J., & Mountjoy, K. (2012). *What You May Not Know About Bartonella, Babesia, Lyme Disease and Other Tick & Flea-Borne Infections: Improving Treatment Speed, Recovery & Patient Satisfaction* [E-book]. Retrieved from www.personalconsult.com. Naples, FL: International University Infectious Disease Press, page 9.
19. Singleton, K. (2008). *The Lyme Disease Solution.* Dallas, TX: Brown Books Publishing Group, pages 360–361.
20. Bransfield, R. (2012). The psychoimmunology of Lyme/tick-borne diseases and its association with neuropsychiatric symptoms. *The Open Neurology Journal,* 6 (Suppl 1), 88–93.
21. Ibid.
22. Horowitz, R. (2013). *Why Can't I Get Better? Solving the Mystery of Lyme and Chronic Disease.* New York, NY: St. Martin's Press, page 308.
23. http://psychiatryonline.org/doi/pdf/10.1176/appi.books.978089042670.
24. Horowitz, R. (2013). *Why Can't I Get Better? Solving the Mystery of Lyme and Chronic Disease.* New York, NY: St. Martin's Press, page 57.
25. Bransfield, R. (2012). The psychoimmunology of Lyme/tick-borne diseases and its association with neuropsychiatric symptoms. *The Open Neurology Journal,* 6 (Suppl 1), 88–93.
26. Ibid.
27. Fallon, B., Levin, E., Schweitzer, P., & Hardesty, D. (2010). Inflammation and central nervous system Lyme disease. *Neurobiology of Disease,* 37 (3), 534–541. doi:10.1016/j.nbd.2009,11.016
28. De Kooker, M. (2008). Mind, immunity and health—The science and clinical application of psychoneuroimmunology: main article. *CME: Your SA Journal of CPD: Psychoneuroimmunology: Mind-body Medicine,* 26 (1), 18–20.
29. Leonard, B., & Myint, A. (2009). The psychoneuroimmunology of depression. *Human Psychopharmacology: Clinical and Experimental,* 24 (3), 165–175. doi:10.1002/hup.1011
30. Segerstrom, S. (2010). Resources, stress, and immunity: An ecological perspective on human psychoneuroimmunology. *Annals of Behavioral Medicine,* 40 (1), 114–125. doi:10.1007/s12160-010-9195-3
31. De Ridder, D., Geenen, R., Kuijer, R., & Van Middendorp, H. (2008). Psychological adjustment to chronic disease. *The Lancet,* 246–255.
32. De Kooker, M. (2008). Mind, immunity and health—The science and clinical application of psychoneuroimmunology: main article. *CME: Your SA Journal of CPD: Psychoneuroimmunology: Mind-body Medicine,* 26 (1), 18–20.
33. Horowitz, R. (2013). *Why Can't I Get Better? Solving the Mystery of Lyme and Chronic Disease.* New York, NY: St. Martin's Press, page 187.
34. Ibid.
35. Ibid. page 315.
36. Bransfield, R. (2012). The psychoimmunology of

Lyme/tick-borne diseases and its association with neuropsychiatric symptoms. *The Open Neurology Journal,* 6 (Suppl 1), 88–93.

37. Fallon, B., Levin, E., Schweitzer, P., & Hardesty, D. (2010). Inflammation and central nervous system Lyme disease. *Neurobiology of Disease,* 37 (3), 534–541. doi:10.1016/j.nbd.2009.11016
38. Bransfield, R. (2012). The psychoimmunology of Lyme/tick-borne diseases and its association with neuropsychiatric symptoms. *The Open Neurology Journal,* 6 (Suppl 1), 88–93.
39. Ibid.
40. Ibid.
41. Ibid.
42. Ibid.
43. Singleton, K. (2008). *The Lyme Disease Solution.* Dallas, TX: Brown Books Publishing Group.
44. Horowitz, R. (2013). *Why Can't I Get Better? Solving the Mystery of Lyme and Chronic Disease.* New York, NY: St. Martin's Press, page 322.
45. Ibid.
46. Ibid. page 325.
47. Singleton, K. (2008). *The Lyme Disease Solution.* Dallas, TX: Brown Books Publishing Group, page 361.
48. Horowitz, R. (2013). *Why Can't I Get Better? Solving the Mystery of Lyme and Chronic Disease.* New York, NY: St. Martin's Press, page 317.
49. Ibid. page 325.
50. Singleton, K. (2008). *The Lyme Disease Solution.* Dallas, TX: Brown Books Publishing Group, page 360.
51. Schaller, J., & Mountjoy, K. (2012). *What You May Not Know About Bartonella, Babesia, Lyme Disease and Other Tick & Flea-Borne Infections: Improving Treatment Speed, Recovery & Patient Satisfaction* [E-book]. Retrieved from www.personalconsult.com. Naples, FL: International University Infectious Disease Press, page 51.
52. Ibid.
53. Singleton, K. (2008). *The Lyme Disease Solution.* Dallas, TX: Brown Books Publishing Group, page 361.
54. Ibid. page 365.
55. Horowitz, R. (2013). *Why Can't I Get Better? Solving the Mystery of Lyme and Chronic Disease.* New York, NY: St. Martin's Press, page 310.
56. www.shcs.ucdavis.edu/wellness.
57. http://www.nationalwellness.org/?page=Six_Dimensions&hhSearchTerms=%22full+and+potential%22.
58. Pert, C. (1997). *Molecules of Emotion.* New York, NY: Scribner, page 189.
59. Lipton, B. (2005). *The Biology of Belief.* Santa Rosa, CA: Mountain of Love/Elite Books, page 145-154.
60. Ibid.
61. Ibid.
62. Marx Hubbard, B. (1998). *Conscious Evolution.* Novato, CA: New World Library, page 48.
63. Buhner, S. (2005). *Healing Lyme: Natural Healing and Prevention of Lyme Borreliosis and its Coinfections.* New York, NY: Raven Press, page 23.
64. Ibid. page 30.
65. Brach, T. (2014, June 13). Feeling overwhelmed? Remember "RAIN": Four steps to stop being so hard on ourselves. Retrieved from http://www.mindful.org/tara-brach-rain-mindfulness-practice.
66. Scaer, R. (2005). *The Trauma Spectrum: Hidden Wounds and Human Resiliency.* New York, NY: W. W. Norton & Company, pages 43–44.
67. Lipton, B. (2005). *The Biology of Belief.* Santa Rosa, CA: Mountain of Love/Elite Books, pages 145–154.
68. Ibid, page 128.
69. Horowitz, R. (2013). *Why Can't I Get Better? Solving the Mystery of Lyme and Chronic Disease.* New York, NY: St. Martin's Press, page 317.
70. Ibid. page 325.
71. Ibid. page 445.
72. Sullivan, J. (2004). *Living Large: Transformative Work at the Intersection of Ethics and Spirituality.* Laurel, MD: Tai Sophia Press.
73. Ibid.
74. St. John, N. (2013). *The Book of Afformations.* Carlsbad, CA: Hay House.
75. Horowitz, R. (2013). *Why Can't I Get Better? Solving the Mystery of Lyme and Chronic Disease.* New York, NY: St. Martin's Press, page 430.
76. Kabat-Zinn, J. (2003). Mindfulness Based Interventions in Context: Past, Present and Future. *Clinical Psychology: Science and Practice,* 10 (2), 144–156. doi:10.1093/clipsy/bpg016.
77. http://www.umassmed.edu/cfm/stress-reduction/faqs/.
78. http://www.energypsych.org.
79. Sternberg, E., & Gold, P. (1997). The mind-body interaction in disease. *Scientific American,* 8–15.
80. Benedetti, F. (2013). Placebo and the new physiology of the doctor-patient relationship. *Physiological Reviews,* 93 (3), 1207–1246. doi:10.1152/physrev.00043.2012
81. Brody, H., & Miller, F. (2011). Lessons from recent research about the placebo effect—From art to Science. *JAMA,* 306 (23), 2612–2613.

82. Finniss, D., Kaptchuk, T., Miller, F., & Benedetti, F. (2010). Biological, clinical and ethical advances of placebo effects. *The Lancet,* 686–695.

83. Singleton, K. (2008). *The Lyme Disease Solution.* Dallas, TX: Brown Books Publishing Group, page 176.

84. Ibid. page 198.

85. Piazza, G., & Piazza, L. (2016). *Recipes for Repair.* Sunapee, NH: Peconic Publishing, LLC.

86. Horowitz, R. (2013). *Why Can't I Get Better? Solving the Mystery of Lyme and Chronic Disease.* New York, NY: St. Martin's Press, page 444.

87. Ibid.

88. Sternberg, E., & Gold, P. (1997). The mind-body interaction in disease. *Scientific American,* 8–15.

89. De Kooker, M. (2008). Mind, immunity and health—The science and clinical application of psychoneuroimmunology: main article. *CME: Your SA Journal of CPD: Psychoneuroimmunology: Mind-body Medicine,* 26 (1), 18–20.

90. Leonard, B., & Myint, A. (2009). The psychoneuroimmunology of depression. *Human Psychopharmacology: Clinical and Experimental,* 24 (3), 165–175. doi:10.1002/hup.1011

91. Lipton, B. (2005). *The Biology of Belief.* Santa Rosa, CA: Mountain of Love/Elite Books, pages 83–84.

92. Pert, C. (1997). *Molecules of Emotion.* New York, NY: Scribner, page 185.

93. Ibid. page 189.

94. Ibid. page 184.

95. Ibid.

96. Lipton, B. (2005). *The Biology of Belief.* Santa Rosa, CA: Mountain of Love/Elite Books, page 132.

97. Ibid.

98. Ibid. page 135.

99. Ibid. page 125.

100. Ibid. page 128.

101. Benedetti, F. (2013). Placebo and the new physiology of the doctor-patient relationship. *Physiological Reviews,* 93 (3), 1207–1246. doi:10.1152/physrev.00043.2012

102. Brody, H., & Miller, F. (2011). Lessons from recent research about the placebo effect—From art to Science. *JAMA,* 306 (23), 2612–2613.

103. Finniss, D., Kaptchuk, T., Miller, F., & Benedetti, F. (2010). Biological, clinical and ethical advances of placebo effects. *The Lancet,* 686–695.

104. Benedetti, F. (2013). Placebo and the new physiology of the doctor-patient relationship. *Physiological Reviews,* 93 (3), 1207–1246. doi:10.1152/physrev.00043.2012

105. Ibid.

106. Brody, H., & Miller, F. (2011). Lessons from recent research about the placebo effect—From art to Science. *JAMA,* 306 (23), 2612–2613.

107. Finniss, D., Kaptchuk, T., Miller, F., & Benedetti, F. (2010). Biological, clinical and ethical advances of placebo effects. *The Lancet,* 686–695.

108. Silverman, M., Heim, C., Nater, U., Marques, A., & Sternberg, E. (2010). Neuroendocrine and immune contributors to fatigue. *PM&R,* 2 (5), 338–346. 10.1016/j.pmrj.2010.04.008.

109. De Kooker, M. (2008). Mind, immunity and health—The science and clinical application of psychoneuroimmunology: main article. *CME: Your SA Journal of CPD: Psychoneuroimmunology: Mind-body Medicine,* 26 (1), 18–20.

110. Ruden, R. (2005). Why tapping works: Speculations from the observable brain. Retrieved from http://www.lifescriptcounseling.com/research/whyitworks.pdf.

111. Lipton, B. (2005). *The Biology of Belief.* Santa Rosa, CA: Mountain of Love/Elite Books.

112. Feinstein, D. (2008). Energy Psychology: A review of the preliminary evidence. *Psychotherapy: Theory, Research, Practice, Training,* 45 (2), 199–213. Retrieved from http://innersource.net/ep/images/stories/downloads/Research_in_EP.pdf.

113. Horowitz, R. (2013). *Why Can't I Get Better? Solving the Mystery of Lyme and Chronic Disease.* New York, NY: St. Martin's Press, page 325.

114. Feinstein, D. (2008). Energy Psychology: A review of the preliminary evidence. *Psychotherapy: Theory, Research, Practice, Training,* 45 (2), 199–213. Retrieved from http://innersource.net/ep/images/stories/downloads/Research_in_EP.pdf.

115. Ruden, R. (2005). Why tapping works: Speculations from the observable brain. Retrieved from http://www.lifescriptcounseling.com/research/whyitworks.pdf.

116. Feinstein, D. (2008). Energy Psychology: A review of the preliminary evidence. *Psychotherapy: Theory, Research, Practice, Training,* 45 (2), 199–213. Retrieved from http://innersource.net/ep/images/stories/downloads/Research_in_EP.pdf.

117. National Institutes of Health, Consensus Development Conference Statement. (1997). *Acupuncture,* 15 (5), 1–34. Retrieved from http://consensus.nih.gov/1997/Acupuncture107html.htm.

118. Feinstein, D. (2008). Energy Psychology: A review of the preliminary evidence. *Psychotherapy: Theory, Research, Practice, Training,* 45 (2), 199–213. Retrieved from http://innersource.net/ep/images/stories/downloads/Research_in_EP.pdf.

119. Ruden, R. (2005). Why tapping works: Speculations from the observable brain. Retrieved from http://www .lifescriptcounseling.com/research/whyitworks.pdf.

120. Hui, K. K. S., Liu, J., Marina, O., Napadow, V., Haselgrove, C., Kwong, K. K., . . . Makris, N. (2005). The integrated response of the human cerebro-cerebellar and limbic systems to acupuncture stimulation at ST 36 as evidenced by fMRI. *NeuroImage*, 27, 479–496. doi: 101016/ j.neuroimage.2005.04.037.

121. Ruden, R. (2005). Why tapping works: Speculations from the observable brain. Retrieved from http://www .lifescriptcounseling.com/research/whyitworks.pdf.

122. Feinstein, D. (2008). Energy Psychology: A review of the preliminary evidence. *Psychotherapy: Theory, Research, Practice, Training,* 45 (2), 199–213. Retrieved from http://innersource.net/ep/images/ stories/downloads/Research_in_EP.pdf.

123. Ruden, R. (2005). Why tapping works: Speculations from the observable brain. Retrieved from http://www .lifescriptcounseling.com/research/whyitworks.pdf.

124. Adolphus, R., Russell, James A., & Tranel D. (1999). A role for the human amygdala in recognizing emotional arousal from unpleasant stimuli. *Psychological Science,* 10 (2), 167–171.

125. Ruden, R. (2005). Why tapping works: Speculations from the observable brain. Retrieved from http://www .lifescriptcounseling.com/research/whyitworks.pdf.

126. Horowitz, R. (2013). *Why Can't I Get Better? Solving the Mystery of Lyme and Chronic Disease.* New York, NY: St. Martin's Press.

127. Ruden, R. (2005). Why tapping works: Speculations from the observable brain. Retrieved from http://www .lifescriptcounseling.com/research/whyitworks.pdf.

128. Feinstein, D. (2009). Facts, paradigms, and anomalies in the acceptance of energy psychology: A rejoinder to Mccaslin's (2009) and Pignotti and Thyer's (2009) comments on Feinstein (2008a). *Psychotherapy Theory, Research, Practice, Training,* 46 (2), 262–269. doi: 10.1037/a0016086

129. McCaslin, D. L. (2009). Comments and rejoinder: A review of efficacy claims in energy psychology. *Psychotherapy Theory, Research, Practice, Training,* 46 (2), 249–256. doi: 10.1037/a0016025

130. Pignotti, M. & Thyer, B. (2009). Some comments on "Energy Psychology: A review of the evidence": premature conclusions based on incomplete evidence? *Psychotherapy Theory, Research, Practice, Training,* 46 (2), 257–261. doi: 10.1037/a0016027

131. Church, D. (2009). Treatment of combat trauma in veterans using EFT (emotional freedom techniques): A pilot protocol. *Traumatology,* 20 (10), 1–11. doi:101177/1534765609347549

132. Lubin, H., & Schneider, T. (2009). Change is possible: EFT (emotional freedom techniques) with life-sentence and veteran prisoners at San Quentin State Prison. *Energy Psychology,* 1 (1), 1–6. Retrieved from http:// www.stressproject.org/documents/lubin-pdf.

133. Feinstein, D. (2008). Energy Psychology: A review of the preliminary evidence. *Psychotherapy: Theory, Research, Practice, Training,* 45 (2), 199–213. Retrieved from http://innersource.net/ep/images/ stories/downloads/Research_in_EP.pdf.

134. Ruden, R. (2005). Why tapping works: Speculations from the observable brain. Retrieved from http://www. lifescriptcounseling.com/research/whyitworks.pdf.

135. Church, D. (2009). Treatment of combat trauma in veterans using EFT (emotional freedom techniques): A pilot protocol. *Traumatology,* 20 (10), 1–11. doi:101177/1534765609347549

136. Church, D., Hawk, C., Books, A., Toukolehto, O., Wren, M., Dinter, I., & Stein, P. (2010, April). Psychological trauma in veterans using EFT (emotional freedom techniques): A randomized controlled trial. Paper presented at the Society of Behavioral Medicine, Seattle, Washington. In peer review.

137. Church, D. (2009). Treatment of combat trauma in veterans using EFT (emotional freedom techniques): A pilot protocol. *Traumatology,* 20 (10), 1–11. doi:101177/1534765609347549

138. Ibid.

139. Ibid.

140. Ruden, R. (2005). Why tapping works: Speculations from the observable brain. Retrieved from http://www .lifescriptcounseling.com/research/whyitworks.pdf.

141. Ibid.

142. Lipton, B. (2005). *The Biology of Belief.* Santa Rosa, CA: Mountain of Love/Elite Books.

143. Ruden, R. (2005). Why tapping works: Speculations from the observable brain. Retrieved from http://www. lifescriptcounseling.com/research/whyitworks.pdf.

144. Feinstein, D. (2008). Energy Psychology: A review of the preliminary evidence. *Psychotherapy: Theory, Research, Practice, Training,* 45 (2), 199–213. Retrieved from http://innersource.net/ep/images/ stories/downloads/Research_in_EP.pdf.

About the Authors

Anita Bains, D.PSc, M.S., APRN, BC, has been a passionate health care practitioner for 25 years. In addition to her training in traditional and cognitive psychotherapies, Anita is an expert practitioner in Eye Movement Desensitization and Reprocessing (EMDR) and Emotional Freedom Techniques (EFT). She lectures internationally, including at the Chengdu University of Traditional Chinese Medicine in China. The practices offered in this workbook have played a major role in Anita's own recovery journey from Lyme/TBDs. She shares these tools of recovery with others so they too experience their benefits and move forward toward healing, wholeness and wellbeing. Anita sees clients individually in person, on Skype and over the phone, and can be reached through her website: anitabains.com.

Tracey Middleton is a Clinical Social Worker (LCSW-C), Licensed Pastoral Therapist and Emotional Freedom Techniques (EFT) Expert. In her integrative therapy practice, she combines energy psychology with traditional clinical approaches such as Cognitive Behavioral Therapy (CBT) and Eye Movement Desensitization and Reprocessing (EMDR) to maximize treatment outcomes and empower clients in diverse populations to achieve optimal wellbeing, including those with Lyme/TBDs. Tracey also uses the self-help tools presented in this workbook to support her own recovery from Lyme/TBDs. Tracey presents EFT to numerous medical establishments and community support groups. She sees clients in person, on Skype and over the phone. You can visit Tracey's website at: traceymiddleton.com.

Made in the USA
Las Vegas, NV
11 May 2021

22820657R00249